International Policy Coordination and Exchange Rate Fluctuations

A National Bureau
of Economic Research
Conference Report

International Policy Coordination and Exchange Rate Fluctuations

Edited by William H. Branson,
Jacob A. Frenkel,
and Morris Goldstein

The University of Chicago Press
Chicago and London

WILLIAM H. BRANSON is the Jacob Viner Professor of International Economics at Princeton University and Director of the Program in International Studies at the NBER. JACOB A. FRENKEL is Economic Counsellor and Director of Research at the International Monetary Fund, and has been the David Rockefeller Professor of International Economics at the University of Chicago. MORRIS GOLDSTEIN is Deputy Director of the Research Department at the International Monetary Fund.

The University of Chicago Press, Chicago 60637
The University of Chicago Press, Ltd., London

© 1990 by the National Bureau of Economic Research
All rights reserved. Published 1990
Printed in the United States of America
99 98 97 96 95 94 93 92 91 90   5 4 3 2 1

Library of Congress Cataloging-in-Publication Data

International policy coordination and exchange rate fluctuations / edited by William H. Branson, Jacob A. Frenkel, and Morris Goldstein.
    p.   cm. — (A National Bureau of Economic Research conference report)
    "Contains the papers and formal discussions presented at a National Bureau of Economic Research conference held at Kiawah Island, South Carolina on October 27–29, 1988"—Pref.
    Includes bibliographical references.
    ISBN 0-226-07141-3 (alk. paper)
    1. Foreign exchange administration—Congresses. 2. International economic relations—Congresses. I. Branson, William H. II. Frenkel, Jacob A. III. Goldstein, Morris. IV. National Bureau of Economic Research. V. Series: Conference report (National Bureau of Economic Research)
HG3851.I545 1990
332.4'564—dc20   90-35942
                                          CIP

Contents

Preface

This volume contains the papers and their formal discussions presented at a National Bureau of Economic Research conference held at Kiawah Island, South Carolina, on October 27–29, 1988. Each paper was assigned two discussants. Authors were given the opportunity to revise their papers after the conference, and discussants to revise after the paper revisions. An introductory chapter by the editors provides a "road map" to the book and highlights the main issues discussed at the conference.

In organizing the conference, the editors invited papers on salient aspects of coordination and exchange rates. One group of papers, by Jacob A. Frenkel, Morris Goldstein, and Paul R. Masson, by Peter B. Kenen, and by Jeffrey A. Frankel, addressed the scope, methods, and effects of coordination. A second pair of papers, by Maurice Obstfeld and by Francesco Giavazzi and Alberto Giovannini, analyzed either specific instruments of coordination, such as foreign-exchange market intervention, or the lessons of ongoing coordination efforts. Reflecting the important role played by exchange rate considerations in recent coordination efforts by the largest industrial countries, the paper by Paul R. Krugman examined the determinants of equilibrium real exchange rates. Finally, the influence of the financial regulatory structure and of multinational corporations in forming the economic environment for coordination was discussed in the papers by David Folkerts-Landau and by Kenneth A. Froot. The volume also contains a background paper on the adequacy of international data by Lois Stekler.

After the Kiawah Island conference, on February 16, 1989, the editors organized a one-day meeting to discuss the main results with policymakers at the Madison Hotel in Washington, D. C. Summary versions of the papers have been made available in typescript form by NBER as a Conference Report.

We would like to thank the Smith Richardson Foundation for financing this project through NBER including research support, a preconference meeting,

and the Washington meeting and Conference Report. Mark Fitz-Patrick assisted
in preparing this volume, and Kirsten Foss Davis and Ilana Hardesty did their
usual excellent job of conference and meeting organizing. As usual, the opinions
expressed in this volume are those of the individual authors and do not necessarily reflect the views of NBER or the IMF.

William H. Branson
Jacob A. Frenkel
Morris Goldstein
January 1990

Introduction

William H. Branson, Jacob A. Frenkel, and
Morris Goldstein

Since the finance ministers and central bank governors of the five largest industrial democracies concluded the Plaza Agreement in New York in September 1985, the theory and practice of international economic policy coordination has become the subject of spirited academic and public policy debate. To some, policy coordination represents a watershed in the way that countries manage increased economic interdependence, and a foundation upon which an improved international monetary system can be constructed. To others, policy coordination constitutes merely a minor extension of the more long-standing process of international economic policy cooperation, and one that carries risks of delaying or otherwise weakening the implementation of macroeconomic and structural policies.

The papers and comments collected in this volume attempt from different vantage points and perspectives to understand: what international policy coordination means today and has meant in the past; under what conditions or circumstances coordination is likely to be beneficial—both to the direct participants and to the rest of the world; what factors most influence the quantitative impact or "effects" of coordination; what obstacles and constraints are most relevant for the exercise of coordination in the current and prospective global economic environment; what methods of coordination are apt to be most or least effective; and, based on the experience of the European Monetary System and of earlier regimes, in what directions the coordination process

William H. Branson is the Jacob Viner Professor of International Economics at Princeton University and Director of the Program in International Studies at the National Bureau of Economic Research. Jacob A. Frenkel is the Economic Counsellor and Director of Research at the International Monetary Fund, and a research associate of the National Bureau of Economic Research. Morris Goldstein is Deputy Director of the Research Department of the International Monetary Fund.

1

might move in the future, including those associated with greater fixity of exchange rates.

A somewhat more specific guide to the volume's contents can be obtained from a snapshot of the key issues that emerged from the papers and the discussion.

(1) *What does policy coordination mean and what conditions its effects?* As the conference proceeded, it became apparent that coordination meant different things to different participants. In addition, even on identical definitions, there remained a divergence of views on the effects of coordination.

One relevant distinction is between less and more ambitious forms of interaction among policy authorities. The former—which some participants preferred to label ''cooperation'' rather than ''coordination''—encompasses adoption of a common data base and the exchange of information regarding recent developments and policy intentions. William Branson introduced and advocated the use of this distinction. There was a consensus that policy co-operation was beneficial. Douglas Purvis, for example, argued that cooperation was essential when a country changed its medium-term objectives and initiated a dramatic change in policies, and when there was an international crisis, financial or otherwise. Policy coordination was interpreted as going further, to include agreements among countries to adjust policies in light of shared objectives and/or to implement joint policy action. It suffices to say that the potential benefits and costs of this more ambitious interaction were subject to diverse appraisal.

The nature of the theoretical case for policy coordination—as a means of internalizing the externalities associated with international spillovers of national policy decisions—was not at the center of debate. Instead, it was the *practice* of policy coordination that garnered the most attention. One issue was whether a perceived need to coordinate increased or decreased pressures on governments to do the right thing. Supporters of coordination maintained that it was hard to see how peer pressure directed at the dangers of the large U.S. budget deficit could have been anything but helpful over the past few years, and similarly helpful with respect to coordination's contribution to motivating structural reform in Europe and Japan. Those who felt that the public emphasis on coordination could be counterproductive, such as Martin Feldstein, stressed that it could provide a political excuse for inaction by shifting the blame for poor domestic policy performance to other countries. In a similar vein, some participants argued that coordinated firefighting could itself postpone policy action. Stanley Fischer offered the view that by supporting the dollar in 1987, concerted foreign-exchange market intervention probably prevented a precipitous fall in the dollar, which might in turn have forced earlier corrective action on the U.S. fiscal deficit.

A number of participants pointed to the limited size of cross-country policy multipliers as suggesting that both the gains from policy coordination and the incentive to coordinate seriously—especially for a relatively closed economy like the United States—would be "small." Others, however, thought this took too narrow an interpretation of the scope and effects of coordination. Fred Bergsten argued that it would be misleading to gauge the effects of, for example, the Plaza Agreement without taking into account the protectionist counterfactual; without Plaza, we could well have gotten a far more protectionist U.S. trade bill than actually ensued. William Branson conjectured that economists adopted a narrow scope for coordination in order to reduce the problem to a size that was manageable with available tools (usually, game theory)—but at a cost of allowing much of the substance to vanish.

Uncertainty about how the world works was yet another factor that gave rise to different views on the feasibility and desirability of coordination. Jeffrey Frankel argued that model uncertainty made it difficult for countries to know which policy changes to ask for and to agree to make. Moreover, because results might turn out to be different from those expected, such uncertainty could lead coordination to reduce welfare rather than increase it. Ralph Bryant felt that one should not exaggerate the degree of our ignorance about the consequences of policy actions. He noted that there was no significant empirical ambiguity about the sign of the spillover effects of fiscal policy actions for the major industrial countries, and that the magnitude of monetary policy spillover effects—whatever the sign—was generally acknowledged to be quite small.

(2) *How frequent and how wide should coordination be?* Some participants put forward the case that coordination would be most effective when it was a regular, ongoing process, which some participants labelled cooperation. Jacob Frenkel, Morris Goldstein, and Paul Masson claimed that multiperiod bargaining improved the incentive to fulfill earlier commitments (i.e., increased the role of "reputation" in policy agreements) and expanded the opportunities for policy bargains. Peter Kenen took a different view. He interpreted the postwar experience as suggesting that true coordination was likely only in those unusual cases where there was a clearly perceived need for regime-preserving action. Because the supply of the true coordination was limited, he also preferred coordination via rules or accepted codes-of-conduct (as under the Bretton Woods regime) since these mechanisms required less discretionary coordination. Stanley Fischer found the distinction between policy-optimizing and regime-preserving coordination suggestive but elusive; he queried what regime was being preserved through current efforts at coordination.

Turning to the width or scope of coordination, most participants saw two conflicting considerations at work. On the one hand, improved policy performance might require action on fiscal, structural, and regulatory policies, as well as on monetary and exchange rate policies. On the other hand, negotiation costs across increasing spheres of jurisdiction can rise rapidly with the number of issues under consideration. John Flemming ventured the opinion that the Cooke Committee was successful in getting an agreement on common capital-adequacy standards for commercial banks because its purview was limited and because the preparation was done by specialists. In his view, prospects for success would have been less favorable if coordination on such financial policy or regulatory issues were handled in a more wide-ranging forum.

(3) *Is it better to coordinate around a single indicator rather than around many?* Jeffrey Frankel argued that the G-7 coordination exercise was flawed. If each country had many indicators to follow but only a few policy instruments, the indicators would almost surely send conflicting signals. National authorities would therefore feel no constraint on their setting of policy instruments. A single indicator would in his view avoid this problem. Among those indicators that provided a nominal anchor, his own choice was for internationally coordinated, nominal-domestic-demand targets (to be pursued by monetary policy). A number of participants took exception to this single-indicator strategy. Ralph Bryant found no convincing need for authorities to focus on a single intermediate variable. He maintained that multiple ultimate targets, the use of a variety of intermediate variables as indicators, and a direct emphasis on the actual instruments of policy did not pose difficult analytical problems. In addition, he felt a nominal-income-targeting strategy paid insufficient attention to coordination between monetary and fiscal policies within a country. Jacob Frenkel, Morris Goldstein, and Paul Masson noted that so long as policy authorities had multiple targets and weighed them differently than their peers do, a multiple-indicator system was probably the only politically feasible one. They also expressed strong reservations about organizing coordination around exchange rate indicators alone. For one thing, exchange rate indicators could send false signals for monetary policy when badly behaved fiscal policies put pressure on exchange rates. Douglas Purvis was prepared to give the G-7 multiple-indicator exercise passing grades if it was seen not as fine-tuning a series of policy targets but rather as putting some structure on the cooperative process of consultation and information exchange.

(4) *Is greater management of exchange rates desirable and, if so, what considerations should guide the identification of equilibrium exchange rates?* A host of questions clustered around this broad issue.

One question was whether greater fixity of exchange rates provided superior insulation against a variety of shocks. This was taken up in three of the conference papers—albeit with alternative underlying theoretical frameworks and, as it turned out, with different findings. Using the IMF's MULTIMOD model (with forward-looking expectations), Jacob Frenkel, Morris Goldstein, and Paul Masson found that policy regimes which performed better in the face of certain kinds of shocks fared worse for others, with no single (exchange rate) regime dominating. A conclusion of Jeffrey Frankel's analysis of shocks was that one has to place a high weight on exchange rate stability itself to demonstrate that a rigid exchange rate rule for monetary policy dominates a rigid nominal GNP rule. Finally, employing a portfolio-balance-type model, Peter Kenen reported that fixed exchange rates are to be preferred to floating rates for a majority of shocks.

A second question is whether the costs of exchange rate misalignment are avoidable and undesirable. Some participants, such as Paul Krugman and Fred Bergsten, thought they were and that authorities should therefore induce nominal rates to move in the direction of the long-run, equilibrium real exchange rate. Some other participants, however, maintained a skeptical view of a more activist role for exchange rate management. Michael Mussa, in particular, argued that it may sometimes be necessary or desirable to countenance exchange rate misalignment in order to allow economic policy to pursue objectives more important than the rapid achievement of current account equilibrium. His case in point was the 1981–85 real appreciation of the dollar. He saw the real appreciation during 1980–82 as an inevitable consequence of tighter U.S. monetary policy which was needed to bring down the U.S. inflation rate. Moreover, the further appreciation during 1983–84 helped, inter alia, to contain inflationary pressures that would otherwise have accompanied the strong recovery of the U.S. economy from the 1981–1982 recession.

The ability of economists to identify the equilibrium real exchange rate also elicited considerable discussion. Those who argued that official estimates of equilibrium rates would be subject to substantial margins of error stressed the difficulty of defining a sustainable current account position as well as the daunting general equilibrium nature of the exercise. The other camp pointed to the successful operation of the European Monetary System and to the larger misalignments that might occur in irrational and unmanaged foreign-exchange markets. After appraising all the evidence on where the dollar needed to go to reach equilibrium, Paul Krugman concluded with a definite "don't know."

Yet another related question was whether equilibrium real exchange rates would be subject to sizable secular trends because of persistent intercountry differences in income elasticities for exports and imports. For example, did the oft-observed higher ratio of export-to-import income elasticity for Japan, relative to the United States, imply a steadily depreciating dollar for equilibrium? Paul Krugman's answer was no—because there was a systematic offset in growth rates: Japan, on average, grows faster than the United States. What counted was the *product* of income elasticities and growth rates—and this product had been relatively stable over time. Moreover, Krugman argued that this stability was consistent with a specialization among industrial countries that reflected increasing returns rather than comparative advantage. Many participants felt that the determinants of the paths of long-run equilibrium real exchange rates was a fruitful area for further study.

The ramifications of uncertainty associated with highly variable floating exchange rates also entered the discussion of exchange rate management. Richard Cooper offered the view that any exchange rate system under which firm profitability was influenced much more by exchange swings than by longer-run cost considerations would prove unacceptable to business interests and would eventually be replaced. The surest way to reduce exchange rate uncertainty was to reduce the number of exchange rates in the world. Larger common currency areas would of course require a high degree of monetary policy coordination within each area. Yet if different regional interests could be accommodated within the Federal Reserve's Open Market Committee, why could they not also in, say, a European central bank? Among the questions raised by participants who were not convinced by Cooper's scenario was how real economic shocks would be handled once the nominal exchange rate was no longer a policy instrument; would labor mobility, or the tax and transfer system, or capital mobility take on an expanded role?

(5) *Has recent experience with (sterilized) foreign-exchange market intervention altered earlier views about its effectiveness?* Most participants seemed to be in general agreement with the main conclusions of Maurice Obstfeld's examination of experience with intervention over the 1985–87 period. He found that: monetary and fiscal actions—not sterilized intervention—had been the dominant determinant of broad exchange rate movements; the scale of intervention had been too small to have significant portfolio effects; the "signalling effect" of intervention had been effective only when backed up by action on policy fundamentals; and the most effective intervention operations had been "concerted" ones. John Flemming was uncomfortable with the notion that bonds in different currencies were perfect substitutes since it would imply that portfolios would typically be undiversified. Shuntaro Namba cited econometric work at the Bank of Japan which suggested that sterilized intervention could affect risk premiums but also that these effects had weakened recently. Hans Genberg was skeptical about the quantitative significance of central banks putting their money where their mouths were and put forward the view that intervention operations may merely serve as a "placebo" for public opinion. Martin Feldstein doubted that either concerted intervention or the policy coordination process more generally had contributed much to the 1985–87 fall of the dollar.

(6) *Can the European Monetary System (EMS) be exported?* A short answer—to judge from the study by Francesco Giavazzi and Alberto Giovannini—is no. They argued that the incentives which countries have to belong to the EMS (and to its exchange rate mechanism)—namely, the high degree of trade interdependence and the more comprehensive design of regional integration of which the EMS is just an element—are not present among the United States, Europe, and Japan. In addition, they see the operation of the EMS as an (imperfect) greater deutsche mark area, where the Federal Republic of Germany practices (near) monetary policy independence. The institution of fixed (but adjustable) exchange rates per se cannot in their view induce international monetary cooperation. While endorsing their main conclusions, Wolfgang Rieke pointed out that the Bundesbank's policy independence can be limited by external imbalances; in fact, he conjectured that the potential inflationary consequences for surplus countries may be more than the corresponding constraining effects on deficit countries arising from reserve losses

through intervention. He also reiterated the view that common decision-making in the area of monetary policy (à la European central bank) would cause unease unless price stability was fully accepted as a priority objective. Richard Marston acknowledged the role that trade interdependence can play in motivating measures to reduce exchange rate variability but emphasized that it was only part of the story. Canada, for example, has over 80 percent of its trade with the United States but has allowed its exchange rate vis-à-vis the United States to vary substantially—probably in order to insulate itself from disturbances originating in its main trading partner.

(7) *Do we need greater international coordination of financial policy?* Here, financial policy refers to policies governing international and domestic transactions, markets, and institutions, including the taxation of transactions or the returns to capital. The case for more coordination was laid out by David Folkerts-Landau. He argued that the ongoing, largely uncoordinated restructuring of financial markets can be unstable because of perverse incentives for risk taking by financial institutions. At the same time that private market participants were exploiting the greater opportunities for arbitraging regulatory and fiscal differences across domestic and international jurisdictions, financial authorities did not reduce—in fact, they significantly extended—implicit and explicit liquidity and solvency guarantees to these participants. Francesco Papadia notes that the implicit "competition in laxity by supervisory authorities" is a particular risk for Europe of 1990. Folkerts-Landau concludes that, if globalization and liberalization of financial markets is not to produce suboptimal prudential regulation, or suboptimal allocation and pricing of risk, greater coordination of financial policy is required. Many participants found this line of argument appealing but nevertheless harbored some reservations. Papadia argued that coordination would be clearly welfare improving only if the regulation were due to market failure. Others were concerned about the feasibility of implementing such coordination on a universal basis when there was always an incentive for one location not to impose the regulation in order to capture a larger share of the world's business. A third concern was how to ensure that efforts at eliminating "over-insurance" for financial institutions did not tie the hands of authorities in coordinating their response to an incipient financial crisis.

(8) *Does the existence of large multinational corporations (MNCs) affect the behavior of exchange rates and capital flows?* Kenneth Froot approached this question by looking both at the financial innovations used by MNCs and at their investment decisions. Adopting a Modigliani-Miller-type argument, he maintained that firm financing techniques are basically a "veil" and that investors will not pay the firm to do anything they can do for themselves. He also found some evidence of a positive relationship between excess volatility of asset prices and trading volume (i.e., "noise trading") at very high frequencies and at short horizons. However, MNCs—as opposed to banks—have been responsible for a dramatic rise in currency trading at longer horizons, where speculation appears

to be stabilizing. Foreign direct investment is, in his view, less sensitive to exchange rate uncertainty than are trade flows. A more powerful instrument that influences foreign investment by MNCs is corporate tax codes. Froot illustrated how change in U.S. corporate tax provisions affected U.S. direct investment inflows and outflows in the 1980s—albeit not enough to explain coincident swings in the dollar. Geoffrey Carliner supported Froot's conclusion that MNCs do not increase exchange rate fluctuations. Since foreign direct investment by MNCs is dwarfed by international flows of portfolio capital, Carliner argued that actions of financial institutions—not MNCs—need to be placed at center stage in any institutional actor story of destabilizing capital flows. He also made a plea for giving more attention to international coordination of tax policies since international tax competition can produce suboptimal outcomes. John Flemming too agreed with the basic thrust of Froot's analysis. He noted that an implication of exchange rate instability militating more strongly against trade than against foreign direct investment is that much of undeterred investment displaces deterred trade. He also took issue with the notion that MNCs could contribute to closer adherence to purchasing power parity on two counts: (a) MNCs are not immune to the costs of adjustment of switching production from one source to another; and (b) to the extent that MNCs have market power, they may be well placed to practice price discrimination between different markets.

(9) *Are data on current account positions and international indebtedness adequate as indicators of the need for policy adjustment?* This issue was examined by Lois Stekler, with particular emphasis on the quality of U.S. data. To be sure, her work indicated a number of areas where the existing data are flawed, ranging from large discrepancies between U.S. and Japanese data on purchases of U.S. securities by Japanese residents, to outdated (World War II) benchmark surveys of U.S. portfolio assets abroad, to the effect of securitization of capital flows on shifting transactions from an on-balance to off-balance-sheet basis. In the end, however, she concluded that the shift of the U.S. current account from near balance in the first three years of the 1980s to a deficit of around $150 billion cannot be accounted for by errors and omissions, and that publicly available data also indicate correctly the direction and rough order of magnitude of the U.S. net international investment position.

1 The Rationale for, and Effects of, International Economic Policy Coordination

Jacob A. Frenkel, Morris Goldstein, and Paul R. Masson

Coordination of macroeconomic policies is certainly not easy; maybe it is impossible. But in its absence, I suspect nationalistic solutions will be sought—trade barriers, capital controls, and dual exchange-rate systems. War among nations with these weapons is likely to be mutually destructive. Eventually, they, too, would evoke agitation for international coordination.

James Tobin (1987, 68)

I believe that many of the claimed advantages of cooperation and coordination are wrong, that there are substantial risks and disadvantages to the types of coordination that are envisioned, and that an emphasis on international coordination can distract attention from the necessary changes in domestic policy.

Martin Feldstein (1988, 3)

1.1 Introduction

This paper discusses the rationale and mechanisms for, and the effects of, international coordination of economic policies. Coordination is defined here, following Wallich (1984, 85), as "a significant modification of national policies in recognition of international economic interdependence."[1] The existence of a number of comprehensive surveys of the literature on coordination makes the task easier.[2] This discussion can, therefore, be selective and focus on a number of key issues that impinge on the advisability and practicality of strengthening policy coordination among the larger industrial countries.

Jacob A. Frenkel is the Economic Counsellor and Director of Research at the International Monetary Fund, and a research associate of the National Bureau of Economic Research. Morris Goldstein is Deputy Director of the Research Department of the International Monetary Fund. Paul R. Masson is an Advisor in the Research Department of the International Monetary Fund, and a research affiliate of the National Bureau of Economic Research.

The views expressed are the authors' alone and do not represent the views of the International Monetary Fund.

This paper is organized as follows. Section 1.2 covers economic policy coordination in the widest sense and addresses various dimensions of the rationale for, and scope of, coordination. The terrain covered includes the applicability of the "invisible hand" paradigm to decentralized economic policy decisions, barriers to coordination, the range and specificity of policies to be coordinated, the frequency of coordination, and the number of participants to be included in the coordination exercise. Section 1.3 narrows the discussion to monetary and fiscal policies and turns to the mechanisms or methods of coordination. The emphasis here is on the two broad issues of rules versus discretion and of single-indicator versus multiple-indicator approaches.[3] A brief discussion is also included on the use of indicators in the ongoing Group of Seven (G-7) coordination process.

Section 1.4 confronts the problem of how to infer the effects of coordination. A number of empirical experiments are carried out using a global macroeconomic model (MULTIMOD) developed in the International Monetary Fund. The policies considered include nominal GNP or money targeting, "smoothing" rules for monetary and fiscal policy that imply only modest international coordination, and more activist "target-zone" proposals that place greater international conditions on national authorities in the conduct of monetary and/or fiscal policies. In one set of "historical" simulations, we compare the results of simulated policies to the actual evolution of the world economy over the 1974–87 period. In the other set of simulations, we analyze the effects of various single shocks to particular behavioral relationships under alternative policy rules.

1.2   Rationale for and Scope of Coordination

The most logical starting point is to ask why international policy coordination would be beneficial in the first place. After all, if in the domestic economy the working of the invisible hand under pure competition translates independent decentralized decisions into a social optimum, why should not the same principle apply to policy decisions by countries in the world economy?

The answer is that economic policy actions, particularly those of larger countries, create quantitatively significant spillover effects or externalities for other countries, and that a global optimum requires that such externalities be taken into account in the decision-making calculus.[4] Coordination is then best seen as a facilitating mechanism for internalizing these externalities.

This conclusion can perhaps be better appreciated by emphasizing the departures from the competitive model in today's global economy. Cooper (1987) has identified several such departures, and his analysis merits some extension here.

Unlike the atomistic economic agents of the competitive model who base their consumption and production decisions on prices that are beyond their control, larger countries exercise a certain degree of influence over prices, including the real exchange rate. This of course raises the specter that they will manipulate such prices to their own advantage and at the expense of others. Two examples are frequently cited—one dealing with inflation, and the other with real output and employment. Under floating rates, a Mundellian (1971) policy mix of tight monetary and loose fiscal policy allows an appreciated currency to enhance a country's disinflationary policy strategy—but at the cost of making it harder for trading partners to realize their own disinflation targets. Similarly, under conditions of high capital mobility and sticky nominal wages, a monetary expansion under floating rates leads to a real depreciation and to an expansion of output and employment at home. But the flip side of the coin is that output and employment contract abroad.[5] Seen in this light, the role of coordination is to prevent—or to minimize—such intentional as well as unintentional "beggar-thy-neighbor" practices. Most international monetary constitutions have injunctions against "manipulating" exchange rates or international reserves.

The existence of public goods constitutes a second important point of departure from the competitive model.

When there are N currencies, there can be only $N-1$ independent exchange rate targets. Similarly, not all countries can achieve independently set targets for current account surpluses. Adherents of decentralized policymaking—sometimes rather inappropriately labelled the "German school"—argue that such inconsistencies provide no justification for coordination. Much as in the competitive model, the economic system will generate signals—in the form of changes in exchange rates, interest rates, prices, and incomes—that will lead to an adjustment of targets such that they eventually become consistent. If, however, the path to consistency involves large swings in real exchange rates, or even more problematically, the imposition of restrictions on trade and capital flows, then reliance on decentralized policymaking may not be globally optimal. Implicit in this conclusion is the notion that a certain degree of stability in real exchange rates and an open international trading and financial system are valued in and of themselves as public goods (in contrast, the market signals that resolve supply/demand inconsistencies in the competitive model, are not regarded as public goods). If that is accepted, there is a positive role for coordination, both to identify target inconsistencies at an early stage and to resolve them in ways that do not produce too little of the public good(s).[6] It is of course possible for groups of countries who value the public good highly to attempt to obtain more of it by setting up "regional" zones of exchange rate stability or of free trade, and some have done just that (including the establishment of the European Monetary System [EMS]).[7] But the essence of a public good is that it will tend to be *under*supplied so long as some large suppliers or users act in a decentralized fashion.

Once the realm of atomistic competitors is left and that of nontrivial spillovers of policies is entered—be it via goods, asset, or labor markets—the possibility arises that choices made independently by national governments would not be as effective in achieving their objectives as policies that are coordinated with other governments.[8] Whereas any single country acting alone may be reluctant to follow expansionary policies designed to counter a global deflationary shock for fear of unduly worsening its external balance, coordinated expansion by many countries will loosen the external constraint and permit each country to move closer to internal balance. In addition, coordination may assist the policymaking process by mobilizing peer pressure to help provide governments with the political will to make difficult choices in the face of opposition from domestic pressure groups. The success of Weight Watchers provides an intuitive parallel: while overweight individuals know what needs to be done to meet their targets and could in principle do it entirely on their own, many apparently find it helpful to subject themselves to peer pressure and to engage the moral support of others in like circumstances.

All of this establishes a presumption that there can be valid reasons for deviating from the tradition of decentralized decision-making when it comes to economic policy, that is, that there is scope for coordination. This presumption is reinforced by two empirical observations. The first is that the world economy of 1990 is considerably more open and integrated than that of 1950, or 1960, or even of 1970. Not only have simple ratios of imports or exports to GNP increased but also—and probably more fundamentally—global capital markets have become more integrated (Fischer 1988; Frenkel 1983, 1986). With larger spillovers, there is more at stake in how one manages interdependence. Second, there is by now widespread recognition that the insulating properties of floating exchange rates are more modest than was suspected prior to their introduction in 1973.[9]

But a presumption that cooperation could be beneficial is not the same as a guarantee—nor does it preclude the existence of sometimes formidable *obstacles* to its implementation.

Suppose national policymakers have a predilection for inflationary policies but are restrained from implementing them by the concern that relatively expansionary monetary policy will bring on a devaluation (or depreciation). Yet, as outlined by Rogoff (1985), if all countries pursue such inflationary policies simultaneously, none has to worry about the threat of devaluation. Here, coordination may actually weaken discipline by easing the balance of payments constraint. In a similar vein, as noted by Feldstein (1988) there is the potential risk that a coordinated attempt to stabilize a pattern of nominal or real exchange rates could take place in an inappropriately high aggregate rate of inflation. Equally troublesome would be a coordination of fiscal policies that yielded an aggregate fiscal deficit for the larger countries that put undue upward pressure on world interest rates. The basic point is straightforward: there is nothing in the coordination process in and of itself that reduces the importance of sound macroeconomic policies (Bockelmann 1988). There can be coordination around good policies and coordination around bad ones—just as with the exchange rate regime, where there are good fixes and bad fixes, and good floats and bad floats (Frenkel 1985). Welfare improvements are not automatic.

It is only realistic, too, to acknowledge that there are barriers to the exercise of coordination. Four of the more prominent ones are worth mentioning. First, international policy bargains that involve shared objectives can be frustrated if some policy instruments are treated as objectives in themselves. Schultze (1988), for example, offers the view that it would have been difficult to have reached a bargain on target zones for exchange rates in the early 1980s given President Reagan's twin commitments to increasing defense spending and cutting taxes. In some other countries, the constraints on policy instruments may lie in different areas—including structural policies—but the implications are the same.

Second, there can at times be sharp disagreements among countries about the effects that policy changes have on policy targets. In some cases, these differences may extend beyond the size to even the sign of various policy impact multipliers.[10] The harder it is to agree on how the world works, the harder it is to reach agreement on a jointly designed set of policies.

Third, while most countries have experienced a marked increase in openness over the past few decades, there remain huge cross-country differences in the degree of interdependence. Large countries—the United States being the classic case in point—are generally less affected than small countries by other countries' policies. Coordination—as Bryant (1987) has recently emphasized—is not a matter of altruism. It is rather the manifestation of mutual self-interest. To the extent that large countries are less beset by spillovers and feedbacks than small ones, the formers' incentive to coordinate on a continuous basis may be lower.[11] In this regard, the high degree of trade interdependence shared by members of the EMS can be seen as a positive factor in reinforcing incentives to coordinate in that group.

Finally, as Polak (1981) has reminded us, in terms of national priorities, international bargaining typically comes after domestic bargaining. More specifically, the compromise of growth and inflation objectives at the national level may leave little room for further compromise on demand measures at the international level.

These barriers to coordination should not be overestimated. One of the clearest examples of true coordination—the Bonn Economic Summit of 1978—occurred just when domestic bargaining over the same issues was most intense.[12] The growing integration of capital markets—of which the global stock market crash of October 1987 is but one reminder—has brought the implications of interdependence home to even large countries, and continued empirical work on multicountry models should be able progressively to whittle down the margin of disagreement on the effects of policies. Still, as readers of Sherlock Holmes will be aware, sometimes the most telling clue is that the hounds *didn't* bark. If the scope for coordination is to expand beyond the efforts of the past, these obstacles will need to be overcome.

Turning from the rationale to the scope for coordination, a key issue concerns the appropriate range and depth of policies to be coordinated.

The case for supporting a wide-ranging, multi-issue approach to coordination is that it increases the probability of concluding some policy bargains that benefit all parties (Putnam and Bayne 1984), that favorable spillover effects are generated across negotiating issues, and that improved economic performance today depends as much on trade and structural policies as on exchange rate and demand policies. Exhibit A is the Bonn Economic Summit of 1978 where commitments to accelerate growth by Japan and the Federal Republic of Germany were exchanged for a commitment by the United States to come to grips with its inflation and oil problems, and where agreement on macroeconomic and energy policies has been credited with reinforcing progress on the Tokyo Round of Multilateral Trade Negotiations (Putnam and Henning 1986).

The defense of a narrower approach to coordination rests on the arguments that negotiation costs rise rapidly with the spread of issues under consideration (Artis and Ostry 1986), that prospects for implementation of agreements dim as the number of jurisdictional spheres expands (i.e., finance ministers can negotiate agreements but fiscal policy is typically the responsibility of legislatures, while monetary policy is the province of independent central banks); and that heated disputes on some issues (such as the stance of monetary and fiscal policies) can frustrate the chance for agreements in other areas (like defense and foreign assistance) where coordination might be more fruitful (Feldstein 1988). In addition, a case could be made that coordination is only likely in areas where there is a consensus about the effects of common policies (Cooper 1988).

In view of these conflicting considerations, it is hard to fault present institutional practices on the range of coordination. Those practices entail high-frequency coordination on narrow issues in a multitude of forums (such as the IMF, the Organization of Economic Cooperation and Development [OECD], the Bank of International Settlements [BIS], and the General Agreement on Tariffs and Trade [GATT]);[13] less frequent (say, biannual) and wider coordination at a higher level in more limited forums (such as the IMF's Interim Committee, or the G-7 major industrial countries); and even less frequent (annual), wider-yet coordination at the highest level (heads of state and of governments at the economic summits). Thus, there are occasional opportunities for multi-issue bargaining, but without the exponential increase in negotiation costs that might ensue if this were the order of the day. All in all, probably not a bad compromise.

The ''depth'' of coordination covers the degree of specificity and disaggregation within a given policy area. Here, two issues arise—one dealing with fiscal policy, and the other with structural policies. A strong implication of recent research is that aggregate measures, such as the central or general government fiscal deficit, are not likely to be a good guide to the effects of *fiscal policies* on macroeconomic variables such as the current account, the exchange rate, and the rate of interest (Frenkel and Razin 1987b). The reason is that such effects depend on *how* the deficit is altered: that is, taxes versus expenditures, expenditures on tradables versus nontradables, taxes on investment versus those on saving, fiscal action by a country with a current account surplus versus a deficit, and anticipated versus unanticipated policies. This suggests that more specificity in coordination—quite apart from its positive effect on the ability to monitor the implementation of agreed upon policies— would be desirable. It is notable that the Louvre Accord of February 1987 among the G-7 specified not only quantitative targets for budget deficits but also some quantitative guidelines for how these overall fiscal targets were to be achieved.[14]

In the area of *structural policies,* a good case can also be made for specificity—but on somewhat different grounds. Here, coordination may often best be interpreted not as the simultaneous application of the same policy instrument in different doses or directions across countries, but rather as the simultaneous application of different policy instruments[15]—with each country adopting the policy best tailored to its particular structural weakness.[16] In some cases, this may imply reducing impediments to labor mobility or to market-determined wages; in others, it may mean increasing incentives for private investment relative to those for private saving; and in still others, it may mean changes in the trade and distribution system. The simultaneous application of the policy measures across countries may be necessary to overcome the blocking tactics of domestic pressure groups and to enhance the credibility of the exercise. Again, the depth or specificity of coordination can be as relevant as the range.

Another salient issue concerns the question of *when* to coordinate. There has been, and continues to be, wide variation in the frequency of coordination across different forums—ranging from one-of-a-kind meetings like the 1971 Smithsonian Conference on exchange rates to the near continuous discussion and decision-making at the executive boards of the IMF and the World Bank.

One position is that, given the constraints, true coordination cannot be expected to be more than an episodic, regime-preserving effort. Dini (1988) has recently argued that international considerations still play only a small factor in policymaking, and that only at times of crisis is a common interest in coordinated action clearly recognized.[17] Some might even go further and argue that the reservoir of international compromise should be conserved for situations where there is a high probability of a policy deal and where failure to reach an agreement would carry a high cost.

Our view is that both the likelihood and effectiveness of coordination will be enhanced when it is a regular, ongoing process—and for at least three reasons. First, the potential for multiperiod bargaining expands the opportunities for policy bargains (by facilitating, for example, phasing of policy measures). What should count in assessing the gains to coordination is the present discounted value of welfare-improving policy agreements over an extended period—not the welfare change in a single period. Second, as suggested in the game-theoretic literature, the existence of repeated bargaining strengthens the role of reputational considerations in coordination.[18] In contrast, when coordination is a once-and-for-all or episodic exercise, there is a higher risk that agreed policies will never be implemented because of the much discussed problem of time inconsistency, that is, the temptation to renege on earlier policy commitments when it later becomes advantageous to do so (Kydland and Prescott 1977; Calvo 1978). To be effective, coordination agreements need to pass through the market filter of credibility, and credibility is more likely if sticking to the agreement enhances reputation, which in turn allows profitable bargains to be struck in the future. Third, once coordination is established as a routine ongoing process, there is apt to be more freedom of policy maneuver for all participants than when negotiations are conducted in a crisis atmosphere and when disagreements—which after all are inevitable— may be inappropriately seen as signaling the collapse of coordination itself.[19]

A final question concerns the size of the coordinating group, that is, *who* should coordinate. Again, existing practice does not provide a definitive answer. Among the industrial countries, we have the Group of Seven and the Group of Ten. For the developing countries, there are the Group of Twenty-Four and the Group of Seventy-Seven. And in the executive board of the Fund—where industrial and developing countries alike are represented—there are twenty-two representatives of various country groupings—a Group of Twenty-Two.

Among the factors that should influence the size of the coordinating group, three would seem to stand out. First, to the extent that the raison d'être of coordination is the internalization of externalities, the group should include those countries whose policies generate the largest externalities. This argues for including the largest industrial countries. Second, there is the general proposition that the costs of negotiation, and conflicts that might endanger the continuity of the exercise, increase significantly with the number of players. This argues for a relatively small group. Third, and pointing in the opposite direction, a small group runs the risk of concluding policy agreements which are beneficial to the direct participants—but which are not satisfactory to those countries not sitting at the coordination table.[20] In this connection, it is relevant that the managing director of the Fund participates in G-7 coordination meetings. Since the Fund's membership includes not only the larger industrial countries but also the smaller industrial countries, as well as most of the developing countries, one rationale for the managing director's participation is that it provides a systemic perspective and evaluation on proposed policy agreements—while still keeping the meeting small enough for administrative efficiency.

1.3   Mechanisms of Coordination

This section shifts the focus from whether to coordinate to *how* to coordinate. More specifically, the advantages and disadvantages of alternative mechanisms of coordination are discussed, with particular attention to the issues of rules versus discretion and of single- versus multi-indicator approaches. The use of economic indicators in the ongoing G-7 coordination process is also outlined.

It is not surprising that many of the issues that emerged during the long and continuing debate on the relative merits of rules versus discretion in domestic economic policy should have resurfaced in the dialogue on international economic policy coordination. After all, the present system of managed floating, even as it has evolved since the Plaza Agreement of September 1985, is much closer to a pure discretion than to a pure rules model. In this regard, the gold standard with its automatic specie flow mechanism, the adjustable peg system with its clear implications for the subordination of domestic monetary policy to the exchange rate (except during fundamental disequilibria), the EMS with its parity grid and divergence indicator, target zone proposals with their trigger for coordination discussions whenever the actual exchange rate threatens to breach the zone, and pure floating with its complete prohibition on all official intervention in the exchange market—all can be considered less discretionary than the present exchange rate system.

Those who support a more rule-based approach to international economic policy rest their case on essentially four arguments. First, the most promising route to eliminating any excess demand for coordination in the world economy is not by increasing the supply, but rather by decreasing the demand (or the need) for coordination (Polak 1981; Kenen 1987). That decrease in demand, in turn, can best be brought about by the application of simple policy rules, such as the maintenance of a fixed exchange rate. In the process, one would eliminate—so the argument goes—most of the negotiation costs and burden-sharing conflicts that are intrinsic to more discretionary systems. Second, rules are regarded as the only viable mechanism for imposing discipline on economic policymakers who might otherwise manipulate the instruments of policy for their own objectives.[21] Third, rules are regarded as enhancing the predictability of policy actions and thereby improving the private sector's ability to make informed resource allocation decisions.[22] Fourth, rules are seen as a way of preventing destabilizing fine-tuning, and thus of providing protection against the lack of knowledge about how the economy operates.

The main counterarguments in favor of a discretionary approach are the following. First, rule-based adjustment systems often turn out to be less automatic in practice than in theory. For example, the automaticity of the specie flow mechanism under the historical gold standard was often undermined by the proclivity of authorities to offset or sterilize the effect of gold flows (Cooper 1982; U.S. Congress 1982).

Second, rules will impart discipline to the conduct of macroeconomic policy only to the extent that the penalties for breaking the rules are significant enough to ensure that the rules are followed. The Bretton Woods rule that countries should consult with the Fund once there was a cumulative parity change of 10 percent or more, while complied with in a technical sense, fell short in a substantive sense of its original purpose. The discussion surrounding the revision of the original Gramm-Rudman deficit reduction targets in the United States is a more recent case in point. History could in fact be seen as being just as kind to the proposition that the policy regime adjusts to the amount of discipline that countries want to have—as to the reverse (Goldstein 1980, 1984; Frenkel 1982; Frenkel and Goldstein 1986). Also, care needs to be taken to separate the effects of policy rules on economic outcomes from other influences. In this connection, the oft-made argument that the EMS was a major determinant of the 1979–85 disinflation in Europe would seem to be based on shaky ground.[23]

Third, it is by no means clear that rules are necessary to obtain the benefits of greater predictability of policy. For example, the practice of preannouncing money-supply targets—sometimes accompanied by announcements of public sector borrowing requirements—provides the markets with information on the authorities' policy intentions, but stops well short of a rigid rule.

Finally, while rules diminish the risk emanating from fine-tuning, they increase the risk stemming from lack of adaptability to changes in the operating environment.[24] The idea of a ''crawling-peg'' rule based on inflation differentials drew quite a few supporters in the 1960s as the right antidote for sticky nominal exchange rates. Yet its neglect of the need for real exchange rate changes now seems more serious in light of the real economic disturbances of the early 1970s.[25] More recently, the crumbling of the link between narrow monetary aggregates and the ultimate targets of monetary policy in the face of large-scale financial innovation and institutional change has reminded us anew of the limitations of policy rules.

In light of all this, there may not be any attractive alternative to conducting economic policy coordination in a judgmental way.

Even after the choice is made about coordinating via rules or discretion, there remains the decision of whether to coordinate around a single indicator or a set of indicators.[26]

There are two main considerations that are typically advanced to support the single-indicator approach. One is that it avoids overcoordination of policies by preserving for each country freedom of action over those policies not used to reach the single target variable. Thus, for example, if the exchange rate is the focus of coordination, monetary policy will be constrained, but other policies will be less affected. Implicit in this line of argument is the view that attempts to place many policies under international coordination will ultimately prove self-defeating and may even induce national authorities to compensate by exercising greater independence in *un*coordinated policy instruments, such as trade policy (Frenkel 1975).

The second, and probably more important, defense of a single-indicator approach is that it sends a clear signal to markets about the course of future policy. If, for example, the monetary authorities commit themselves to maintain a fixed exchange rate within a given band, then movements of the exchange rate provide an unambiguous guide for monetary policy. A similar message would derive from a nominal income target for monetary or fiscal policy, with the exchange rate left to determination of the market. In contrast, a multi-indicator approach increases the authorities' scope for discretion since they can appeal to the conflicting messages coming from different indicators. In cases where the authorities' past record of policy performance has been weak and where a single objective of policy is predominant (such as disinflation), a single-indicator framework for coordination can carry significant advantages in the battle to restore credibility to policy.

But relying on a single policy indicator can also carry substantial risks. Perhaps the most serious one is that the single indicator can send weak—or even false signals—about the need for changes in other policies that are not being coordinated. This is perhaps best illustrated by considering the problem of errant fiscal policy under a regime of fixed exchange rates or of target zones.

First, consider fixed rates. With high capital mobility, a fiscal expansion will yield an incipient positive interest rate differential, a capital inflow, and an overall balance of payments surplus—not a deficit. Here, exchange rate fixity helps to finance—and by no means disciplines—irresponsible fiscal policy (Frenkel and Goldstein 1988a). Only if and when the markets expect fiscal deficits to be monetized will they force the authorities to choose between fiscal policy adjustments and devaluation.[27] The better the reputation of the authorities, the longer in coming will be the discipline of markets, that is, the exchange rate will provide only a weak and late signal for policy adjustment. In this connection, it is worth observing that whereas the EMS has produced a notable convergence of monetary policy, convergence of fiscal policy has not taken place (Tanzi and Ter-Minassian 1987; Holtham, Keating, and Spencer 1987).

Next, rerun the same fiscal expansion under a target zone regime, where the zones are to be defended by monetary policy. In such a scenario, the appreciation of the currency induced by the fiscal action will prompt a loosening of monetary policy to keep the rate from breaching the zone. Here, coordination around a single indicator, namely, the exchange rate, will have exacerbated—not corrected—the basic cause of the problems.[28] The single indicator would have sent the wrong signal for policy adjustment.

In contrast, a multi-indicator approach to coordination—assuming that the list of indicators included monetary and fiscal policy variables—would not be susceptible to this weak or false signal problem. This is because such an approach goes directly to the basic stance of fiscal and monetary policies, rather than passing through the medium of the exchange rate. If, for example, the impetus for coordination was a misalignment of exchange rates, and if the root cause of the misalignment was an inappropriate stance and/or mix of monetary and fiscal policies, the multi-indicator approach would be appealing.

But all is not a bed of roses here either. While all effective approaches to coordination require a consistency of policy instruments and targets within and across countries, this requirement of consistency or compatibility can take an added prominence when authorities make public a set of targets and intended courses for policy instruments.

Two aspects merit explicit mention. One is that exchange rate targets—or even concerted views on the existing pattern of exchange rates—must be consistent with the announced course of monetary and fiscal policies. Without that consistency, attempts to provide the market with an anchor for medium-term exchange rate expectations are likely to prove fruitless.

The second point is that the credibility of multiple policy targets also hinges on the constraints on policy instruments. Two such constraints are the striking inflexibility of fiscal policy in almost all industrial countries (Tanzi 1988), and the limited ability of sterilized exchange market intervention to affect the level of the exchange rate over the medium-term, unless of course it provides a signal about the future course of policies (Mussa 1981; Jurgensen 1983). A relevant concern is that limitations on other policy instruments may wind up with monetary policy being asked to carry too heavy a burden—with primary responsibility for maintaining internal and external balance. In such a case, any contribution that a multi-indicator approach to coordination could make to enhancing the predictability of policies would also be diminished. This is so because a shock to the system—such as the October 1987 global stock market crash—might raise in the minds of market participants the question of whether monetary policy would serve its internal or external master.

Some of the broad issues dealing with mechanisms of coordination can be more concretely illustrated by reviewing several of the salient features of the use of indicators in the ongoing G-7 coordination process.

Indicators assist the policy coordination process in at least four ways. First, they are used to help identify likely inconsistencies between prospective policies and targets, as well as among targets themselves—both within and across countries. Second, they serve as a monitoring device to ascertain whether short-term policy actions and performance are "on track" with respect to earlier announced medium-term projections and objectives. Third, indicators are employed to help gauge the international implications of domestic policies and performance for variables such as external payments positions and exchange rates, and to help reach judgments about whether such implications are desirable and sustainable. Finally, indicators serve as a common data base and terms of reference for assessing the current economic situation and policy options; in their absence, policy discussions could become bogged down by disagreements on "what is"—to say nothing about what should be.

The idea of using indicators in multilateral surveillance predates the recent strengthening of coordination. In 1972–74, a working group of the Committee of Twenty on Reform of the International Monetary System examined how objective indicators might be used to allocate the burden of adjustment to international payments disequilibriums (IMF 1974). That work was abandoned with the move to floating exchange rates because it was thought—erroneously, with the benefit of hindsight—that problems of balance of payments adjustment would henceforth be less serious (Crockett 1987). In the wake of the Plaza Agreement, new life was breathed into the use of indicators at the April 1986 meeting of the Interim Committee. Its communiqué suggested, inter alia, that "An approach worth exploring further was the formulation of a set of objective indicators related to policy actions and economic performance, having regard to a medium-term framework" (IMF 1986). The Tokyo Economic Summit of May 1986 gave further support to the use of indicators in the G-7 coordination process. The Tokyo Economic Declaration also specified that the list of indicators should include: GNP and domestic demand growth, inflation, unemployment, trade and current account positions, monetary conditions, fiscal balances, exchange rates, and international reserves.

In terms of our earlier discussion, the application of indicators within the G-7 coordination exercise is better characterized as a discretionary, multiple-indicator approach than as a rule-based, single-indicator one. As hinted at earlier, these two characteristics of the present approach are related: so long as countries have multiple objectives and weight them differently, a multiple-indicator approach may be the only politically feasible one; and once a multiple-indicator approach is adopted, the more likely it is to be discretionary than rule-based. Indeed, there has been widespread agreement in official circles that indicators should be used as an analytical framework for coordination discussions rather than as automatic triggers for policy actions.

Mention should also be made of two recent initiatives in the use of indicators. As proposed at the Venice Economic Summit in 1987 and incorporated in subsequent coordination meetings, aggregate indicators for the G-7 as a whole have been added to the list of individual-country indicators. Aggregate indicators for the group may include such variables as the growth rates of real GNP and of domestic demand, the current account position, and the real exchange rate. Aggregate indicators are intended to fulfill two purposes: to capture the effects of policies of G-7 countries on countries not directly sitting at the table, and to gauge whether the overall stance of policies in major countries is biased toward expansion or contraction. On the first point, alternative policy packages among the larger industrial countries may have quite different implications for developing countries, depending on how they affect such variables as world interest rates, world economic activity, and the volume of world trade. Aggregate indicators are a shorthand mechanism for inferring the magnitude of these linkages between the industrial and developing countries. On the second point, focus on individual-country indicators— for instance, on real exchange rates—does not give a reading on whether aggregate policy is too inflationary or deflationary. In fact, it was this very concern that coordinated policies might lead to either global inflation or global contraction which prompted former U.S. Treasury Secretary Baker and U.K. Chancellor Lawson, at the 1987 Fund-Bank Annual Meeting, to propose a commodity-price basket indicator. This aggregate indicator is intended to serve as a potential "early warning signal" of emerging inflationary or deflationary pressures. The basket includes prices of primary commodities that are traded on world markets and are widely consumed. Issues arise in the construction of the basket about the treatment of oil, the relative weights to be applied to the component commodities, and the currency denomination of the index. Preliminary econometric work suggests that a commodity-price indicator does have some value as a leading indicator of movements in G-7 consumer prices (Boughton and Branson 1988).

1.4 The Effects of Coordination

Identifying key issues related to the rationale and mechanisms for economic policy coordination is one thing; attempting to infer its effects is quite another. The latter is obviously an empirical question that requires for analysis some type of quantitative economic model.

Efforts to gauge the effects of international economic policy coordination or of alternative international monetary arrangements fall into two categories. One strand of the literature compares the value of a welfare function where each country maximizes welfare independently with that where the countries maximize a joint welfare function. Two controversial findings are that the gains from coordination are likely to be "small" for the largest countries and that the gains can even be negative if countries coordinate using the "wrong" model of the world economy.[29]

These findings should not be used as an indictment of coordination—for at least five reasons. First, a comparison of optimal uncoordinated with optimal coordinated policies may not be generalizable to the more relevant comparison of suboptimal uncoordinated with suboptimal coordinated policies. In partic-ular, the link between pressures for protectionism on the one hand, and recession and exchange rates on the other, could result in quite a different counterfactual (i.e., what would happen in the absence of coordination) from that assumed in these studies.[30] To take a specific example, in evaluating the effects of the Plaza Agreement of September 1985, one should ask how protectionist pressures in the U.S. Congress might have evolved in its absence. Second, some of the gains from coordination may be unobservable (unwritten pledges to alter policies in the future), or difficult to separate from less ambitious forms of cooperation (exchange of information across countries), or may extend beyond the realm of macroeconomic policy (joint measures to combat terrorism, to harmonize international fare schedules for air travel, and so on). Third, a judgment that gains from coordination are small presupposes some standard of comparison. Would the gains from international coordination be small relative to the gains from coordination of policies across different economic agencies within a national government?[31] Fourth, empirical estimates of gains from coordination have typically compared policies that do not exploit the incentive governments have to adhere to agreements in order to enhance their reputation for consistency. Currie, Levine, and Vidalis (1987) argue, in contrast, that comparison of "reputational" policies shows large gains. Fifth, the danger that coordination may reduce welfare because policymakers use the wrong model(s) is greatest if they ignore model uncertainty. If, however, policymakers recognize that they do not know the true model and take this uncertainty into account, policy may be set in a more cautious fashion, with positive effects on the gains from coordination (Ghosh and Masson 1988).

The second strain of the empirical literature attempts to quantify the effects of specific policy proposals (such as the introduction of target zones) by comparing them either with a baseline that describes the current policy stance, or with historical values for the macroeconomic variables of interest. This typically involves the simulation of a global econometric model. To date, most attention has been paid to rule-based proposals for policy coordination that focus on real effective exchange rates. Two examples of such studies are Edison, Miller, and Williamson (1987) and Currie and Wren-Lewis (1987). They compare simulated outcomes of cooperative policy rules to recent historical experience. Both of these studies, however, are open to the classic Lucas (1976) critique that, due to the endogeneity of expectations of economic agents, as well as other endogenous responses to the policy regime, estimates of "structural parameters" will differ under different policy regimes; in these studies, expectations are formed in a mechanistic fashion—independent of the policy regime.

In this paper, we present some preliminary rule-based simulations derived from a global macroeconomic model developed in the research department of the IMF and called MULTIMOD. Two sets of simulations results are reported. The first set might be called *historical* simulations. Here, we address two questions: (a) whether a smoother path of monetary and fiscal policies would have produced a smoother path for real exchange rates, real output, and inflation than that observed historically; and (b) what the variability of policy instruments would be under a simple or extended "target zone" scheme where the real effective exchange rate is treated as an intermediate target (Williamson 1985 [1983]; Williamson and Miller 1987). In these historical simulations, the "effects" of coordination are generated by comparing the counterfactual simulations to a baseline simulation where MULTIMOD is constrained to replicate the historical data over 1974–87 by including the appropriate residuals in each equation. These same residuals are also used in the counterfactual simulations, each of which postulates that policy would have been different in some way from its historical stance. Our second set of simulations—for convenience, labeled single-shock simulations—disregard the historical record and focus instead on hypothetical individual shocks to particular behavioral relationships in the model. More specifically, we consider shocks to the demand for money, to aggregate supply, to aggregate demand, to export demand, and to portfolio preferences. Responses to these shocks are then examined under alternative policy rules. In addition to the coordinated rules of simple and extended target zones, we also study monetary targeting and nominal GNP targeting. In short, the objective is to see if, when, and how certain rules are likely to perform better than others.

It could be objected that the rules we consider do not constitute "coordination" in the sense of joint utility maximization, which is the focus of the first strand of literature discussed above. While true, there is certainly an element of coordination in such rules, in the usual meaning of the term (see Frenkel, ch. 3 in this volume). In particular, target zones would have to involve agreement concerning a consistent set of targets; because of the $N - 1$ problem, targets for real effective exchange rates cannot be chosen independently.

By virtue of using MULTIMOD for the simulations, our approach differs from most earlier work in two important respects. One is that expectations are forward-looking and reflect the stance of policy. This permits expectations to differ across different policy regimes.[32] For instance, if it is known that the monetary authorities will resist movements away from an "equilibrium" level for the exchange rate, then this will condition the value expected for the exchange rate in the future. In this sense, the results are less subject to the Lucas critique than most of previous work.[33] In a related vein, the model attributes complete credibility to the government's policy stance and assumes that the private sector forms its expectations in a fashion that turns out to be correct ex post. Thus, it gives a potentially powerful influence to changes in present and future policies. Second, although this paper concentrates on the larger industrial countries, MULTIMOD contains a fully specified developing country block.

Before proceeding to a capsule summary of MULTIMOD and to the simulations themselves, it is worth emphasizing a caveat. We are in a still early stage of applying MULTIMOD to policy coordination issues. The results should, therefore, be considered tentative, preliminary, and relevant only to a few rule-based proposals. Much more will need to be learned over time about which aspects of the simulations are quite model specific, about the sensitivity of the conclusions to particular parameter values, and about the effects of alternative coordination proposals—including those that rely on a judgmental or discretionary application of policies.[34]

MULTIMOD is documented fully elsewhere (Masson and others 1988), and we will therefore limit ourselves here to describing its main features. The model contains separate submodels for the three largest industrial countries— that is, for the United States, Japan, and the Federal Republic of Germany—for the remaining four G-7 countries as a group (France, the United Kingdom, Italy, and Canada), and for the remaining smaller industrial countries as a group. Developing countries (excluding the high-income oil exporters) are modeled as one region, but with some industrial disaggregation. Each of the country or regional submodels has equations explaining the components of aggregate demand as well as the supply of the various goods produced. The submodels are linked through trade and financial flows. The parameters of the behavioral equations are in most part estimated using annual data available since the early 1960s.

In the case of industrial countries, financial markets are assumed to exhibit both perfect capital mobility and perfect substitutability between assets denominated in different currencies.[35] Consequently, arbitrage conditions link the returns on long- and short-term bonds and on domestic and foreign bonds. Moreover, as suggested earlier, expectations are assumed to be forward-looking and to be consistent with the model's solution in future periods. Thus interest parity holds both ex ante and ex post in model simulations where future variables are correctly anticipated—that is, where there are no "surprises" after the first simulation period.[36] As a result, the change in the exchange rate between two currencies from one period to the next is determined by their interest differential prevailing in the first period.

Similarly, expected long-term bond rates and rates of inflation are also consistent with the model's solutions for future periods in the absence of further shocks. The rate of inflation—unlike prices in financial markets—is not assumed perfectly flexible. Instead, rigidities in wage and product markets make for persistent effects on output as a result of purely monetary shocks; only in the medium to long run will full employment result.[37] Thus, both monetary and fiscal policies of the industrial countries have significant and persistent effects on real variables, both in the country undertaking the policy change and in other countries.

In order to provide some feel for the properties of MULTIMOD, table 1.1 shows the effects of monetary and fiscal policies in each of the three major countries on itself, on the other three major countries, and on the remaining G-7 countries.[38] These policy changes are assumed to be *un*anticipated at the time of initiation. Two comments are in order about the results. First, and not surprisingly, policy actions taken by the United States have much larger spillover effects than those undertaken in Japan or in the Federal Republic of Germany. This reflects the large size of the U.S. economy and the fact that, while it is a relatively closed economy to imports, a relatively large share of its imports come from other G-7 countries. Japan is only roughly half as large (in terms of GNP) and obtains more of its imports from outside the G-7 sources. Germany is the most open but is smaller than Japan; the spillovers of its actions primarily affect other European countries. Second, while both monetary and fiscal policies have strong effects on domestic real output over the medium term, fiscal policy has a much larger own-effect on the current account than does monetary policy.[39] This is because the output and relative-price effects go in the *same* direction for a fiscal policy change, whereas they

Table 1.1   Spillovers from Changes in Fiscal and Monetary Policies in MULTIMOD

Country Taking Action	Real GDP[a]				Current balance[b]				Real effective exchange rate[a]			
	United States	Japan	Germany	Other G-7 Countries	United States	Japan	Germany	Other G-7 Countries	United States	Japan	Germany	Other G-7 Countries
	Government Spending Increase of 1% of GNP in 1988[c]											
United States	1.2	0.5	-0.1	0.2	-13	3	-1	3	1.5	-0.3	-0.1	-0.5
	0.6	0.6	0.1	0.6	-18	6	—	7	1.8	-0.2	-0.4	-0.6
Japan	—	1.5	-0.1	0.1	1	-5	—	2	0.1	0.5	0.1	-0.3
	0.1	0.6	—	0.3	1	-8	1	4	-0.1	0.9	—	-0.4
Germany	0.1	0.1	0.8	0.2	1	1	-6	2	-0.3	-0.2	0.7	-0.2
	0.1	0.2	0.3	0.2	—	2	-5	3	-0.4	-0.3	0.9	-0.2
	Increase in Money Supply Target by 5% Relative to Baseline											
United States	1.2	-0.5	-0.3	-0.1	6	5	5	—	-3.8	0.6	1.4	0.6
	0.8	-0.2	-0.1	-0.1	6	5	6	-1	-2.1	0.3	1.0	0.3
Japan	-0.1	1.1	—	—	-1	3	—	-1	0.4	-2.2	0.3	0.6
	-0.1	1.0	-0.1	-0.3	-1	6	-1	-4	0.3	-1.2	—	0.4
Germany	-0.1	—	2.1	—	-1	—	—	1	1.2	0.8	-3.5	1.0
	—	-0.1	1.1	-0.2	—	-1	-1	-1	0.7	0.5	-1.8	0.5

Note: First and second rows for each entry correspond to first and third year domestic and foreign effects.

[a]Percentage deviation from baseline.

[b]Deviation from baseline, billions of dollars.

[c]Temporary; each successive year is 70% of previous year's.

offset each other in the case of monetary policy. A fiscal expansion, for example, induces an appreciation of the real exchange rate and an increase in domestic demand—both of which lead to a fall in net exports.[40] In contrast, a monetary expansion yields a depreciation of the real exchange rate—which promotes net exports—and an increase in domestic demand—which penalizes them; because the relative-price effect dominates—at least in the case of the United States and Japan—the result is a small improvement in the current account.

1.4.1   Historical Simulations

One rather minimalist interpretation of coordination is that large countries should use their monetary and fiscal policies in a largely independent de-centralized way but should avoid sharp changes in policy stance that would, in turn, generate sharp changes in real exchange rates. Such a concession to internalizing externalities would not affect the ultimate size of the stock adjustment of actual to desired policies but would constrain the speed of adjustment—much in the same spirit that speed limits in boat marinas discourage large boats from producing wakes that would topple smaller boats. One exponent of "smoothing" guidelines is Corden (1986, 431), who states:[41]

> If we accept that the spillover effects of a foreign fiscal policy change can be defined as the adverse effects of the destabilization of the real exchange rate, two implications follow.
>
> The most important implication is that each country benefits the other by maintaining relatively stable policies, meaning policies which will minimize real exchange-rate changes in either direction. Coordination consists essentially of a reciprocal agreement to modify policies that generate real exchange-rate instability.

Figures 1.1 to 1.3 summarize developments for some indicators of policy stance since the first full year of generalized floating (1974), while figure 1.4 gives a measure of real effective exchange rates for the G-7 countries.[42] There are well-known difficulties in getting good policy indicators, including the problem that each of the series—money growth, the share of government purchases on goods and services in GNP, and the ratio of tax receipts less noninterest transfer payments to net national product and interest receipts—are all endogenous to some extent. It should also be emphasized that this historical period contains several different policy regimes, ranging from targeting of monetary aggregates over much of the earlier part of the period, to the strengthening of international economic policy coordination since the Plaza Agreement of September 1985.

Nevertheless, some useful stylized facts emerge from an examination of historical data. First, money growth rates are quite volatile and appear to be positively correlated across economies. Second, taxes net of transfers seem to exhibit more variation than government spending; evidence of fiscal stimulus

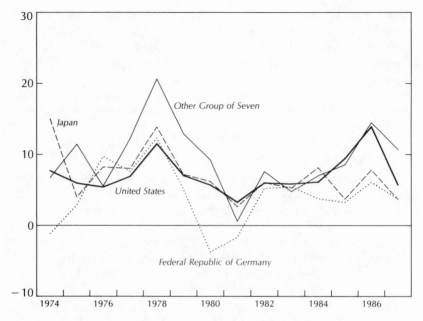

Fig. 1.1   Money growth rates: actual values (percent change)

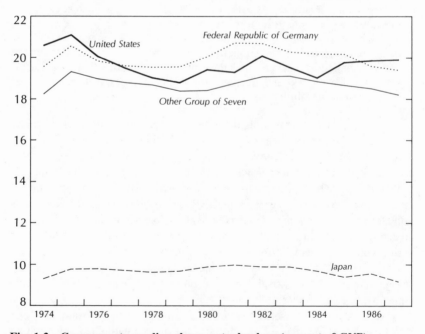

Fig. 1.2   Government spending share: actual values (percent of GNP)

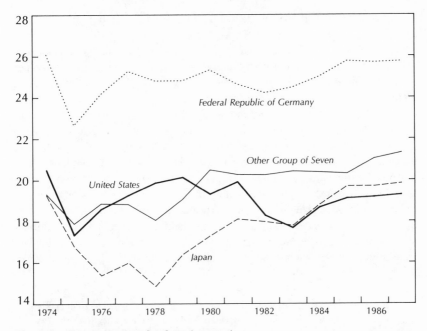

Fig. 1.3   Tax rates: actual values (percent)

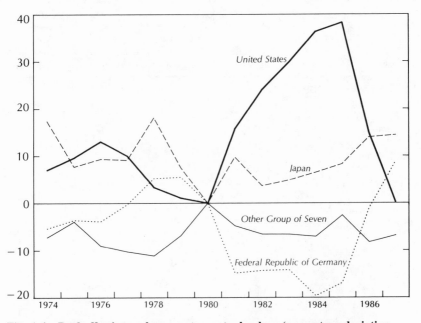

Fig. 1.4   Real effective exchange rates: actual values (percentage deviation from 1980 value)

in the United States in 1983 is clear. Finally, real exchange rates exhibit large fluctuations, especially for the United States.

To estimate the effects of "smoother" policies, each of the variables in figures 1.1 to 1.3 was replaced by its five-year moving average. Those values then were input as exogenous variables into MULTIMOD, and the values of endogenous variables were calculated.

Table 1.2 presents the mean and standard deviation of several macroeconomic indicators, comparing their historical values with those resulting from a simulation of smoother policies. Interestingly enough, smoothing of policy variables is nowhere near sufficient to produce smooth values for major macroeconomic variables. On the contrary, such a simple smoothing rule tends to accentuate some of the fluctuations in the historical data. For example, though the average growth of real gross domestic product is about the same as in the historical data, its standard deviation is higher in the policy smoothing simulation. Real effective exchange rates are somewhat less variable with smoothing, but real short-term interest rates are considerably more variable.

Table 1.2   MULTIMOD Simulations: Comparisons of Historical Policy Stance with Values of Endogenous Variables when Money Growth, Tax Rates, and the Stance of Government Spending in GDP are Smoothed, 1974–1987

	Mean Values		Standard Deviations	
Variable	Historical Values	Simulated Values under Smoothing	Historical Values	Simulated Values under Smoothing
Growth rate of real GDP				
United States	2.5	2.6	2.8	4.6
Japan	3.7	3.8	1.8	2.9
Germany	1.9	2.0	1.9	3.6
Other Group of Seven	2.2	2.4	1.4	3.0
Rate of inflation				
United States	6.5	7.4	3.0	3.0
Japan	5.0	6.5	6.0	5.9
Germany	3.9	4.5	2.1	1.9
Other Group of Seven	10.2	11.4	5.4	6.1
Real effective exchange rate (1980=0)				
United States	14.6	16.3	12.9	11.7
Japan	9.4	9.3	5.2	5.1
Germany	−5.4	−5.1	9.1	8.9
Other Group of Seven	−6.6	−8.6	3.0	3.1
Real short-term interest rate				
United States	2.1	2.5	3.6	4.4
Japan	2.7	2.5	3.5	4.6
Germany	2.9	2.7	2.4	3.1
Other Group of Seven	2.3	2.4	5.7	6.8

This simulation illustrates that smoothing policy instruments may lead to less, not more, smoothness in target variables. Other variables exogenous to the model are also a source of variation in output and exchange rates. The model simulation suggests that the random shocks over the historical period, including changes in nonpolicy variables such as oil production, have had a greater influence in producing swings in exchange rates and in economic activity than economic policy variables. The role of policy has been to accommodate partially those shocks. For instance, money growth rates were increased initially after the first and second oil price shocks, but a permanent increase was resisted. The basic point is that the variability of policy instruments has to a large degree been a response to shocks, rather than an exogenous source of instability;[43] put in other words, the historical period already contains considerable smoothing—albeit of a discretionary rather than rule-based variety—and therefore attempts to impose additional smoothing on top of it do not produce salutary effects.

Note also that real effective exchange rates take on values in this simulation that are very similar to the historical data, though they are somewhat less volatile when policy is smoothed. There seems to be little support here for the notion that exchange rate stability can be achieved solely through the application of simple mechanical smoothing rules. Recall, however, that the smoothing simulation has only considered a change in the path of policy variables—leaving their end points unchanged—rather than a permanent change in those variables. A permanent increase in the rate of money growth or in the shares of taxes or government spending in output might have more powerful effects.

A more activist approach to the coordination of economic policies would go beyond smoothing. One such approach would be to postulate that monetary authorities resist movements of an intermediate variable—in particular the real effective exchange rate—from their long-run equilibrium levels. A system of target zones for exchange rates has been proposed by Williamson (1985 [1983]) and extended by Williamson and Miller (1987). The original proposal calculated "fundamental equilibrium exchange rates" and advocated the use of monetary policies to resist movements away from those rates. As explained by Williamson:

> The basic focus of exchange rate management should be on estimating an appropriate value for the exchange rate and seeking to limit deviations from that value beyond a reasonable range. (1985 [1983, 47])
>
> While other techniques, like sterilized intervention, may be able to give limited assistance, a serious commitment to exchange rate management leaves no realistic alternative to a willingness to direct monetary policy at least in part toward an exchange rate target. (56)

More recently, Williamson and Miller (1987, 7) supplement the prescription that monetary policies be used to target real effective exchange rates with the assignment of fiscal policies to targets for the growth in domestic demand for the G-7 countries: "The basic argument is that a nominal income target fulfills the same function as a money supply rule, providing a "nominal anchor" to prevent inflation from taking off and a guide to expectations, while avoiding the shocks to demand that come from variations in velocity." In addition, the proposal, or "blueprint," specifies that "the average level of world (real) short-term interest rates should be revised up (down) if aggregated growth of nominal income is threatening to exceed (fall short of) the sum of the target growth of nominal demand for the participating countries." (2)

Earlier simulation studies of target zones have been undertaken by Williamson and Miller (1987, App. C), based on Edison, Miller, and Williamson (1987). Those studies employed the Federal Reserve Board's multicountry model (MCM), which is characterized by adaptive expectations. As emphasized earlier, MULTIMOD uses model-consistent forward-looking expectations—a difference that should, in our view, produce more firmly grounded answers.

Two simulations were performed—one for the original target zone proposal (labeled "target zones"), and one for target zones augmented by a rule for fiscal policy (labeled "blueprint"). The attempt was made to stay close to the spirit of the original proposals while still making a few minor modifications.

Much of the action in a target-zone scheme centers around the monetary reaction function since it is monetary policy that is typically assigned to the exchange rate. In the standard version of MULTIMOD, the reaction function for short-term interest rates involves resisting movements away from an exogenous target for base money. The demand for base money, in turn, is assumed to depend on real GNP and on its deflator with elasticities close to unity. When the effects of target zones are simulated, this term is retained but with a much lower weight than normal.[44] The "target-zone" element in the reaction function is represented by the assumption that the short-term interest rate deviates from the baseline depending on the cube of the deviation of the real effective exchange rate from its target value (Edison, Miller, and Williamson 1987, 97). Thus, the monetary policy rule used in both the target-zone and blueprint simulations takes the following algebraic form:

$$R = R^b + [(c - \bar{c})/n]^3 + a[\bar{m} - m],$$

where, as in Edison and others (1987), R is the short-term rate, R^b is its baseline value, c is the log of the real effective exchange rate, $\bar{c}$ its target value, and n is half the width of the target zone, (namely, 10 percent); $\bar{m}$ is the target for the (log of the) monetary base, m the long-run demand for the monetary base with baseline interest rates but simulated output and prices, and a is a negative constant.[45]

Targets for the real effective rate were taken from Williamson (1985 [1983]).[46] As in Edison, Miller, and Williamson (1987), an adjustment to the level of the target real effective rate is made to keep it compatible with the definition used in the model, but the constraint is imposed that the translated target exchange rate variable follow the same path as in Williamson (1985 [1983]).[47]

As mentioned earlier, the "blueprint" proposes that fiscal policy follow a rule targeted on nominal domestic demand growth. As such, the equations in MULTIMOD for real government spending on goods and services had to be endogenized along such lines. The target paths for nominal domestic demand growth were taken from Williamson and Miller (1987) for the period 1980–87; outside that period, we used their formula to calculate targets.

The main results of interest are portrayed in figures 1.5 to 1.8, where actual (historical) values are compared to simulated values for the target-zone proposal and for the blueprint proposal. The figures cover real effective exchange rates, real GNP growth rates, rates of inflation, and current account balances. Bands 10 percent each side of Williamson's (1985 [1983]) fundamental equilibrium exchange rates have been drawn on figure 1.5.

Several interesting—albeit tentative—conclusions emerge from the simulations.

First, there is surprisingly little success in limiting real exchange rate movements away from their targets, especially for the United States.[48] This is apparent for both the more limited assignment of monetary policy to target exchange rates and the case where fiscal policy is made endogenous, though not specifically for exchange rate targeting. Also, the cost of resisting exchange rate movements in terms of greater variability of nominal interest rates appears to be quite high in the model. In 1985, the short-term rate in the United States is 370 basis points below its baseline value in the target-zone simulation, and 260 basis points above in Germany. An attempt to increase the feedback onto interest rates of real exchange rates produced explosive behavior in the model and negative nominal interest rates. Why is the movement in real effective exchange rates so small? In the model, this is the result of the long-run neutrality of real variables with respect to monetary policy, of the relatively small impact of interest rates on exchange rates when exchange rates are anchored by perfect foresight, and of the fact that monetary policy changes are anticipated in advance. A nominal depreciation resulting from anticipated monetary expansion leads quite soon to increases in import prices and domestic inflation, reducing the amount of real depreciation. Such a scenario has been discussed by Feldstein (1988, 7) in the following terms:

> If the United States had agreed in 1983 to stop the dollar's rise, the easiest way would have been for the Federal Reserve to ease monetary policy. . . . The easier monetary policy would produce inflation and the inflation would cause the dollar's nominal value to decline. In the end, there would have been no change in the real exchange rate or the trade deficit but a higher price level and a high rate of inflation.

With perfect foresight of policy changes, the required movements in monetary policy may be quite large for even small, and transitory, real exchange rate changes. It can be seen from figure 1.5 that the dollar's real

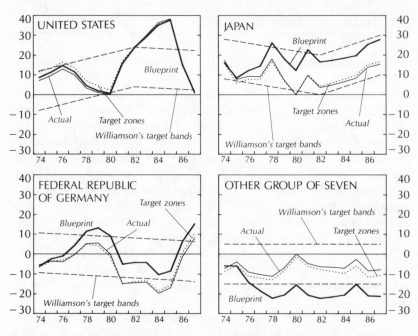

Fig. 1.5   Real effective exchange rates: actual and simulated values (percentage deviation from 1980 value)

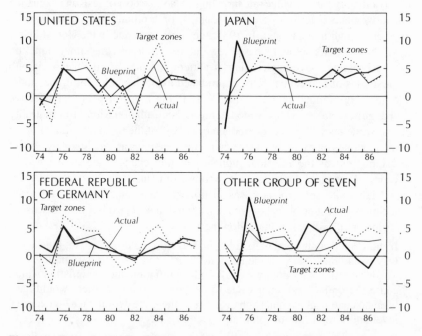

Fig. 1.6   Rate of growth of GNP: actual and simulated values (percent change)

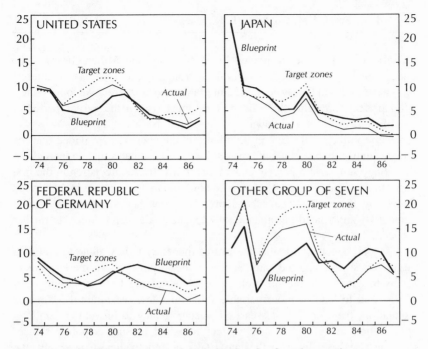

Fig. 1.7 Rate of inflation: actual and simulated values (percent)

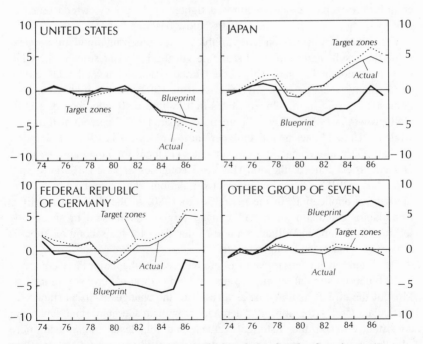

Fig. 1.8 Current account balance: actual and simulated values (percent of GNP)

effective exchange rate is judged by Williamson and Miller (1987) to be undervalued in 1978–80, but overvalued from 1982 to 1985. Thus, interest rates have to rise in the earlier period but fall in the latter (relative to baseline). With perfect foresight, the amount they must rise in the earlier period is amplified because it is known that they will be lower later.[49] Note that monetary policy is effective in the model in the short run, provided that the money supply change is *un*anticipated. Table 1.1 indicates that an increase in the money supply of 5 percent causes a real effective depreciation in the first year ranging from 2 percent in the case of Germany to 4 percent in the United States; by the second year, the depreciation has been reduced to 1 to 2 percent. If anticipated beforehand, the extent of the depreciation is further reduced.

A second conclusion is that the use of monetary policy alone to maintain target zones—keeping the same stance of fiscal policy as in the baseline— seems to exacerbate the inflationary pressures of the late 1970s and early 1980s, and to lead to more variable inflation rates; see figure 1.7. In this simulation, the United States eases monetary policy to prevent the dollar's appreciation in 1980–85; with perfect foresight of such a policy stance, inflation rises somewhat in the late 1970s in anticipation. Conversely, the dollar's undervaluation in 1987 (according to the calculated fundamental equilibrium exchange rate) requires a tightening of policy, which tends to lower inflation rates in the mid-1980s below baseline levels.

The substantial effects on real variables in the blueprint simulation appear to be the result mainly of the fiscal rule. In the blueprint simulation, GNP growth is smoothed considerably in the United States and the Federal Republic of Germany (see fig. 1.6). The recession of 1982 and the high growth of domestic demand in the United States in 1984 are both smoothed out; U.S. GNP growth in 1984 is only 2.7 percent, compared to 7.2 percent historically, while the United States no longer experiences a recession in 1982. Moderation of sharp GNP movements is however not so evident for Japan and the other G-7 countries. Indeed, the non-U.S. G-7 countries experience large output variations in 1975–76 in the blueprint simulations. This may be a result of a mechanical application (in the period up to 1980) of the Williamson-Miller formula for calculating nominal demand targets; if adjusted in an ad hoc fashion (as is done in Williamson and Miller 1987 for the second oil shock), a more reasonable path might result.

Third, current account imbalances are reduced for the major three countries in the blueprint simulation, in the sense of being closer to zero; see figure 1.8. Most of the effects again come as a result of the changes in fiscal stance. In particular, targets for domestic demand growth in Germany and Japan are consistently above the historical values, and this leads to a much more stimulative fiscal policy in these countries (see Williamson and Miller 1987, figs. 4 and 5). But again, there is a cost. General government fiscal deficits reach 10 percent of GNP in Germany and 8 percent in Japan in the early 1980s!

By the same token, it is the fiscal stimulus—rather than the monetary policy change—that is the cause of the sizable appreciation of the yen and deutsche mark in the 1980s relative to baseline. Clearly, such large deficits would be neither desirable—nor tolerable politically. It is also noteworthy that the counterpart to the smaller current account surpluses in Germany and Japan is larger surpluses in the other G-7 countries, rather than a reduction of U.S. deficits. This occurs because a weighted average of domestic demand targets for France, the United Kingdom, Italy, and Canada in Williamson and Miller (1987) is consistently lower than actual demand over the period 1974–87.

1.4.2   Single-Shock Simulations

In our view, the results of the historical simulations are instructive. Still, it is not clear to what extent these results reflect either the specific shocks that were present in the 1974–87 historical episode or the assumption made that all exogenous variables—including the shocks—were known prior to their occurrence. Furthermore, because the historical data contain a great variety of shocks, interpretation of the simulation results is blurred. In what follows we do a set of simpler experiments with the model, where only one shock to a particular behavioral relationship is assumed to occur. The shock, which is assumed to have been unanticipated when it occurred, is an innovation that applies to a single period. Though temporary, the shock nevertheless has persistent effects because errors are serially correlated and because the structural equations of the model include lagged effects. Expectations are assumed to be formed in the model in a way that properly takes into account the subsequent dynamics; that is, once the shock has occurred, perfect foresight is assumed to prevail.

No more than the historical simulations, results from single shocks do not allow a complete evaluation of policy rules. Clearly, the relative variance of various shocks should influence the choice among policy rules (Poole 1970; Henderson 1979). The historical simulations that were discussed above do capture the relative importance of the different shocks, but only for one historical episode. More informative perhaps would be evaluation of policy rules under a series of drawings from the distribution describing the shocks—a subject that we hope to investigate in a forthcoming paper. Nevertheless, analyses of single shocks do permit some intuition to be brought to bear on the issue of policy choice; they should shed some light on when particular rules are likely to perform better than others. Ranking the rules would, however, generally require an explicit objective function that specifies the weights attached to output fluctuations, inflation, and other objectives.

In the simulations reported below, we expand the set of policy rules to include not only simple and extended target-zone schemes, but nominal GNP and money targeting as well. It is implicitly assumed that nominal GNP and money targeting involve less coordination than target zones, although there is no reason to rule out the possibility that nominal GNP (or nominal domestic demand or money) targets might be internationally coordinated. The four policy rules can be compactly summarized as:

1. *Money targeting:* the short-term interest rate is aimed at a target for the monetary base; real government expenditure is exogenous.
2. *Nominal GNP targeting,* using the short-term interest rate. Again, government expenditure is exogenous.
3. *Target zones,* using the short-term interest rate; the level of world interest rates is also adjusted up or down as a function of world nominal income. Government expenditure is exogenous.
4. *Blueprint proposal:* As for target zones, but in addition government expenditure is aimed at a target for nominal domestic demand (i.e., absorption).

To be more precise about the implementation of the alternative policy rules, consider the following equations where lower-case variables denote logs and upper-case variables represent levels. In particular, M is the monetary base (m is its logarithm), u is a random shock to the demand for money, Y is nominal GNP, WY is aggregate nominal income (in dollars) of industrial countries taken together, Q is real GNP, P is the GNP deflator, A is nominal domestic absorption, G is real government expenditure on goods and services, C is competitiveness (the relative price of domestic to foreign output), and R is the short-term interest rate. A b superscript indicates baseline values, which are also assumed to be the target values of the relevant variables. Implicitly then, the simulations start from a position of equilibrium, which is disturbed by the shock being considered. The goal of each of the rules should be to return the economy as quickly and smoothly as possible to the initial equilibrium.

(1) *Money targeting:*

$$R = R^b + 13.5 \left[m^d - m^b \right]$$

where m^d is long-run money demand, ignoring the effect of interest rates; m^d is given by:

$$m^d = p + .970 \, q + 5.15 \, u$$

(2) *Nominal GNP targeting:*

$$R = R^b + 25 \left[y - y^b \right]$$

(3) *Target zones:*

$$R = R^b + \left[(c - c^b)/0.1 \right]^3 + 25 \left[wy - wy^b \right]$$

(4) *Blueprint:*

$$R = R^b + \left[(c - c^b)/0.1 \right]^3 + 25 \left[wy - wy^b \right]$$
$$(G - G^b)/Q^b = (A^b - A)/A^b$$

The form of the policy rules requires some explanation, especially since they differ slightly from those performed for the historical period. In general, we have attempted to follow as closely as possible the intentions of their advocates. The form selected resulted from some experimentation that identified inadequacies with alternative specifications or with feedback parameters. In particular, since policy changes have lagged effects on their targets, "instrument instability" may result if one attempts to hit the targets too closely period by period (Holbrook 1972). This applies most forcefully to the interest rate instrument, where caution needs to be exercised not to set the feedback coefficient too high.

Rule (1), for *money targeting,* used the same specification as in the standard version of MULTIMOD. If a money target were exactly achieved, an implication would be an explosive, sawtooth pattern for short-term interest rates. For this reason, equation (1) allows interest rates to equate the long-run demand for money (conditional on observed GNP) to the money stock target. The short-run demand for money can be written as:

$$m = p + .1883 \, q - .0070 \, R - .0074 \, R_{-1} + .8058 \, (m - p)_{-1} + u,$$

where u is an error term. Setting $m = m^b$ and solving for R, on the assumption that $R = R_{-1}$ and $m - p = (m - p)_{-1}$, yields

$$R = -13.5 \, (m^b - p) + 13.1 \, q - 69.4 \, u$$

A rearrangement of this equation, on the assumption that the equation also holds in the baseline, gives rule (1) above.

Nominal GNP targeting has been proposed by Tobin (1980) and others as preferable to money targeting because it avoids an inappropriate tightening or easing of monetary policy in response to velocity shocks. The form that such a nominal GNP target might take has been discussed by Taylor (1985b), Fischer (1988), and Tobin (1980). Rule (2) was specified in terms of a target for the *level* of nominal GNP, rather than its rate of change, because of the potential instability of the latter identified in Taylor (1985b). Some experimentation with feedback coefficients led to a value of 25. Since the interest rate is in percent, this implies that a 1 percent deviation from the nominal GNP target leads to a 25 basis point increase in the interest rate. Such a value yields a flatter aggregate demand schedule (in $Q - P$ space) for nominal GNP targeting than for money targeting (Taylor 1985b). Since the coefficient of real income is approximately unity in equation (1), the money rule can also be framed in terms of nominal GNP with the difference that the error in the demand-for-money equation would then also affect the setting of interest rates.

Target zones, rule (3), follow the form described in Williamson and Miller (1987) and in Edison, Miller, and Williamson (1987). There are some slight modifications relative to the historical simulations, such that the feedback rules are closer to those proposed in the "blueprint." Specifically, the width of the target zone is taken here to be 10 percent, not the 20 percent used in the historical simulation. The problems of nonconvergence that were present in our historical simulations did not surface here, allowing us to increase the reaction of short-term interest rates to deviations from fundamental equilibrium exchange rates. Also, the nominal anchor for prices is the target level of world nominal income—rather than money supply targets. Note that it is the level, not the rate of change of world nominal GNP that appears in the equation, again reflecting Taylor's (1985b) findings. The feedback coefficient on world nominal GNP was taken to be the same as for domestic nominal GNP targeting.

The *extended target zones* or *"blueprint"* proposal, rule (4), contains an equation for government spending that does not hit domestic-demand targets exactly. However, since the first-year multiplier effect on output of G is close to one, the rule allows approximate achievement of domestic-demand targets.

So much for the policy rules. The (transitory) shocks that we consider are the following:

(A) A shock to the *demand for money*—that is, to velocity—in the United States of 2 percent.
(B) An *aggregate supply shock* in the United States; in particular, the residual in the equation for the rate of change in the nonoil GNP deflator is increased by 2 percent.
(C) An *aggregate demand shock* in the United States: a positive innovation in consumption equal to 1 percent.
(D) A *shift in demand* towards U.S. goods, equal to 10 percent of U.S. exports.
(E) A *portfolio preference shift* out of U.S. dollar assets, leading to an increase in the required rate of return on dollar assets by 10 percentage points.

Each of the rules is simulated subject to each of the five shocks, one at a time. Figures 1.9 to 1.12 give the main results of interest.

The *money demand shock* is not plotted because the results are straightforward to describe. It is only in the case of money targeting that the money shock has any effect on policy settings and on other endogenous variables (there is a small effect of the money shock on consumption because money is a component of net wealth, but the magnitude is negligible). In the case of money targeting, the positive innovation to money demand leads to temporarily higher short-term interest rates, and as a consequence, to temporarily lower economic activity. Other rules ignore the money demand shock and maintain policy instruments unchanged; macroeconomic variables therefore remain at their equilibrium levels. This points up the superiority of these rules in the face of money demand shocks—an argument similar to that made by the advocates of nominal GNP targeting (Tobin 1980). Of course, if shifts in money demand could be identified, then the rule for targeting money could be modified to target a "shock-corrected" money stock that omitted the term u.

The *aggregate supply shock* (or cost-push inflation shock) yields a variety of responses (fig. 1.9). This shock tends to put upward pressure on the domestic output price relative to the absorption deflator, leading to some

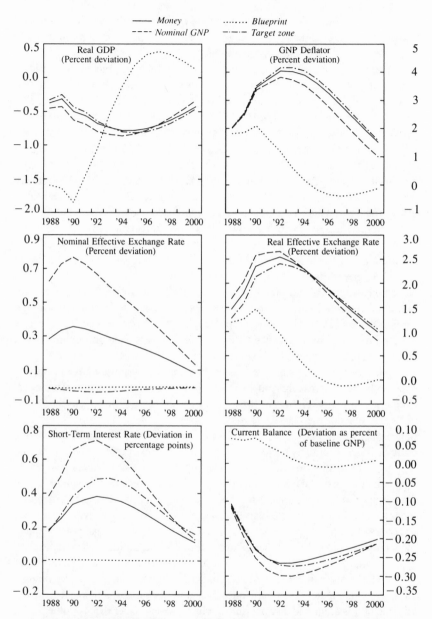

Fig. 1.9   Simulated effects of U.S. aggregate supply shock (deviations of U.S. variables from baseline)

(short-run) stimulus to consumption as well as higher inflation. As mentioned above, the greater flatness of the aggregate demand curve under nominal GNP targeting—vis-à-vis money targeting—leads to a greater response of interest rates and hence greater short-run output losses but smaller increases in prices. Which of the two rules is preferable depends on the trade-off between the two objectives of output and price level stability, as well as on the discount rate that captures intertemporal trade-offs.[50] There is also a considerable difference between responses under the target-zone and blueprint rules. Using monetary policy to counteract the real appreciation of the U.S. dollar requires *lower,* not higher, U.S. nominal interest rates. However, for both the target-zone and blueprint rules, there is an additional term (with admittedly an arbitrarily imposed coefficient) that tends to raise interest rates if world nominal GNP grows too fast, which is the case here. Under target zones, the result is that U.S. interest rates rise but by somewhat less than interest rates in other industrial countries. This leads to a small nominal dollar depreciation, which tends to add to inflationary pressures but limits output losses. In contrast, under the blueprint rule U.S. government spending contracts to counteract the stimulus to consumption, helping to limit the real appreciation of the dollar. The net effect on output is negative because domestic demand is close to its baseline value, but foreign demand falls. However, output is actually higher after seven years, by which time prices have returned to their baseline levels. The bottom line is that an aggregate supply shock causes a dilemma for the first three rules because one instrument has to wear two hats: that is, monetary policy has not only to resist inflationary pressures but also to neutralize output effects or resist the real exchange rate appreciation in the country experiencing the shock.[51]

Next, consider the *aggregate demand shock,* namely, a 1 percent increase in U.S. consumption (see fig. 1.10). Again, the effects differ under alternative policy rules. Absent any policy changes, such a shock will increase output and put upward pressure on prices, as well as appreciate the real exchange rate and lead to a decline in the current account. It also generates positive spillovers for the output of other countries. Since nominal GNP rises, as does the demand for money, both rules (1) and (2) cause interest rates to rise; again, given the relative steepness of the aggregate demand curves, the output and price increases are more moderate under nominal GNP targeting. Turning to the coordinated rules, the real appreciation of the U.S. dollar leads to a smaller rise in interest rates in the United States than in other industrial countries under target zones. However, by limiting the interest rate increases in the United States in response to a demand increase, this rule builds in inflationary pressures, which persist longer than for other rules. In contrast, the extra degree of freedom accorded by fiscal policy in the blueprint rule allows the aggregate demand shock to be almost completely offset by lower government spending. As a result, the output, price, and real exchange rate effects are smallest for this rule.

Figure 1.11 presents results from an aggregate demand shock that corresponds to a shift towards U.S. goods and away from other countries' goods.

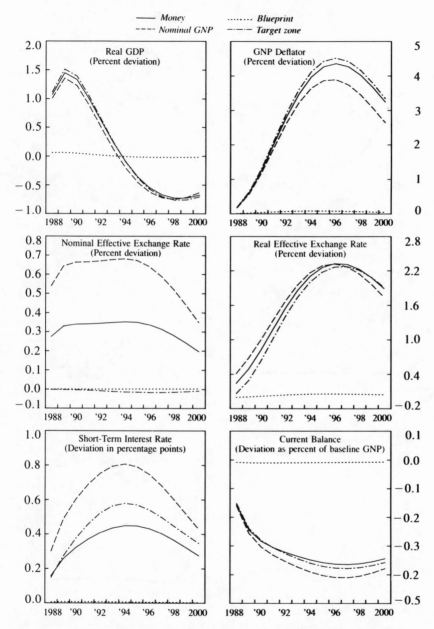

Fig. 1.10   Simulated effects of a shock to U.S. consumption (deviations of U.S. variables from baseline)

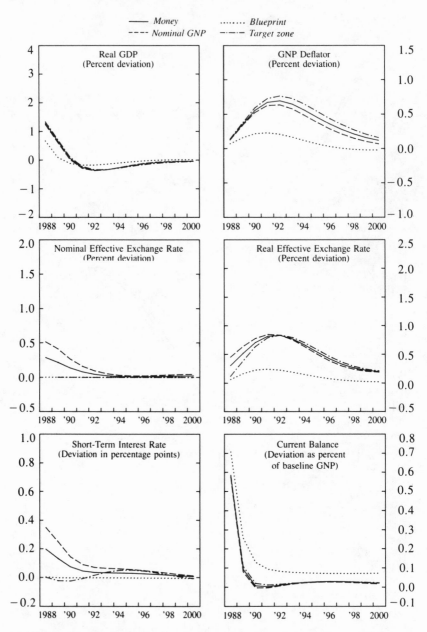

Fig. 1.11   Simulated effects of a shock to U.S. exports (deviations of U.S. variables from baseline)

The positive shock to U.S. exports of 10 percent shows up in lower exports of other countries in proportions that correspond to their shares in world trade;[52] the U.S. current account improves by some $30 billion in the first period. For all policy rules, U.S. real output rises initially, and price increases are relatively small. The contrast is greatest in the behavior of short-term interest rates. Neither real exchange rates nor world nominal GNP change much, so that there is little effect on interest rates under target zones or the blueprint. However, money and nominal GNP targeting resist the rise in activity and prices in the U.S. by raising interest rates.

The final shock is to the *exchange rate of the dollar* (against the yen, the deutsche mark, and other industrial country currencies) brought about by a 10 percent increase in the required return on dollar assets. Output effects are largest for the two uncoordinated rules (money and nominal GNP targeting) and least for the coordinated rule (the blueprint) that uses both monetary and fiscal instruments. The exchange rate overshoots under all four rules, with the U.S. nominal effective exchange rate depreciating by about 15 percent in the first year. Under target zones, the GNP deflator shows no signs of stabilizing (fig. 1.12). Under the blueprint, higher domestic demand results from the income effect of higher exports; as a result, government spending must fall to achieve the nominal domestic-demand target. This leads to a *greater* real depreciation of the dollar in the years 1990–96 than under the other rules, and a larger current account balance.

To sum up, there are five basic conclusions that emerge from these simulations of individual shocks.

First, as in the historical simulations, monetary policy is relatively ineffective when its subsequent effects are anticipated. This conclusion seems to follow whether or not the shocks themselves are anticipated. Conversely, fiscal policy—in particular, variations in government spending—seems to be quite powerful in influencing real output, real exchange rates, and current accounts. Clearly, then, a comparison of rules that use both fiscal and monetary policy with those that just use monetary policy will favor the former. But there is a catch. The use of fiscal policy may not have the flexibility that is assumed for it in, say, the blueprint rule. It may be constrained by other objectives— including the need to reduce budget deficits or to limit the importance of government in the economy. As such, fiscal policy may not be able to react immediately to shocks, at least not within the one-year period assumed here.

Second, it does appear that the behavior of alternative policy rules in response to different shocks is quite different. Rules that perform best for some shocks may perform least well for others. In some cases, however, it is clear which rule dominates (or which rules dominate). For instance, if money demand shocks are prevalent, then monetary targeting is not appropriate. Somewhat surprisingly, even when portfolio preference shifts are frequent, our results do not suggest that target zones—implemented through monetary policy changes—would be preferred. Reliance on monetary policy to ensure that real exchange rates remain within target bands may not be effective.

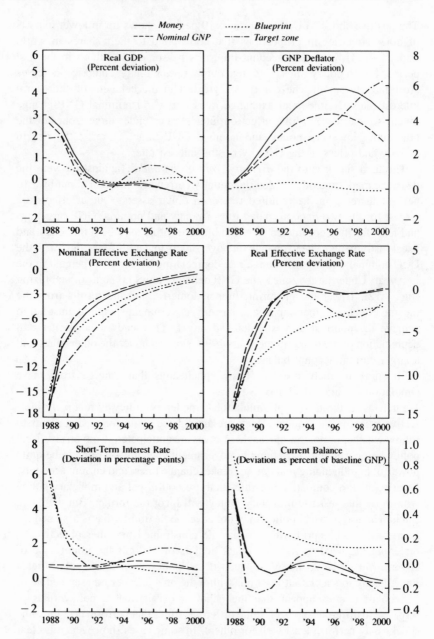

Fig. 1.12   Simulated effects of a shock to the value of the U.S. dollar (deviations of U.S. variables from baseline)

Third, nominal GNP targeting—while it dominates money targeting if velocity shocks are prevalent—may be subject to acute problems of instrument instability, implying that an attempt at close control would involve large swings in interest rates from period to period. Because of the relative ineffectiveness of monetary policy to affect real magnitudes in the model, using monetary policy to target nominal GNP would have to allow for large deviations from targets. It is therefore unlikely to be very precise. As a consequence, the advantages for credibility of framing policy on a single indicator are apt to be diluted by the inability of the authorities to achieve close control of that indicator. Nominal GNP targeting could also make it too easy for authorities to walk away from their targets by citing forces "beyond their control."

Fourth, the simple target-zone proposal is also subject to the ineffectiveness of monetary policy. As a result, target zones that rely solely on monetary policy do not seem capable of maintaining real effective exchange rates within bands that are even 10 percent on either side of the target. While, we have considered only arbitrary shocks, a comparison with estimated variances suggests that they are not out of line with historical experience. This relatively small impact of interest rates on real exchange rates in the model is due in large part to the twin properties that exchange rates are anchored by perfect foresight and that perfect foresight is assumed to prevail following the shocks. If the equilibrium level of the exchange rate were uncertain, or there were extrapolative expectations, then target zones might have greater effectiveness. Another important consideration is that for some shocks—in particular, a supply shock—the target zone would move monetary policy in a perverse direction. By resisting the real appreciation resulting from an inflationary shock, it would exacerbate those inflationary pressures.

Fifth and finally, target zones augmented by the use of the fiscal instrument—as outlined in the blueprint proposal—are more successful in limiting the effects of shocks. Its greater success in limiting movements away from long-run equilibrium real exchange rates derives mainly however from the use of fiscal policy. As suggested earlier, if fiscal policy is constrained by other objectives—or cannot be used flexibly—then the implied ability to counteract shocks may be illusory. Our results are an illustration of the point that it is clearly desirable to improve the flexibility of the budgetary process, whatever the objectives that guide fiscal policy.

Notes

1. Other definitions of coordination include: "decisionmaking that maximizes joint welfare and thus enables international interdependencies to be positively exploited" (Artis and Ostry 1986, 14); and "agreements between countries to adjust their policies in the light of shared objectives or to implement policies jointly" (Horne and Masson

1988, 261). A more general term is "cooperation," which includes policy coordination, but also extends to exchange of information and consultation among countries. We do not address these issues of terminology in this paper.

2. See the surveys by Artis and Ostry (1986), Cooper (1985), Fischer (1988), Hamada (1979), Horne and Masson (1988), Kenen (1987), Polak (1981), and Wallich (1984).

3. Another key issue relating to mechanisms for coordination is that of hegemonic versus more symmetric systems; on this, see Frenkel, Goldstein, and Masson (1988).

4. Evidence on the size of spillover effects from policy actions by the major industrial countries is discussed in the latter part of this section and in Table 1.1.

5. The conclusion that a monetary expansion under floating rates affects real output in opposite directions at home and abroad is associated with the Mundell-Fleming model (Mundell 1971; Fleming 1962). For a recent evaluation of this model, see Frenkel and Razin (1987a); a broader survey of the international transmission mechanism can be found in Frenkel and Mussa (1985). Econometric models are more divided on whether a monetary expansion under floating rates has negative transmission effects on real output abroad; see Helliwell and Padmore (1985) and Bryant and others (1988).

6. Corden (1986) has recently argued that there may be a case for asking large countries to slow their speed of adjustment to desired policy targets so as to dampen movements in real exchange rates that could cause difficulties for others (see sec. 1.4).

7. Another constraint on regional attempts to create more of the public good is that they may divert or discourage its production outside the region; the argument here is analogous to the concepts of "trade creation" and "trade diversion" in the customs union literature.

8. To reach this conclusion, it is necessary to assume that each player does not have sufficient policy instruments to achieve all its policy targets simultaneously, and that coordination alters the trade-offs among policy targets; see Gavin (1986). Without those assumptions, the motivation for coordination would disappear.

9. See Goldstein (1984). This is not to say that the insulating properties of floating rates are inferior to those of alternative regimes. Indeed, it is hard to see any other exchange rate regime surviving the shocks of the 1970s without widespread controls on trade and capital.

10. See Bryant and others (1988) and Helliwell and Padmore (1985) for a comparison of open-economy multipliers from different global econometric models. Frankel and Rockett (1988) illustrate the sensitivity of welfare effects of coordination to the selection of the "right" versus the "wrong" economic model.

11. See Fischer (1988). Dini (1988) goes further to argue that when the incentives to coordinate differ widely among group members, there may be a tendency for bilateral bargains to take place among those who have the most to trade.

12. See Putnam and Bayne (1984). At the same time, the Bonn Economic Summit of 1978 is regarded in some quarters as illustrative of the pitfalls of coordinating macroeconomic policies when the economic outlook is changing rapidly.

13. Another example of high-frequency coordination is that among central banks of the largest countries on exchange-market intervention tactics.

14. For example, the Louvre Communiqué states that: "The United States Government will pursue policies with a view to reducing the fiscal 1988 deficit to 2.3 percent of GNP from its estimated level of 3.9 percent in fiscal 1987. For this purpose, the growth in government expenditures will be held to less than 1 percent in fiscal 1988 as part of the continuing program to reduce the share of government in GNP from its current level of 23 percent;" see IMF (1987).

15. Because coordination of structural policies typically involves different policy instruments, individual country actions cannot—unlike in the case of coordination of

fiscal policies—be evaluated with reference to an aggregate policy indicator that would be desirable from a global perspective.

16. This is not to deny the helpful role that harmonization of structural policies—ranging from adopting similar tax provisions to implementing common regulations concerning movements of goods, labor, and capital—could play in certain circumstances.

17. Those who hold the view that international factors have minimal influence on policymaking sometimes also argue that countries' policy commitments in coordination agreements represent policies that would have occurred even in the absence of such agreements. Under this view, coordination affects only the timing of policy announcements, with countries delaying such announcements until coordination meetings so that they can present a dowry to the others.

18. See the papers in Buiter and Marston (1985).

19. As Poehl (1987, 19–20) notes: "international cooperation does not necessarily imply that all parties must agree on all details at all times. It is important that we regard it as a process of maintaining stability in our increasingly interrelated world economy. . . . The process of international cooperation may be difficult and burdensome, even frustrating at times, but there is no alternative to it."

20. It is precisely because of the risk of "collusion" among the coordinating countries that Vaubel (1985) favors decentralized decision-making.

21. It is in this context that the problems of time inconsistency and moral hazard often surface.

22. Advocates of rules also argue that once the public knows better what the authorities will do, markets will demand less of a risk premium to hold the authorities' financial obligations.

23. Kenen (1987) cites a regression of the change in the inflation rate between 1979 and 1985 on the level of the inflation rate in 1979 and a zero-one dummy variable denoting participation in the exchange rate mechanism of the EMS. The sample comprised twenty-two industrial countries. The EMS dummy variable was *not* statistically significant, whereas the level of the inflation rate in 1979 was. Note that this finding does not preclude a helpful role of the EMS in disinflation since participation could still have reduced the output cost of disinflation (Giavazzi and Giovannini 1988); but this is a different story.

24. As developed in Polak (1988), the need for rules to guard against the dangers of fine-tuning has receded in any case since economic policy in most industrial countries is now oriented much more toward the medium term. Fischer (1988) makes the complementary point that the state of our knowledge about the effects of monetary and fiscal policy is too rudimentary to justify policy rules. Niehans (1987) expresses doubts that rules could be relied upon to reduce international disturbances.

25. On the limitations of purchasing-power-parity rules, see Frenkel (1981).

26. Multiple indicators can reflect multiple targets and/or multiple instruments employed to reach a smaller number of targets.

27. The literature on "speculative attacks" deals with just this phenomenon; see, for example, Flood and Garber (1980).

28. See Frenkel and Goldstein (1986). This missing link between exchange rate movements and fiscal policy under target zones is being increasingly recognized. Whereas first-generation target-zone proposals spoke only of monetary policy, second-generation proposals have added a policy rule or guideline for fiscal policy; contrast Williamson (1985 [1983]) with Williamson and Miller (1987). Also, see the simulations of simple versus extended target-zone rules in section 1.4.

29. See Oudiz and Sachs (1984), McKibbin and Sachs (1988), and Taylor (1985a) for evidence on the size of the gains, and Frenkel and Rockett (1988) for the effects of using the "wrong" model.

30. See Schultze (1988) and Bryant and others (1988). As an example of the difficulties associated with identifying the "counterfactual," contrast Feldstein's (1988) appraisal of the likely evaluation of exchange rates in the absence of the Plaza Agreement with that of Lamfalussy (1987).

31. Frankel and Rockett (1988), however, show that, for a set of models compared in Bryant and others (1988), gains from knowing the "true" model (assuming that one is correct) dominate gains from coordination.

32. Another recent paper, Taylor (1986), considers different exchange rate arrangements in a rational expectations model; however, only completely fixed and freely floating exchange rates are compared, and the model is limited to the seven major industrial countries.

33. The model simulations do not, however, allow for two other ways in which private sector behavior may be affected by changes in policy regimes. First, the variance of output, prices, or exchange rates may be different, leading to different degrees of substitutability among goods or assets. For example, it has been argued that the greater variability of exchange rates has led to a lower level of international trade than would have prevailed under fixed rates. Second, expectations may contain "speculative bubbles" in some circumstances, and hence may not solely reflect economic fundamentals. For example, the rise of the U.S. dollar early in 1985 despite declining interest rate differentials in favor of dollar-denominated assets is hard to explain.

34. Although simulation studies of judgmental coordinated policies are somewhat more difficult to design than analyses of rule-based proposals, a start in this direction has been made in some internal studies by Fund staff.

35. In contrast to the industrial countries, developing countries are not assumed to face perfect capital markets. Instead, the availability of financing reflects their ability to service debt, as measured by a ratio of their inflation-adjusted interest payments to the value of their exports. It is assumed that there is an upper limit to this ratio, beyond which the risk of nonrepayment becomes high, and consequently creditors would refuse to grant further new lending. As a result of the financing constraint, imports by developing countries are also constrained, tending to reduce both consumption and investment. The constraint on financing is, however, not solely based on current developments, but also reflects an assessment of future export prospects of developing countries; expected future exports are made to be consistent with the model's solution for those future exports.

36. This is a feature that will be relaxed in future work—in particular, by imposing shocks to residuals in successive periods.

37. Labor markets do not appear explicitly in the model, but features of wage bargaining, such as those due to overlapping multiperiod contracts, are reflected in the equation estimated for inflation.

38. The properties of MULTIMOD for these policy changes are quite similar to the average for other existing multicountry models; see Fischer (1988, 16).

39. One strong implication of this empirical regularity is that any "assignment rule" that assigns monetary policy to the current account—for example, Williamson and Miller's (1987) blueprint—is going to face problems; on this point, see Genberg and Swoboda (1987) and Boughton (1988).

40. It is assumed here that fiscal expansion is *not* accommodated by an increase in money growth. Current account effects also reflect the impact of interest rate changes on net investment income.

41. Niehans (1987, 215) also stresses the importance of steady policies: "The first, and most promising, step to reducing international disturbances must surely be the avoidance of the policy shifts that produce them. Especially for the dominant economy, the United States, the most important part of cooperation is steadiness."

42. The measure of real effective exchange rate is the country's manufactured export price, divided by a weighted average export price of its competitors, including developing countries. Thus, an increase indicates appreciation.

43. Corden (1986, 431) recognizes this to some extent: "[Coordination] means, incidentally, that if private investment in a country declines there should be some compensating increase in its fiscal deficit to modify the current account effect. It does not necessarily mean that a fiscal policy stance should be stable."

44. The role of this variable is to give a nominal anchor to the system. The inclusion of this term is also consistent with the intent of the blueprint proposal to make the level of interest rates depend (in an unspecified fashion) on the growth of aggregate GNP.

45. In implementing the rule, the value given by Edison, Miller, and Williamson (1987) to n, 10 percent, was initially tried, but the model either would not solve or gave negative nominal interest rates. Consequently, a higher value, 20 percent, was used, implying a lower feedback of exchange rate misalignments on interest rates.

46. Again, we adopt Williamson's (1985) estimates of target or equilibrium real effective exchange rates merely to stay as close as possible to the original proposals. There should be no implication that we agree or disagree with those estimates. For a discussion of some of the difficulties associated with calculating equilibrium exchange rates, see Frenkel and Goldstein (1988b).

47. It should also be noted that MULTIMOD's definition of real effective exchange rates is wider than most measures, since it allows for competition from manufactures produced in developing countries.

48. It is also the case in Edison, Miller, and Williamson (1987), that real exchange rates under a target zone regime differ little from their historical values.

49. Suppose there are three time periods and that interest parity relates interest rates and exchange rates. Suppose also that the exchange rate is unchanged in the third period. In each period, the interest rate differential is equal to the appreciation that is expected for (and actually occurs in) the next period. Thus, in terms of deviations from baseline, $d_t = e_{t+1} - e_t$, where $e_3 = 0$. Then in the second period, the interest differential will have to be equal to the desired change in the exchange rate; if it is overvalued by 5 percent, interest rates will have to be 5 percentage points lower. If in the first period the exchange rate is undervalued by 5 percent, then interest rates will have to be not 5, but 10 percentage points, higher.

50. As shown in Buiter and Miller (1982), if the model has the natural rate property, then the cumulative output losses from different disinflation policies are the same when discounting is ignored.

51. If there is no feedback of inflation onto monetary policy—such as through world nominal income—then the target-zone rule cannot be simulated in MULTIMOD because of the absence of a nominal anchor.

52. The shock is distributed using the weights that serve to allocate the world trade discrepancy in MULTIMOD. As a result, the shock to the United States is also reduced by the U.S. share of world trade, so that U.S. exports rise on impact by 8.6 percent, not the full 10 percent.

References

Artis, Michael, and Sylvia Ostry. 1986. *International economic policy coordination.* Chatham House Papers, no. 30, Royal Institute of International Affairs. London: Routledge and Kegan Paul.

Bockelmann, H. 1988. The need for worldwide coordination of economic policies. Paper presented at Conference on Financing the World Economy in the Nineties, School for Banking and Finance, Tilburg University.

Boughton, James. 1988. Policy assignment strategies with somewhat flexible exchange rates. IMF Working Paper no. 88/40.

Boughton, James, and William Branson. 1988. Commodity prices as a leading indicator of inflation. IMF Working Paper no. 88/87.

Bryant, Ralph. 1987. Intergovernmental coordination of economic policies. In P. B. Kenen, ed., *International monetary cooperation: Essays in honor of Henry C. Wallich*. Essays in International Finance no. 169 (December): 4–15. Princeton: International Finance Section, Princeton University.

Bryant, Ralph, and others, eds. 1988. *Empirical macroeconomics for interdependent economies*. Washington, DC: Brookings Institution.

Bryant, Ralph, and Richard Portes, eds. 1987. *Global macroeconomics: Policy conflict and cooperation*. London: Macmillan.

Buiter, Willem, and Marcus H. Miller. 1982. Real exchange rate over-shooting and the output cost of bringing down inflation. *European Economic Review* 18 (May/June): 85–123.

Buiter, Willem H., and Richard C. Marston, eds. 1985. *International economic policy coordination*. New York: Cambridge University Press.

Calvo, Guillermo A. 1978. On the time consistency of optimal policy in a monetary economy. *Econometrica* 46 (November): 1411–28.

Cooper, Richard N. 1982. The gold standard: Historical facts and future prospects. *Brookings Papers on Economic Activity* 1:1–45.

———. 1985. Economic interdependence and coordination of economic policies. In R. W. Jones and P. B. Kenen, eds., *Handbook of international economics*, vol. 2, 1194–1234. Amsterdam: North-Holland.

———. 1987. International economic cooperation: Is it desirable? Is it likely? Lecture presented at International Monetary Fund (October).

———. 1988. U.S. macroeconomic policy, 1986–88: Are the models useful? In Ralph Bryant, and others, eds., *Empirical macroeconomics for interdependent economies*, 255–66. Washington, DC: Brookings Institution.

Corden, W. Max. 1986. Fiscal policies, current accounts and real exchange rates: In search of a logic of international policy coordination. *Weltwirtschaftliches Archiv* 122 (no. 3): 423–38.

Crockett, Andrew. 1987. Strengthening international economic cooperation: The role of indicators in multilateral surveillance. IMF Working Paper no. 87/76.

Currie, David, Paul Levine, and Nicholas Vidalis. 1987. International cooperation and reputation in an empirical two-bloc model. In R. C. Bryant and R. Portes, eds., *Global macroeconomics: Policy conflict and cooperation*, 75–127. London: Macmillan.

Currie, David, and Simon Wren-Lewis. 1987. Conflict and cooperation in international macroeconomic policymaking: The past decade and future prospects. International Monetary Fund (December). Typescript.

Dini, Lamberto. 1988. Cooperation and conflict in monetary and trade policies. Paper presented at International Management and Development Institute, U.S.–European Top Management Roundtable. Milan, February 19.

Edison, Hali J., Marcus H. Miller, and John Williamson. 1987. On evaluating and extending the target zone proposal. *Journal of Policy Modeling* 9 (Spring): 199–224.

Feldstein, Martin. 1988. Distinguished lecture on economics in government: Thinking about international economic coordination. *The Journal of Economic Perspectives* 2 (Spring): 3–13.

Fischer, Stanley. 1988. International macroeconomic policy coordination. In Martin Feldstein, ed., *International economic cooperation,* 11–43. Chicago: University of Chicago Press.

Fleming, J. Marcus. 1962. Domestic financial policies under fixed and under floating exchange rates. *IMF Staff Papers* 9 (November): 369–79.

Flood, Robert, and Peter Garber. 1980. Market fundamentals versus price level bubbles: The first tests. *Journal of Political Economy* 88 (August).

Frankel, Jeffrey, and Katherine Rockett. 1988. International macroeconomic policy coordination when policymakers do not agree on the true model. *American Economic Review* 78, no. 3 (June): 318–40.

Frenkel, Jacob A. 1975. Current problems of the international monetary system: Reflections on European monetary integration. *Weltwirtschaftliches Archiv* 111 (no. 2): 216–21.

———. 1981. The collapse of purchasing power parities during the 1970's. *European Economic Review* 16 (May): 145–65.

———. 1982. Turbulence in the market for foreign exchange and macroeconomic policies. The Henry Thornton Lecture, City University Centre for Banking and International Finance, London.

———. 1983. International liquidity and monetary control. In George M. von Furstenberg, ed., *International money and credit: The policy roles.* Washington, DC: International Monetary Fund.

———. 1985. A note on "the good fix" and "the bad fix." *European Economic Review* 1–2 (June–July).

———. 1986. International interdependence and the constraints on macroeconomic policies. *Weltwirtschaftliches Archiv* 122 (no. 4).

Frenkel, Jacob A., and Morris Goldstein. 1986. A guide to target zones. *IMF Staff Papers* 33 (December): 633–70.

———. 1988a. The international monetary system: Developments and prospects. Paper presented at the Cato Institute Conference, February 1988. *Cato Journal* 8 (Fall).

———. 1988b. Exchange rate volatility and misalignment. In *Financial Market Volatility.* Kansas City: Federal Reserve Bank of Kansas City.

Frenkel, Jacob A., Morris Goldstein, and Paul R. Masson. 1988. International coordination of economic policies: Scope, methods, and effects. In Wilfried Guth, ed., *Economic Policy Coordination,* 149–91. Washington, DC: International Monetary Fund.

Frenkel, Jacob A., and Michael Mussa. 1985. Asset markets, exchange rates and the balance of payments. In R. W. Jones and P. B. Kenen, eds., *Handbook of international economics,* vol. 2, 679–747. Amsterdam: North-Holland.

Frenkel, Jacob A., and Assaf Razin. 1987a. The Mundell-Fleming model: A quarter century later. *IMF Staff Papers* 34 (December) 567–720.

———. 1987b. *Fiscal policies and the world economy.* Cambridge, MA: MIT Press.

Gavin, Michael. 1986. Macroeconomic policy coordination under alternative exchange rate regimes. Federal Reserve Board (September). Typescript.

Genberg, Hans, and Alexander Swoboda. 1987. The current account and the policy mix under flexible exchange rates. IMF Working Paper no. 87/70.

Ghosh, Atish R., and Paul R. Masson. 1988. International policy coordination in a world with model uncertainty. *IMF Staff Papers* 35 (June): 230–58.

Giavazzi, Francesco, and Alberto Giovannini. 1988. Interpreting the European disinflation. The role of the exchange rate regime. *Informacion Comercial Espanola* (May).

Goldstein, Morris. 1980. *Have flexible exchange rates handicapped macroeconomic policy?* Special Papers in International Economics no. 14 (June). Princeton: Princeton University Press.

_____. 1984. *The exchange rate system: Lessons of the past and options for the future.* IMF Occasional Paper no. 30 (July).

Hamada, Koichi. 1979. Macroeconomic strategy and coordination under alternative exchange rates. In R. Dornbusch and J. Frenkel, eds., *International economic policy: Theory and evidence,* 292–324. Baltimore: Johns Hopkins University Press.

Helliwell, John F., and Tim Padmore. 1985. Empirical studies of macroeconomic interdependence. In R. W. Jones and P. B. Kenen, eds., *Handbook of international economics,* vol. 2, 1107–51. Amsterdam: North-Holland.

Henderson, Dale. 1979. Financial policies in open economics. *American Economic Review* 69 (May): 232–39.

Holbrook, Robert S. 1972. Optimal economic policy and the problem of instrument instability. *American Economic Review* 62 (March): 57–65.

Holtham, Gerald, Giles Keating, and Peter Spencer. 1987. *EMS: Advance or face retreat.* London: Credit Suisse First Boston Ltd.

Horne, Jocelyn, and Paul R. Masson. 1988. Scope and limits of international economic cooperation and policy coordination. *IMF Staff Papers* 35 (June): 259–96.

IMF. 1974. Documents of the Committee of 20. Washington, DC: International Monetary Fund.

_____. 1986. *IMF Survey* (May 19): 157.

_____. 1987. *IMF Survey* (March 9): 73.

Jurgensen, Philippe. 1983. *Report of the working group on exchange market intervention.* Washington, DC: U.S. Treasury.

Kenen, Peter B. 1987. Exchange rates and policy coordination. Brookings Discussion Paper no. 61 (October). Washington, DC: Brookings Institution.

Kydland, F., and E. Prescott. 1977. Rules rather than discretion: The inconsistency of optimal plans. *Journal of Political Economy* 85 (June): 473–91.

Lamfalussy, Alexandre. 1987. Current account imbalances in the industrial world: Why they matter. In P. B. Kenen, ed., *International monetary cooperation: Essays in honor of Henry C. Wallich.* Essays in International Finance no. 169 (December): 31–37. Princeton: International Finance Section, Princeton University.

Masson, Paul R., and others. 1988. MULTIMOD: A multi-region econometric model. *Staff studies for the world economic outlook* (July). Washington, DC: International Monetary Fund.

McKibbin, Warwick J., and Jeffrey D. Sachs. 1988. Coordination of monetary and fiscal policies in the industrial countries. In Jacob A. Frenkel, ed., *International aspects of fiscal policy,* 73–113. Chicago: University of Chicago Press.

Mundell, Robert A. 1971. *The dollar and the policy mix.* Essays in International Finance no. 85 (May). Princeton: Princeton University Press.

Mussa, Michael. 1981. *The role of official intervention.* Occasional Paper no. 6. New York: Group of Thirty.

Niehans, Jurg. 1987. Generating international disturbances. In Y. Suzuki and M. Okabe, eds., *Toward a world of economic stability: Optimal monetary framework and policy,* 181–218. Tokyo: University of Tokyo Press.

Oudiz, Gilles, and Jeffrey D. Sachs. 1984. Macroeconomic policy coordination among the industrial economies. *Brookings Papers on Economic Activity* 1: 1–75.

Poehl, Karl Otto. 1987. Cooperation—A keystone for the stability of the international monetary system. First Arthur Burns Memorial Lecture, at the American Council on Germany, New York (November).

Polak, Jacques J. 1981. *Coordination of National Economic Policies.* Occasional Paper no. 7. New York: Group of Thirty.

_____. 1988. Economic policy objectives and policymaking in the major industrial countries. In Wilfried Guth, ed., *Economic policy coordination,* 1–43. Washington, DC: IMF.

Poole, William. 1970. Optimal choice of monetary policy instruments in a simple stochastic macro model. *Quarterly Journal of Economics* 84 (May): 197–216.

Putnam, Robert D., and Nicholas Bayne. 1984. *Hanging Together: The Seven-Power Summits.* Cambridge, MA: Harvard University Press.

Putnam, Robert D., and C. Randall Henning. 1986. The Bonn summit of 1978: How does international economic policy coordination actually work? Brookings Discussion Papers in International Economics no. 53 (October). Washington, DC: Brookings Institution.

Rogoff, Kenneth. 1985. Can international monetary policy cooperation be counterproductive? *Journal of International Economics* 18 (May): 199–217.

Schultze, Charles. 1988. International macroeconomics coordination—Marrying the economic models with political reality. In Martin Feldstein, ed., *International Economic Cooperation,* 49–60. Chicago: University of Chicago Press.

Tanzi, Vito. 1988. Fiscal policy and international coordination: Current and future issues. Paper presented at Conference on Fiscal Policy, Economic Adjustment, and Financial Markets. Boconni University, January 27–30.

Tanzi, Vito, and Teresa Ter-Minassian. 1987. The European monetary system and fiscal policies. In Sijbren Cnossen, ed., *Tax coordination in the European community,* ch. 13. Series on International Taxation no. 7. Boston: Kluwer Law and Taxation Publishers.

Taylor, John. 1985a. International coordination in the design of Macroeconomic policy rules. *European Economic Review* 28 (June–July): 53–81.

———. 1985b. What would nominal GNP targeting do to the business cycle? In K. Brunner and A. H. Meltzer, eds., *Understanding monetary regimes.* Carnegie-Rochester Conference Series on Public Policy 22: 61–84.

———. 1986. An econometric evaluation of international monetary policy rules: Fixed versus flexible exchange rates. Stanford University. Typescript.

Tobin, James. 1980. Stabilization policy ten years after. *Brookings Papers on Economic Activity* 1: 19–71.

———. 1987. Agenda for international coordination of macroeconomic policies. In P. B. Kenen, ed., *International monetary cooperation: Essays in honor of Henry C. Wallich.* Essays in International Finance no. 169 (December): 61–69. Princeton: International Finance Section, Princeton University.

U.S. Congress. 1982. *Report to the congress of the commission on the role of gold in the domestic and international monetary systems.* Washington, DC: Government Printing Office (March).

Vaubel, Roland. 1985. International collusion or competition for macroeconomic policy coordination? A restatement. *Recherches Économiques de Louvain* 51 (December): 223–40.

Wallich, Henry C. 1984. Institutional cooperation in the world economy. In Jacob Frenkel and Michael Mussa, eds., *The world economic system: Performance and prospects,* 85–99. Dover, MA: Auburn House.

Williamson, John. 1985[1983]. *The exchange rate system.* 2d ed. Policy Analyses in International Economics no. 5. Washington, DC: Institute for International Economics.

Williamson, John, and Marcus H. Miller. 1987. *Targets and indicators: A blueprint for the international coordination of economic policy.* Policy Analyses in International Economics no. 22 (September). Washington, DC: Institute for International Economics.

Comment   Martin Feldstein

Jacob Frenkel and his colleagues at the International Monetary Fund have presented not just an interesting paper, but what are essentially two very interesting, but quite incompatible, papers. In the first of these, they analyze

Martin Feldstein is the George F. Baker Professor of Economics at Harvard University and President and Chief Executive Officer of the National Bureau of Economic Research.

different types of macroeconomic coordination, summarizing the arguments for and against coordination, but focusing on the arguments in favor of coordination of the type now practiced by the G-7 finance ministers: discretionary ad hoc agreements, the absence of any explicit policy response rules, a vague multitarget process, and an emphasis on exchange rate targets.

In their second "paper," the authors present a fascinating empirical analysis of the results of five possible ways to formalize exchange rate stabilization and, more generally, macroeconomic coordination. My reading of their evidence is that none of these rules would lead to satisfactory economic performance. In the historic simulations that they present, the proposed rules lead to wild fluctuations of exchange rates or interest rates. Moreover, the fiscal policies that would be required to stabilize real exchange rates would call upon the Federal Republic of Germany and Japan to have budget deficits of more than 8 percent of GNP. The single-shock simulations also give little reason to be sanguine about coordination efforts unless fiscal policy can be coordinated, something that clearly has not been achieved between the United States and Germany and, as the authors note, has not even been achieved among the countries that participate in the EMS.

I describe these as two incompatible papers because I do not see how, given the evidence of these simulations, Frenkel, Goldstein, and Masson (FGM) can be at all sanguine about the usefulness of macroeconomic coordination and attempts at exchange rate stabilization.

Indeed, even without their simulation analyses, I cannot agree with their optimistic view of the potential advantages of macroeconomic coordination. There may be a case for quiet information exchange and discussion of the type that takes place at the monthly meetings of the Bank for International Settlements or the periodic meetings of the OECD's Working Party 3. But the attempts to go beyond the exchange of information and to coordinate macroeconomic policy and exchange rates in the manner of the G-7 meetings is, I believe, unwise.

It could, of course, be argued that the FGM empirical evidence against explicit coordination is not very persuasive because the econometric model (IMF's MULTIMOD) is, as the authors stress, still very preliminary. Moreover, the perfect foresight character of the model and the assumption that announcements of government policies are completely believed are both substantial departures from reality. And, although the authors refer to the Lucas (1976) critique, they do not deal with it even though it is particularly important in the present context, in which the proposed policies are very different in character from the ones that prevailed during the period that generated the data on which their estimates are based.

But the inadequacy of existing modeling capability should hardly be comfort to advocates of coordination. If the best model that the IMF has is still preliminary and far from reliable, it is hard to see how governments can have the analytic capability to do macroeconomic coordination.

Although FGM offer the common observation that the growth of trade has increased economic interdependence, the evidence that they present in table 1.1 shows that the interdependence is so small it can hardly be used to support the case for U.S. participation in a macroeconomic coordination process. For example, if Germany and Japan both increase their government spending by 1 percent of GNP, the impact in the United States would be a real GNP rise of only 0.2 percent or about $10 billion.

The large fiscal changes that would be needed to have any substantial real impact are likely to be strongly resisted unless they also serve domestic goals (in which case they would be achieved without the coordination process). The authors implicitly recognize this when they say that fiscal instruments may enter the social welfare functions of countries. And well they should, since changes in tax rates alter excess burdens and income distribution; changes in government spending increase or decrease benefits to current citizens; and changes in deficits imply changes in future debt service, with the corresponding excess burdens.

I believe that FGM are also overly optimistic about the nature of the G-7 agreements. They write as if they believe that the official communiqués issued reflect what ministers actually believe and what governments will actually do. A more accurate assessment would regard the G-7 communiqués as politically convenient declarations. Let us look at the two examples which FGM select to illustrate their case.

In 1978, at the Bonn Summit, Germany and other governments committed to accelerate their growth rates in exchange for a commitment by the United States to come to grips with its inflation problem. In fact, U.S. inflation continued to rise for three more years. It was eighteen months after the Bonn Summit that Paul Volcker persuaded the Federal Reserve and President Carter to impose a tighter monetary policy, and even this was soon reversed under pressure from President Carter. The Reagan administration's support in 1981 for tough anti-inflationary policies was totally unrelated to the earlier Summit discussions.

FGM also cite the specific promise of the United States at the February 1987 Louvre meeting of the G-7 finance ministers. The communiqué not only promised a reduction of the U.S. budget deficit, but also specified that it would be reduced to 2.3 percent of GNP in fiscal year 1988 by containing the growth of government spending. This was, of course, only a restatement of the recently proposed Reagan budget for FY1988 and not at all a reflection of the likely outcome of the upcoming negotiations with Congress. In the end, the FY1988 deficit was 3.2 percent of GNP, despite surprisingly fast economic growth between 1987 and 1988. The actual deficit rose between these two years.

Although I understand that there are ambiguities in interpreting economic policies, I doubt that any budget action that the United States has taken since the Louvre meeting was the result of its international agreements. Moreover, the American system of government makes it clear that the U.S. Treasury secretary cannot reliably promise any change in either monetary or fiscal policy.

I am also very skeptical of the credit that the authors give to the 1985 Plaza Accord (see sec. 1.4) for either the reduction of the dollar or the reduction of protectionist pressures in the United States. Even a cursory examination of the exchange rate data shows that the value of the dollar fell as rapidly in the six months before the Plaza meeting as it did in the six months after the Plaza meeting. Although it is hard to assess what protectionist pressures would have been if the dollar had not fallen, there can be no doubt that the 1988 trade bill is a remarkably protectionist piece of legislation.

In my judgment the G-7 summits and finance ministers, meetings and communiqués are basically empty political gestures that are useful to the political figures involved, but of no substantive importance. That in itself is probably a good thing, because effective coordination of policy would probably have increased inflationary pressures during the past several years. For example, the pressure on the United States to reduce the value of the dollar during 1982 through 1984, if it had been effective, would have forced the Federal Reserve to adopt a more inflationary monetary policy.

There are several other ways in which the current G-7 process is actually counterproductive.[1] First, the emphasis on macroeconomic coordination and exchange rate management deflects attention from other less glamorous areas where cooperation could be helpful, including the LDC debt problem, trade conflicts, and cross-border environmental issues.

Second, the emphasis on interdependence and the responsibilities of ''other countries'' to contribute to the solution of our macroeconomic problems causes antagonism. Now the United States tells other countries that they must change their monetary and fiscal policies to assist us or accept the adverse consequences that we can impose on them. Secretary Baker repeatedly asserted in 1986 that if Germany and Japan did not pursue more expansionary policies, the United States would punish them by depressing the value of the dollar and thus the trade balances of those countries. How will Americans react if the Japanese tell us in some future year that we must change our domestic policies to help them or suffer the consequences that they can impose on us?

Third, the emphasis on interdependence provides a political excuse for inaction. The coordination process provides domestic policy with a handy scapegoat. If the U.S. economy performs badly, the blame is shifted from domestic policies to the actions of Germany and Japan.

Finally, business and portfolio investors can be frightened into inappropriate action by the notion that our economy will suffer unless we have active cooperation from other major industrial countries. That sentiment contributed to the stock market crash in October 1987. Fortunately, immediately after the crash both Alan Greenspan and James Baker indicated that the value of the dollar would no longer be a goal of economic policy, which would instead focus on the domestic economy.

As these comments indicate, my reading of the paper by Frenkel, Goldstein, and Masson has only reinforced my skepticism about international macroeconomic coordination. The analytic arguments offer no new reasons to favor integration; the measures of interdependence show that we can easily achieve the desired shifts in macroeconomic stimulus without foreign assistance; and the simulation results show that no policy reaction process that FGM could devise would improve either the historic performance of the world's economy or the prospective reaction to individual shocks.

Quiet discussions of economic policy among key government officials of the major countries are no doubt a good thing. Times may even exist when joint action is clearly of mutual interest. But the current public proclamations of macroeconomic coordination as a regular aspect of policy and formal schemes for exchange rate management are a bad idea. There is nothing in this paper to make us believe otherwise.

Note

1. For a more complete statement of these views, see M. Feldstein, Distinguished lecture on economics in government: Thinking about international economic coordination. *Journal of Economic Perspectives* 2 (Spring 1988): 3–13.

Comment   William H. Branson

This paper by Jacob Frenkel, Morris Goldstein, and Paul Masson (FGM) is broad-ranging and informative. It thoroughly covers the rationale, scope, and mechanisms of coordination, or rather, as I argue below, cooperation, as seen from the perspective of the IMF or the G-7. This is in contrast to much of the literature on coordination in economics, which focuses on technical aspects of game theory. In a sense, here we see coordination as perceived by practitioners who are fully aware of the technical issues that are involved in its analysis, but leave them submerged. As a result, the paper is very readable and will be widely read. The paper also gives us a nice exercise in the use of the IMF's MULTIMOD world model to analyze alternative policy regimes. This, too, is clear and readable, and provides good exposure for MULTIMOD. Thus both the discussion of coordination issues and the simulation study are useful additions to our knowledge.

William H. Branson is the Jacob Viner Professor of International Economics at Princeton University, and Director of the Program in International Studies at the NBER.

I will begin with FGM's definition of coordination, and put it in a broader context of international economic cooperation. FGM, in my view, generally discuss the looser concept of cooperation rather than coordination as the authors define it. As I go through my comments on the paper's substance, I will point out why this is my view. This does not detract at all from the value of the paper's discussion of cooperation, but it does refocus the paper somewhat. At the end of the comment, I will come back to some thoughts about why economists have such peculiar difficulties with the concept of coordination.

The paper begins with the well-known definition by Henry Wallich of coordination as "a significant modification of national policies in recognition of international economic interdependence." This is a useful definition, which the following quotation from Lamberto Dini (1988, 1) puts into a broader context:

> I find it useful . . . to distinguish between cooperation and coordination. Cooperation basically involves information exchange, consultation among authorities, and possibly common assessments of the international repercussions of national policies. Coordination means that policy-makers in a number of countries agree on common objectives and together take joint policy decisions that differ from those they would have taken on their own. Conflict is . . . the opposite of coordination. It may arise . . . when no consideration is given to the international dimension of national policies. . . . We can view international cooperation as a continuum ranging from coordination, the highest level of cooperation, to conflict, when cooperation breaks down.

In the context set by Dini, the FGM paper is mainly about cooperation.

The discussions in the numerous international forums that are examined in the paper are examples of cooperation, using the Dini and the Wallich definitions. The argument for an ongoing process is a persuasive one, if applied to cooperation, with occasions within the process that call for coordinated action. The discussion of rules versus discretion seems to be half about coordination (rules) and half about cooperation (discretion), and the choice between single and multiple indicators is applicable to an ongoing process of cooperation.

The simulations using MULTIMOD provide some interesting and surprising results. FGM's table 1.1 shows the basic policy multipliers from MULTIMOD solutions for the United States, Japan, and the Federal Republic of Germany. The GDP results show minimal interdependence between the United States and Germany, and substantial effects on Japan from the United States, but not vice versa. One can see here the source of some results that indicate that the gains from coordination would be small. It would be interesting to see these multipliers with Germany replaced by a European aggregate. I would expect to see larger spillovers involving Europe in that case.

The second set of interesting results comes from the exercise in which the policy variables in the history are smoothed in the simulation, on the supposition that smoother policy would give smoother outcomes. This supposition is suspect on at least two grounds. First, there were substantial exogenous shocks, such as oil price changes, during the 1974–87 simulation period. Second, with forward-looking expectations, which MULTIMOD features, the announcement of a gradual policy shift in the future should cause interest rates and exchange rates to jump at the time of the announcement. We saw this effect with the Reagan budget program in 1981. As FGM note, the result of the simulations is the opposite of the supposition. In FGM's table 1.2 we see that smoothing policy has little effect on the mean outcomes for the target variables, but that it generally increases the standard deviations! Thus during the 1974–87 period, on average, monetary and fiscal policy were stabilizing, according to MULTIMOD. This is an encouraging result for new-Keynesian activists.

Next, FGM go on to simulations of target zones and the Williamson-Miller blueprints. The most notable result here is the effect of the blueprints on current account balances, shown in FGM's figure 1.8. FGM note that the target zones and blueprints reduce the current imbalances of the three major countries, but the effect on the United States is very small. My impression from figure 1.8 is that the target zones or blueprints shift the counterpart of the U.S. deficit from Germany and Japan to the other G-7 countries. The last set of simulations shows the effects of various single shocks in the United States under four alternative policy rules. The results are shown in FGM's figures 1.9–1.12. The blueprint results mainly stand out due to the stabilizing effects of the flexible U.S. fiscal policy that they assume. Since MULTIMOD appears to be a new-Keynesian model, this is not surprising. But the results do emphasize how important this assumption about fiscal policy is for the operation of the blueprints.

Finally, I return to the question of why economists have such difficulty with the idea of coordination. After all, theorists and practitioners in many disparate fields find coordination to be the natural state of affairs. Arms negotiators, international health officials, air traffic controllers, museum curators, and even the International Olympic Committee all coordinate; why shouldn't economic policymakers? I think an indication of the resolution of this seeming conundrum can be found in the two quotations that begin the FGM paper.

Martin Feldstein focuses on a very narrow scope for coordination, namely macroeconomic policy, and the possibility that international coordination will distract attention from the effort needed to get domestic policy right. Presumably the cost of this distraction is larger than the small gains from macroeconomic policy coordination, in Feldstein's view. James Tobin takes a wider view, with economic warfare within his horizon. He, like the international health officials, thinks some form of coordination is almost inevitable.

The economist's problem seems to come from narrowing the scope for coordination so much that the gains from trade are virtually eliminated. Why do we do this? Perhaps, in order to reduce the problem to a size that is manageable with the available tools, usually game theory, we have to squeeze it down so much that the substance vanishes. This difficulty shows up in FGM's inability to stick to their own definition of coordination. To make things interesting, as they do, and go beyond a game-theoretic analysis, they properly expand their horizon to cooperation, as Lamberto Dini defined it. The next step would be an analysis of the optimal scope for coordination.

Reference

Dini, Lamberto. 1988. Cooperation and conflict in monetary and trade policies. International Management and Development Institute, U.S.–European Top Management Roundtable. Milan, February 19.

2 The Coordination of Macroeconomic Policies

Peter B. Kenen

2.1 Introduction

For the last three years, beginning with the Plaza Communiqué of September 1985, governments have been hard at work on policy coordination, including the improvement of the process itself. We have seen nothing like it since the mid-1970s and the run-up to the Bonn Economic Summit of 1978. Economists have also been at work, modeling and measuring the gains from policy coordination and devising new approaches. But some have turned against it. The obstacles are large, they say, the potential gains are small, and there is the risk that governments will get it wrong—that macroeconomic coordination will make matters worse.

Some economists were skeptical initially. In 1981, for example, Max Corden argued that coordination is not needed because the international monetary ''non-system'' has a logic of its own:

> The key feature of the present system is that it is a form of international *laissez-faire*. First of all, it allows free play to the private market, not just to trade in goods and non-financial services but, above all, to the private capital market. Secondly, it allows free play to governments and their central banks to operate in the market and—if they wish and where they can—to influence and even fix its prices or its quantities. Thus it is a fairly free market where many governments, acting in their own presumed interests and not necessarily taking much account of the interests of other governments, are participants. (60).

Peter B. Kenen is Walker Professor of Economics and International Finance and Director of the International Finance Section at Princeton University.

This paper is based partly on research conducted while the author was Visiting Fellow at the Royal Institute of International Affairs, supported by a fellowship from the German Marshall Fund. An earlier version appears as the concluding chapter in Kenen (1988a).

Roland Vaubel (1981) went even further, arguing that governments should compete in providing the most attractive economic environment, measured primarily by price stability, and that policy coordination is harmful because it reduces competition among governments. Coordination can also raise the costs of policy mistakes because governments will do the same wrong things collectively rather than make mutually canceling errors.

On Corden's "market" view, each government can and should be free to choose its own monetary and fiscal policies but also to choose its exchange rate arrangements and decide for itself whether to borrow or lend on international capital markets. This sort of policy decentralization would probably be optimal if all economies were very small; each country's decisions regarding its exchange rate would have only trivial effects on other countries' effective exchange rates, and its decisions to borrow or lend would not have much influence on world interest rates.

What happens, however, when economies are large? Each country's policies affect other countries, and structural interdependence gives rise in turn to policy interdependence. The conventional case for coordination starts here.[1] But the strength of the case depends on the extent of the underlying structural interdependence, the governments' policy objectives, and the number of policy instruments at their command.

Stanley Fischer (1988) has surveyed recent research on these issues and has joined the skeptics:

> The notion of international policy coordination is appealing and appears to hold out the promise of major improvements in economic performance. However, estimates of the quantitative impacts of policy decisions in one economy on other economies are quite small. These results, together with explicit calculations of the benefits of coordination, suggest the gains will rarely be significant. Furthermore, theoretical analysis finds many circumstances under which coordination worsens rather than improves economic performance.
>
> The interest in policy coordination in the United States has been strongest when advocates of coordination were hoping to use international policy agreements to bring about changes in domestic policies that they regarded as either undesirable or eventually untenable. It is entirely possible though that formal coordination would sometimes require a country to undertake policy actions of which it disapproved.
>
> So long as exchange rates remain flexible—and they will likely remain flexible among the three major currency areas—macroeconomic policy coordination among the major blocs is unlikely to advance beyond the provision of mutual information and occasional agreements for specific policy trade-offs. Both information exchanges and occasional policy agreements when the circumstances are right are useful and should be encouraged.
>
> But more consistent ongoing policy coordination in which countries, including the United States, significantly modify national policies "in recognition of international policy interdependence" is not on the near hor-

izon. Fortunately, the evidence suggests that the potential gains from coordination are in any event small: the best that each country can do for other countries is to keep its own economy in shape. (38–39).

Martin Feldstein was even blunter in comments written shortly after the stock market crash of October 1987:

> Unfortunately, ever since the 1985 Plaza meeting, the [U.S.] administration and the governments of other industrial nations have emphatically asserted that international economic coordination is crucial to a healthy international economy in general and to continued U.S. growth in particular. Since such assertions are not justified by the actual interdependence of the industrial economies, Americans have been inappropriately worried about whether coordination would continue.
>
> Because foreign governments will inevitably pursue the policies that they believe are in their own best interests, it was inevitable that international coordination would eventually collapse. . . . But what contributed to the market decline was not the collapse of international macroeconomic coordination per se but the false impression created by governments that healthy expansion requires such coordination.
>
> The U.S. should now in a clear but friendly way end the international coordination of macroeconomic policy. We should continue to cooperate with other governments by exchanging information about current and future policy decisions, but we should recognize explicitly that Japan and Germany have the right to pursue the monetary and fiscal policies that they believe are in their own best interests.
>
> It is frightening to the American public and upsetting to our financial markets to believe that the fate of our economy depends on the decisions made in Bonn and Tokyo. Portfolio investors, business managers and the public in general need to be reassured that we are not hostages to foreign economic policies, that the U.S. is the master of its own economic destiny, and that our government can and will do what is needed to maintain healthy economic growth (Feldstein 1987).

When thoughtful economists like Fischer and Feldstein express themselves this forcefully, policymakers should listen. But when they listen carefully, they are likely to conclude that two quite different concepts of coordination are at issue. The critics of coordination are castigating governments for pursuing objectives that bear very little resemblance to the objectives that actually animate the governments' own efforts.

Economists typically adopt what can be described as a policy-optimizing approach to coordination,[2] and their use of game-theoretic methods to represent that process has led them to treat the participating governments as antagonists engaged in what Putnam and Henning (1986) have described as policy barter—the trading of commitments about policy instruments without any trading of analyses or forecasts. In this particular framework, moreover, exchange rate stabilization does not play a central role; it is at most a *method* for optimizing policies and is usually a second-best method at that.

Governments, by contrast, appear to adopt what can be described as a regime-preserving or public goods approach to policy coordination. It has different implications for the ways in which governments interact and for the role of exchange rate stabilization. Mutual persuasion takes the place of adversarial bargaining; exchange rate stabilization becomes a public good rather than a rule for optimizing policies. Furthermore, the regime-preserving approach sheds light on certain puzzling questions: Why does policy coordination move in and out of fashion? Why are disagreements about policy objectives cited so often as "obstacles" to coordination, when they can be expected to raise the gains from policy-optimizing coordination? Why do governments argue about sharing the "burdens" of coordination, when each of them should be expected to benefit from policy optimization?

2.2   Perspectives on Policy Coordination

Governments engage in many forms of economic cooperation. They exchange information about their economies, policies, and forecasts. They provide financial assistance to other governments, bilaterally and multilaterally, ranging from balance of payments support to long-term development aid. They act jointly to supervise or regulate various sorts of economic activity.

Coordination is the most rigorous form of economic cooperation because it involves mutually agreed modifications in the participants' national policies. In the macroeconomic domain, it involves an exchange of explicit, operational commitments about the conduct of monetary and fiscal policies. Commitments of this sort can be framed contingently, with reference to mutually agreed norms or targets; a government can promise to cut taxes, for example, if the growth rate of real GNP or nominal demand is lower than the rate it has promised to deliver. But commitments to targets, by themselves, do not constitute coordination. Commitments about instruments are the distinguishing feature of coordination, setting it apart from other forms of economic cooperation.[3]

2.2.1   Forms of Coordination

Coordination can result from episodic bargaining about specific policy packages or from a once-for-all bargain about policy rules or guidelines.

The Bonn Summit of 1978 is usually cited as the leading instance of episodic bargaining, although the Bonn bargain was not confined to macroeconomic matters. The Federal Republic of Germany and Japan made promises about their fiscal policies, and the United States made promises about its energy policies (Putnam and Bayne 1987, ch. 4). The Bretton Woods Agreement of

1944 is sometimes cited as a once-for-all bargain about rules, although it was too vague to meet my definition of full-fledged coordination. The exchange rate obligations were explicit; the corresponding policy commitments were implicit. The latter became somewhat tighter, however, as the Bretton Woods system evolved. The International Monetary Fund (IMF) began to attach strict policy conditions to the use of its resources, and Working Party 3 of the Organization for Economic Cooperation and Development (OECD) devoted close attention to the macroeconomic side of the exchange rate system.

These arrangements began to resemble rule-based policy coordination, but some would say that they were not symmetrical enough. The obligations of deficit countries were more clearly defined and commonly accepted than those of surplus countries. But symmetry is different from reciprocity or mutuality. The Bretton Woods system was *not* symmetrical—although the most striking asymmetries arose from the special role of the dollar rather than the imbalance between obligations borne by deficit and surplus countries. Nevertheless, the obligations were mutual in the important contingent sense emphasized earlier. They applied in principle to every country when it ran a balance of payments deficit. (Concern to preserve this contingent mutuality explains the reluctance of the IMF to depart from the uniform treatment of its members when attaching conditions to the use of its resources.)

The Louvre Accord of 1987 can be described as a combination of the two techniques for policy coordination. There were rule-based obligations, too loosely defined perhaps, which linked the use of interest rate policies to the maintenance of exchange rate stability. There was an ad hoc bargain about fiscal policies, although it served mainly to codify the goals that governments had already chosen unilaterally.[4]

A number of rule-based systems have been proposed in recent years, including those of McKinnon (1984, 1988), Meade (1984), and Williamson and Miller (1987). McKinnon proposes a gold standard without gold. The major central banks would choose an appropriate growth rate for the global money stock and would then conduct their monetary policies to realize that growth rate. Each of them would also use nonsterilized intervention to peg its exchange rate, causing its national money stock to grow faster than the global stock when its currency was strong and more slowly than the global stock when its currency was weak. The system would work symmetrically, however, so that exchange rate pegging would not affect the growth rate of the global money stock. The Williamson-Miller proposal would not peg exchange rates but is more comprehensive than McKinnon's proposal; it covers fiscal policies as well as interest rate or monetary policies.[5] Because it would involve a rule-based bargain to coordinate national policies, and we will discuss it later, the Williamson-Miller framework is reproduced as figure 2.1.

The distinction between types of policy bargains—between ad hoc agreements on policy packages and long-lasting agreements on policy rules—is helpful in sorting out arguments and issues. But it is far less fundamental than the distinction drawn in the introduction to this paper, which pertains to the rationale for policy coordination.

2.2.2   The Policy-Optimizing Approach

Many economists look upon policy formation as an optimizing process and are thus inclined to treat policy coordination as an extension of that process. Each government is deemed to have a welfare function defined in terms of its policy targets, and it sets its policy instruments to maximize that function. Its actions may affect other governments' decisions, but it disregards that possibility. When all governments behave this way, however, they end up in a suboptimal situation, the noncooperative or Nash equilibrium. They have neglected the policy interdependence resulting from structural interdependence, and they can bargain their way to a better situation, the cooperative or Pareto equilibrium. By changing the settings of their policy instruments in a mutually agreed manner, they can get closer to their policy targets and raise each country's welfare.[6]

The Blueprint

The participating countries [the Group of Seven] agree that they will conduct their macroeconomic policies with a view to pursuing the following two intermediate targets:

(1) A rate of growth of domestic demand in each country calculated according to a formula designed to promote the fastest growth of output consistent with gradual reduction of inflation to an acceptable level and agreed adjustment of the current account of the balance of payments.

(2) A real effective exchange that will not deviate by more than [10] percent from an internationally agreed estimate of the "fundamental equilibrium exchange rate," the rate estimated to be consistent with simultaneous internal and external balance in the medium term.

To that end, the participants agree that they will modify their monetary and fiscal policies according to the following principles:

(A) The *average level* of world (real) short-term interest rates should be revised up (down) if aggregate growth of national income is threatening to exceed (fall short of) the sum of the target growth of nominal demand for the participating countries.

(B) *Differences* in short-term interest rates among countries should be revised when necessary to supplement intervention in the exchange markets to prevent the deviation of currencies from their target ranges.

(C) National *fiscal policies* should be revised with a view to achieving national target rates of growth of domestic demand.

The rules (A) to (C) should be constrained by the medium-term objective of maintaining the real interest rate in its historically normal range and of avoiding an increasing or excessive ratio of public debt to GNP.

Figure 2.1   The Williamson-Miller blueprint for a target zone system
Source: Williamson and Miller (1987, 2); brackets and italics in original.

Viewed from this standpoint, policy coordination serves to internalize the effects of economic interdependence, which no single government can capture on its own by setting its policies unilaterally. To use a different metaphor, policy coordination gives each government partial control over other governments' policy instruments. Therefore, it relieves the shortage of instruments that prevents each government from reaching its own targets (see, e.g., Buiter and Eaton 1985, and Eichengreen 1985).

No one can quarrel with the logic of the policy-optimizing approach. It has given precise operational meaning to the notion of policy interdependence, provided a framework for measuring the costs of neglecting it, and linked this special subject with the much larger literature on macroeconomic theory and policy. But it tends to be more normative than positive. It tells us what governments can hope to achieve by multinational optimization and warns against some of the risks. It is less useful, however, in helping us to understand what governments are actually trying to accomplish, the obstacles they face, and the institutional arrangements they employ.

2.2.3   The Regime-Preserving Approach

Some economists, many political scientists, and most policymakers look at policy coordination from a different standpoint.[7] It is needed to produce certain public goods and defend the international economic system from economic and political shocks, including misbehavior by governments themselves.

Much of this important work was done by the United States in the first two postwar decades. It was the hegemonic power, having the ability and self-interested concern to stabilize the world economy by its actions. Furthermore, it had been largely responsible for writing the rules of the system and designing the institutions. It could thus be expected to defend them whenever they were threatened. Equally important, other governments could not accomplish very much without American cooperation. Matters are different now. It is still difficult to get very far without American cooperation, and little is likely to happen until Washington decides that something must be done. But the United States cannot act alone. The economic and political costs are too high.

It is easy to find examples of regime-preserving cooperation in recent economic history. They include the mobilization of financial support for the dollar and sterling in the 1960s and the joint management of the London gold pool, the ''rescue'' of the dollar in 1978, the speedy provision of bridge loans to Mexico at the start of the debt crisis in 1982, and the Plaza Communiqué of 1985, which was meant to defend the trade regime rather than alter the exchange rate regime.

The bargain struck at Bonn in 1978 can likewise be described as regime-preserving coordination. It reflected an agreed need for collective action on two fronts: for more vigorous recovery from the global recession of 1974–75, to combat rising unemployment, especially in Europe, and for energy conservation to reduce the industrial countries' dependence on imported oil and limit the ability of OPEC to raise oil prices.

When viewed from this different perspective, policy coordination becomes the logical response to the dispersion of power and influence that ended American hegemony. Public goods must be produced and institutional arrangements defended by common or collective action. When seen this way, moreover, disagreements about the benefits and costs of policy coordination take on a different but familiar aspect. They become debates about burden sharing.

2.3 Two Views of Exchange Rate Management

The two views of policy coordination yield different ways of looking at exchange rate management. Seen from the policy-optimizing viewpoint, it involves the use of a simple policy rule to internalize the effects of economic interdependence. Seen from the regime-preserving viewpoint, it embodies a commitment by governments to improve the global economic environment by pursuing exchange rate stability as a policy objective (strictly speaking, an intermediate objective conducive to the pursuit of stable and liberal trade policies and an efficient allocation of resources nationally and globally).

2.3.1 Exchange Rates in the Policy-Optimizing Framework

The earliest theoretical work on policy-optimizing coordination dealt mainly with the pegged rate case. Recent work has taken the opposite tack, partly because of the change in the actual exchange rate regime and partly because mathematical tractability exerts an unfortunate influence on the economist's research agenda.

Although many economists doubt that exchange rate expectations are truly rational, they tend to disparage any other view. Yet it is hard to solve a theoretical model in which rational expectations are combined with imperfect capital mobility. Accordingly, most such models assume that foreign and domestic assets are perfect substitutes. On this assumption, however, exchange rate pegging precludes any other use of monetary policy, greatly reducing the scope for policy coordination.[8] Therefore, exchange rate pegging is typically viewed as a second-best alternative to fully optimal coordination. It is attractive mainly because a simple, rule-based regime is less vulnerable to cheating or reneging, which many economists have regarded as a major obstacle to fully optimal coordination (see, e.g., Canzoneri and Gray 1985, and McKibbin and Sachs 1986).

When foreign and domestic assets are imperfect substitutes, however, the case for exchange rate pegging becomes much stronger, even in the policy-optimizing framework. Purchases and sales of foreign assets (intervention) can be used to peg the exchange rate; purchases and sales of domestic assets (open market operations) can be used to pursue domestic policy objectives. Using this framework to ask how exchange rate arrangements affect the need for policy-optimizing coordination, I have reached an unorthodox conclusion (Kenen 1987a, 1988c). A simple agreement to peg exchange rates, without any additional coordination, is better from each government's national standpoint than an agreement to let rates float and pursue fully optimal coordination. This is because exchange rate arrangements affect the ways in which exogenous shocks influence outputs and prices.

Working with a standard portfolio-balance model, I have studied the effects of various exogenous shocks, including fiscal policy shocks, under pegged and floating rates and asked how those two exchange rate regimes affect each government's ability to stabilize its output and price level on its own, without attempting to coordinate its monetary policy with those of other countries. In effect, I have used the policy-optimizing framework to look anew at an old question, whether a floating exchange rate can confer policy autonomy on the governments of interdependent economies. It cannot. On the contrary, a pegged exchange rate proves to be superior in three of the five cases studied (a permanent shift in demand between the countries' bonds, a temporary increase in one country's saving reflecting a permanent increase in desired wealth, and a balanced budget increase in one government's spending). The ranking of exchange rate regimes is ambiguous in the other two cases (a permanent switch in demand between the countries' goods and a permanent increase in one country's stock of debt resulting from a temporary tax cut).

My model is summarized in the appendix to this paper. It contains two countries, the U.S. and EC, each with its own good, bond, and currency. The two goods and bonds are traded and are imperfect substitutes; each currency is held only in the issuing country. Asset markets and goods markets clear continuously, but goods prices are sticky. An increase in demand for the U.S. good, for example, does not raise its dollar price immediately. There is instead a temporary increase in U.S. output. But wages and prices start to rise in response to the increase in output, and they go on rising until output returns to its long-run equilibrium level. U.S. bonds are dollar bonds issued by the U.S. government when it runs a budget deficit; EC bonds are ecu bonds issued by the EC government. The two countries' money supplies are managed by their central banks, using open market operations in their own bond markets. When the exchange rate is pegged, however, money supplies are affected by intervention in the foreign-exchange market; intervention can be sterilized when, as here, two countries' bonds are imperfect substitutes, but sterilization is not automatic.

Expectations are static, and the model begins in long-run equilibrium, where there is no saving or investment, budgets and trade flows are balanced, and prices are constant. When this situation is disturbed, moreover, the two economies move gradually to a new long-run equilibrium, driven by changes in wealth induced by transitory saving and, in the floating rate case, by capital gains or losses on holdings of foreign-currency bonds. Governments are well behaved. They do not try to move their economies away from the stationary state but use their monetary policies merely to optimize the adjustment process initiated by an exogenous shock. Furthermore, each government has enough confidence in the other's integrity to give it open-ended access to reserves.

Casting these assumptions in game-theoretic terms, each government may be said to start at the bliss point defined by its own social welfare (loss) function, and their bliss points will be identical initially even if the governments have different preferences. Therefore, the Nash and Pareto equilibria will coincide. When the situation is disturbed, however, each government will seek to minimize the welfare loss resulting from the output and price effects of the shock. But there are two sorts of shocks. Some can be shown to shift both bliss points together, so that the Nash and Pareto equilibria will continue to coincide. In these special cases, each government can use its own monetary policy to neutralize completely the output and price effects of the shock and thus move directly to its new bliss point. There is no welfare loss and no need for policy coordination. Other shocks can be shown to shift the bliss points differently, so that the Nash and Pareto equilibria will no longer coincide, and monetary policies cannot be expected to neutralize the output and price effects of those shocks. Each government must then settle for a second-best solution, involving a departure from its bliss point and a welfare loss, and policy coordination is needed to minimize that loss.[9]

This strategy is illustrated in figures 2.2 and 2.3, which focus on the pegged rate case. The vertical axis in figure 2.2 measures the permanent change in the U.S. price level resulting from an open market operation or exogenous shock, and the horizontal axis measures the temporary change in U.S. output. As the U.S. economy starts in long-run equilibrium and the U.S. government wants to stay there, the origin in figure 2.2 represents the U.S. bliss point in output and price space, and points on the elliptical indifference curve surrounding it are welfare-inferior to it. (There is, of course, one such curve for each value of the U.S. social welfare function.) The line BB and arrows on it show what happens to the U.S. economy when the U.S. central bank makes an open market purchase. Output rises temporarily, and the price level rises permanently. The line FF and arrows on it show what happens when the EC central bank makes an open market purchase. Under a pegged exchange rate, the case considered here, the change in the U.S. price level will be the same when the size of the open market purchase is the same, but the change in U.S. output will be smaller. Therefore, FF is steeper than BB.

The apparatus in figure 2.2. can be used to derive a reaction curve showing how the U.S. central bank responds to the effects of an open market purchase by the EC central bank. An EC open market purchase takes the U.S. economy to a point such as T', and the options open to the U.S. central bank are shown by the line B'B', parallel to BB. The best option is at H', where B'B' is tangent to the indifference curve; the U.S. central bank must make an open market sale

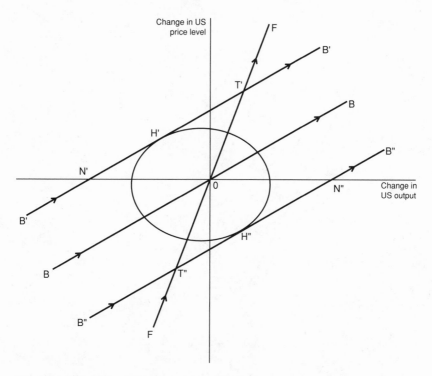

Fig. 2.2   U.S. policy preferences and policy responses

to minimize the welfare loss resulting from the EC open market purchase. But the U.S. price level is higher at H' than at the origin, which says that the U.S. open market sale is smaller than the EC open market purchase. (The global money supply has risen, raising both countries' prices.)

Turning to figure 2.3, the vertical axis measures holdings of EC bonds by the EC central bank, and the horizontal axis measures holdings of U.S. bonds by the U.S. central bank. The point P is the initial U.S. bliss point and the EC bliss point too, because the EC economy also starts in long-run equilibrium and the EC government wants to stay there. The line I_1 is the U.S. reaction curve, showing how the U.S. central bank responds to an EC open market purchase. It is negatively sloped, because the U.S. central bank will make an open market sale, reducing its holdings of U.S. bonds. It is steeper absolutely than a 45° line, because the U.S. open market sale is smaller than the EC open market purchase. The line I_2 is the EC reaction curve, derived from the EC counterpart of figure 2.2.

Returning to figure 2.2, consider the effects of an exogenous shock that drives the U.S. economy to a point such as N', depressing U.S. output temporarily but having no permanent effect on the U.S. price level. (That is what actually happens with a permanent switch in demand from the U.S. bond

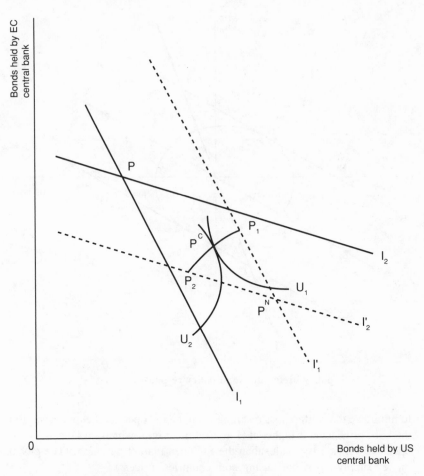

Fig. 2.3   Policy reactions curves for the U.S. and EC

to the EC bond.) The U.S. central bank could go again to H′, accepting a permanent increase in the U.S. price level in order to reduce the size of the temporary cut in U.S. output. But there is another possibility. Suppose that the U.S. central bank makes an open market purchase large enough to take the U.S. economy from N′ to T′ and the EC central bank makes an open market sale large enough to take the U.S. economy from T′ to the origin. The output and price effects of the shock will be neutralized completely. This outcome is shown in figure 2.3 by shifting the U.S. bliss point to P_1, where the EC central bank holds fewer bonds and the U.S. central bank holds more bonds, then shifting the U.S. reaction curve from I_1 to I'_1 making it pass through the new U.S. bliss point.[10]

Now suppose that the same exogenous shock drives the EC economy to the EC counterpart of point N″ in figure 2.2, raising EC output temporarily and having no permanent effect on the EC price level. The effects of the shock can be neutralized completely if the EC central bank makes an open market sale large enough to take the EC economy from N″ to T″ and the U.S. central bank makes an open market purchase large enough to take the EC economy from T″ to the origin. In figure 2.3, the EC bliss point shifts to P_2, where the EC central bank holds fewer bonds and the U.S. central bank holds more bonds, and the new EC reaction curve must be I_2'.

If each central bank optimizes its policy independently, without taking account of the other's decisions, the two will wind up in Nash equilibrium at P^N. If they coordinate their policies by some sort of bargaining, they will wind up in Pareto equilibrium at a point such as P^C, lying on the so-called contract curve connecting P_1 and P_2, and it is easy to prove that P^C is better than P^N from each country's standpoint. Bliss points such as P_1 and P_2 are surrounded by elliptical indifference curves, and two such curves are drawn in figure 2.3. They are the curves whose tangency defines the point P^C. But U_1, the U.S. indifference curve, cuts I_1' between P^N and P_1, which says that the U.S. welfare loss is smaller at P^C than at P^N, while U_2, the EC indifference curve, cuts I_2' between P^N and P_2, which makes an analogous statement about EC welfare. These are the gains from policy-optimizing coordination.

This sort of policy coordination cannot neutralize completely the output effects of the shock; it can only minimize the resulting welfare losses. The effects of a shock are neutralized completely only when a government can reach its new bliss point, and P^C lies between those bliss points. If the bliss points shifted together, however, they would continue to coincide, and the new reaction curves would intersect at the new common bliss point, just as they did initially. That is precisely what happens under a pegged exchange rate. The bliss points shift together in three of the five cases studied, permitting the two central banks to neutralize completely the output and price effects of the shocks without having to coordinate their policies.

2.3.2   Exchange Rates in the Regime-Preserving Framework

In the previous section, the policy-optimizing framework was used to prove that exchange rate pegging can substitute for more ambitious forms of policy coordination. But two strong assumptions were needed. First, the two economies were well behaved. They began in long-run equilibrium and returned to it after every shock. Disturbances were permanent but did not have permanent effects on output. Second, governments were well behaved. They did not defy or try to manipulate the long-run properties of their economies in ways that might have interfered with the viability of a pegged exchange rate. When these assumptions are violated, we step through the looking glass, from a world in which exchange rate pegging reduces the need for policy coordination to one in which coordination is required merely to achieve exchange-rate stability.

When we take that step, moreover, we have to change our frame of reference—to shift from the policy-optimizing framework to the regime-preserving framework. Unless we treat exchange rate stability as an international public good, something that governments want but cannot produce individually, it is hard to explain how exchange-rate stability can become the rationale for policy coordination. The critics of coordination go wrong here, but so do the defenders. They debate the merits of the Louvre Accord for being something different than it was. The G-7 governments were not trying to manage the global economy. They were trying to manage exchange rates. They started rather tentatively, hoping to keep the dollar from "overshooting" and thus allow the adjustment process to work itself out, but became more ambitious as time wore on. They deserve to be graded fairly, however, for what they were trying to accomplish and how they set about it, not by an extraneous standard.

There is enough to debate even when the issues are narrowly defined by the regime-preserving framework. How much importance should governments attach to the production of exchange rate stability? What should they be willing to sacrifice in order to produce it? How much can they achieve by intervention? How closely must they coordinate their monetary and fiscal policies? How frequently should they revise their exchange rate targets? Can they continue to depend on informal understandings of the sort embodied in the Louvre Accord, or must they adopt more formal rules? Should exchange rate bands be hard and narrow, as in the Bretton Woods system and EMS, or soft and wide, as proposed by Williamson (1985 [1983])? Can governments reform exchange rate arrangements without reforming reserve arrangements?

I have explored most of these issues elsewhere (Kenen 1987c, 1988a) and tried to show how they are linked. Thus, judgments about the feasibility of revising exchange rate targets must condition one's judgments about the appropriate size of the exchange rate band, and the width of the band cannot be chosen without knowing whether it should be hard or soft. If a hard band is appropriate, moreover, intervention must play a major role in exchange rate management; a hard band cannot be defended merely by manipulating short-term interest rates. But changes in reserve arrangements may be needed to facilitate and finance large amounts of intervention.

There have been remarkable changes in the importance that governments attach to exchange rate stability and in their self-confidence—what they think they can achieve by altering or challenging the market's expectations.

At the Versailles Summit of 1982, the G-7 governments created a working group to study the role of intervention, and the group's report was predictably critical of using it extensively. Intervention could be helpful in some special circumstances, but mainly for drawing the market's attention to the implications of monetary policies. Intervention could not and should not be used to oppose market forces (Working Group 1983). The same view was expressed in a second, more comprehensive report on the monetary system commissioned by the Williamsburg Summit in 1983. It worried about the volatility of floating exchange rates and warned that "large movements in real exchange rates may lead to patterns of international transactions that are unlikely to be sustainable," but it laid most of the blame for exchange rate instability on "inadequate and inconsistent policies that have led to divergent economic performance" (Deputies 1985, paras. 17, 20). In effect, governments endorsed the view then prevalent among economists that foreign-exchange markets process information efficiently and should not be blamed for the policies on which they are asked to pass judgment. That would be shooting the messenger who brings embarrassing news (Frenkel 1987).

A few months later, however, governments took a different view. On September 22, 1985, in the Plaza Communiqué, they sent the messenger back to the market to say that the market was not doing its job:

> The Ministers and Governors agreed that exchange rates should play a role in adjusting external imbalances. In order to do this, exchange rates should better reflect fundamental economic conditions than has been the case. They believe that agreed policy actions must be implemented and reinforced to improve the fundamentals further, and that in view of the present and prospective changes in fundamentals, some further orderly appreciation of the main non-dollar currencies against the dollar is desirable. They stand ready to cooperate more closely to encourage this when to do so would be helpful.

And they took the next step in the Louvre Accord of February 22, 1987:

> The Ministers and Governors agreed that the substantial exchange-rate changes since the Plaza Agreement will increasingly contribute to reducing external imbalances and have now brought their currencies within ranges broadly consistent with underlying economic fundamentals, given the policy commitments summarized [earlier] in this statement.
> Further substantial exchange-rate shifts among their currencies could damage growth and adjustment prospects in their countries.
> In current circumstances, therefore, they agreed to cooperate closely to foster stability of exchange rates around current levels.

In the months that followed, the G-7 governments intervened massively to support the dollar. They let it depreciate slightly in the spring but held it to a very narrow range thereafter, until the stock market collapse in October.

The rationale for trying to stabilize exchange rates can be summed up in two statements. Those who produce exchange rates in the foreign-exchange market are differently motivated from those who consume them in the markets for goods, services, and long-term assets. Furthermore, exchange rates are very flexible, like other asset prices, whereas goods prices are sticky, so that nominal and real exchange rates move together.

A growing body of evidence supports the first assertion. Inhabitants of the foreign-exchange market have been shown to behave myopically, even irrationally,[11] and this would be reason enough to challenge the conventional wisdom of the early 1980s, which held that markets are wiser than governments. But the second assertion is more important. If goods prices were perfectly flexible, there would be little cause to worry about exchange rate arrangements. Goods markets would optimize relative prices continuously, including real exchange rates, even if they had to cope with nonsensical messages from the foreign-exchange market. Governments could then stabilize their money stocks and allow the foreign-exchange market to determine nominal exchange rates, or they could peg exchange rates and allow the market to determine national money stocks. It is the stickiness of goods prices that makes the exchange rate regime important. When nominal exchange rates affect real exchange rates, they also affect economic activity—its level, location, and composition.

The strength of the connection between nominal and real exchange rates is shown clearly in figure 2.4, which draws attention to the huge swing in real rates during in the 1980s. This may have been the most expensive round-trip in recent history, save perhaps for the swing in oil prices that began and ended earlier. It would have been expensive even if the effects of the strong dollar had been fully reversed once the exchange rate movement was reversed. According to Branson and Love (1988), the appreciation of the dollar from 1980 to 1985 wiped out more than one million jobs in U.S. industry, affecting more than 5.3 percent of the work force in manufacturing. But the costs of the swing may prove to be even bigger because its effects may not be reversed completely.

Whole industries and regions in the United States may be affected permanently because plants that were shut down when they became uncompetitive will not be reopened. They were not inefficient in 1980, when the

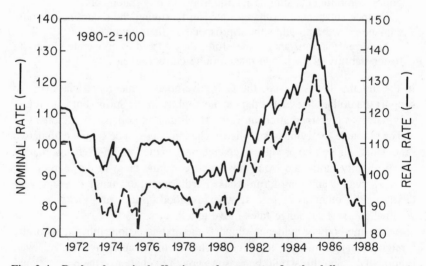

Fig. 2.4   Real and nominal effective exchange rates for the dollar
Source: J. P. Morgan, *World Financial Markets*, various issues; includes currencies of fifteen industrial countries weighted by bilateral trade in manufactures.

exchange rate swing began, but have been rendered obsolete by decisions and events resulting from that swing. Export and domestic markets have been lost to foreign competitors, who invested heavily to capture them and will not give them up, even though they are less profitable than they were initially.[12] This is not a mercantilist dirge. It is a lament for lost resources—for the physical and human capital that has been misallocated, not only in the United States but in other countries too.

These real resource costs have been compounded by permanent damage to the trading system. Although it was deeply opposed to protectionism, the Reagan administration was unable to resist pressures from industries severely hurt by the appreciation of the dollar. It imposed new trade restrictions or tightened old ones on imports of automobiles, steel, textiles, and apparel, and most of them remain in place.

But was this trip unnecessary, or was the foreign-exchange market doing a job that goods markets could not do because goods prices are not flexible enough? That is the key question.

Krugman (1989) dismisses the question curtly, saying that there was no fundamental reason for raising the real value of the dollar in 1984 only to reduce it in 1985. He argues persuasively that this part of the round-trip reflected irrational behavior by the foreign-exchange market. But it is hard to blame the *whole* round-trip on that sort of behavior. The appreciation of the dollar began with the tightening of U.S. monetary policy in 1979. It was driven thereafter by the capital inflow induced by the combination of tight money with a growing budget deficit. In this simple but meaningful sense, the first part of the trip was unavoidable under a floating exchange rate.

Suppose that Louvre Accord had been in force at the start of the 1980s. What would have happened to the dollar? A number of economists have played back this period using different policies or policy rules and a different exchange rate regime (see, e.g., Currie and Wren-Lewis 1988, Williamson and Miller 1987, and Frenkel, Goldstein, and Masson, ch. 1 in this volume). All of them conclude that the world would have been a better place. But most of the improvement can be traced to the modification of U.S. policies, not to the modification of the exchange rate regime. In fact, the exchange rate rules used in most such exercises are too loose to have much influence. The point at issue, moreover, has to do with the behavior of exchange rates under the policies actually followed rather than the modification of those policies. There are two reasons. First, it is hard to believe that the Reagan administration would have forsworn its idiosyncratic fiscal experiment in deference to policy rules or guidelines endorsed by an earlier administration. Second, and more generally, it is wrong to contrast the existing exchange rate regime under imperfect policies with an alternative regime under perfect policies.

If the G-7 governments had been committed to exchange rate management at the start of the 1980s, the new U.S. policy mix would have forced them to intervene heavily to prevent the dollar from appreciating, which would have put strong upward pressure on the U.S. money supply and strong downward pressure on other countries' money supplies.[13] These monetary side effects of exchange rate stabilization would have produced political pressures that might perhaps have forced the U.S. government to act earlier and more decisively on the budgetary front. At the same time, the G-7 governments would have been warned of the need to adjust exchange rates—to revalue the dollar gradually in small steps, but by less than it rose in fact under the influence of market forces.

How, then, should we apportion blame for the whole round-trip? Some blame must be borne by U.S. policies, which would have caused the dollar to appreciate significantly whether exchange rates were floating freely or closely managed. But much blame must be borne by the foreign-exchange market, not just for producing the speculative bubble of 1984–85 but also for taking a myopic view two or three years earlier. If the inhabitants of the market had been endowed with the marvelous attributes displayed by those who populate many economists' models, they would have known that the U.S. budget and trade deficits could not last indefinitely and that the dollar would have to return eventually to something near its 1980 level. When the dollar started to appreciate, then, they would have bet against it, selling dollars rather than buying them and reducing the net capital inflow. In other words, they would have engaged in stabilizing speculation on a scale sufficiently large to keep nominal and real exchange rates from changing substantially.[14]

The basic lesson taught by the experience of 1980–87 has to do with the high cost of imperfect policies under floating exchange rates. The core of the case for exchange rate management is the simple but sad fact that policies and markets are usually imperfect and interact in costly ways under freely floating rates.

2.4 Obstacles to Policy Coordination

Economists have used the policy-optimizing framework to measure the potential gains from policy coordination. An early attempt by Oudiz and Sachs (1984) found that the gains were disappointingly small. In one of their exercises, for example, the coordination of fiscal and monetary policies by Germany, Japan, and the United States had very little influence on the fiscal instruments and rather small effects on economic performance; when measured in units equivalent to percentage point changes in real income, the welfare gains were smaller than 1 percent of GNP. But subsequent studies have produced bigger numbers. Holtham and Hughes Hallett (1987) have reported welfare gains, measured in income-equivalent units, as large as 6 or 7 percent of GNP and not smaller than 3 or 4 percent, depending on the model used. There would thus seem to be large unexploited gains from policy-optimizing coordination.

Why don't governments exploit those gains? Four reasons are commonly given. First, governments are apt to renege on their bargains and cannot trust each other. Second, governments subscribe to different views about economic behavior and the workings of the world economy. Third, governments have different policy targets. Fourth, political and constitutional constraints interfere with the bargaining process.

The first explanation has been demolished. The rest make sense. But they seem more cogent when they are invoked to explain the apparent scarcity of regime-preserving coordination than when they are used to account for a shortage of policy-optimizing coordination.

2.4.1 Reneging and Reliability

The concern about reneging derives in large part from the stylized way in which economists have represented public and private decision-making and the resulting concern with the problem of time consistency. The issue is illustrated neatly by the Barro-Gordon (1983) model, in which wages and prices are set by the private sector in light of its expectations concerning the inflation rate, which depends in turn on its expectations concerning the money supply. If the government promises to raise the money supply by, say, 5 percent and the private sector expects the government to keep its word, wages and prices will rise immediately by 5 percent, in line with the expected growth rate of the money supply. At this point, the government has two options. If it keeps its promise, it will exactly validate the actual inflation rate, and there will be no change in output or employment. If it breaks its promise and raises the money supply by, say, 10 percent, it will stimulate output and employment, because the inflation rate cannot change until wages and prices can be adjusted. If it breaks its word frequently, however, it will lose credibility. The private sector will cease to pay attention to the government's promises; it will start to base its expectations on the actual growth rate of the money supply, not the rate that the government keeps promising. The inflation rate will rise, and the rapid growth rate of the money supply will serve merely to validate the higher inflation rate. It will no longer stimulate output and employment.[15]

The argument, however, depends on three assumptions: (1) the private sector makes binding decisions about wages and prices; (2) the government can and should make promises about its own behavior to facilitate planning by the private sector; and (3) the "game" played by the government vis-à-vis the private sector is the only game in town.

The assumption about binding private sector decisions is unexceptional. In fact, the resulting stickiness of wages and prices is one basic reason for wanting to stabilize nominal exchange rates. The case for predictable behavior by governments is equally hard to challenge in principle but has to be qualified carefully. Governments may need to keep markets guessing by creating uncertainty about their tactics; they need short-term flexibility, which is not necessarily incompatible with medium-term predictability. Furthermore, governments cannot be rigidly predictable in an uncertain world. If they were the only source of uncertainty facing the private sector, governments could produce economic stability by being perfectly predictable. When governments and the private sector are *both* plagued by uncertainties, the rigid pursuit of predictable policies can cause instability.[16] But the third feature of the Barro-Gordon (1983) model is far too restrictive. Governments play many games simultaneously, including the all-important political game. If a government cheats on any other player, all of them can punish it. In fact, they can choose a new government at the next election. In the international context, moreover, governments can commit themselves rather firmly because the costs of cheating are very high. A government that breaks its promises to other governments cannot make more bargains with them. This consideration is particularly important for the major industrial countries, which have to cooperate not only in macroeconomic matters but in many economic, political, and strategic domains.[17]

Governments try to refrain from making commitments they cannot expect to honor and try to honor those they make:

> If we take seriously the claim that policy-makers in an anarchic world are constantly tempted to cheat, certain features of the [1978] Bonn story— certain things that did *not* happen—seem quite anomalous. We find little evidence that the negotiations were hampered by mutual fear of reneging. For example, even though the Bonn agreement was negotiated with exquisite care, it contained no special provisions about phasing or partial conditionality that might have protected the parties from unexpected defection. Moreover, the Germans and the Japanese both irretrievably enacted their parts of the bargain in September [1978], more than six months before [President Carter's] action on oil price decontrol and nearly two years before decontrol was implemented.
>
> Once the Germans and Japanese had fulfilled their parts of the bargain, the temptation to the President to renege should have been overpowering, if the standard account of international anarchy is to be believed. Moreover, the domestic political pressure on him to renege was clearly very strong. But virtually no one on either side of the final decontrol debate dismissed the Bonn pledge as irrelevant. (Putnam and Henning 1986, 100)

But these results seem natural enough when we treat the Bonn bargain as an exercise in regime-preserving coordination and bear in mind the complex and continuing relationships among the participating governments. Each stood to gain from its own ''concessions'' as well as those of its partners, and each was concerned to preserve its reputation for reliability. In President Carter's own words, ''Each of us has been careful not to promise more than he can deliver'' (Putnam and Henning 1986, 100).

2.4.2 Disagreements about Economic Behavior

Governments *do* disagree about economic behavior. German and American governments have disagreed for years about the responsiveness of unemployment to aggregate demand and even about the way that aggregate demand responds to fiscal and monetary policies. For a time, moreover, U.S. officials denied that there was any connection between the American budget and trade deficits, while other governments connected them simplistically, without leaving enough room for the role of the exchange rate.[18] But economists disagree in turn about the way that disagreements among governments affect policy coordination.

Frankel and Rockett (1988) have tried to show that misperceptions about economic behavior can lead to welfare-worsening policy bargains. They use ten large multicountry models to represent U.S. and European views about economic behavior and assume that each party uses its own model to measure the welfare effects of striking a bargain with the other. The governments do not exchange information. Instead, they engage in policy barter, agreeing to coordinate their policies whenever each government's own calculations lead it to believe that coordination will be beneficial, given its own model and objectives.

After they have taken the governments through the bargaining process and know the new settings of the policy instruments, Frankel and Rockett ask what will happen to each country, using the "true" model of the world economy. Because they must measure the effects of every bargain using all ten models, they must analyze 100 potential bargains and 1,000 possible outcomes. They find that the United States gains in 494 cases, loses in 398, and is unaffected in the remaining 108, while Europe gains in 477 cases, loses in 418, and is unaffected in the remaining 105. The parties' "success rates" are about 60 percent.

These are interesting results, but they must be interpreted cautiously. Frankel (1988, 27) himself concludes that "ministers in Group of 7 and Summit meetings might do better to discuss their beliefs directly rather than telling the others how to adjust their policies." But that is what governments have been doing all along, and there is a simple way to represent the outcome.

Suppose as before that each government believes in one model and also knows the other's model. If it is not perfectly confident about the rightness of its views, prudential considerations should lead it to ask how a policy bargain would affect its welfare on the working supposition that the other government is using the right model; it should not strike a bargain unless it can expect to gain under both governments' models. If it wants to persuade its partner to accept its own proposals, an important part of the actual bargaining process, reputational considerations should lead it to make sure that its own proposals would raise its partner's welfare under both governments' models. These concerns, taken together, impose a strong condition on the bargaining process. It should not even start unless both governments can expect to gain under both governments' models.

Holtham and Hughes Hallett (1987) came to this conclusion by a different route and applied the strong condition to the Frankel-Rockett (1988) bargains.

They used six models, not ten, and had thus to analyze thirty-six possible bargains.[19] But they ruled out twenty of those bargains because they violated the strong condition. (Three were ruled out because Europe would be worse off on the U.S. view of the world, eight because the United States would be worse off on the European view, and the other nine because both sides would be worse off on the other's view.) This leads me to my first conclusion: disagreements about economic behavior can be a major obstacle to policy-optimizing coordination. They can keep governments from getting together. But Holtham and Hughes Hallett went on to measure the welfare effects of the other sixteen bargains and found that the success rate was quite high. It was 73 percent for the United States and 83 percent for Europe.[20] This leads to my second conclusion: when prudential and reputational considerations block bargains that should not take place, policy coordination is not very dangerous to the participants' health.

It would be hard to conduct this sort of exercise for an instance of regime-preserving coordination. But one would expect the same sort of result. When governments disagree about the workings of the world economy, they are bound to hold different views about the costs of policy coordination, even when they agree completely about the benefits. Suppose that two governments are considering the use of interest rate policies for exchange rate stabilization. If they hold different views about the way that interest rates affect aggregate demand, they will also disagree about the costs of exchange rate stabilization.

Disagreements about economic behavior may be very potent in blocking this sort of coordination. When governments are willing to contemplate policy-optimizing coordination, it must be because they believe that a suitable policy bargain will allow them to make welfare-improving changes in their own national policies. When they are made to contemplate regime-preserving coordination, they may still believe that their national policies continue to be optimal and will thus want their partners to make the policy changes required for the common good.

2.4.3 Disagreements about Policy Objectives

The same possibility arises when governments have different policy objectives—the third in the list of reasons for the scarcity of coordination. In fact, such differences cannot explain why governments fail to engage in policy-optimizing coordination. On the contrary, they make it more attractive.

An example drawn from Eichengreen (1985) illustrates this point. Indeed, it makes a stronger point. Governments that have incompatible objectives can nevertheless benefit from policy-optimizing coordination.

Consider two identical economies with rigid wage rates and greedy governments. Each government wants to hold three-quarters of the global gold stock. If they pursue their targets independently, raising their interest rates competitively to attract capital inflows and gold, they will wind up with identical gold stocks but high unemployment rates. There are two ways to deal with this outcome. The two governments can agree to reduce their interest rates without even talking about their targets. That is the sort of policy barter that many economists have in mind when they talk about policy-optimizing coordination. Alternatively, the governments can reveal and modify their policy targets. But what if they reveal them and refuse to modify them? That is when conflicts or differences in targets obstruct coordination.

This case is too simple to take seriously—or is it? It does not differ from the case in which governments pursue incompatible current account targets, and they seem to do that frequently. It does not differ from the case in which they attach different weights to different targets, including the common or collective targets that they can achieve only at some cost in terms of their domestic targets. When collective targets are at issue, moreover, debates about objectives are unavoidable. The aims of the exercise have to be identified, and differences in preferences are bound to surface. When governments engage in policy barter, they can agree on means without discussing ends. When they engage in mutual persuasion—which is what normally happens—it is hard to agree on means without agreeing on ends.

2.4.4   Political and Constitutional Constraints

The fourth reason for the shortage of coordination applies to both varieties. Once again, however, it provides a more compelling explanation for the scarcity of regime-preserving coordination. There are political and constitutional obstacles to every sort of international cooperation, but they are hardest to surmount when the costs are clear and close to home and the benefits are not.

The political obstacles to policy coordination have been dramatized by the budgetary problems of the United States. How can the United States engage in international bargaining about fiscal policies when congressional leaders can say that the president's budget is ''dead on arrival'' on Capitol Hill? In the last days of World War I, the German general staff was said to believe that the situation was serious but not hopeless, while the Austrian general staff thought that it was hopeless but not serious. The Viennese view may be more appropriate here. The budgetary deadlock of the 1980s does not signify permanent paralysis. Nor should we neglect the political problems faced by other major countries in making and adjusting fiscal policies:

> The political system in Japan has traditionally restrained the powers of the Prime Minister to a far greater degree than the U.S. constitution limits the power of the American President. Always conscious of factional politics, the Prime Minister must answer to ''policy tribes'' which are groups of politicians committed to one-dimensional special interests. The Prime Minister must also placate vast armies of bureaucrats, not always from a position of strength. In Japan, it has often been said, politicians reign, but bureaucrats rule. (Funabashi 1988, 91)

The German situation is similar for different reasons:

> Although the ruling coalition has no difficulty in obtaining sufficient parliamentary support for its taxing and spending priorities, in practice its

control over fiscal policy is undermined by the following two factors. First, since the 1970s . . . the SPD has received control of the Ministry of Finance, while the FDP has staffed the Ministry of Economics, an arrangement that has weakened the federal government's ability to undertake comprehensive or drastic measures. Second, the federal government controls less than 50 percent of public investment, and only about 15 percent of the nation's total public spending and investment, the remainder coming from the *land* and local governments. (Funabashi 1988, 117)

There is, of course, a fundamental difference between these situations and the U.S. situation. Once the German and Japanese governments have decided to make a policy change, they can commit themselves formally, and the U.S. government cannot, because it cannot commit the Congress. But the record is not so very bad. President Carter was careful not to promise more than he could deliver—and he did deliver eventually. In another context, moreover, the White House obtained in advance a promise of rapid congressional action on the trade policy bargain produced by the Tokyo round of GATT negotiations— the "fast track" that Congress would follow in agreeing to accept or reject those parts of the bargain requiring new legislation. The Bush administration should perhaps propose a similar standby arrangement in the fiscal policy package it takes to Capitol Hill to break the budgetary deadlock.

The basic problems are political, not constitutional. No democratic government can make major policy changes without working hard to persuade the public that the new policies will be better than the old, if not indeed the best of all possible policies. When the time comes to coordinate policies, "Each national leader already has made a substantial investment in building a particular coalition at the domestic [game] board, and he or she will be loath to construct a different coalition simply to sustain an alternative policy mix that might be more acceptable internationally" (Putnam and Bayne 1987, 11). In brief, fiscal policies are not very flexible in any democracy, regardless of its constitution.

Policy coordination is made more difficult by jurisdictional divisions within governments. The problem is most serious on the monetary side, especially in Germany and the United States which have independent central banks. Here again, however, constitutional arrangements matter less than political realities, and independent central banks maintain their independence by being extremely astute politically. They cannot permit politicians to precommit them or to take their consent for granted, and they can be expected to make their views known, privately or publicly. Once they have given their consent, however, they are apt to be very reliable partners, because credibility is their most important asset. Furthermore, they rely on each other to protect their independence. On a number of recent occasions, central banks have refused to make interest rate changes until they could be sure that foreign central banks were ready to move with them.[21]

Finally, monetary policies can be altered rapidly and incrementally, without building a new political consensus. That is why a change in monetary policy is usually the first signal of a change in official thinking about the economic outlook. Therefore, monetary policies can be coordinated more deftly than fiscal policies, despite jurisdictional divisions in some countries.

2.5   The Framework for Policy Coordination

Rigidities in making fiscal policies and differences of view about the ways in which they work are probably sufficient to account for the apparent scarcity of policy-optimizing coordination—why governments fail to exploit all of the potential gains. They may even account for a more important failure. Quantitative studies of policy coordination have to start with a benchmark— the counterpart of the noncooperative equilibrium. They must therefore define fully optimal policies for each government acting unilaterally, and this is an instructive exercise. The welfare gains obtained by optimizing policies are often larger than the gains obtained thereafter by moving from noncooperative to cooperative policies. Dealing with policy coordination between the United States and Europe, Hughes Hallett (1987) obtains these welfare measures:

Simulation	United States	Europe
Baseline	466.2	346.2
Noncooperative	103.6	81.3
Cooperative	96.2	55.8

These are loss-function calculations, measuring the welfare costs of the governments' failure to reach their targets, so reductions are good things. But the biggest reductions occur on the way from the actual (baseline) situation to optimal noncooperative policies, not from noncooperative to cooperative (coordinated) policies. Political and institutional rigidities combine with the uncertainties of the real world to interfere with any sort of optimization, let alone optimal coordination.

The same rigidities and disagreements also help to account for the apparent scarcity of regime-preserving coordination, and disagreements about targets are important too. They combine to produce disagreements about burden sharing. But disagreements of this sort are more readily susceptible to resolution than those which arise when one government tries to tell another how to pursue its own self-interest. For this reason, if no other, we can perhaps be optimistic about the prospects for the sorts of policy coordination required to support exchange rate management.

What sorts of coordination are needed? The Williamson-Miller (1987) framework supplies an appropriate starting point. Intervention and interest rate differences would be used to stabilize exchange rates, while the global average of real interest rates and national fiscal policies would be used to regulate nominal expenditure. Conflicts between external and internal balance would be reconciled in the usual way, by periodic adjustments in real exchange rates. This is a far more sensible assignment than the one proposed by McKinnon (1988), who believes that fiscal policies should regulate current account balances because real exchange rates do not affect them, that the global money supply should be used to control the global price level, and that nonsterilized intervention should keep nominal exchange rates in line with purchasing power parity. Fiscal policies cannot control current account balances without imposing unemployment on deficit countries and inflationary pressures on surplus countries. They may be needed to validate changes in real exchange rates but cannot replace them.[22]

Yet the Williamson-Miller (1987) framework fails to address some difficult issues. While monetary policies must be coordinated closely to influence capital flows and offset expectations of exchange rate realignments, they cannot be assigned to that task exclusively, nor can fiscal policies be assigned exclusively to managing nominal demand. On the one hand, fiscal policies affect current account balances and, therefore, the size of the task faced by monetary policies. On the other hand, fiscal policies cannot be adjusted frequently enough to stabilize aggregate demand. Monetary policies must do some of the work that fiscal policies could do if they were more flexible, and exchange rate changes must do the rest.

It is important to distinguish between exchange rate management and the rigid defense of pegged exchange rates within very narrow bands. In my own view, the bands should be hard but wide and should be adjusted frequently to rectify disequilibria, including those that result from rigid fiscal policies. It is also important to distinguish between fiscal differences and fiscal shocks. International differences in fiscal policies do not necessarily destabilize exchange rates. They have not done so in the EMS, even though they continue to be quite large (see Gros and Thygesen 1988, 7). In fact, differences in fiscal policies can compensate for differences in national savings rates that would otherwise produce current account imbalances. The lessons to be learned from the 1980s relate to the effects of large fiscal shocks, which are bad news indeed, and the framework for multilateral surveillance currently being developed by the G-7 governments should focus very sharply on that problem.

Appendix

This appendix presents the model used to derive the results reported in the text. The model contains two countries, the U.S. and EC, but is written entirely in U.S. dollar terms. All nominal variables are dollar denominated except those with primes and those pertaining to the EC bond (F, F^c, etc.) which are denominated in EC ecu. The subscripts 1 and 2 denote U.S. and EC variables respectively; asterisks denote long-run values and exogenous shifts in demands for goods and assets.

The U.S. Economy

U.S. households hold U.S. money, U.S. bonds, and EC bonds. Their wealth is

(1) $$W_1 = L_1 + B_1 + \pi F_1,$$

where W_1 is U.S. wealth, L_1 and B_1 measure U.S. holdings of U.S. money and bonds, F_1 measures U.S. holdings of EC bonds denominated in ecu, and π is the exchange rate in dollars per ecu. (An increase in π is a depreciation of the dollar.) The time path of U.S. wealth is

(2) $$(dW_1/dt) = S_1 + F_1(d\pi/dt),$$

where S_1 is U.S. saving, and the last term measures the capital gain conferred by a depreciation of the dollar.

The U.S. money supply is

(3) $$L_1 = B^c - R,$$

where L_1 is the money supply, B^c is the central bank's holdings of U.S. bonds, and R measures its reserve liabilities to the EC central bank. (An increase in B^c reflects an open market purchase by the U.S. central bank; an increase in R reflects nonsterilized intervention in the foreign-exchange market—a dollar purchase by the U.S. or EC central bank to keep π from rising.)

The supply of dollar bonds can change only gradually as the U.S. government runs a budget deficit or surplus. The market-clearing equation for the U.S. bond is

(4) $$B = B_1 + B_2 + B^c,$$

where B_1 and B_2 are the quantities held by U.S. and EC residents and B^c is the quantity held by the U.S. central bank. The evolution of B is governed by a stylized fiscal policy:

(5) $$(dB/dt) = g(B^* - B), 0 < g < 1.$$

The U.S. government chooses a target level of debt, B^*, and runs a budget deficit or surplus until target and actual debt levels are equal. The government cuts taxes to run a deficit, then rescinds the tax cut gradually to satisfy equation (5). The government's budget is

(6) $\quad g(B^* - B) = G_1 + r_1 B - T_1 - T_{12} - r_1 B^c, T_{12} = r_1 B_2 - r_2 \pi F_1,$

where G_1 is the government's spending on U.S. and EC goods, r_1 and r_2 are the interest rates on U.S. and EC bonds, T_1 is the lump sum tax that the government adjusts continuously to run the desired surplus or deficit, and T_{12} is an intergovernmental transfer payment from the EC to the U.S. that removes all interest income terms from the definitions of the current account balance and disposable income.

The demand for money by U.S. households is defined with reference to the value of U.S. output and varies inversely with the U.S. interest rate around $\bar{r}$, its initial level:

(7) $\qquad L_1 = (1/v)\mathrm{Exp}[-\delta_1(r_1 - \bar{r})]p_1 Q_1, \delta_1 > 0,$

where Q_1 is U.S. output and p_1 is its price. The demand for the EC bond by U.S. households is defined with reference to U.S. wealth and varies with the difference between U.S. and EC interest rates:

(8) $\qquad \pi F_1 = \beta_1 \mathrm{Exp}[-\frac{1}{2}\phi(r_1 - r_2)]W_1, 0 < \beta_1 < 1, \phi > 0.$

The demand for the U.S. bond by U.S. households is defined residually by equations (1), (7), and (8).

Saving depends on the difference between desired and actual wealth:

(9) $\qquad S_1 = s(W_1^* - W_1), 0 < s < 1.$

Desired wealth, in turn, depends on the domestic interest rate and on disposable income:

(10) $\qquad W_1^* = \alpha \mathrm{Exp}[\Theta_1(r_1 - \bar{r})]Y_1^d, 0 < s\alpha < 1, 0 < \Theta_1 < \phi.$

The term $s\alpha$ is the marginal propensity to save out of disposable income (and must thus lie between zero and unity); the restriction on Θ_1 puts a lower bound on capital mobility. Disposable income is

(11) $\quad Y_1^d = p_1 Q_1 + r_1 B_1 + r_2 \pi F_1 - T_1 = p_1 Q_1 - G_1 + g(B^* - B),$

where equation (6) has been used to replace the lump sum tax T_1.

Households and the government have identical preferences with regard to goods, and a_1 measures the share of the EC good in total U.S. spending. Therefore,

(12) $\quad p_1 c_{11} = (1 - a_1)(Y_1^d - S_1 + G_1), p_2 c_{21} = a_1(Y_1^d - S_1 + G_1).$

On these same assumptions, the U.S. consumer price index is

(13) $$q_1 = p_1^{1-a_1} p_2^{a_1}.$$

Finally, the market-clearing equation for the U.S. good is

(14) $$Q_1 = c_{11} + c_{12},$$

where c_{12} is the quantity of the U.S. good imported by the EC for household and government consumption.

The EC Economy

It is not necessary to write out all of the EC equations, since they resemble their U.S. counterparts. The equations for EC wealth, however, look different because they are written in terms of the dollar (the foreign currency) rather than the ecu:

(1') $$W_2 = \pi(L_2' + F_2) + B_2,$$

(2') $$(dW_2/dt) = S_2 + (L_2' + F_2)(d\pi/dt),$$

where W_2 is EC wealth, L_2' and F_2 measure holdings of EC money and bonds in ecu, B_2 measures holdings of U.S. bonds in dollars, and S_2 is EC saving in dollars. The supplies of the two ecu assets are given by

(3') $$L_2' = F^c + (1/\pi)R,$$

(4') $$F = F_1 + F_2 + F^c,$$

(5') $$(dF/dt) = g(F^* - F),$$

where F, F^c and F^* play the roles that B, B^c, and B^* played in the U.S. equations. The EC budget equation is

(6') $$g(F^* - F) = G_2' + r_2 F - T_2' + (1/\pi)T_{12} - r_2 F^c,$$

where G_2' and T_2' play the roles that G_1 and T_1 played in the U.S. budget equation. The EC demands for money and the U.S. bond are

(7') $$L_2 = (1/v)\mathrm{Exp}[-\delta_2(r_2 - \bar{r})]p_2 Q_2$$

(8') $$B_2 = \beta_2 \mathrm{Exp}[\tfrac{1}{2}\phi(r_1 - r_2)]W_2$$

The EC demand for the EC bond is defined residually. The remaining EC equations, for saving, desired wealth, disposable income, levels of EC spending on the U.S. and EC goods, and the consumer price index, are identical to their U.S. counterparts, equations (9) through (13), apart from subscripts. The market-clearing equation for the EC good is made redundant by Walras's Law.

Strategic Simplifications

Four conditions are imposed on the initial situation. Prices are normalized at unity $(p_1 = p_2' = \pi = 1$, so that $p_2 = \pi p_2' = q_1 = q_2 = \pi q_2' = 1)$. Interest rates are equalized $(r_1 = r_2 = \bar{r})$. Net reserves are zero $(R = 0)$. Both economies start in a stationary state $(S_1 = S_2 = 0, B^* = B$, and $F^* = F)$, so trade is balanced initially $(p_1 c_{12} = p_2 c_{21})$.

Two restrictions are imposed on economic behavior. Each country's spending is biased toward its own home good, so that $a_1 < \frac{1}{2}$ and $(1 - a_2) < \frac{1}{2}$, where a_1 and a_2 are the shares of the EC good in U.S. and EC spending, espectively. When the U.S. and EC interest rates are equal, as they are to start, the share of the foreign-currency asset in each country's wealth is equal to the share of the imported good in that country's spending, so that $\beta_1 = a_1$ and $\beta_2 = (1 - a_2)$.

Finally, outputs and levels of government spending are the same in the U.S. and EC $(Q_1 = Q_2 = Q$, and $G_1 = G_2' = G)$, and all behavioral parameters are the same $(\delta_1 = \delta_2 = \delta$, and $\Theta_1 = \Theta_2 = \Theta)$. Under these assumptions, moreover, $W_1 = W_2$, and $a_1 = (1 - a_2) = a$, because trade is balanced initially.

The model is solved for the short-run and long-run effects of six disturbances: open market purchases of the domestic bond in the U.S. and EC $(dB^c > 0$ and $dF^c > 0)$, a permanent shift by U.S. or EC households from the EC bond to the U.S. bond $(dB_2^* > 0)$, a permanent shift in U.S. or EC spending from the U.S. good to the EC good $(dc_2^* > 0)$, permanent increases in government spending in the U.S. and EC matched by increases in lump sum taxes $(dG_1 > 0$ and $dG_2' > 0)$, permanent increases in desired wealth causing temporary increases in saving $(dW_1^* > 0$ and $dW_2^* > 0)$, and temporary tax cuts in the U.S. and EC causing permanent increase in stocks of debt $(dB^* > 0$ and $dF^* > 0)$. As prices are sticky in both countries, p_1 and p_2' are held at unity to obtain the short-run solutions, but Q_1 and Q_2 vary. As outputs return eventually to their natural levels, Q_1 and Q_2 are held at their initial levels to obtain the long-run solutions, but p_1 and p_2' vary.

The Short-Run Solutions

The pegged rate solutions are obtained by holding π at unity and allowing R to vary:

(15) $dR = (1/H)\{aW\phi[n(vdB^c - vdF^c) - (1 - 2a)(dx_1 - dx_2) + 2dc_2^*]$

$- [s(1 - 2a)W\Theta + nQ\delta]dB_2^*\}$,

where

$$H = s(1 - 2a)J + 2a(Q\delta + nvW\phi),$$

$$n = 2a + s\alpha(1 - 2a),$$

$$J = W\Theta + \alpha Q\delta,$$

$$dx_1 = s(\alpha dG_1 - dW_1^*) + (1 - s\alpha)gdB^*,$$

$$dx_2 = s(\alpha dG_2' - dW_2^*) + (1 - s\alpha)gdF^*.$$

An open market purchase of domestic bonds reduces the reserves of the country involved; so do the two forms of fiscal expansion and a permanent fall in desired wealth (a temporary decrease in household saving). A switch in demand to the U.S. bond raises U.S. reserves. A switch in demand to the EC good raises EC reserves.

The changes in outputs are

(16) $dQ_1 = (1/H)(1/J)\{[H_1 vdB^c + H_2 vdF^c + v(H_1 - H_2)dB_2^*]$
$$+ (1/s)(M_1 dx_1 + M_2 dx_2) - J[(Q\delta + 2avW\phi)dc_2^* - H_f d\bar\pi]\},$$

(16') $dQ_2 = (1/H)(1/J)\{[H_1 vdF^c + H_2 vdB^c - v(H_1 - H_2)dB_2^*]$
$$+ (1/s)(M_1 dx_2 + M_2 dx_1) + J[(Q\delta + 2avW\phi)dc_2^* - H_f d\bar\pi]\},$$

where

$$H_1 = [s(1 - 2a)J + a(Q\delta + nvW\phi)]W\Theta, \quad H_2 = a(Q\delta + nvW\phi)W\Theta,$$

$$M_1 = s(1 - 2a)J(Q\delta + avW\phi) + aQ\delta (Q\delta + nvW\phi),$$

$$M_2 = a[Q\delta(Q\delta + 2avW\phi) - s(1 - 2a)W\Theta(vW\phi)],$$

$$H_f = a[(Q\delta + 2avW\phi)U_f + 2v(1 - a)Ws(1 - 2a)W\Theta],$$

$$U_f = Q + s(1 - 2a)W.$$

These effects are unambiguous, with one exception noted shortly. An open market purchase of the domestic bond raises both countries' outputs but raises domestic output by more than foreign output ($H_1 > H_2$). Both forms of fiscal expansion raise domestic output but can raise or lower foreign output, and a reduction in desired wealth has the same effects. A switch in demand to the U.S. bond raises U.S. output and reduces EC output, and a switch in demand to the EC good has the opposite effects. The final terms in equations (16) and (16') describe the effects of a once-for-all devaluation of the dollar, which raises U.S. output and reduces EC output.

The floating rate solutions are obtained by holding R at zero and allowing π to vary:

(17) $$d\pi = (1/a)(A/U)dR,$$

where dR is the vector of changes in reserves given in equation (15), and

$$U = 2\{(1 - a)[s(1 - 2a)J + 2aQ\delta] + a\phi U_f\}.$$

These effects are unambiguous, because those in equation (15) were unambiguous. The dollar depreciates under a floating rate whenever U.S. reserves would fall under a pegged rate.

The changes in outputs are

(18) $dQ_1 = (1/U)\{(1/J)[U_1 vdB^c - U_2 vdF^c - (1/W)JQ\delta U_f dB_2^*]$
$+ (1/J)(1/s)Q\delta[V_1 dx_1 + V_2 dx_2] - 2Q\delta(1 - a)dc_2^*,$

(18') $dQ_2 = (1/U)\{(1/J)[U_1 vdF^c - U_2 vdB^c + (1/W)JQ\delta U_f dB_2^*]$
$+ (1/J)(1/s)Q\delta[V_1 dx_2 + V_2 dx_1] + 2Q\delta(1 - a)dc_2^*\},$

where

$$U_1 = 2(1 - a)W\Theta[s(1 - 2a)J + aQ\delta] + a(J + W\Theta)\phi U_f,$$
$$U_2 = aQ\delta[\alpha\phi U_f - 2(1 - a)W\Theta],$$
$$V_1 = 2(1 - a)[s(1 - 2a)J + aQ\delta] + a\phi U_f,$$
$$V_2 = a[2(1 - a)Q\delta + \phi U_f].$$

These terms are unambiguous (even U_2, as $\phi > \Theta$). An open market purchase of the domestic bond raises domestic output but reduces foreign output. Both forms of fiscal expansion raise both outputs, as does a permanent fall in desired wealth. A switch in demand to the U.S. bond reduces U.S. output and raises EC output, and a switch in demand to the EC good has the same effects.

The Long-Run Solutions

These are the long-run solutions for the pegged rate case:

(19) $dR = (1/2N)\{[(1 - 2a)W\Theta + 2aW\phi](vdB^c - vdF^c)$
$- 2(Q\delta)dB_2^* + Q\delta[(1 - 2a)(\alpha dG_1 - dW_1^*)$
$- (1 - 2a)(\alpha dG_2' - dW_2^*) + (dB^* - dF^*)]$
$+ [(1 - 2a)J + 2aW\phi](1/a)dc_2^*\},$

where

$$N = v(1 - 2a)W\Theta + 2avW\phi + Q\delta.$$

There is an important difference between the signs of these effects and those in equation (15), pertaining to the short run. In the short run, both forms of fiscal expansion raise the reserves of the country involved, and a permanent fall in desired wealth has the same effect; in the long run, however, they reduce its reserves. The changes in the two price indexes are

(20) $dq_1 = (1/2JQ)[W\Theta(vdB^c + vdF^c) + Q\delta(dB^*$

              $+ \alpha dG_1 - dW_1^*) + Q\delta(dF^* + \alpha dG_2' - dW_2^*)]$

              $- (1/2Q)(1 - 2a)(1/a)dc_2^* + (1/2)d\bar{\pi},$

(20') $dq_2' = (1/2JQ)[\ldots] + (1/2Q)(1 - 2a)(1/a)dc_2^* - (1/2)d\bar{\pi},$

where the term [. . .] in equation (20') is identical to the corresponding term
in equation (20). A switch in demand to the U.S. bond has no permanent effect
on the countries' price levels; it does not appear in equations (20) and (20').
A switch in demand to the EC good drives them apart, raising the EC price
level and reducing the U.S. price level, and a devaluation has the opposite
effects, but all of the other disturbances raise them by the same amounts.

These are the long-run solutions for the floating rate case:

(21) $d\pi = (2N/QK)dR,$

where dR is the vector of changes in reserves given in equation (19) and

$$K = (1 - 2a)J + 2aW(\delta + \phi).$$

The changes in the two price indexes are

(22) $dq_1 = (1/JQK)\{K_1 vdB^c - K_2 vdF^c - Q\delta JdB_2^* + JK_0 dc_2^*$

           $+ Q\delta[(1 - 2a)J + aW(\delta + \phi)](dB^* + \alpha dG_1 - dW_1^*)$

           $+ aQ\delta[W(\delta + \phi) - J]dF^* + aQ\delta W(\delta + \phi)(\alpha dG_2' - dW_2^*)\},$

(22') $dq_2' = (1/JQK)\{K_1 vdF^c - K_2 vdB^c + Q\delta JdB_2^* - JK_0 dc_2^*$

           $+ Q\delta[(1 - 2a)J + aW(\delta + \phi)](dF^* + \alpha dG_2' - dW_2^*)$

           $+ aQ\delta[W(\delta + \phi) - J]dB^*$

           $+ aQ\delta W(\delta + \phi)(\alpha dG_1 - dW_1^*)\},$

where

           $K_1 = W\Theta[(1 - 2a)J + aW(\delta + \phi)] + (aW\phi)J,$

           $K_2 = aW\delta(\alpha Q\phi - W\Theta),$

           $K_0 = (1 - 2a)\alpha\delta G + aW(\delta + \phi).$

An open market purchase of the domestic bond raises the domestic price level
and reduces the foreign price level (as $\phi > \Theta$). A temporary tax cut causing
a permanent increase in debt raises the domestic price level but can raise or
lower the foreign price level. A balanced budget increase in government
spending raises both price levels, as does a permanent fall in desired wealth.
A switch in demand to the U.S. bond reduces the U.S. price level and raises

the EC price level, and a switch in demand to the EC good has the opposite effects.

The Bliss-Point Shifts

To obtain the countries' bliss-point shifts, we would set $dQ_1 = dQ_2 = dq_1 = dq_2' = 0$ and solve the appropriate output and price equations for the requisite changes in B^c and F^c. Under a pegged exchange rate, for example, equations (16) and (20) would be solved for the U.S. bliss-point shifts, and equations (16') and (20') would be solved for the EC bliss-point shifts. This is laborious and not really necessary. It is simpler to set $dQ_1 = dQ_2$ and solve the appropriate output equations for the changes in B^c and F^c that stabilize Q_1 and Q_2. These will represent common bliss-point shifts if it can be shown that $dq_1 = d_2' = 0$ when the changes in B^c and F^c are inserted in the price equations.

Here is the simplest illustration. With a switch in demand from the EC bond to the U.S. bond ($dB_2^* > 0$) and a pegged exchange rate, equations (16) and (16') say that $dB^c = - dF^c = dB_2^*$ will stabilize both countries' outputs. But the switch in demand does not affect price levels, and when $dB^c + dF^c = 0$, equations (20) and (20') say that $dq_1 = dq_2' = 0$. Therefore, the bliss points shift together. But the changes in B^c and F^c that stabilize Q_1 and Q_2 with a floating exchange rate, obtained from equations (18) and (18'), do not stabilize q_1 and q_2' when used in equations (22) and (22').

The same results obtain with balanced budget changes in government spending and changes in desired wealth. They do not obtain in the remaining cases, with temporary tax cuts leading to permanent changes in supplies of debt, and switches in demand between goods. With a U.S. tax cut, for example, outputs are stabilized with a pegged exchange rate when

$$dB^c = - (1/v)(1/W\Theta)(Q\delta + avW\phi)(1/s)(1 - s\alpha)gdB^*,$$

$$dF^c = (1/v)(1/W\Theta)(avW\phi)(1/s)(1 - s\alpha)gdB^*.$$

But these solutions give $dq_1 = dq_2' = - (1/2)\delta(1/s)[(1 - s\alpha)g - s]dB^*$, which goes to zero when $g = s/(1 - s\alpha)$ but not otherwise.

Notes

1. Corden examines these issues in a subsequent paper (Corden 1986), paying particular attention to the interdependence of fiscal policies. He concedes that large countries' budget deficits can have large effects on real exchange rates and interest rates. But he does not depart substantially from his earlier conclusion. Governments should mitigate the adverse effects of their neighbors' policies by making compensatory changes in their own domestic policies rather than rely on agreed rules or procedures to limit or correct fiscal policy differences.

2. In earlier papers (Kenen 1987a, 1987b, 1988b), I used different names for the approaches described in this and the next paragraph, but each attempt to label them ran into difficulties.

3. Similar definitions are used by Bryant (1980, 465), Artis and Ostry (1986, 75) and Frankel (1988, 1). The varieties of cooperation are discussed in Kenen (1987a). Some authors are less emphatic about including commitments about instruments in the definition of coordination. But the concept becomes too elastic without them. At the start of the 1980s, governments firmly agreed to combat inflation but said nothing about the settings of their monetary and fiscal policies, and the outcome was unsatisfactory — huge movements in real exchange rates and in current account balances. No one would want to identify that outcome with policy coordination. In fact, the subsequent revival of full-fledged coordination was partly a reaction to that outcome.

4. Describing the negotiations that led to the Louvre Accord, Funabashi (1988, chs. 5–8) depicts it differently: Japan and the Federal Republic of Germany agreed reluctantly to take new fiscal measures in exchange for a commitment by the United States to help stabilize dollar exchange rates by joint intervention. There were no commitments about monetary policies. This characterization is not wholly accurate. The United States was also pressed to make fiscal policy commitments, and it had agreed to the stabilization of the yen-dollar exchange rate some months before the Louvre Accord (even before Japan agreed to take new fiscal measures). Furthermore, the disagreement about German interest rates that cropped up in October 1987, the "collapse" of coordination to which Feldstein refers, suggests that the Louvre Accord included understandings about interest rate policies, even if there were no formal undertakings.

5. The most recent version of Meade's proposal, developed in Blake, Vines, and Weale (1988), is even more comprehensive than the Williamson-Miller proposal, having a wealth target as well as a GDP target, and it uses a different rule to define the exchange rate target.

6. Following Hamada (1974, 1976), the Nash and Pareto equilibria are usually depicted by reaction curves, as in figure 2.3. These curves appear to say that governments respond directly to changes in other governments' policies. If that were true, however, the Nash equilibrium would degenerate; each government would soon notice that other governments do not stand pat when it alters its own policies. Therefore, reaction curves should be deemed to say that governments respond to the *effects* of their partners' policies. They can then react repeatedly to each others' policies without becoming aware of policy interdependence. For surveys of research on policy-optimizing coordination, see Cooper (1985), Kenen (1987a), and Fischer (1988); on recent theoretical developments, see Oudiz and Sachs (1985).

7. Cooper (1985) and Kindleberger (1986) are prominent among the economists; for the views of political scientists and policymakers, see Putnam and Bayne (1987, ch. 1), and the sources cited there. Paul Krugman has persuaded me that the policy-optimizing framework can be used to represent regime-preserving coordination by including the international public good in the governments' welfare functions. That, indeed, is done in some recent papers; a measure of exchange rate variability is included in the governments' loss functions to represent their collective interest in exchange rate stability. I still believe, however, that the regime-preserving approach is sufficiently different in its implications to justify the sharp distinction drawn in this paper.

8. It is still necessary to decide what should be done with one country's money supply or with the global money supply. In many representations of pegged rate regimes, that decision is left to a single country (the United States in the Bretton Woods system and Germany in the EMS); McKinnon (1984) would handle the problem collectively, as would Williamson and Miller (1987), who would use the global money supply to manage the average short-term interest rate (see fig. 2.1). This is the fundamental issue

facing the designers of a European central bank. The question of substitutability, central to the functioning of policy coordination under pegged exchange rates, is also central to the functioning of official intervention in foreign-exchange markets; see Marston, ch. 6 in this volume.

9. Other economists have suggested or used the same basic approach. Buiter and Eaton (1985) show that Nash and Pareto equilibria are both bliss-point equilibria when policy targets and instruments are equal in number; Giavazzi and Giovannini (1986) anticipate my approach to the ranking of exchange rate regimes but do not carry it out; Turnovsky and d'Orey (1986) adopt the same strategy but deal only with temporary disturbances.

10. The size of the bliss-point shift does not depend on the particular shape of the ellipse in figure 2.2 (on the preferences of the U.S. government); it depends only on the slopes of the BB and FF curves (on the structures of the U.S. and EC economies).

11. See, for example, Dominguez (1986), Frankel and Froot (1986, 1987), and Krugman (1989); recent research on this issue is surveyed by Dornbusch and Frankel (1987).

12. This theme is developed by Krugman (1989), drawing partly on work by Dixit (1989) concerning the effects of uncertainty about the future exchange rate. A firm that has made the investment required to enter a market may decide to remain in that market even when the exchange rate turns against it, even though it cannot cover its variable costs, if the firm is sufficiently uncertain about the permanence of the new exchange rate. Conversely, a firm that has left a market may decide not to make the investment required to reenter it when the exchange rate moves in its favor. For more on the allocational effects of the exchange rate swing, see Marris (1987, 54–60).

13. These tendencies would have developed even under existing institutional arrangements, which automatically sterilize the effects of foreign official intervention on the U.S. money supply (and likewise sterilize the effects of U.S. intervention when conducted by the U.S. Treasury rather than the Federal Reserve); see Kenen (1988a, ch. 5). To prevent the dollar from appreciating, foreign official institutions would have been forced to sell dollars and thus to sell the U.S. government securities in which they invest their dollar reserves. To prevent U.S. interest rates from rising sharply under the influence of those sales and thus enlarging the capital inflow to the United States, the Federal Reserve System would have been compelled to undertake open market purchases of government securities, and these would have raised the U.S. money supply. Furthermore, foreign central banks could not have sterilized the domestic money-supply effects of their own and U.S. intervention without reducing their interest rates and thus enlarging the capital flow. These monetary effects of exchange rate management have also been cited by Frenkel (1987) and Dornbusch (1988) in criticizing McKinnon's rules for exchange rate management and by Williamson and Miller (1987) in defending their own proposals from those, like myself, who favor tighter arrangements.

14. In this case, however, the current account deficit would have been smaller, and interest rates might have risen in the United States, in order to crowd out domestic investment and thus make room for the budget deficit.

15. Taken to its logical conclusion, the Barro-Gordon model restates the basic proposition of the ''new'' macroeconomics—that monetary policy cannot affect the real economy—but casts it as a long-run tendency. If a government protects its reputation by keeping its promises, it can never alter output or employment. If it risks its reputation by breaking its word, it will vitiate its ability to surprise the private sector. Rogoff (1985) uses the same basic model to show why international policy coordination can be welfare-worsening, but his results have been challenged by Currie, Levine, and Vidalis (1987) and by Carraro and Giavazzi (1988).

16. Bryant (1987) has made the same point and applied it more generally to the problems of time consistency and reneging. He points out that all policy promises are contingent on forecasts about the state of the world, explicitly or implicitly. It is therefore impossible for anyone to know whether a government is reneging on previous promises or adapting to new circumstances.

17. These considerations are finding their way into the formal literature on policy-optimizing coordination; see Canzoneri and Henderson (1987). But the emphasis is still too narrow; it treats policy coordination as a repeated game but neglects the broad context in which the game is played.

18. Some of these disagreements may really testify to disputes about objectives. It may be more convenient for governments to say "That won't work" than to say "We don't like that." If this is true, however, apparent disagreements about behavior should not interfere with policy-optimizing coordination because disagreements about objectives can actually enhance the gains from that sort of coordination. An illustration follows shortly.

19. Holtham and Hughes Hallett used an early version of the Frankel-Rockett paper, which gave complete results for six models. The final version of the paper shows results that differ appreciably from those in the early version but gives complete results for only four models. It is therefore impossible to update the calculations reported in the text. (When they are updated for the four models shown in tables 4 and 5 of the final version, seven of the sixteen bargains violate the strong condition, and the success rates for the remaining nine approach 75 percent, up from 69 percent for all twenty-four bargains.)

20. These numbers cannot be compared directly to the 60 percent success rate reported by Frankel and Rockett, which covered all ten models. The corresponding rate for the six models used by Holtham and Hughes Hallett was 62 percent.

21. See Funabashi (1988, chs. 2 and 7). But his assessment of monetary cooperation is more critical than mine. He seems to regard the central bankers' silence at certain G-5 meetings as reflecting a reluctance to coordinate their policies. It should perhaps be seen as reflecting their reluctance to endorse the rather ambitious commitments made by finance ministers.

22. See Dornbusch (1988) and Krugman (1989). Simulations by Currie and Wren-Lewis (1988) support this view; feedback rules based on the Williamson-Miller framework do better than rules that use fiscal policies to regulate current account balances and monetary policies to regulate aggregate demand.

References

Artis, M., and S. Ostry. 1986. *International economic policy coordination.* London: Royal Institute of International Affairs.

Barro, R. J., and D. Gordon. 1983. Rules, discretion, and reputation in a model of monetary policy. *Journal of Monetary Economics* 12:101–21.

Blake, A., D. Vines, and M. Weale. 1988. Wealth targets, exchange rate targets, and macroeconomic policy. CEPR Discussion Paper no. 247. London: Centre for Economic Policy Research.

Branson, W. H., and J. P. Love. 1988. U.S. manufacturing and the real exchange rate. In R. C. Marston, ed., *Misalignment of exchange rates: Effects on trade and industry.* Chicago: University of Chicago Press.

Bryant, R. C. 1980. *Money and monetary policy in interdependent nations.* Washington, DC: Brookings Institution.

———. 1987. Intergovernmental coordination of economic policies. In P. B. Kenen, ed., *International monetary cooperation: Essays in honor of Henry C. Wallich.* Essays in International Finance no. 169. Princeton: International Finance Section, Princeton University.

Buiter, W. H., and J. Eaton. 1985. Policy decentralization and exchange rate management in interdependent economies. In J. S. Bhandari, ed., *Exchange rate management under uncertainty.* Cambridge, MA: MIT Press.

Canzoneri, M. B., and J. A. Gray. 1985. Monetary policy games and the consequences of noncooperative behavior. *International Economic Review* 26:547–564.

Canzoneri, M. B. and D. B. Henderson. 1987. Is sovereign policymaking bad? Paper presented at the NBER conference on the European Monetary System. Cambridge, MA: National Bureau of Economic Research.

Carraro, C., and F. Giavazzi. 1988. Can international policy coordination really be counterproductive? CEPR Discussion Paper no. 258. London: Centre for Economic Policy Research.

Cooper, R. N. 1985. Economic interdependence and coordination of economic policies. In R. W. Jones and P. B. Kenen, eds., *Handbook of international economics,* vol. 2. Amsterdam: North Holland.

Corden, W. M. 1981. The logic of the international monetary non-system. In F. Machlup, G. Fels, and H. Muller-Groeling, eds., *Reflections on a troubled world economy: Essays in honor of Herbert Giersch.* London: St. Martins Press.

———. 1986. Fiscal policies, current accounts, and real exchange rates: In search for a logic of international policy coordination. *Weltwirtschaftliches Archiv* 122 (no.3):423–38.

Currie, D., P. Levine, and N. Vidalis, 1987. International cooperation and reputation in an empirical two-block model. In R. C. Bryant and R. Portes, eds., *Global macroeconomics: Policy conflict and cooperation.* London: Macmillan.

Currie, D., and S. Wren-Lewis, 1988. A comparison of alternative regimes for international macropolicy coordination.

Deputies of the Group of Ten. 1985. *Report on the functioning of the international monetary system.* Reprinted in *IMF Survey: Supplement* (July). Washington, DC: International Monetary Fund.

Dixit, A. 1989. Entry and exit decisions of firms under uncertainty. *Journal of Political Economy* 97:620–38.

Dominguez, K. M. 1986. Are foreign exchange forecasts rational? New evidence from survey data. International Finance Discussion Paper no. 281. Washington, DC: Board of Governors of the Federal Reserve System.

Dornbusch, R. 1988. Doubts about the McKinnon standard. *Journal of Economic Perspectives* 2 (Winter):105–12.

Dornbusch, R., and J. Frankel. 1987. The flexible exchange rate system: Experience and alternatives. NBER Working Paper no. 2464. Cambridge, MA: National Bureau of Economic Research.

Eichengreen, B. 1985. International policy coordination in historical perspective. In W. H. Buiter and R. C. Marston, eds., *International economic policy coordination.* New York: Cambridge University Press.

Feldstein, M. 1987. The end of policy coordination. *The Wall Street Journal,* November 9.

Fischer, S. 1988. Macroeconomic policy. In M. Feldstein, ed., *International economic cooperation.* Chicago: University of Chicago Press.

Frankel, J. A. 1988. *Obstacles to international macroeconomic policy coordination.* Princeton Studies in International Finance no. 64. Princeton: International Finance Section, Princeton University.

Frankel, J. A. and K. A. Froot. 1986. Explaining the demand for dollars: International rates of return and the expectations of chartists and fundamentalists. Department of Economics Working Paper no. 8603. University of California at Berkeley.

———. 1987. Using survey data to test standard propositions regarding exchange rate expectations. *American Economic Review* 77:133–53.

Frankel, J. A. and K. E. Rockett. 1988. International macroeconomic policy coordination when policymakers do not agree on the true model. *American Economic Review* 78:318–40.

Frenkel, J. A. 1987. The international monetary system: Should it be reformed? *American Economic Review* 77 (May):205–10.

Funabashi, Y. 1988. *Managing the dollar: From the Plaza to the Louvre.* Washington, DC: Institute for International Economics.

Giavazzi, F., and A. Giovannini. 1986. Monetary policy interactions under managed exchange rates. CEPR Discussion Paper no. 123. London: Centre for Economic Policy Research.

Gros, D., and N. Thygesen. 1988. The EMS: Achievements, current issues and directions for the future. CEPS Paper no. 35. Brussels: Center for European Policy Studies.

Hamada, K. 1974. Alternative exchange rate systems and the interdependence of monetary policies. In R. Z. Aliber, ed., *National monetary policies and the international financial system.* Chicago: University of Chicago Press.

———. 1976. A strategic analysis of monetary interdependence. *Journal of Political Economy* 84:677–700.

Holtham, G., and A. J. Hughes Hallett. 1987. International policy cooperation and model uncertainty. In R. C. Bryant and R. Portes, eds., *Global macroeconomics: Policy conflict and cooperation.* London: Macmillan.

Hughes Hallett, A. J. 1987. Macroeconomic policy design with incomplete information: A new argument for coordinating economic policies. CEPR Discussion Paper no. 151. London: Centre for Economic Policy Research.

Kenen, P. B. 1987a. Exchange rates and policy coordination. Brookings Discussion Papers in International Economics no. 61. Washington, DC: Brookings Institution.

———. 1987b. What role for IMF surveillance? *World Development* 15:1445–56.

———. 1987c. Exchange rate management: What role for intervention? *American Economic Review* 77 (May):194–99.

———. 1988a. *Managing exchange rates.* London: Royal Institute of International Affairs.

———. 1988b. International money and macroeconomics. In K. A. Elliott and J. Williamson, eds., *World economic problems.* Washington, DC: Institute for International Economics.

———. 1988c. Exchange rates and policy coordination in an asymmetric model. CEPR Discussion Paper no. 240. London: Centre for Economic Policy Research.

Kindleberger, C. P. 1986. International public goods without international government. *American Economic Review* 76:1–13.

Krugman, P. 1989. *Exchange Rate Instability.* Cambridge, MA: MIT Press.

McKibbin, W. J., and J. D. Sachs. 1986. Comparing the global performance of alternative exchange rate arrangements. Brookings Discussion Papers in International Economics no. 49. Washington, DC: Brookings Institution.

McKinnon, R. I. 1984. *An international standard for monetary stabilization.* Policy Analyses in International Economics no. 8. Washington, DC: Institute for International Economics.

———. 1988. Monetary and exchange rate policies for international stability: A proposal. *Journal of Economic Perspectives* 2 (Winter):83–103.

Marris, S. 1987. *Deficits and the dollar: The world economy at risk.* rev. ed. Policy Analyses in International Economics no. 14. Washington, DC: Institute for International Economics.

Meade, J. E. 1984. A new Keynesian Bretton Woods. *Three Banks Review* (June).

Oudiz, G., and J. Sachs. 1984. Macroeconomic policy coordination among the industrial economies. *Brookings Papers on Economic Activity* 1:1–64.

————. 1985. International policy coordination in dynamic macroeconomic models. In W. H. Buiter and R. C. Marston, eds., *International economic policy coordination.* New York: Cambridge University Press.

Putnam, R. D., and N. Bayne. 1987. *Hanging together: The seven-power summits.* 2d ed. London: Sage Publications.

Putnam, R. D. and C. R. Henning. 1986. The Bonn summit of 1978: How does international economic policy coordination actually work? Brookings Discussion Papers in International Economics no. 53 (October). Washington, DC: Brookings Institution.

Rogoff, K. 1985. Can international monetary cooperation be counterproductive? *Journal of International Economics* 18:199–217.

Turnovsky, S. J., and V. d'Orey, 1986. Monetary policies in interdependent economies with stochastic disturbances. *Economic Journal* 96:696–721.

Vaubel, R. 1981. Coordination or competition among national macroeconomic policies? In F. Machlup, G. Fels, and H. Muller-Groeling, eds., *Reflections on a troubled world economy: Essays in honor of Herbert Giersch.* London: St. Martins Press.

Williamson, J. 1985 [1983]. *The Exchange Rate System.* 2d ed. Policy Analyses in International Economics no. 5. Washington, DC: Institute for International Economics.

Williamson, J. and M. H. Miller. 1987. *Targets and indicators: A blueprint for the international coordination of economic policies.* Policy Analyses in International Economics no. 22 (September). Washington, DC: Institute for International Economics.

Working Group on Exchange Market Intervention 1983. *Report.* Washington, DC: U.S. Treasury.

Comment   Richard N. Cooper

The Bretton Woods system can be said to have begun de facto in 1959, when West European currencies first became fully convertible for current account transactions. Before a decade had passed it was under severe pressure, accompanied by widespread calls within the economics profession for its abandonment in favor of some form of flexible exchange rates. Over fifteen years after the inauguration of widespread exchange rate flexibility, in March 1973, there are increasing calls within the economics profession for some form of exchange rate management. Although many economists still favor relatively unmanaged floating, the weight of argument and evidence is shifting away from the conditions that must be met for free floating to be optimal, or even

Richard N. Cooper is the Maurits C. Boas Professor of International Economics at Harvard University.

superior, to extensive official management of exchange rates, if not outright rigidity.

Peter Kenen has added to the weight of argument. In a simple portfolio-balance model in which assets are imperfect substitutes, Kenen finds that, for three of the five generic disturbances he examines, fixed exchange rates permit national policymakers to achieve their objectives on their own, without formal coordination among countries, whereas freely floating exchange rates do not. For the other two generic disturbances, neither fixed nor floating exchange rates lead to such a result; some coordination of policy among countries will lead to an outcome superior to that arising from decentralized national decision-making. Kenen's results thus scotch the notion, once prevalent among economists, that freely floating exchange rates will generally insulate countries from international influences, especially those arising in the financial sector.

Kenen provides a thoughtful review of the recent literature on policy co-ordination among countries, as well as adding to it, and offers his judgements, with which I generally agree, on a number of points in that literature. First, exchange rate cooperation in the late 1980s among the major countries is not best interpreted in terms of most academic literature on coordination, since that literature typically assumes a policy-optimizing framework for analysis; rather, it should be interpreted in terms of what Kenen calls regime-preservation. Two relevant aspects to those cooperative efforts, not emphasized by Kenen, were the desire in 1985 to push the dollar down sharply in order to protect the liberal trading system by reducing protectionist pressures in the United States, and the desire in 1987 to reestablish some stability in exchange rates on the grounds that significant movements in exchange rates can themselves be a source of disturbance to national economies, what Kenen calls the public goods aspect of exchange rate stability. (It must be said, however, that the Louvre Accord of 1987 resulted in part from Japanese concern that a further sharp rise in the yen from the late 1986 level would put severe adjustment strains on Japanese firms, and an American concern that further sharp depreciation of the dollar would revive inflationary expectations in the United States, both notions that could be encompassed in a policy-optimizing framework.)

Second, the widely cited Frankel-Rockett (1988) simulations on policy coordination under different perceived models of how economies work exaggerate the risks of policy coordination, since those results do not allow for acknowledgement by policymakers that their preferred model might be wrong. The caution that is appropriate to uncertain knowledge would reduce substantially the number of instances in which policymakers would coordinate policies to their own ultimate disadvantage.

Third, the preoccupation in the technical literature with so-called time inconsistency, or the likelihood that governments will renege on commitments previously made, while interesting from a technical point of view, is misplaced.

Governments at any time are playing many "games" and expect to continue doing so in the future. To renege on clear past commitments would compromise their positions in other current and subsequent negotiations. They thus have ample reason—to preserve credibility—for keeping their past commitments unless there are plausible and well-understood reasons for not doing so.

Fourth, disagreements on objectives are probably not a significant obstacle to macroeconomic cooperation among major market-oriented economies; indeed, disagreements on certain kinds of objectives (e.g., current account targets) may substantially enhance the gains from cooperation. Rather, disagreements on the behavioral responses of economies to specified policy actions are a much more serious obstacle to coordination of macroeconomic policies, as indeed was also the case for international cooperation in preventing the spread of contagious diseases until scientific developments resulted in consensus on the etiologies of the important diseases (Cooper 1989).

Kenen's paper does not focus on the debate over the exchange rate regime, but his analysis raises new questions about the desirability of free floating. I would like to take the occasion to go further and reopen an old but still unsettled question concerning the use of nominal exchange rates as either a free endogenous variable in the economy or as a policy tool.

That is perhaps best done by posing an operational question: would it be desirable to depreciate the North German mark against the South German mark? Or should the New England dollar be appreciated against other U.S. dollars? Each of these actions had something to be said for it in 1987 and early 1988. North Germany was relatively depressed, while South Germany was buoyant, yet wages were determined at the national level so that North German wages were too high relative to South German wages. A depreciation of the North German mark could possibly correct for this and stimulate economic activity in the north, while dampening it somewhat in the south.

Similarly, New England in 1987–88 was booming, with house prices and other prices of nontradables rising especially rapidly. The oil and gas regions of the U.S. economy and to a lesser extent the industrial midwest were somewhat depressed. Appreciating the New England dollar against other U.S. dollars, and in particular against the Texas dollar, would redistribute economic activity in a desirable direction.

Since these actions would be generally desirable, why do we not think about them? The answer probably lies in their total political impractability. They run strongly against the national unity that a unified currency area both fosters and symbolizes, and which the Federal Republic of Germany and the United States of America have each established. The proposals are simply too radical, even quixotic.

But I suggest there is another, more analytical reason for not seriously thinking about these changes in exchange rates. To depreciate the North German mark against the South German mark, or to appreciate the Boston dollar against the Dallas dollar, would jar economic relations within each country badly. It would create a major new source of uncertainty in making contracts and in investing on the basis of future expected demand. Businessmen must worry about the real value of money, but the rate of inflation changes slowly compared with real exchange rates under a system of flexible exchange rates. Movements in exchange rates can wipe out—or double—a 5 percent profit margin in a week. Movements in nominal exchange rates, which as we have learned in recent years do more than simply correct for differential rates of inflation, introduce great uncertainty for prospective investors who are exposed to international—or in this context, interregional—trade. In reaching an overall judgement on the merits of a regime of exchange rate flexibility, the possible negative effects of this uncertainty on investment must be balanced against the occasionally favorable effect of exchange rate flexibility on reducing the costs of adjustment.

References

Cooper, Richard N. 1989. International cooperation in public health as prologue to macroeconomic cooperation. In R. N. Cooper et al., *Can nations agree?* Washington, DC: Brookings Institution.
Frankel, J. A., and K. E. Rockett. 1988. International macroeconomic policy coordination when policymakers do not agree on the true model. *American Economic Review* 78, no. 3 (June):318–40.

Comment   Stanley Fischer

Peter Kenen argues in this interesting and stimulating paper that much of the policy coordination literature misses the point. Drawing a distinction between policy-optimizing and regime-preserving coordination, he develops the argument that policy coordination in practice is directed mainly to regime preservation, and not to policy optimization.

The distinction between policy-optimizing and regime-preserving coordination is suggestive but elusive. Policy optimization is the standard approach followed in the coordination literature. In that framework, the gains to coordination may be examined under either fixed or floating rates. The analyst would then be able to rank outcomes in a two-by-two matrix, resulting from combinations of coordination versus noncoordination under fixed and floating exchange rates.

Kenen's *analysis* in this paper confines itself to two of the possible four boxes in that matrix, namely those in which countries do not coordinate

Stanley Fischer is Vice President, Development Economics, and Chief Economist at the World Bank, on leave from the Massachusetts Institute of Technology, and a Research Associate of the National Bureau of Economic Research.

policies. His analysis implies that fixed exchange rates are, in this noncoordinated mode, preferable to floating in the face of three types of shocks (a permanent shift in portfolio preferences between the countries' bonds, a temporary increase in one country's saving rate, and a balanced budget increase in one government's spending) and not clearly worse in the face of two other shocks (a permanent switch in demand for the goods of the two countries and a permanent increase in the stock of bonds in one of the countries). The analysis is carried out in a portfolio-balance-type model with static expectations.

Kenen's conclusion is that fixed exchange rates are preferable to floating rates. He assumes that governments will share this conclusion and that they will therefore engage in policies designed to preserve fixed exchange rates. This behavior, he suggests, is better thought of as cooperative rather than coordinating. He also argues that we should more generally interpret various types of policy coordination or cooperation as resulting from governments' attempts to preserve institutional arrangements that they regard as being on the whole helpful.

The distinction between the choice of regime and the question of whether coordination is preferable within a given regime is worth emphasizing. Decisions about coordination may be necessary in some regimes, but handled automatically in others: for instance, the issue of fiscal policy harmonization has to be negotiated within the European Community, but is handled automatically in the U.S. federal system. Similarly, one of the benefits of a fixed exchange rate system may be that it calls forth automatically the monetary and/or fiscal policies necessary to maintain fixed rates.

Nonetheless, Kenen's analysis does not directly address the important question of how the regime is chosen. He shows that fixed exchange rates are better in some circumstances (namely, with noncoordination, in his model) and then suggests that is why we observe governments cooperating to smooth exchange rates. But why do governments not cooperate, having the best of both worlds by holding exchange rates fixed in response to some shocks and varying them in response to others? The answer must have to do with: the simplicity for the government of carrying out a fixed exchange rate rule compared with the difficulties of coordinating on a more complicated rule; the difficulties of identifying particular shocks; and the effects on expectations of adopting a simple rule.

It is suggested in Kenen's note 7 that the public goods aspect of exchange rate stability could be included in the ordinary policy optimization literature by including exchange rate stability as an argument of the utility function of each government. This is formally true, but it would not make sense to do so unless the conclusion that exchange rate stability is desirable came from some economic or broader political economy analysis rather than being arbitrary.

Beyond the analytics, the paper also presents insightful comments on the literature and on the current debate on policy coordination. In doing so, Kenen takes issue with the relevance of the Barro-Gordon analysis of dynamic inconsistency to the international context. He suggests that governments do not renege on agreements they have reached with other governments, using the Bonn Economic Summit Agreement as an example. While governments are reluctant to renege on formal agreements, it appears that the U.S. government has held out the prospect of a reduction in its fiscal deficit as its share of the repeated agreements to support the dollar since 1985 but has not actually moved fast on this front.

It is not entirely clear how the distinction between regime-preserving and policy-optimizing coordination relates to the current debate. We are in the current situation because governments were not willing in the late sixties and early seventies to preserve the fixed exchange rate regime. They are undoubtedly trying to preserve or maximize something through their current efforts at coordination, but it is difficult to see what regime is being preserved. It is not the fixed exchange rate regime; perhaps as Kenen suggests, modern coordination is intended to preserve the international trading system.

Current differences in attitudes to policy coordination are colored most strongly by views of the success or failure of the Bonn Summit of 1978, and on the consequences of international policy coordination since 1985. Proponents of policy coordination regard the Bonn Summit as a success, even though it soured German policymakers' views of the process. They believe that their expansionary moves in 1978 were partly responsible for the high inflation in 1979. Their failure to expand in 1986 despite urgings from abroad can be attributed to the earlier experience, and can also be regarded ex post as appropriate.

One view of coordination since 1985 is that it has succeeded by bringing the dollar down smoothly, preventing a hard landing, and permitting continued growth of the international economy. Alternatively, coordination has been the cover under which other countries finance the U.S. budget and trade deficits, thereby protecting the United States from the consequences of its fiscal policy. I believe the latter view is more appropriate, and that without the particular type of coordination practised since 1985, the U.S. would already have been forced into more fundamental fiscal contraction.

However, there is not too much point in blaming policy coordination for this outcome. It is not coordination per se that is to blame, but rather the fact underlying the coordination—the desire of other countries not to have the dollar depreciate too rapidly against their currencies.

One can compare the effects of exchange rate coordination since 1985 with international policy coordination over the debt crisis. In each case, coordination prevented rapid adjustment of an underlying disequilibrium. In the debt crisis, debtors and creditors would by now have reached a settlement had official intervention not occurred. In each case, international policy coordination reduced the risks to the international economy but did so at the cost of prolonging a situation that needed to be changed.

It is these tendencies that lead critics to suggest that the reflex belief in the values of international policy coordination is unwise. In principle, optimal international policy coordination cannot hurt. In practice it sometimes does. This view is strengthened by the fact that proponents of international policy coordination are at their most vociferous when they want to change domestic policies of which they disapprove, and which they hope to affect through international action.

The right approach to international policy coordination is suggested by the analysis on which Peter Kenen embarks in this paper: first design a system which is robust to noncoordination, undertake automatically those policies that are needed to sustain the system, and consider other policies and coordinated policy actions on a case-by-case basis.

3 Obstacles to Coordination, and a Consideration of Two Proposals to Overcome Them: International Nominal Targeting (INT) and the Hosomi Fund

Jeffrey A. Frankel

3.1 Introduction: Plans for World Monetary Reform Should Be Politically Practical

Designing proposals for world monetary reform was in the 1960s a popular "parlor game" among economists. We will perhaps see a revival of this sport in the 1990s.

The impetus behind such proposals is a serious one. Exchange rate volatility turned out to be higher than was anticipated before the move to floating exchange rates in 1973, and the swings were particularly large in the 1980s, prompting proposals for government action to stabilize exchange rates. Among the (allegedly) promised fruits of floating exchange rates that have failed to materialize is insulation of each country's economy from disturbances originating among its partners. This insulation property was supposed to allow countries to set their policies independently. Meanwhile, the need to correct the large macroeconomic imbalances that arose in the 1980s, without setting off a world recession, has reinforced support for the idea that interdependence may be inevitable, and that countries should set their policies cooperatively rather than independently. Proposals for coordination draw support from a burgeoning academic literature that, until recently, was almost unanimous in claiming that each country's economic welfare was necessarily higher under a regime of coordination than under a noncooperative (Nash) regime in which countries set their policies independently.[1]

Jeffrey A. Frankel is a professor of economics at the University of California, Berkeley, and a research associate of the National Bureau of Economic Research.

The author would like to thank Julia Lowell for efficient research assistance and Ralph Bryant, Geoff Carliner, Doug Purvis, and John Williamson for comments and suggestions. It should be noted that, under the procedures of the National Bureau of Economic Research, papers do not take policy positions or make recommendations.

Plans for full-fledged coordination, in the sense of cooperative maximization of some joint welfare function, are likely to be too complex to be implemented as literally proposed. Hence the motivation for simpler more practical schemes,[2] for example focusing on a few key "economic indicators." But the ultimate reason for skepticism that coordination proposals will in fact be implemented is that they require nations to give up some degree of sovereignty over policymaking for the sake of cooperation. Looking forward from 1990, it is unlikely for many years to come that countries will be ready for such a commitment. In the first place, enforcement is a problem even when everyone benefits relative to the Nash equilibrium (because each country could do still better by deviating unilaterally from the agreement). In the second place, given uncertainties about policies and about future disturbances, a coordination regime that guarantees higher welfare for each country ex ante will nevertheless probably entail ex post losses for some countries in some years, creating a great temptation for them to break the agreement. An American government, for example, would be unlikely to maintain policies sacrificing U.S. economic welfare for the sake of an international agreement, for fear of losing political support.

If a cooperative regime is to be successful, it must be built on an accumulation of trust. If countries are in every year to resist the short-run advantages of deviating from the agreement for the sake of the longer-run gains of maintaining the cooperative regime, it is necessary that there be either explicit sanctions for violations or implicit effects on their long-term reputations. The reputations route requires a passage of time during which countries can establish track records by which they can be judged. The sanctions route requires a commitment to give up national sovereignty, for which, again, countries will not be politically ready for some time. This is one major problem with a proposed return to fixed exchange rates, a gold standard, and other ambitious plans for world monetary reform. They presuppose a world of surrendered sovereignty, and there is no evident pathway leading there from our current world. "You can't get there from here."

The most we can anticipate is that coordination would begin on a small scale in the 1990s, with countries giving up just a small amount of sovereignty in return for small expected gains. Such coordination could be pronounced successful if announced international economic agreements were not completely devoid of substance, if the agreements actually caused countries to modify their policies—even if only a little—from what they otherwise would have been, and if the results can be seen to have raised economic welfare—again, even if only a little.

If coordination on a small scale is successful in the 1990s, then it will establish the prerequisites of trust and confidence needed for coordination on a moderate scale in the 21st century: national track records of compliance with the international agreements, or perhaps sufficient consensus as to the benefits to allow the establishment of sanctions for future noncompliance. The point is that, at each stage, a record of successful coordination will allow an increase in the degree of political commitment to coordination in the next stage. What is needed, then, is a proposal for a sequence of coordination regimes, an overall plan in which the degree of coordination can begin at a small "epsilon" and be gradually raised from there (in theory, someday reaching the level of full coordination of policies).

This paper contains, in addition to a review of the obstacles to future progress toward coordination, a preliminary examination of two modest proposals for the form that successful coordination might take. One is an international version of targeting nominal GNP (or aggregate demand). The proposal will be called INT, for international nominal targeting.[3] The other is a supranational bank, sometimes called a Hosomi Fund, which could intervene in the foreign-exchange markets, without national central banks surrendering their own rights to operate in the markets. In each case—INT and a Hosomi Fund—a key element of the proposal is that it could begin on a very small scale, build up trust and confidence in the institution slowly, and thus progress to higher degrees of coordination.

The essence of the argument for the need for coordination is that there are international externalities or spillover effects. If these externalities did not exist, that is, if each country was unaffected by changes in other countries, then the decentralized noncooperative solution would be optimal; there would be little role for international meetings or a supranational institution to coordinate policies (just as there would be little role for government intervention in the domestic economy if domestic markets functioned competitively and without externalities).

One cannot know whether or what kind of coordination is desirable without first knowing the nature of the externalities. Is the Nash noncooperative equilibrium too contractionary, because of a proclivity toward "beggar-thy-neighbor" policies? Then joint expansion is called for. This, of course, was the logic of the "locomotive theory" that gave rise to the 1978 Bonn Summit. Or, on the other hand, is the existing equilibrium overly inflationary? In that case, joint discipline would be called for. This is the apparent motivation underlying the European Monetary System (EMS). Perhaps the problem is that each country seeks by its policy mix to raise real interest rates, attract capital inflows, and appreciate its currency, thereby reducing the consumer price index for any given level of output and employment. This description seemed to characterize some major countries in the early 1980s. Or perhaps the problem, rather than "competitive appreciation," is "competitive depreciation," as was feared at Bretton Woods in 1944 on the basis of the experience of the 1930s. Each kind of externality would imply a different kind of appropriate coordination to address it.

In section 3.2 we address problems concerning the overall degree of expansion of macroeconomic policies, whether monetary and fiscal policies are too tight or too loose, rather than the proper mix of the two. In section 3.3, more briefly, we address the problem of exchange rate variability.[4] It is left as a topic for future work to consider problems of the degree of expansion simultaneously with problems of the monetary/fiscal policy mix, real interest rates, and the exchange rate.

3.2   Overcoming Obstacles to Coordinated Expansion or Contraction

3.2.1   Domestic Policymaking

Macroeconomic policymaking is always a tradeoff between the advantages of discretion on the one hand and rules on the other. In the past, writers concerned with either one of the two problems often simplistically assumed away the other. If the aim is to maximize economic welfare (a function of output and inflation) only for a given period, ignoring long-run implications for expected inflation, discretion can be shown to be unambiguously superior to rules; after all, how can one possibly gain by agreeing to limit beforehand one's abilities to respond to developments in the economy? If one ignores the possibility of short-run disturbances, on the other hand, rules can be shown to be unambiguously superior to discretion in a long-run equilibrium; macro-economic policy cannot affect output in the long run anyway, and precommitting to a nominal anchor can reduce expected inflation and thereby reduce actual inflation.

There are a few excellent surveys of the literature concerning time inconsistency, precommitment and reputations, and its implications for the older debate over rules versus discretion. See, for example, Barro (1986), Fischer (1988a), and Rogoff (1987). It should be clear by now that neither extreme in the debate represents the complete correct answer. On the one hand, if the political system's policymaking process is allowed to optimize on a purely short-run basis, the outcome will be overexpansion. Thus some degree of longer-term commitment to resist inflationary temptations is indicated, even if it is a decision to insulate the central bank from the political process rather than formal commitment to a nominal anchor or rule.[5] On the other hand, in a world where new disturbances come along, it is important that the government retain at least some ability to respond to stabilize the economy. The solution is *some* degree of commitment, but less than 100 percent, to some nominal anchor.[6]

In the context of domestic policymaking, this paper makes no judgment on the desirable degree of precommitment to a nominal target. (Analogously, when we turn to international coordination, we take as given by the political process the degree of commitment to coordination.)

But it can be argued that, whatever the degree of precommitment to a nominal target, nominal GNP (or nominal demand) makes a more suitable target than the four other nominal variables that have been proposed: the money supply, the price level, the price of gold, or the exchange rate. The argument has been well made by others.[7] In the event of disturbances in the banking system, disturbances in the public's demand for money, or other disturbances affecting the demand for goods, a policy of holding nominal GNP steady insulates the economy; neither real income nor the price level need be affected. In the event of disturbances to supply, such as the oil price increases of the 1970s, the change is divided equiproportionately between an increase in the price level and a fall in output. For some countries, this is roughly the split that a discretionary policy would choose anyway.[8] In general, unless the objective function puts precisely equal weights on inflation and real growth, fixing nominal GNP will not give precisely the right answer. *But if the choice is among the available nominal anchors, nominal GNP gives an outcome characterized by greater stability of output and the price level.* An Appendix to this paper shows that a nominal GNP target strictly dominates a money-supply target, in the sense of minimizing a quadratic loss function, regardless how important inflation-fighting credibility is.

To take an example from recent history, the Federal Reserve, citing large velocity shifts, decided beginning in late 1982 to allow M1 to break firmly outside their preannounced target zone. M1 grew 10.3 percent per year from 1982:2 to 1986:2. Some observers have suggested that the Federal Reserve was following a general policy of targeting nominal GNP. For four years the monetarists decried the betrayal of the money growth rule and warned that a major return of inflation was imminent. Nobody can doubt in retrospect that the Federal Reserve chose the right course. Even with the recovery that began in 1983 and continued through the four years and beyond, nominal GNP grew more slowly than the money supply: 8.0 percent per year. Thus velocity declined at 2.3 percent per year, in contrast to its past historical pattern of *increasing* at roughly 3 percent a year. If the Federal Reserve had followed the explicit monetarist prescription of rigidly precommitting to a money growth rate lower than that of the preceding period, such as 3 percent, and velocity had followed the same path, then nominal GNP would have grown at only 0.7 percent a year. This number is an upper bound because, with even lower inflation than occurred, velocity would probably have fallen even more than it did. The implication seems clear that the 1981 – 82 recession would have lasted another five years!

3.2.2   Obstacles to International Policy Coordination

After the initial enthusiasm for the gains from coordination, especially at the theoretical level, a number of economists have in recent years been pointing out some of its difficulties (beginning, at the public level, with Feldstein 1983, 1988).

The obstacles to implementing a successful regime of macroeconomic policy coordination are of three sorts: uncertainty, enforcement, and time-consistent inflation-fighting credibility. Difficulties of enforcement and credibility have received the most attention from economists. Even when a coordination package guarantees that each country will be better off than it would be in the noncooperative equilibrium, the country will be able to do better still if it "cheats" on the agreement. That is, it will be able to do better in the short-run, assuming that the other countries leave their policies as agreed; in future periods, the other countries will presumably retaliate by also abandoning the agreement. But economists have probably overemphasized the difficulties of enforcement (see Kenen 1987, 31–36, on this point[9]) and underemphasized the difficulties of uncertainty. If policymakers could be certain as to how various policy changes would affect their economic objectives, it might not be very difficult to enforce cooperative agreements. But uncertainty is in fact endemic to international macroeconomic policy-making.

As we will see, uncertainty is of three kinds: uncertainty regarding the current and future position of the economy, uncertainty regarding the desirable optima for the target variables, and uncertainty regarding the effects on the target variables of changes in those policy instruments which the policymakers directly control. Each of these areas of uncertainty makes it difficult for policymakers in one country to know what policy changes to ask of its trading partners, and to know what policy changes it should be willing to make in return. Even assuming that there are no problems of enforcement, a cooper-ative package of policy changes that each country thinks will benefit itself could, ex post, easily turn out to make things worse rather than better. This could be the outcome if the baseline level of output, for example, turns out to be different than expected, or if the optimum level (e.g., potential output) turns out to be different than expected, or if a foreign expansion of monetary policy, for example, turns out to have a different effect on domestic output than expected.

Uncertainty greatly complicates the enforcement problem as well. In the first place, policymakers do not have direct control over the variables that we refer to as their "policies." Central banks cannot determine the money supply precisely because of disturbances within the banking system or in the wider economy's demand for money. Nor can a specific policymaker who is engaged in international negotiations determine his country's fiscal policies precisely. For this reason, it can be difficult to hold policymakers accountable for deviations of the policy variables from the cooperative bargain that they agree to.

In the second place, ex ante uncertainty means that there will be some states of the world in which the temptation to cheat is especially great because a country turns out ex post to lose a lot from abiding by the agreement (relative to unilaterally violating the agreement, and perhaps also relative to never having made the agreement to begin with). In such circumstances, the short-run gains from abrogating may outweigh the longer-term gains from continued cooperation.

A third kind of obstacle has been pointed out by Rogoff (1985a). A cooperative agreement that succeeds in raising economic welfare in one period will, if it takes the form of joint reflation, raise expectations of future inflation and may thus reduce economic welfare in the longer run. In such a circumstance, renouncing cooperation may be a way that countries can precommit to less inflationary policies.

This part of the paper examines these different obstacles to successful international coordination and then argues that INT, an international version of targeting nominal GNP (or nominal aggregate demand), is more likely than other types of coordination to surmount these obstacles.

Problems of Uncertainty

There are three things that a country ideally needs to know before it even can enter negotiations with other countries on coordinated policy changes. (1) What is the initial position of the domestic economy, relative to the optimum values of the target variable? (2) What are the correct weights to put on the various possible target variables? (This includes the question of which variables should be excluded altogether from consideration and which included.) (3) What effect does each unit change in the domestic (and the foreign) macroeconomic policy variables have on the target variables; that is, what is the correct model of the world economy?

These three elements follow simply from the algebraic expression for the economic objective function. We specify here a function of three target variables, although we could as easily have more or fewer.

(1) $$W = (\tfrac{1}{2}) (y^2 + w_x x^2 + w_p p^2),$$

(1') $$W^* = (\tfrac{1}{2}) (y^{*^2} + w^*_{x^*} x^{*^2} + w^*_{p^*} p^{*^2}),$$

where W is the quadratic loss to be minimized, y is output (expressed in log form and relative to its optimum), x is the current account (expressed as a percentage of GNP and again relative to its optimum), p is the inflation rate, w_x is the relative weight placed on the current account objective, w_p is the relative weight placed on the inflation objective, and an asterisk (*) denotes the analogous variables for the foreign country. We will refer to two policy instruments: the money supply m (in log form), and government expenditure g (as a percentage of GNP).

The marginal welfare effects of changes in these policy variables are then given by:

(2) $$dW/dm = (y)y_m + w_x(x)x_m + w_p(p)p_m,$$

(3) $$dW/dg = (y)y_g + w_x(x)x_g + w_p(p)p_g,$$

(4) $$dW/dm^* = (y)y_{m^*} + w_x(x)x_{m^*} + w_p(p)p_{m^*},$$

$$(5) \qquad dW/dg^* = (y)y_{g*} + w_x(x)x_{g*} + w_p(p)p_{g*},$$

$$(2') \qquad dW^*/dm = (y^*)y^*_m + w^*_{x*}(x^*)x^*_m + w^*_{p*}(p^*)p^*_m,$$

$$(3') \qquad dW^*/dg = (y^*)y^*_g + w^*_{x*}(x^*)x^*_g + w^*_{p*}(p^*)p^*_g,$$

$$(4') \qquad dW^*/dm^* = (y^*)y^*_{m*} + w^*_{x*}(x^*)x^*_{m*} + w^*_{p*}(p^*)p^*_{m*},$$

$$(5') \qquad dW^*/dg^* = (y^*)y^*_{g*} + w^*_{x*}(x^*)x^*_{g*} + w^*_{p*}(p^*)p^*_{g*},$$

where the policy multiplier effect of money on output is given by y_m, the effect of money on the current account by x_m, etc. If we wished to solve for the optimum, we would set these derivatives equal to zero (with the target variables (y), (x), etc., first expressed as linear functions of the policy variables m, g, etc. In the Nash noncooperative equilibrium (in which each country takes the other's policies as given), we would need only equations (2), (3), (4') and (5') for the solution. Each country ignores the effect that its policies have on the other country, so equations (4), (5), (2'), and (3') do not enter. Indeed, this is precisely the standard reason why the noncooperative equilibrium is suboptimal. These cross-country effects enter only in the determination of the cooperative solution.

Before they decide on a policy change, policymakers must at least know the sign of the corresponding derivative. Equation (2), or any other of the eight derivatives above, neatly illustrates the three kinds of uncertainty. First is uncertainty about the initial position, the variables, y, x, and p. Position uncertainty in turn breaks down into three parts: (a) uncertainty about the current value of the target variable in question;[10] (b) uncertainty over how the target variables are likely to move during the forthcoming year or more in the absence of policy changes, the "baseline forecast";[11] and (c) uncertainty as to the location of the optimum value of the target variable.[12]

The point is clear. The policymaker's estimates of the current values of y, x, or p in his country could easily be off by several percentage points in either direction, which could flip the signs of the corresponding three terms—any one of which could change the sign of the derivative of the objective function—in each of equations (2)–(5). Thus it is entirely possible that the country could ask its partners in negotiations to expand, or that it could agree to a partner's request that it itself expand, when these changes would in fact move the economy in the wrong direction.

To take one historical example, in the late 1970s the U.S. policymakers, looking at the available economic data, concluded that insufficient growth in the world economy was the problem of the time. This assumption was the basis of the 1978 Bonn Summit agreement for coordinated expansion with Japan and Europe, the Federal Republic of Germany in particular. By the end of the decade, the consensus had become that fighting inflation was the top priority, not accelerating real growth. A natural way of interpreting the view—widely held in Germany at least—that the results of the Bonn coordinated expansion turned out in retrospect to have been detrimental is to say that unanticipated developments, particularly the large increase in oil prices associated with the sudden Iranian crisis of 1979, moved the world economy to a highly inflationary position where expansion was no longer called for.[13]

The second sort of uncertainty present in the equations is uncertainty regarding the proper weights w_x and w_p to put on the target variables in the objective function.[14] This issue is even more subjective than the issue of the optimal values of the target variables. In a society where the weights that individual actors place on inflation (or the current account) vary from zero to infinity, the likelihood must be judged very high that any given government is using weights that differ from the "correct" ones that would follow from any given criterion. One can see from the equations that putting insufficient weight on fighting inflation, for example, can have the same effect as underestimating the baseline inflation rate: the policymaker in coordination exercises may ask his trading partners to adopt expansionary policies when contractionary policies are in fact called for. This is precisely the mistake that by 1980 some concluded had been made by the United States. From the viewpoint of the Republicans who were elected to the presidency in that year, or the Social Democrats who came to power in Germany soon thereafter, the policymakers who had agreed to coordinated reflation at the Bonn Summit of 1978 had put insufficient weight on the objective of price stability.

The third sort of uncertainty pertains to the policy multipliers, the derivatives y_m, y_g, etc., in equations (2)–(5'), telling the effect of changes in the money supply and government expenditure on the target variables. Any given government is likely to be using policy multipliers that differ substantially from the "true" ones, and that may even be incorrect in sign. One way of seeing this is to note the tremendous variation in multipliers according to different schools of thought, or even according to different estimates in models of "mainstream" macroeconomists. They cannot all be correct, and it seems highly probable that no single model is in fact exactly right.[15]

It is possible to illustrate the potential range of multiplier estimates in some detail. In a recent exercise conducted at the Brookings Institution, twelve leading econometric models of the international macroeconomy simulated the effects of specific policy changes in the United States and in the rest of the OECD.[16] The models participating were the Federal Reserve Board's Multi-country model, the European Economic Community's Compact model, the Japanese Economic Planning Agency model, Project Link, Patrick Minford's Liverpool model, the McKibbin-Sachs Global model, the Sims-Litterman VAR model, the OECD's Interlink model, John Taylor's model, the Wharton Econometrics model, and the Data Resources, Inc., model. The variation in the estimates is large, not just in magnitude but also in sign. The effect of fiscal or monetary expansion on domestic output and inflation is usually at least of the positive sign that one would expect. (Even here there are exceptions as regards inflation: the VAR, Wharton, and Link models sometimes show expansion causing a *reduction* in the CPI, probably due to effects via markup pricing.) But disagreement among the models becomes much more common when we turn to the international effects.

The areas of greatest disagreement among the econometric models regarding international transmission are not the same as one might expect from the theoretical literature. A U.S. fiscal expansion is transmitted positively to the rest of the OECD in ten out of eleven models, and an expansion in the other countries is transmitted positively to the United States in nine out of ten models, whereas in theory fiscal transmission can easily be negative.[17] The greatest amount of disagreement occurs, rather, on the effect of a monetary expansion on the domestic current account, and therefore on the foreign current account and output level. There are two conflicting effects. On the one hand, the monetary expansion raises income and therefore imports. On the other hand, it depreciates the currency, which tends to improve the trade balance. (In the Mundell-Fleming model the net effect on the current account must be positive.[18]) It turns out that a U.S. monetary expansion worsens the current account in eight out of eleven models, and a monetary expansion in the other OECD countries worsens their current accounts in five out of ten models. (In most models the rest of the Mundell-Fleming transmission mechanism is reversed as well: the foreign current account and foreign income rise rather than fall.)

What happens if U.S., European, and Japanese policymakers proceed with coordination efforts despite disagreements such as these? In Frankel and Rockett (1986, 1988) and Frankel (1988a), we use the Brookings simulations (and the welfare weights from Oudiz and Sachs 1984) to consider the possibilities when governments coordinate using conflicting models. Countries will in general be able to find a package of coordinated policy changes that each believes will leave it better off, even though each has a different view of the effects and thus may not understand why the other is willing to go along with the package. The actual effects depend on what the true model is. If we consider ten possible models, there are 1,000 combinations of models that can be used to represent the beliefs of the U.S. policymakers, the beliefs of non–U.S. policymakers, and reality. We find that monetary coordination results in gains for the United States in 546 cases, losses in 321 cases, and no effect on the objective functions (to four significant digits) in 133 cases. Coordination results in gains for the rest of the OECD countries in 539 cases, as against losses in 327 and no effect in 134.

A number of authors have taken exception to this finding and to its implication that uncertainty constitutes a serious obstacle to successful international policy coordination. Holtham and Hughes Hallett (1987), Frenkel, Goldstein, and Masson (1988, 31–32), and Ghosh and Masson (1988a, b) argue that, in a world in which different models abound, it is not sensible to assume that each policymaker acts as if he knows with certainty the correct model. Such criticisms could be applied to the original paper, Frankel and Rockett (1986). But extensions in the published Frankel and Rockett (1988, 337–338) and Frankel (1988a, 19–21) papers relax the assumption that each policymaker acts as if he or she is certain as to the correct model. Policymakers are assumed to assign probability weights to each of the possible models and then to maximize their expected welfare.[19] Coordination then turns out to raise U.S. welfare in only 20 percent of the cases, and to raise non–U.S. welfare in 60 percent of the cases.

Ghosh (1987) and Ghosh and Masson (1988) claim that the presence of model uncertainty—far from rendering coordination unattractive as in my results—actually furnishes an argument in favor of coordination, provided that policymakers recognize that they do not know the true model. Their argument is essentially that if the policymaker has rational expectations, then the probability weights he assigns to the possible models ($\frac{1}{10}$ to each of 10 in our experiment) will correspond to the best weights available. This argument is correct (1) assuming that governments do in fact assign the best weights to alternative models (which among other things implies that all governments share the same perceptions, which does not seem to be the case), and (2) as a statement about ex ante welfare only. If governments do not agree on the correct set of weights to assign the models, the implications even for correct ex ante welfare are precisely the same as the original implications of disagreement as to the correct model are for true ex post welfare: coordination could make the country worse off in expected value. Furthermore, even if the countries do know the best weights, it is still quite possible that the true model will turn out to lie far from the weighted-average model and coordination will reduce ex post welfare. It is ex post welfare that should be the ultimate criterion; to argue otherwise essentially would be to argue that what matters is that the president blithely perceives that he has made the best decision, even if the consequences for the economy may in fact be calamitous.

Holtham and Hughes Hallett (1987) and Kenen (1987) argue that we should rule out coordination (i.e., that it will not take place) in cases where the bargain is not "sustainable," defined as cases where one party expects that the other—even though happy to go along with the bargain—will in fact lose from it. The supposition is that the first party will expect the other policymaker to abrogate the agreement next period, when the error becomes evident. To this, one can make two possible responses. First, one can point out that throughout the exercise (that considered by Holtham and Hughes Hallett 1987, as much as by Frankel and Rockett 1988), it is assumed that policymakers do not revise their multiplier estimates just because the target variables turn out in the next period to take different values from the ones they expected. (Implicitly, they assign the error to a transitory disturbance. This is the alternative to assuming that they gradually update their multiplier estimates in a Bayesian way until they converge on the true model.[20] It would certainly be foolish to represent anyone as completely revising his multiplier estimates each period so that his model fits perfectly the latest data point.) It follows that it would not be rational to expect the other policymaker to abrogate the agreement next period, because the other policymaker is known to believe in a model that will continue to make the agreement appear advantageous. It is not as if the other policymaker will be able to accuse the first of bad faith. If the first keeps his promise to set his policy instruments in the way agreed upon, it is not his fault if the economy responds in an unexpected way.

The second possible response to the point is to admit that policymakers in international negotiations are less likely to reach agreement on a coordination package if they have profoundly different views of the world and thus have difficulty communicating at all. This argument does not change the conclusion that uncertainty constitutes a serious obstacle to successful policy coordination. It simply reclassifies some of the 1,000 combinations as cases where coordination does not even get past the talking stage. And there is nothing to guarantee that those "sustainable" cases where the coordination does take place will have a higher incidence of welfare gains than that reflected in the statistics that count all 1,000 cases.[21]

Carrying this logic one step further, we can consider the subset of 100 cases where the two countries agree on a single model. Again, this does not necessarily improve the chances that the chosen model is the correct one. In Frankel and Rockett (1988, 330), for the subset where the countries agree, coordination turns out to result in U.S. gains in 65 percent of the cases, and rest-of-world gains in 59 percent of the cases. Holtham and Hughes Hallett (1987, 25) reach a similar conclusion: judged by the correct model, only slightly over half the agreement cases result in gains.

Frenkel, Goldstein, and Masson (1988, 30–31) offer some further defenses of coordination, these in response to the point made by Oudiz and Sachs (1984) and others that the gains from coordination are empirically found to be small, even under the normal certainty assumption (which is the best case in that the gains are necessarily positive). First, they cite a finding of Holtham and Hughes Hallett (1987) that the gains from coordination turn out larger when other target variables such as the exchange rate are included in the objective function. Against this finding must be balanced the problems that uncertainty poses for choosing the exchange rate as one of the target variables; the econometric record shows even greater uncertainty as to the effects of macroeconomic policies on exchange rates than on output, inflation, and the trade balance.

Frenkel, Goldstein, and Masson point out two further limitations of the Oudiz-Sachs (1984) approach: that it does not provide an explicit standard of comparison when it pronounces the gains from coordination "small," and that it assumes that the "counterfactual" (what would happen in the absence of coordination) is optimization by policymakers in the Nash noncooperative equilibrium, which is not necessarily realistic. These two points are simultaneously addressed by an experiment reported in Frankel and Rockett (1988,

332, table 7) and Frankel (1988a, tables 13 and 14). There the gains from coordination, under the best-case assumption that the policymaker knows the true model, are compared to the gains to a single policymaker, who may previously have believed an incorrect model, of discovering the true model and unilaterally adjusting his policies accordingly (while staying within the Nash noncooperative equilibrium). In a majority of cases, the gains from coordination are small compared to the gains from a unilateral switch to the correct model (nine to six for the U.S. and twelve to four for the rest of the OECD, in each case assuming that the partner knows the correct model all along).

Thus it remains true that the obstacles to successful coordination are formidable, even in a simplified one-period framework with enforcement assumed to be automatic.

Problems of Enforcement and the G-7 Indicators

Coming from our consideration of the problems of uncertainty, several conditions would seem to be essential for any cooperative agreement to "stick." First, each round of coordination must specify clearly what is expected of each party. It is hard enough to enforce a clear-cut agreement because each party has an incentive to cheat; enforcement is hopeless if the parties have not even spelled out what is required of them. (When OPEC ministers come out of a Vienna meeting without having agreed upon oil production quotas for their countries, it is probably a safe bet that the members will not be withholding output in the common interest; enforcement is hard enough even when the agreement is explicit.)

Second, for the parties to be held accountable, the variables that they commit to must, to the maximum extent possible, be both observable and under the control of the governmental authorities, and in particular under the control of those authorities involved in the international negotiations. It is for this reason that when the IMF negotiates a "letter of intent" with the finance minister of a borrowing country, the "performance criteria" that are agreed upon tend to be variables directly under the control of the authorities, such as the growth rate of the monetary base, rather than variables that are harder to control like the broad money supply, let alone the ultimate target variables like inflation. Otherwise, the national authorities could always claim that a subsequent failure to satisfy a performance criterion was beyond their control.

It is not essential that the variables be under the precise short-run control of the authorities, especially if compliance with the agreement is to be checked only on a basis of, say, once a year at annual reviews by the IMF ("Article IV Consultations") or at summit meetings of the heads of state, or twice a year at meetings of the finance ministers. It is only essential that there be an unambiguous sign to the relationship between the policy instruments that *are* under direct control and the variable to which the parties commit, and that the lags in the relationship not be too long. When the variable begins to deviate seriously from the agreed-upon range, the policymakers begin to adjust the policy instruments accordingly. Then the policymaker at the end of the year can be held accountable for any large deviations from the agreement.

The third necessary condition pulls the opposite direction from the second. The variables that the parties commit to must be closely enough tied to the target variables in their ultimate objective function that if there turns out to be an unexpected disturbance in one of the economic relationships (or if one of the multipliers belonging to an agreed policy change turns out to be different than expected), the country will not be too drastically harmed. If the country commits to a specific number for the monetary base or the money supply, and there are shifts in the money multiplier or velocity that translate that number into a severe and needless recession, it is obvious that the country will break its commitment. There must also be a similar link between the variables that each party commits to and the *other* country's target variables. A country will not be as impressed when its partner sticks to its money growth target if this turns out to be disadvantageous to it (for example because a disturbance moves it to the overly inflationary side of full employment, or because the partner's money growth turns out to be transmitted negatively rather than positively).

At the Tokyo Summit of May 1986, it was decided that the G-5 countries, or thenceforth the G-7, would focus in their meetings on a set of ten "objective indicators": the growth rate of GNP, interest rate, inflation rate, unemployment, ratio of the fiscal deficit to GNP, current account and trade balances, money growth rate, international reserve holdings, and exchange rate. No pretense was made that the members would rigidly commit to specific numbers for these indicators, in the sense that sanctions would be imposed on a country if it deviated far from the values agreed upon. But the plan did include the understanding that appropriate remedial measures would be taken whenever there developed significant deviations from the "intended course." The indicators are viewed as prototypes of the variables that representatives would bargain over if coordination were to become more serious. The current G-7 system could be viewed as an attempted case of the "epsilon-small" degree of coordination mentioned at the beginning of this paper, a necessary stage for building confidence before moving on to more binding forms of coordination.

The list has been further discussed, and trimmed down, at subsequent G-7 meetings. By the time of the Venice Summit in June 1987, the list had been reduced to six indicators: growth, inflation, trade balances, government budgets, monetary conditions, and exchange rates.[22] Treasury Secretary James Baker, however, in October 1987 told the IMF Annual Meeting that "the United States is prepared to consider utilizing, as an additional indicator in the coordination process, the relationship among our currencies and a basket of commodities, including gold. . . ." At the Toronto Summit of June 1988, "the G-7 countries welcomed the addition of a commodity price indicator and the progress made toward refining the analytical use of indicators."[23]

The French Finance Minister Edouard Balladur singled out five indicators after the G-7 meeting of December 23, 1987 (a "Louvre Agreement II"). He writes of "a system based on international cooperation building on the spirit of the Louvre Agreements. Their enforcement requires close surveillance of each of the major economies on the basis of such economic indicators as growth rates, fiscal balance, balance of payments, interest rates, and exchange rates. This surveillance is already being established gradually."[24]

It is somewhat difficult to reconcile these optimistic statements that some amount of substantive coordination is already taking place with the fact that G-7 meetings do not publicly announce the targets agreed to for the indicators. How can any pressure be brought to bear on countries that stray from the agreed-upon targets (whether it is moral suasion, embarrassment, the effect on long-term reputations, or outright sanctions) if the targets themselves are not made public?[25]

Indeed, the G-7 guards with tremendous secrecy the values of the indicators, even more so than the central banks guard the secrecy of their foreign-exchange market interventions. Theory says that the success of a target zone, for exchange rates for example, is enhanced when speculators are made aware of the boundaries.[26] Why does the G-7 keep them secret? One possible answer—drawn from the central banker's, and not the economist's, view of the financial markets—is that the G-7 countries believe that short-term foreign-exchange speculation is destabilizing, and that creation of short-term uncertainty as to what the authorities will do is a way of discouraging such speculation.[27] Another possible answer is that they do not want to lose face when the exchange rate subsequently breaks outside the band. This answer fits in well with one's suspicion that the G-7 meetings may in fact reach no substantive agreements, but find it politically useful to issue communiqués nevertheless; the communiqués are sufficiently vague that each member can interpret them to his own advantage.[28]

The G-7 list of indicators is not especially well-suited to the desirable conditions for workable coordination stated above. It is difficult to imagine a G-7 meeting applying moral censure to one of its members for having experienced a higher rate of real growth during the year than had been agreed upon in the preceding meeting, or a lower rate of inflation.

The main problem with the list is that it is too long to be practical. When each country has ten indicators but only two or three policy instruments, it is virtually certain that the indicators will give conflicting signals and that the national authorities will feel no constraint on their setting of policy instruments. Frenkel, Goldstein, and Masson (1988, 22) note that one argument in favor of choosing a single indicator is the point that when multiple indicators send conflicting signals, authorities can hide behind the confusion. They also observe that multiple indicators can encourage "overcoordination:" setting a single indicator allows each country to retain some degree of freedom in setting its monetary and fiscal policies. In this light, a serious coordination scheme might begin in the 1990s by setting only one indicator, and then only progress to commitments to multiple variables when and if sufficient political consensus and confidence has developed to justify that degree of sacrifice of sovereignty.

Perhaps the true list has been, or will be, winnowed down to a smaller number of indicators? No item on the list is a good candidate to be the single variable on which negotiation under a future coordination regime would focus. Each would seem to be dominated by nominal GNP (or nominal demand). We consider each in turn. Real output, employment, inflation, and the trade balance are less directly affected by policy instruments than is nominal GNP, aside from the fact that focusing exclusively on any one would destabilize the others. The money supply is more under the control of the authorities (at least on an annual basis), but is much less directly linked to target variables: it is one unambiguous step further away from the two fundamental target variables of real output and the price level than is nominal GNP (that step, of course, being the existence of shifts in velocity, as discussed in sec. 2.1 and demonstrated in the Appendix). Furthermore we saw in the preceding section that the effects of money on all three target variables (output, price level, and trade balance) in the other country are completely ambiguous in sign. Thus it is an even less suitable choice of focus for international coordination than for domestic policymaking.

Fiscal policy is more easily linked to the foreign target variables (or would be, if the high-employment deficit were used as the indicator). But it is less directly under the control of the policymakers than is the money supply. Among G-7 countries, the inability to control the budget deficit has been most striking in the case of the United States in the 1980s. Feldstein (1988, 10) offers a reason why the United States will never be able to participate in serious international bargaining over fiscal policy:

> A primary reason why such macroeconomic policy coordination cannot work as envisioned is that the United States is constitutionally incapable of participating in such a negotiation. The separation of powers in the American form of government means that the Secretary of the Treasury cannot promise to reduce or expand the budget deficit or to change tax rules. This power does not rest with the President or the administration but depends on a legislative agreement between the President and the Congress.

Exchange rate policy is of course a very large topic in itself, to be considered briefly in the last part of this paper. But we can note some difficulties with the exchange rate being the single indicator that G-7 countries commit to in policy coordination agreements. If the dollar/mark rate begins to stray outside the announced target zone, which of the two governments should suffer sanctions or a loss in reputation? The "$n-1$" problem means that one country would have to sit out, presumably the United States, which is not what is wanted.[29] Countries could commit to certain targets for their foreign-exchange intervention, or more generally to monetary and fiscal policies, which in theory would determine the exchange rate. But—as already noted—the link from macroeconomic policies to the exchange rate is fraught with even greater uncertainty than the link to output and inflation, even if one were to assume that the exchange rate might have as great a claim to being in the objective function as the other target variables.

In the second part of the Appendix to this paper, the exchange rate is added in to the objective function along with output and the price level. It is shown that the penalty that goes with stabilizing the exchange rate is to be saddled with a monetary policy that destabilizes the overall price level, relative to a regime of stabilizing nominal GNP. Within this framework, to opt for a fixed exchange rate regime, one has to put tremendous weight on the exchange rate objective. (One has to be prepared to argue that a 10 percent fluctuation in the exchange rate causes greater trouble than a 10 percent fluctuation in the price level.) The only other way out would be to assume that much of the disturbance in the exchange rate equation will disappear when the regime changes, rather than having to be accommodated by the money supply.[30] If we were to make the more practical comparison of exchange rate target zones with nominal GNP target zones, rather than literally fixed exchange rates with fixed nominal GNP, the advantages of INT would be further boosted by the accountability point: if a country's exchange rate strays outside the target zone to which it has committed itself, it can always claim that the movement is beyond its control. Such claims would be completely credible, in light of the large disturbances in the exchange rate equation.

As for the remaining three indicators on the G-7 list, the interest rate, international reserves, and the price of gold, the last is the only one that has been proposed as a candidate for the sole variable around which countries should coordinate. Proponents of a central role for gold do not seem to appreciate the analytical point that shifts in the demand function for gold, and in the other economic relationships that link it to the target variables that we ultimately care about, are even more unstable than shifts in the demand for money or the demand for foreign exchange, and are likely to remain so in the future.

This does not mean that the price of gold and other commodities is not a good indicator, in the sense of an early warning signal as to the likely future course of a true target variable, namely the overall price level.[31] In this sense it belongs with the money supply, the interest rate, and the yield curve, and many other leading indicators, on the list of variables that policymakers may want to monitor on a short-term basis in attempting to hit their targets, whether under a regime of coordination (e.g., international nominal GNP targeting), decentralized national policymaking with some commitment to a nominal anchor (e.g., regular nominal GNP targeting), or complete discretion.

In short, if coordination is to begin—on a scale that is small, but goes beyond the stage of mere rhetoric—by some degree of commitment to a single variable, then nominal GNP (or nominal demand) would seem to dominate each of the eleven indicators that the G-7 has apparently been discussing as the natural candidate for that variable.

Problems of Inflation-fighting Credibility

The third of the existing critiques of international coordination, after problems of uncertainty and problems of enforcement and political practicality, is the point made by Ken Rogoff (1985a): if governments set up the machinery for joint welfare maximization period by period, the cooperative equilibrium in each period is likely to entail a greater degree of expansion, and thereby in the long run undermine the governments' inflation-fighting credibility, and to result in a higher inflation rate for a given level of output. In the Rogoff view, renouncing the machinery of coordination is one of the ways that governments can credibly precommit to less inflationary paths.

It is important to realize that the introduction of longer-term issues of credibility, time inconsistency, and precommitment can just as easily run in favor of coordination as against it.[32] If the perceived externality or shortcoming of the Nash noncooperative equilibrium is that it is overly expansionary, then the coordination equilibrium, even when arrived at on a period-by-period basis, will entail less expansion, not more. This is often argued to be the basis underlying the EMS. The rhetoric that Chancellor Schmidt and President Giscard d'Estaing originally used in proposing the EMS in the late 1970s suggested that they were doing so because the United States was neglecting its duty to supply to the world the public good of a stable, noninflating, currency. Ten years later, many observers of the EMS have decided that its success lies precisely in giving inflation-prone countries like Italy and France a credible nominal anchor for their monetary policies.[33] Committing to an exchange rate parity or band vis-à-vis a hard-currency country like Germany constitutes precisely the sort of time-consistent low-inflation policy sought by those who worry that central bankers left to their own discretion will be overly expansionary.

In the case of the EMS, there is an asymmetry. It is accepted that Germany is simply known to place very large weight on price stability, due to its history or for whatever other reasons. The weaker-currency countries can then peg to the "greater mark area," if they wish to import inflation-fighting credibility. (There is a close analogy with the idea in Rogoff 1985b that if a particular individual—say Paul Volcker—is known to have an extreme aversion to inflation, then the country can gain by appointing him as central banker, even if the country's objective function puts less weight on fighting inflation; his tight-money credibility will reduce the public's expectations of inflation, and in long-run equilibrium will produce a lower level of actual inflation for any given level of output.) In the case of proposals for worldwide coordination, there is no presumption that the United States (the natural "Stackleberg" leader) in fact has as much inflation-fighting credibility as Germany and Japan. Thus there is no automatic presumption that year-by-year coordination would lower the average world inflation rate rather than raise it.

The implication of the credibility issue is that a scheme for coordination is more likely in the long run to produce gains if the plan has the national governments making, not just commitments to each other on a period-by-period basis, but also some degree of commitment to a nominal anchor on a longer-term basis. Hence the arguments for coordinating around the price of gold (by James Baker, Robert Mundell, and others) or around the global money supply (Ronald McKinnon's proposal). But then all the arguments from the closed-economy context (discussed in sec. 3.2.1), as to why nominal GNP as a nominal anchor dominates the money supply, price of gold, or overall price level, apply equally to the world economy.

3.2.3   How International Nominal GNP Targeting (INT) Would Work

The INT framework laid out in Frankel (1988c,d) is a very simple one. The G-7 would put aside their list of ten indicators and would instead focus on nominal demand (defined as nominal GNP minus the balance on goods and services). At each meeting, the national authorities would (a) commit themselves, without any obsessively great degree of firmness, to target rates of growth, or ranges, for their countries' levels of nominal demand for five years into the future, and (b) commit themselves, with somewhat greater firmness, to targets for the coming year. In the first stage, that is, the early 1990s, there would be no explicit enforcement mechanism. But the targets would be publicly announced, and if a country's rate of growth of nominal demand turned out to err significantly in one direction or the other, the fact would be noted disapprovingly at the next G-7 meeting. This does not happen under the current system. If the first stage were successful, a future stage might add another variable or two to the list, or might even commit countries firmly to specific policy responses in the event that their level of nominal demand begins to stray from the year's target.

A plan that called for targeting nominal GNP rather than nominal demand might be more readily and more widely understood, and thus might stand a better chance of succeeding politically. The advantage of focusing on nominal demand is the assumption that when the cooperative equilibrium entails expansion, countries need to be discouraged from the temptation to accomplish the expansion of output through net foreign demand, for example through protectionist trade measures, as opposed to domestic demand. In some years the cooperative equilibrium may entail contraction rather than expansion, and then a nominal GNP target might be preferable to a nominal demand target. But it is usually thought that the political pressure for protectionist trade remedies is greater in recessions than in expansions,[34] which points to nominal demand as the superior choice.[35]

Countries could attain their nominal GNP or nominal demand targets through any of several routes. One possibility, for example, is the Williamson-Miller (1987) "blueprint", which assigns fiscal policy in each country the responsibility for attaining a nominal demand target (and assigns monetary policy in each country responsibility for the exchange rate[36]). But at least one serious problem arises if fiscal policy is explicitly specified as the policy instrument with which countries are expected to attain the nominal demand targets that they agreed to. When their economies stray away from the target, the authorities will claim that it is not politically possible to adjust fiscal policy quickly. Such claims will be completely credible because they will generally be true.[37]

An agreement is more likely to stick if monetary policy, rather than fiscal policy, is specified as the policy instrument that countries are expected to use. Even if fiscal policy is assumed to be no more subject to lags and political encumbrances than is monetary policy, there is another reason for assigning monetary policy to the nominal demand target. If countries also pursue trade balance targets (and it seems that they do, whether or not they should), then the classic "assignment problem" is relevant. The general rule is to assign responsibility for the trade balance target to that policy instrument which has a relatively greater effect on it (Mundell 1962). I agree with Boughton (1989) that under modern conditions of floating exchange rates, which work to decrease the effectiveness of monetary policy with respect to the trade balance and increase the effectiveness of fiscal policy, this means assigning fiscal policy to the trade balance target and monetary policy to the domestic target.

What is the precise instrument of monetary policy that should be adjusted when nominal demand drifts away from the target? The monetary base or level of unborrowed reserves would be better than the broader monetary aggregates because the central bank controls them more directly. (The short-term interest rate is another possible instrument.) McCallum (1988b, 15) has suggested a specific feedback rule in the context of closed-economy policymaking that might do well here. His proposal is that for each 1 percent that nominal GNP deviates from its target in a given quarter, the monetary base be expanded an additional 0.25 percent over the subsequent quarter. He suggests setting a trend growth rate in the target of 3 percent per year, and subtracting from this the average growth rate of base velocity over the preceding four years. An alternative possibility would be to replace the 3 percent target with "a number to be negotiated for each member of the G-7 each year, with a planned long-run tendency of 3 percent."

The central bank would be better able to hit its annual nominal demand target if it were allowed to respond to other available information, besides just the most recent monthly figure for nominal demand itself. Ben Friedman (1984, 183–84), for example, shows that such indicators as the money supply and the stock of credit can be used to predict more accurately deviations from a nominal income target. Many other "leading indicators" could be added to the list. The conclusion seems to be that it would be better in practice to leave the means of attaining the nominal demand target up to the national authorities, rather than require that they follow a particular rule like McCallum's (1987).

It might be objected that this entire discussion of coordination via INT has neglected important questions of the mix between monetary and fiscal policy, the real interest rate, and the exchange rate.[38] These questions are briefly considered next.

3.3   Policy Independence and Exchange Rate Flexibility

One measure of the degree of macroeconomic policy convergence among countries is the magnitude and variability of the real interest differential.

Rogoff (1985c) for example shows that real interest rates are not perfectly correlated across European countries, and argues that this shows that European countries retain some policy independence. One question, posed by observers of the EMS in particular, is whether such independence is attributable to capital controls and other remaining barriers to the free movement of capital across national boundaries, or whether it is attributable to exchange rate flexibility.[39]

3.3.1   Financial Integration, Monetary Integration, and Independence

Frankel and MacArthur (1988) studied real interest differentials for twenty-four countries, from 1982 up to early 1987, and decomposed them into a component attributable to imperfect financial integration (the "country premium") and a component attributable to exchange rate variability (the "currency premium"). Table 3.1 shows real interest differentials for twenty-five countries, vis-à-vis the Eurodollar, updated through the beginning of 1988. (It is taken from Frankel 1989.) Both the mean of the differential and the measures of variability show substantial independence for each of the countries. Table 3.2 uses forward exchange rate data for each currency to separate out the covered interest differential, which represents the component due to imperfect financial integration. The covered interest differential is very small for the G-10 countries (including Switzerland) except for France and Italy, and is also very small for Austria, Singapore, and Hong Kong. Even for the other countries, which often have significant barriers to international financial integration, the country premium is in most cases smaller than the currency premium. This says that for the major countries, and many others as well, exchange rate variability is a greater source of policy independence than is imperfect financial integration.

Different views are possible on whether or not policy independence makes for a more smoothly-running world economy. Corden (1983) argues that decentralized decision-making among countries is more efficient, because each country knows better its own situation. His is an argument in favor of the current floating-rate system. McKinnon (1988), on the other hand, takes it for granted that world economic efficiency requires that real interest rates be equalized across countries (presumably so that the marginal product of capital is equalized across countries). His is an argument in favor of reform of the system so as to reduce exchange rate variability.

3.3.2   A Proposal for Beginning to Stabilize Exchange Rates: The "Hosomi Fund"

Would-be reformers of the world monetary system have a choice. If they wish to allow each country enhanced policy independence, they can seek to decrease the degree of financial market integration. Alternatively, like McKinnon (1984, 1988) and Williamson (1983), they can opt for increased policy convergence and exchange rate stability. (Frenkel, Goldstein, and Masson 1988 refer to a choice between decreasing the demand for policy coordination and increasing the supply.) Frankel (1988b) considers one of the most

Table 3.1   Real Interest Differentials (Local − Dollar)[a]

	No. of Observations	Mean	Standard Error	Series Standard Deviation	Root Mean Squared Error	95% Band
Open Atlantic DCs						
Canada	63	0.09	0.38	2.09	2.09	3.96
Germany	63	−1.29*	0.65	2.77	3.06	5.95
Netherlands	62	−0.71	0.86	3.91	3.97	7.63
Switzerland	62	−2.72*	0.81	3.39	4.36	8.43
United Kingdom	62	0.46	0.79	3.45	3.48	5.69
Group	313	−0.83	0.66	3.16	3.46	
Liberalizing Pacific LDCs						
Hong Kong	62	−2.89*	0.94	4.80	5.62	11.61
Malaysia	62	0.83	1.00	4.61	4.68	8.19
Singapore	61	0.08	0.68	3.33	3.34	6.71
Group	185	−0.67	0.82	4.28	4.62	—
Closed LDCs						
Bahrain	60	2.19	1.46	7.10	7.44	12.93
Greece	56	−9.22*	1.91	9.36	13.19	21.77
Mexico	62	−20.28	9.43	21.19	29.45	52.13
Portugal	61	−3.90	2.97	11.28	11.95	23.62
South Africa	61	−4.84*	1.17	4.85	6.88	11.16
Group	300	−7.25*	1.30	12.16	16.06	—
Closed European DCs						
Austria	64	−2.20*	0.38	2.09	2.09	3.96
Belgium	63	0.53	0.68	2.90	2.95	4.99
Denmark	61	−3.42*	0.90	4.34	5.54	9.64
France	64	−0.48	0.72	2.94	2.98	5.54
Ireland	61	1.53	1.03	3.95	4.24	7.13
Italy	61	1.01	0.86	3.62	3.76	5.83
Norway	50	−0.64	0.84	3.23	3.29	6.83
Spain	63	0.53	1.44	5.92	5.95	11.90
Sweden	63	−0.21	1.07	4.52	4.53	8.28
Group	550	−0.37	0.81	4.00	4.29	—
Liberalizing Pacific DCs						
Australia	60	1.16	0.90	3.69	3.87	7.43
Japan	63	−0.58	0.62	3.41	3.46	6.03
New Zealand	60	1.04	1.83	7.15	7.23	11.36
Group	183	0.52	0.73	5.00	5.09	—
All Countries	1,531	−1.74	—	6.47	8.07	—

Source: Frankel (1989).

[a]Interest differential less realized inflation differential for the period September 1972 to January 1988.

*Mean is significant at the 95% level.

Table 3.2   **Covered Interest Differentials (Local − Dollar)[a]**

	No. of Observations	Mean	Standard Error	Series Standard Deviation	Root Mean Squared Error	95% Band
Open Atlantic DCs						
Canada	68	−0.10*	0.03	0.21	0.24	0.44
Germany	68	0.35*	0.03	0.24	0.42	0.75
Netherlands	68	0.21*	0.02	0.13	0.25	0.45
Switzerland	68	0.42*	0.03	0.23	0.48	0.79
United Kingdom	68	−0.14*	0.02	0.20	0.25	0.41
Group	340	0.14*	0.01	0.21	0.34	—
Liberalizing Pacific LDCs						
Hong Kong	68	0.13*	0.03	0.28	0.31	0.60
Malaysia	63	−1.46*	0.16	1.28	1.95	3.73
Singapore	64	−0.30*	0.04	0.31	0.43	0.73
Group	195	−0.52*	0.05	0.76	1.14	—
Closed LDCs						
Bahrain	64	−2.15*	0.13	1.06	2.41	4.17
Greece	58	−9.39*	0.80	6.08	11.26	20.39
Mexico	43	−16.47*	1.83	12.01	20.54	28.86
Portugal	61	−7.93*	1.23	9.59	12.49	27.83
South Africa	67	−1.07	1.17	9.55	9.61	2.68
Group	293	−6.64*	0.48	8.23	11.82	—
Closed European DCs						
Austria	65	0.13*	0.05	0.39	0.41	0.39
Belgium	68	0.12*	0.03	0.26	0.29	0.59
Denmark	68	−3.53*	0.19	1.57	3.89	6.63
France	68	−1.74*	0.32	2.68	3.20	7.18
Ireland	66	−0.79	0.51	4.17	4.24	7.80
Italy	68	−0.40	0.23	1.92	1.96	4.11
Norway	50	−1.03*	0.11	0.76	1.29	2.10
Spain	67	−2.40*	0.45	3.66	4.39	7.95
Sweden	68	−0.23*	0.06	0.45	0.51	0.81
Group	588	−1.10*	0.09	2.25	2.77	—
Liberalizing Pacific DCs						
Australia	68	−0.75*	0.23	1.94	2.08	2.59
Japan	68	0.09*	0.03	0.21	0.23	0.43
New Zealand	68	−1.63*	0.29	2.42	2.92	5.24
Group	204	−0.76*	0.12	1.78	2.96	—
All Countries	1,620	−1.73*	0.09	3.81	5.36	—

Source: Frankel (1989).

[a]Interest differential less forward discount for the period September 1982 to April 1988.

*Mean is significant at the 95% level.

mentioned proposals for decreasing the degree of financial integration, the "Tobin tax" on foreign-exchange transactions. Here I discuss another particular proposal that others have made for stabilizing exchange rates.[40]

Several years ago, Takashi Hosomi (1985) proposed the creation of a new supranational fund that could intervene in foreign-exchange markets. The Japanese Vice-Minister of Finance for International Affairs, Toyoo Gyoten, has recently floated precisely this sort of proposal.[41] Some recent talk of a European Central Bank, heard both in official and academic circles, strikes a similar note.[42]

The proposal envisions a fund that could undertake operations in the open international markets, but would not replace the individual countries' central banks. A plausible motivation for this approach is precisely the one presented in the introduction to this paper: the need for proposals for monetary reform that are politically practical in that they could begin on a very small scale, gradually build up confidence among the players, and then increase the scale of coordination accordingly. In this case, the size of the fund constitutes the variable that would begin with a small "epsilon" and subsequently increase to reflect however much political consensus exists.

Decisions could be made by an "Open Market Committee" consisting primarily of representatives of the individual central banks, with votes presumably awarded in proportion to the size of their economies or the size of their contribution of international reserves to the fund, as is the case with the IMF, but with operations decided by a median voter rule. (The Bank for International Settlements [BIS] could also serve as a model; indeed it is conceivable that an expanded BIS could serve, in place of founding yet another international institution.) In the event that France, say, wishes to dampen depreciation of the franc against the dollar but is outvoted by a majority in favor of dollar purchases, the Bank of France is still free to intervene in the opposite direction on its own. Countries will at first be giving up very little sovereignty when they agree to the establishment of such a fund because it will be on a small scale. Only if all parties are happy with the outcome would the size of the portfolio—and therefore the potential loss of national sovereignty—be increased.

3.4 Conclusion

This paper has examined two possible reforms of the world monetary system. Both are designed to try to overcome the serious obstacles to successful coordination that are outlined in section 3.2.2. In particular, both are designed in such a way that they can begin on a small scale, and then grow as the degree of political consensus grows.

The INT proposal is appropriate if the shortcoming of the Nash noncooperative equilibrium is thought to be either insufficient or excessive expansion. The Hosomi proposal is appropriate if the shortcoming is thought to lie with the exchange rate. The question arises whether the two are compatible, whether they can be implemented simultaneously if the noncooperative equilibrium is thought to be characterized by both sorts of shortcomings.

If the Hosomi Fund is foreseen to affect exchange rates only via changes in money supplies, and monetary policy is also foreseen to be the instrument whereby countries attain their nominal demand targets, it might seem that there is an overdeterminacy in the system. But I am not sure that there is in fact a problem. There are some obvious policy instruments that would introduce extra degrees of freedom into the system: the Hosomi Fund's intervention could be nonsterilized, thus changing the international supplies of bonds rather than supplies of money, or the countries could use fiscal policy alongside monetary policy to attain their nominal demand targets.

Even if money supplies are the only available policy instruments, there are n money supplies to be determined and n national opinions as to what they should be. So it sounds like there is no overdeterminacy problem. At any given time, the median voter on the International Open Market Committee will simply receive extra weight in determining what the money supplies will be. It is true that if the median voter wants the fund to buy a particular currency to increase its exchange value, at the same time that the country in question is obligated to increase its monetary base in order to correct slower than targeted growth in its nominal GNP, then the country will be put in an untenable position. It seems unlikely that the International Open Market Committee would choose to "pick on" a particular member in this way. But this is merely speculation at this stage. It would be desirable for future research to study the implications of such a Hosomi Fund with a median voter rule, just as it would be desirable for future research to study a regime of cooperative ex ante setting of nominal demand targets. This paper has only tried to point the way, with an examination of some advantages of these two approaches.

Appendix

In this appendix we compare four possible policy regimes: (1) floating exchange rates, with full discretion by national policymakers (the current regime), (2) a rigid money supply rule, (3) a rigid nominal GNP rule, and (4) a rigid exchange rate rule. (In the case of each of the three possible nominal anchors, proponents sometimes have in mind a target zone system; the assumption of a rigid rule just makes the analysis simpler.) The approach, incorporating the advantages both to rules and discretion, follows Rogoff (1985b) and Fischer (1988a), who in turn follow Kydland and Prescott (1977) and Barro and Gordon (1983).

Throughout, we assume an aggregate supply relationship:

(A1) $$y = y^* + b(p - p^e) + u,$$

where y represents output, y^* potential output, p the price level, p^e the expected price level (or they could be the actual and expected inflation rates, respectively), and u a supply disturbance, with all variables expressed as logs.

Output and the Price Level in the Objective Function

We begin without the exchange rate. The loss function is simply:

(A2) $$L = ap^2 + (y - ky^*)^2,$$

where a is the weight assigned to the inflation objective, and we assume that the lagged or expected price level relative to which p is measured can be normalized to zero. We impose $k > 1$, which builds in an expansionary bias to discretionary policymaking.

(A3) $$L = ap^2 + [y^*(1 - k) + b(p - p^e) + u]^2.$$

1. *Discretionary Policy*

Under full discretion, the policymaker each period chooses aggregate demand so as to minimize that period's L, with p^e given:

(A4) $\quad (½)\, dL/dp = ap + [y^*(1 - k) + b(p - p^e) + u]b = 0;$

(A5) $\quad p = [-y^*(1 - k)b + b^2p^e - bu] / [a + b^2].$

Under rational expectations,

(A6) $$p^e = Ep = -y^*(1 - k)b/a.$$

So we can solve (A5) for the price level:

(A7) $$p = -y^*(1 - k)[b/a] - ub/[a + b^2].$$

From (A2), the expected loss function then works out to:

(A8) $\quad EL = (1 + b^2/a)[y^*(1 - k)]^2 + [a/(a + b^2)]\, \text{var}(u).$

The first term represents the inflationary bias in the system, while the second represents the effect of the supply disturbance after the authorities have chosen the optimal split between inflation and output.

2. *Money Rule*

To consider alternative regimes, we must be explicit about the money market equilibrium condition (in case 1, it was implicit that the money supply m was the variable that the authorities were using to control demand):

(A9) $$m = p + y - v,$$

where v represents velocity shocks. (We assume v uncorrelated with u.) If the authorities precommit to a fixed money growth rule in order to reduce expected inflation in long-run equilibrium, then they must give up on affecting y. The optimal money growth rate is the one that sets Ep at the target value for p, namely 0. Thus they will set the money supply m at Ey, where in this case is y^*. The aggregate demand equation thus becomes

$$(A10) \qquad\qquad p + y = y^* + v.$$

Combining with the aggregate supply relationship (A1), the equilibrium is given by

$$(A11) \quad y = y^* + (u + bv)/(1 + b), \qquad p = (v - u)/(1 + b).$$

Substituting into (A2), the expected loss function is

$$(A12) \quad EL = (1 - k)^2 y^{*^2} + [(1 + a)\text{var}(u) + (a + b^2)\text{var}(v)]/(1 + b)^2.$$

The first term is smaller than the corresponding term in the discretion case, because the precommitment reduces expected inflation; but the second term is probably larger, because the authorities have given up the ability to respond to money demand shocks. Which regime is better depends on how big the shocks are, and how big a weight (a) is placed on inflation fighting.

3. *Nominal GNP Rule*

In the case of a nominal GNP rule, the authorities vary the money supply in such a way as to accommodate velocity shocks. Equation (A10) is replaced by the condition that $p + y$ is constant. The solution is the same as in case 2, but with the v disturbance dropped. Thus the expected loss collapses from equation (A12) to

$$(A13) \qquad EL = (1 - k)^2 y^{*^2} + [(1 + a)/(1 + b)^2]\text{var}(u).$$

This unambiguously dominates the money rule case. It is still not possible, without knowing var(u), or (a), to say that the rule dominates discretion. It is quite likely, especially if the variance of u is large, that an absolute commitment to a rule would be unwisely constraining. Hence the argument for a target zone rather than a single number, and for subjecting the central bank chairman to a mere loss of reputation rather than a firing squad if he misses the target. But it seems clear that, to whatever extent the country chooses to commit to a nominal anchor, nominal GNP dominates the money supply as the candidate for anchor.

Adding the Exchange Rate to the Objective Function

We reconsider here a likely objection to choosing nominal GNP or nominal demand as the focus of international coordination, that it neglects the exchange rate. The alternative of setting monetary policy so as to stabilize the exchange rate will not look attractive unless the exchange rate enters the objective function, perhaps indirectly via the consumer price index or the trade balance. Here we confront the argument head on and include the exchange rate directly in the loss function along with output and the price level. Thus we replace (A2) with

(A14) $$L = ap^2 + (y - ky^*)^2 + cs^2,$$

where s is the spot exchange rate measured relative to some equilibrium or target value and c is the weight placed on exchange rate stability per se.

There is no point in specifying an elaborate model of the exchange rate. All the empirical results say that most of the variation in the exchange rate cannot be explained (even ex post; we say nothing of prediction) by measurable macroeconomic variables, and thus can only be attributed to an error term that we here call e. But we must include the money supply in the equation; otherwise we do not allow the authorities the possibility of affecting the exchange rate. Our equation is simply

(A15) $$s = m - y + e.$$

(We assume that e is uncorrelated with the other disturbances.) From (A9),

(A16) $$s = p - v + e.$$

We assume that the same aggregate supply relationship, equation (A1), holds as before. So we can write the loss function (A14) as:

(A17) $$L = ap^2 + [(1 - k)y^* + b(p - p^e) + u]^2 + c(p - v + e)^2.$$

We proceed as before to consider possible regimes.

1. *Discretionary Policy*

$$(\tfrac{1}{2})\, dL/dp = ap + [y^*(1 - k) + b(p - p^e) + u]b + c(p - v + e) = 0.$$

(A18) $$p = [-y^*(1 - k)b + b^2 p^e - bu + c(v - e)] / (a + b^2 + c).$$

The rationally expected p is given by $p^e = Ep$:

(A19) $$p^e = -(1 - k)by^*/(a + c).$$

Substituting into equation (A19) yields

(A20) $$p = -(1 - k)y^*[b/(a + c)] + [c(v - e) - bu]/(a + b^2 + c).$$

The loss function is

(A21) $EL = [(1 - k)y^*]^2 (a + b^2 + c)/(a + c) + \{(a + c)\text{var}(u)$
$+ c(a + b^2) [\text{var}(v) + \text{var}(e)]\}/(a + b^2 + c).$

2. *Money Rule*

As when we considered a money rule before, so that expected inflation is zero, the authorities set m at y^* and (A10) applies. Thus the same solution (A11) for y and p also applies. The exchange rate is given by substituting the solution for p from (A11) into (A16):

(A22) $s = e - [(u + bv)/(1 + b)]$

The additional s term is the only difference from (A12) in the expected loss function:

(A23) $EL = [y^*(1 - k)]^2 + [(1 + a + c)/(1 + b^2)] \text{var}(u)$
$+ [(a + b^2 + cb^2)/(1 + b)^2]\text{var}(v) + (c)\text{var}(e).$

Again the comparison with discretion depends on the various magnitudes.

3. *Nominal GNP Rule*

When the monetary authorities are able to vary m so as to keep $p + y$ constant, the velocity shocks v drop out. The expected loss function becomes

(A24) $EL = [y^*(1 - k)]^2 + [(1 + a + c)/(1 + b)^2] \text{var}(u) + c \text{ var}(e).$

As before, the nominal GNP rule unambiguously dominates the money rule.

In practice, the e shocks in the exchange rate equation are very large. They certainly dwarf the u shocks in the aggregate supply equation. (The exchange rate often moves 10 percent in a year, without corresponding movements in the money supply or other observable macroeconomic variables; try to imagine similar movements of real output.) If the weight c on the s target is substantial, then the last term in the expected loss equation may be important.

4. *Exchange Rate Rule*

Again, the authorities cannot affect y in long-run equilibrium. But now it is the exchange rate that they peg in such a way that $Ep = 0$, which from (A16) is $s = 0$. The ex post price level is then given by

(A25) $p = v - e.$

From (A1),

(A26) $$y = y^* + b(v - e) + u.$$

From (A14),

(A27) $EL = (a + b^2)\mathrm{var}(v - e) + [y^* (1 - k)]^2 + \mathrm{var}(u).$

The coefficient on var (e) is $(a + b^2)$, as compared to the coefficient c in the expected loss equation (A24) under the nominal GNP rule. We made the point above that e shocks in practice dwarf u shocks. Reasoning on this basis, even if v shocks are also small and $a = c$ (the objective function puts no greater weight on a 10 percent fluctuation of the price level than on a 10 percent fluctuation of the exchange rate), which is extremely conservative, the expected loss from fixing s is greater than the expected loss from fixing nominal GNP. The reason is that, under an exchange rate rule, e shocks are allowed to affect the money supply and therefore the overall price level. Once we allow for v shocks (which are probably in between u and e shocks in magnitude), the case for nominal GNP targeting is even stronger. One would have to put extraordinarily high weight on the exchange rate objective to prefer an exchange rate rule.

Notes

1. Fischer (1988b) surveys much of the coordination literature.
2. Levine, Currie, and Gaines (1989) present a general methodology for analyzing the sustainability of coordination agreements that take the form of simple rules.
3. The INT proposal appears in brief form in Frankel (1988c). Frankel (1990) offers a version of the proposal of the same length as the present paper.
4. If the problem with the Nash noncooperative equilibrium is thought to be competitive appreciation or depreciation, then an agreement to move to a regime of greater exchange rate stability will solve the problem. If, on the other hand, the problem is thought to be overly contractionary or overly expansionary monetary policy, then such a switch in regimes may exacerbate the problem by increasing the degree of international transmission of disturbances.
5. While Milton Friedman has justifiably had more influence on this issue than one human being is usually able to have, there have long been two aspects of his campaign against the Federal Reserve Board that are puzzling. First, his argument against discretion in monetary policymaking is largely based on the analysis in Friedman and Schwartz (1963) that the Federal Reserve made the Depression of the 1930s much worse than it otherwise would have been by "allowing" the M1 money supply to fall. Yet in recent decades he has campaigned for the Federal Reserve to do precisely what he accuses them of doing in the 1930s: set a firm target for the monetary base rather than for M1. The second, even more puzzling, aspect is that Friedman and his fellow monetarists claim to believe that U.S. money growth would be slower and more stable if monetary policy were placed more under the control of the democratic political process, via the Treasury or the U.S. Congress, than under the control of elitist control bankers like Paul Volcker. It is particularly ironic that, when a member of the monetarist Shadow Open Market Committee finally became Treasury Under-secretary for Monetary Affairs in the early 1980s, his view that the money growth rate was dangerously high

was overruled by a Treasury Secretary and White House who sought to pressure the Federal Reserve for faster money growth leading up to the 1984 election.

6. Rogoff (1985b) shows that some intermediate degree of commitment to a target is optimal for monetary policy.

7. Gordon (1985), Hall (1985), Taylor (1985), and McCallum (1987, 1988a,b), for example, argue in favor of targeting nominal GNP in the closed economy context. The idea also has proponents in the United Kingdom: Bean (1983), Meade (1984), and Brittan (1987). Williamson and Miller (1987, 7–10) propose targeting nominal demand as part of their "blueprint" for exchange rate target zones.

8. In 1974, Switzerland can be given as an example of a country that chose to take the adverse supply shock almost entirely in the form of lost income and employment in order to restore price stability; Sweden, as an example of a country that chose to take it almost entirely in the form of inflation in order to preserve output and employment; and the United States, as an example in between.

9. Holtham and Hughes Hallett (1987, 130) agree: "Economists have perhaps focused on moral hazard problems because of their interesting logical character rather than because of their empirical importance. It seems likely that uncertainty and model disagreement are greater obstacles to international cooperation."

10. For example, Mankiw and Shapiro (1986) find that the standard deviation of the revision from the preliminary estimate of the real growth rate to the final number is 2.2 percentage points.

11. Kenen and Schwartz (1986) have studied the accuracy of current year forecasts by the IMF *World Economic Outlook* for the last fifteen years. They find that the root mean squared error among the Summit Seven countries is 0.773 percentage points for real growth and 0.743 percentage points for inflation. These prediction errors, relatively small, are in themselves large enough to reverse the signs of the derivatives of the welfare function equations (2)–(5). Errors would presumably be much larger for the horizons of two years or more that are probably most relevant for policymaking. (Many major international econometric models show the effects of monetary and fiscal policy peaking in the second year in the case of output, and not reaching a peak within six years in the case of the price level or current account. See Bryant et al. 1988.)

12. Economists disagree as to the correct estimate of the natural rate of unemployment or the level of potential output, for example.

13. Another unexpected development in the late 1970s was the downward shift in the demand for money in the United States. This disturbance, like the oil shock, meant that the planned growth rate of money turned out ex post to be more inflationary than expected.

14. One way to obtain estimates for the weights is to follow Oudiz and Sachs (1984), who assume that as of 1984 policymakers were optimizing their objective functions in a Nash equilibrium, and infer the welfare weights that they must have had in order to produce the observed outcomes for output, inflation, and the current account. The estimates turn out to be very sensitive to such things as the model of the economy that the policymakers are assumed to have. (To equate the inferred weights with the correct rates, as Oudiz and Sachs do, of course requires not only that the policymakers were indeed seeking to optimize in a Nash equilibrium in that particular year, but also that they know the correct model, the correct weights, and the correct position of the economy relative to the optimum.)

15. The German view that the 1978 Bonn Economic Summit entailed joint reflation which, in retrospect, was inappropriate has been used above to illustrate, alternatively, uncertainty about the baseline forecast (the unanticipated oil shock of 1979) or uncertainty about the objective function (the proper weight to be placed on inflation versus growth). A third possible interpretation is model uncertainty: the Germans believe that the slope of their aggregate supply curve turned out to be steeper than they,

or at least the Americans, thought it would at the time. This interpretation is plausible if one believes that the German labor market is characterized by a high degree of real wage rigidity, as was pointed out by Branson and Rotemberg (1980).

16. See the volume edited by Bryant et al. (1988).

17. For example, if capital mobility is sufficiently low and a depreciation of the domestic currency is contractionary for the foreign country.

18. A reduction in interest rates causes a net capital outflow which, under a floating exchange rate, implies an increase in the current account balance.

19. In the case where the weights are uniform, each policymaker is playing by the same "compromise" model. One possible way of interpreting such a compromise on the model is as a type of cooperation that consists of negotiating over the correct view of the world rather than negotiating over policies. See Frankel (1988a). Kenen (1987, 8–9) and Bryant (1987, 8) stress that exchange of information is a useful function of international cooperation broadly defined.

20. Ghosh and Masson (1989) examine the implications of having the policymakers update their models in a Bayesian way, an interesting extension of the original problem.

21. In any case it would not hurt to try the count on the subset of cases where the countries believe that both will gain. I have not yet done this for all ten models (100 combinations). But the tables in Frankel and Rockett (1988) can be used to do the count for four models. Out of the sixteen combinations, eight cases are eliminated if it is assumed that coordination does not take place when one partner thinks that the other would lose by the proposed package. Out of the eight remaining "sustainable" cases, and the corresponding thirty-two possible outcomes, the United States turns out to gain in twenty-four cases and the rest of the OECD in twenty-two cases. These are only slightly better odds in favor of coordination than result when all combinations are considered admissible.

22. This list did not appear in the communiqué, but rather in comments to the press by U.S. Treasury Assistant Secretary David Mulford. Funabashi (1988, esp. 130ff.) offers a fascinating account of the machinations of the G–7 mechanism from 1985 to 1987.

23. *IMF Survey* (26 September 1988): 292.

24. "Rebuilding an International Monetary System," *Wall Street Journal,* 23 February 1988, p. 28.

25. To take a recent example, in the Baker-Miyazawa Agreement reached in San Francisco in September 1986 (and subsequently broadened to include the Federal Republic of Germany and the other countries at the Louvre in February 1987), the Japanese apparently agreed to a fiscal expansion in exchange for a promise from the U.S. Treasury Secretary that he would stop "talking down" the dollar (plus the usual U.S. promise to cut the budget deficit). In the months that followed, each side viewed the other as not living up to the agreement. (The episode is described in Funabashi 1988). But it was difficult for anyone to verify the extent of compliance, because the precise terms of the original agreement had not been public.

26. See Krugman (1988) for the application of the latest "smooth pasting" technology to this problem.

27. Dornbusch and Frankel (1988, sec. III.6).

28. It is clear from Funabashi (1988) that the various members held differing views as to which indicators were most important, what responses were called for if indicators strayed from the agreed-upon path, and how binding the agreement should be. It is also clear that each was able to interpret the Plaza and Louvre agreements afterwards so as to reflect his own views.

29. Williamson and Miller (1987) address the $n - 1$ problem.

30. Williamson and Miller (1987, 54–55) and Miller and Williamson (1988) do precisely this: assume that there is a large "fad" component to exchange rate fluctuations under the current floating regime, and that it would disappear under their target zone

proposal. (The idea is not absurd. But it certainly "stacks the deck" in an empirical comparison of the two regimes.)

31. Indeed there is some evidence that the prices of gold and other commodities react instantaneously to changes in expectations regarding whether monetary policy will be tight or loose in the future. (Frenkel and Hardouvelis 1985.)

32. Another of Frenkel, Goldstein, and Masson's (1988) arguments against the claim that the gains from coordination are small is to cite results of Currie, Levine, and Vidalis (1987) to the effect that a comparison of the cooperative equilibrium *allowing scope for governments to establish reputations* with the analogous noncooperative equilibrium shows large gains to coordination.

33. For example, Giavazzi and Pagano (1988).

34. Dornbusch and Frankel (1987) note some qualifications, relevant for the U.S. political process, to this standard view of protectionist pressures.

35. Besides subtracting from total GNP that part going to the foreign sector (the trade balance), it might also be a good idea to subtract that part going to inventories as suggested by Gordon (1985).

36. The Williamson-Miller blueprint also specifies that the G-7 should set the *average* level of their interest rates so as to attain a target for the *aggregate* level of their GNPs. This part of their plan is similar to part (a) of my proposal. It is my part (b), cooperative yearly setting of each country's nominal demand target to be attained primarily through monetary policy, that differs the most from their plan (aside from my treatment of exchange rate stability as a separable issue).

37. For attempts to evaluate empirically the stabilizing properties of the blueprint plan, see Miller and Williamson (1988) and Frenkel, Goldstein, and Masson (1988, 33–49). Frenkel and Goldstein (1986) survey target zone proposals. Miller and Williamson also consider a floating rate regime and the McKinnon (1984) proposals to use monetary policy to target the aggregate money supply—or in a later version the aggregate price level—among the G-3 countries. McKibbin and Sachs (1988) also compare these regimes. As yet, I am not aware of empirical work evaluating the likely outcome if countries cooperatively set nominal GNP targets (and use monetary policy to attain them).

38. A related objection is that a plan for using monetary policy to target nominal GNP would have done little to prevent the major disequilibrium that arose in the early 1980s, the U.S. budget and trade deficits. But I agree with Feldstein (1983) that this disequilibrium was not a "coordination failure," that the U.S. administration did not to any extent pursue the policies it did as a result of insufficient expansion by trading partners. Indeed the administration did not even want Europe and Japan to expand, until after 1985. No international bargain would have brought about a U.S. fiscal correction. Only a recognition by the administration and Congress of the link between their fiscal policies and the trade deficit (together with the political will necessary to make difficult budget choices) would have done so. By the same token, neither INT nor any other proposals for coordination should now be allowed to distract attention from the point that the most important policy changes to be made in 1989 can be made unilaterally by the United States. Such thoughts are supported by the findings in Frankel and Rockett (1988) and Frankel (1988a) that the gains from coordination are usually smaller than the gains from the United States discovering the true model and unilaterally adjusting its policies accordingly.

39. A number of authors, including Rogoff (1985c) and Giavazzi and Giovannini (1988), have pointed out that European plans to decrease both the remaining degree of exchange rate flexibility and the remaining level of barriers to financial integration may run into trouble if the individual countries are not ready to give up their remaining policy independence.

40. Dornbusch and Frankel (1988) discuss ten proposals for world monetary reform. Four entail decentralized policy rules: new classical fatalism, a gold standard, national

monetarism, and national nominal income targeting as discussed in section 3.2.1. Four foresee enhanced coordination: the G-7 indicators as discussed in section 3.2.2, Williamson's target zones, McKinnon's "world monetarism," and the Hosomi Fund. Two propose enhanced independence: the Tobin tax on transactions and the Dornbusch proposal for a dual exchange rate.

41. "A New Collar for Currency Markets," *The International Economy* (May/June 1988): 36–38. (See also *Wall Street Journal,* 25 September 1987, p. 22.)

42. In the case of Europe, it seems that a unified currency is the ultimate goal (and a strengthened role for the ecu is considered the first step). In August 1988, a European Community summit meeting agreed to establish a committee that would study creation of a monetary union and to examine the issue at a Madrid meeting scheduled for June 1989. See Casella and Feinstein (1988) for a theoretical analysis.

References

Barro, Robert. 1986. Recent developments in the theory of rules versus discretion. *The Economic Journal* 96, 23–37.

Barro, Robert, and David Gordon. 1983. A positive theory of monetary policy in a natural rate model. *Journal of Political Economy* 91, no. 4 (August): 589–610.

Bean, Charles. 1983. Targeting nominal income: An appraisal. *Economic Journal* 93 (December): 806–19.

Boughton, James. 1989. Policy assignment strategies with somewhat flexible exchange rates. In B. Eichengreen, M. Miller, and R. Portes, eds., *Blueprints for exchange rate management.* London: Academic Press.

Branson, William, and Julio Rotemberg. 1980. International adjustment with wage rigidity. *European Economic Review* 13, no. 3 (May): 309–37.

Brittan, Samuel. 1987. *The role and limits of government.* rev. ed. London: Wildwood House.

Bryant, Ralph. 1987. Intragovernmental coordination of economic policies: An interim stocktaking. In P. B. Kenen, ed., *International monetary cooperation: Essays in honor of Henry C. Wallich.* Essays in International Finance no. 169. Princeton: International Finance Section, Princeton University.

Bryant, Ralph, et al. 1988. *Empirical macroeconomics for interdependent economies.* Washington, DC: Brookings Institution.

Casella, Alessandra, and Jonathan Feinstein. 1988. Alternative monetary systems between two countries. Paper written for conference on European monetary integration, Castelgandolfo, Italy, June.

Corden, W. Maxwell. 1983. The logic of the international monetary nonsystem. In F. Machlup, G. Fels, and H. Muller-Groeling, eds., *Reflections on a troubled world economy: Essays in honor of Herbert Giersch,* 59–74. London: St. Martin's Press.

Currie, David, Paul Levine, and Nicholas Vidalis. 1987. International cooperation and reputation in an empirical two-bloc model. CEPR Discussion Paper Series no. 198 (July). London.

Dornbusch, R., and J. Frankel. 1988. The flexible exchange rate system: Experience and alternatives. NBER Working Paper no. 2464. Cambridge, MA: NBER. In S. Borner, ed., *International finance and trade in a polycentric world.* London: Macmillan, 1989.

Feldstein, Martin. 1983. The world economy. *The Economist* (June 11).

———. 1988. Distinguished lecture on economics in government: Thinking about international economic coordination. *Journal of Economic Perspectives* 2, no. 2 (Spring): 3–13.

Fischer, Stanley. 1988a. Rules vs. discretion in monetary policy. NBER Working Paper no. 2518 (February). Cambridge, MA: NBER.

———. 1988b. International macroeconomic policy coordination. In M. Feldstein, ed., *International policy coordination*. Chicago: University of Chicago Press.

Frankel, Jeffrey. 1988a. *Obstacles to international macroeconomic policy coordination*. IMF Working Paper no. 87/28. *Studies in International Finance* no. 64 (December). Princeton: Princeton University.

———. 1988b. International capital mobility and exchange rate variability. In N. Fieleke, ed., *International payments imbalances in the 1980s*. Boston: Federal Reserve Bank of Boston.

———. 1988c. A proposal for policy coordination: International nominal targeting (INT). In N. Fieleke, ed., *International payments imbalances in the 1980s*. Boston: Federal Reserve Bank of Boston.

———. 1989. Quantifying international capital mobility in the 1980s. NBER Working Paper no. 2856. Forthcoming in D. Bernheim and J. Shoven, eds., *Saving*. Chicago: Univ. of Chicago Press.

———. 1990. International nominal targeting (INT): A proposal for overcoming obstacles to policy coordination. UC Berkeley Working Paper no. 90-135, January. Forthcoming in J. McCallum and R. Mundell, eds., *Global disequilibrium*. Montreal: McGill-Queen's Univ. Press.

Frankel, Jeffrey, and Gikas Hardouvelis. 1985. Commodity prices, money surprises, and Fed credibility. *Journal of Money, Credit and Banking* 17, no. 4 (November): 425–38.

Frankel, Jeffrey, and Alan MacArthur, 1988. Political vs. currency premia in international real interest differentials: A study of forward rates for 24 countries. *European Economic Review* 32: 1083–1121.

Frankel, Jeffrey, and Katharine Rockett. 1986. International macroeconomic policy coordination when policy-makers disagree on the model. NBER Working Paper no. 2059 (October). Cambridge, MA: NBER.

———. 1988. International macroeconomic policy coordination when policymakers do not agree on the true model. *American Economic Review* 78, no. 3 (June): 318–40.

Frenkel, Jacob, and Morris Goldstein. 1986. A guide to target zones. *IMF Staff Papers* 33, no. 4 (December).

Frenkel, Jacob, Morris Goldstein, and Paul Masson. 1988. International coordination of economic policies: Scope, methods and effects. Conference on National Economic Policies and Their Impact on the World Economy, International Monetary Fund, May.

Friedman, Benjamin. 1984. The value of intermediate targets in implementing monetary policy. In *Price stability and public policy,* 169–91. Kansas City, MO.: Federal Reserve Bank of Kansas City.

Friedman, Milton, and Anna Schwartz, 1963. *A monetary history of the United States, 1867–1960*. Princeton: Princeton University Press.

Funabashi, Yoichi. 1988. *Managing the dollar: From the Plaza to the Louvre*. Washington, DC: Institute for International Economics, May.

Ghosh, Atish, and Paul Masson. 1988. International policy coordination in a world with model uncertainty. *IMF Staff Papers* 35 (June).

Ghosh, Atish, and Paul Masson. 1989. Model uncertainty, learning, and the gains from coordination. International Monetary Fund (May).

Ghosh, Swati. 1987. International policy coordination when the model is unknown. M. Phil. Thesis, Oxford University.

Giavazzi, Francesco, and Alberto Giovannini. 1988. *Limiting exchange rate flexibility: The European Monetary System.* Cambridge, MA: MIT Press.

Giavazzi, Francesco, and Marco Pagano. 1988. The advantage of tying one's hands: EMS discipline and central bank credibility. *European Economic Review* 32 (June): 1055–82.

Gordon, Robert. 1985. The conduct of domestic monetary policy. In A. Ando and others, eds., *Monetary policy in our times,* 45–81. Cambridge, MA: MIT Press.

Hall, Robert. 1985. Monetary policy with an elastic price standard. In *Price stability and public policy.* Kansas City, MO: Federal Reserve Bank of Kansas City.

Holtham, Gerald, and Andrew Hughes Hallett. 1987. International policy coordination and model uncertainty. In R. Bryant and R. Portes, eds., *Global macroeconomics: Policy conflict and cooperation.* London: Macmillan.

Hosomi, T. 1985. Toward a more stable international monetary system. In T. Hosomi and M. Fukao, *A second look at foreign exchange market interventions.* Tokyo: Japan Center for International Finance.

Kenen, Peter. 1987. Exchange rates and policy coordination. Brookings Discussion Papers in International Economics no. 61 (October). Washington DC: Brookings Institution.

Kenen, Peter, and Stephen Schwartz. 1986. An assessment of macroeconomic forecasts in the International Monetary Fund's world economic outlook. Working Paper in International Economics no. G-86-04 (December). Princeton: Princeton University.

Krugman, Paul. 1988. Target zones and exchange rate dynamics. NBER Working Paper no. 2481 (January). Cambridge, MA: NBER.

Kydland, F., and E. Prescott. 1977. Rules rather than discretion: The inconsistency of optimal plans. *Journal of Political Economy* 85 (June): 473–91.

Levine, Paul, David Currie, and Jessica Gaines. 1989. Simple rules for international policy agreements. In B. Eichengreen, M. Miller, and R. Portes, eds., *Blueprints for exchange rate management.* London: Academic Press.

McCallum, Bennett. 1987. The case for rules in the conduct of monetary policy: A concrete example, Federal Reserve Bank of Richmond. *Economic Review* (September/October): 10–18.

———. 1988a. Robustness properties of a rule for monetary policy. Revised in K. Brunner and A. Meltzer, eds., Carnegie-Rochester Conference Series on Public Policy (February).

———. 1988b. The role of demand management in the maintenance of full employment. NBER Working Paper no. 2520 (February). Cambridge, MA: NBER.

McKibbin, Warwick, and Jeffrey Sachs. 1988. Coordination of monetary and fiscal policies in the industrial economies. In Jacob Frenkel, ed., *International aspects of fiscal policies,* 73–120. Chicago: University of Chicago Press.

McKinnon, Ronald. 1984. *An international standard for monetary stabilization.* Washington, DC: Institute for International Economics.

———. 1988. Monetary and exchange rate policies for international financial stability. *Journal of Economic Perspectives* (Winter): 83–103.

Mankiw, Gregory, and Matthew Shapiro. 1986. News or noise: An analysis of GNP revisions. *Survey of Current Business* (May): 20–25.

Meade, James. 1984. A new Keynesian Bretton Woods. *Three Banks Review* (June).

Miller, Marcus, and John Williamson. 1988. The international monetary system: An analysis of alternative regimes. Centre for Economic and Policy Research Discussion Paper no. 266 (July). *European Economic Review* 32, no. 5 (June): 1031–48.

Mundell, Robert. 1962. The appropriate use of monetary and fiscal policy under fixed exchange rates. *IMF Staff Papers* 9 (March): 70–77.

Oudiz, Gilles, and Jeffrey Sachs. 1984. Macroeconomic policy coordination among industrial economies. *Brookings Papers on Economic Activity* 1: 1–75.

Rogoff, Kenneth. 1985a. Can international monetary policy coordination be counter-productive? *Journal of International Economics* 18: 199–217.

————. 1985b. The optimal degree of commitment to an intermediate monetary target. *Quarterly Journal of Economics* 100 (November): 1169–89.

————. 1985c. Can exchange rate predictability be achieved without monetary convergence?—Evidence from the EMS. *European Economic Review* 28 (June/July): 93–115.

————. 1987. Reputational constraints on monetary policy. In K. Brunner and A. Meltzer, eds., Carnegie-Rochester Conference Series on Public Policy 26 (Spring, Supplement to the *Journal of Monetary Economics*).

Taylor, John. 1985. What would nominal GNP targeting do to the business cycle? Carnegie-Rochester Conference Series on Public Policy 22: 61–84.

Williamson, John. 1983. *The exchange rate system.* Washington, DC: Institute for International Economics.

Williamson, John, and Marcus Miller. 1987. *Targets and indicators: A blueprint for the international coordination of economic policy.* Policy Analyses in International Economics no. 22 (September). Washington, DC: Institute for International Economics.

Comment   Ralph C. Bryant

A General Reaction to the Paper[1]

I found this paper stimulating. It contains many observations that strike me as sensible and interesting. And I was gratified to see that Frankel seems to be subtly shifting gears in his research on the problems of international cooperation. (Note, however, that there is some disjuncture between the first and second halves of the paper. The "new Frankel" only appears in the second half after paying obeisance to the old Frankel in the first half.)

Despite sharing many of the views expressed in the paper, I also find myself in disagreement on a number of points. The general drift of his argument takes Frankel to a position that I cannot share. Frankel advocates, it seems to me, a second, or even third, best position on the subject of intergovernmental coordination of economic policies; he believes that a first best approach cannot work, and hence that the first best is the enemy of the attainable second best. I am more optimistic about making progress, albeit slowly, toward a first best approach. So on balance I come out in rather a different place on how nations should be trying to cooperate with each other about macroeconomic policies.[2]

"Uncertainty" and the Obstacles It Poses for Coordination

In section 3.2 of the paper, Frankel stresses the obstacles to cooperation and coordination that stem from model uncertainty.[3] For my taste, he oversells some of the points and has some of the nuances wrong.

Ralph C. Bryant is a Senior Fellow in the Economic Studies program at the Brookings Institution in Washington, DC.

Uncertainty about sign of spillover effects.   For example, he exaggerates the degree of our ignorance about the consequences of policy actions. He asserts flat-footedly that models are all over the block in what they say about the effects of one country's policy actions on other countries. In this paper, as in several of his other papers (for example, Frankel and Rockett 1988), he argues that policymakers cannot even be sure of the signs of various cross-border spillovers. He points especially to monetary policy (see his table 3.1), stating that "the effects on all three target variables [output, price level, and trade balance] in the other country are completely ambiguous in sign."

In my opinion, there is no significant empirical ambiguity about the sign of the spillover effects of fiscal actions for the major industrial countries. Fiscal expansions cause an appreciation of the own-country currency and lead to an expansion of real activity abroad (vice versa for fiscal contractions). For a large majority of models, the "positive" transmission is substantial in the first three years following a fiscal action.[4]

Frankel is literally correct about the signs of the monetary policy spillover effects: some are small negative, and some are small positive. But he ought to acknowledge the more important point that the magnitude of the effect, of whatever sign, is probably quite small. Even theory suggests that the effects might be fairly small.[5] The 1986 Brookings conference results, which are the ones cited in his table 3.1, showed that the absolute sizes of monetary spillover effects tend to be empirically small. Further results from later conferences, such as the one at the Federal Reserve in May of 1988, confirm that conclusion. For the time being, the best guess one can make about the consequences of monetary actions on output in foreign countries is to assume a zero effect. The implications for potential policy coordination of that generalization are less dramatic than Frankel suggests.

Is coordination just as likely to make things worse?   Frankel answers this question: possibly yes. Here is another place where, for my taste, he has been overselling his conclusions. In the Frankel and Rockett (1988) paper, the analysis is too much of a mechanical bean-counting exercise. It classifies outcomes as welfare increasing or reducing merely by looking at the signs of the effects; it gives very small gains or losses the same weight as large gains and losses. Even in the final version of the analysis as published in the *American Economic Review,* which does include a discussion of treating policymakers' attitudes about the models as uncertain, this rather mechanical classification persists.

Frankel mentions but then downplays some recent important research by Ghosh and Masson (1988a, 1988b). Ghosh and Masson conclude that model uncertainty, far from precluding policy coordination, may in fact provide a strong incentive for countries to coordinate their macroeconomic policies (a conclusion virtually the opposite from that reached by Frankel). There is much more validity in the Ghosh and Masson analysis, I believe, than Frankel's brief discussion acknowledges.

Similarly, Frankel remains doubtful about making a distinction between "strong bargains" and "weak bargains," as suggested by Holtham and Hughes Hallett (1987). I believe that this distinction is significant and that taking it into account somewhat mitigates the proposition that attempts at policy coordination could make things worse rather than better.[6]

Possible gains from the "mere" exchange of information.   Another respect in which Frankel and I differ is on the gains from consultation and information exchange. These gains could include sizable benefits from consultations about differences among analytical models, with a resulting convergence of analytical views (Bryant 1987). Such gains as have resulted from intergovernmental meetings in the past can in large part be attributed to "mere" consultations. I believe that the potential gains of this sort could be considerable and deserve greater weight than Frankel gives to them. Others such as Feldstein (1988) are even less prone than Frankel to give such points adequate due.

An overall judgment.   As a series of recent papers by Frankel and other authors have emphasized, it is of course possible that attempted coordination of economic policies could be mistaken and lead to welfare losses. In particular, if policymakers use a seriously incorrect model, they are likely to get into hot water and do damage to welfare. But this conclusion is scarcely surprising or controversial!

Moreover, what practical options are open to policymakers in a world in which all models are highly uncertain? They plainly do not have the option of not using any model at all—unless they believe that sucking their thumbs is an acceptable substitute. Policymakers cannot set all their policy instruments at "zero" settings, so to speak, and just decide to have no policy at all. Cross-border spillovers will exist, and may sometimes be large, even if the policymakers decide to ignore such effects when they make decisions.

All things considered, I am unwilling to go along with Frankel in stressing model uncertainty as a reason for hesitating to encourage greater cooperative efforts among national governments about their macroeconomic policies.

Nominal GNP Targeting: A Variant of an Intermediate-Target Strategy

I come now to the part of Frankel's paper putting forward his proposal for nominal income targeting.

The first point deserving attention is that Frankel's proposal is essentially a variant of what in the domestic monetary literature is known as an intermediate-target strategy. This is true both for the closed-economy variants of nominal GNP targeting and for Frankel's suggestion to use nominal GNP targets as the focus for international coordination.

The basic features of an intermediate-target strategy are essentially different from strategies that focus directly on the ultimate targets of policy. In an intermediate-target strategy, policymakers select a variable to use as a surrogate ("intermediate") target that (1) is thought to have a "reliable" relationship to the variables that are the ultimate targets of policy, and (2) will be capable of being fairly closely "controllable" by the policy authority. Furthermore, policymakers decompose the complete decision problem they face into two stages, with different periodicities of decision-making for the two stages. At a first stage, reasoning backwards from their ultimate-target variables, they decide on the path for the surrogate target only infrequently—for example, only once a year. In the second stage, however, they vary the instruments of policy much more continuously in the shorter run, focusing attention on deviations of the intermediate-target variable from its selected path.

Why a Nominal GNP Targeting Strategy is Problematic in a Purely "Domestic" Context

One serious problem with a two-stage, intermediate-target strategy is the inevitable trade-off between the reliability criterion and the controllability criterion. The two criteria point in opposite directions. The more reliable a variable is in its linkages to the ultimate-target variables, the less easily and closely it can be controlled by the adjustment of policy instruments. Conversely, the more closely an intermediate variable is tied to policy instruments, the more complex and numerous the behavioral relationships between it and the ultimate-target variables. There is no way out of this dilemma, and no one ideal intermediate-target variable. The price that has to be paid for selecting a surrogate target that can be controlled closely is to accept greater uncertainty about the links between the surrogate and the ultimate targets, and vice versa.[7]

Why, it must be asked, should policymakers put themselves in the box of focusing on only one surrogate target as the focus of their short-run decisions? There are a variety of conceivable justifications that have been advanced, mainly in connection with using one or another definition of the money stock as the surrogate target. An information-flow justification asserts that such a strategy makes better use of up-to-date information about the economy. An uncertainty justification asserts that such an approach copes better with uncertainty about how the economy functions. Two other possibilities are a game-theoretic, expectational justification (announcing a surrogate target induces favorable effects on private sector behavior) and an "insulation" justification (surrogate targets insulate policy from the short-run vagaries of the political process or from the incompetence of policymakers).

None of these conceivable justifications is analytically convincing when subjected to analysis. Several of them have been shown to be flatly wrong.[8] Logically, there is no need to focus on a single intermediate variable. Multiple ultimate targets, the use of a variety of intermediate variables as indicators, and a direct emphasis on the actual instruments of policy do *not* pose difficult analytical problems. For any given degree of model uncertainty—that is, basic uncertainty about the behavioral relationships that link instruments to ultimate-target variables—policymakers can always do at least as well if they implement policy with a single-stage strategy as with a two-stage, intermediate-target strategy.

Paradoxically, Frankel sees the disadvantage of using the money stock as an intermediate target and is a vigorous critic of so doing. I believe he gives far too little weight to the analogous arguments that undercut his case for nominal GNP targeting. I can agree with him that a nominal domestic-demand target would be preferable, internationally and domestically, to a monetary aggregate target, or an exchange rate target, *if policymakers were to choose to focus on only one variable as a target.* But the premise is unfortunate: I cannot see any valid reason for policymakers to constrain their choice problem in that manner.

I dislike the Frankel INT strategy for another reason, stemming from its likely treatment of fiscal policy. Advocates of nominal GNP targeting typically think of monetary policy as *the* instrument of macroeconomic policy. It is all very well to speak about monetary policy needing to focus on a "nominal anchor." I too believe that monetary policy needs to pay a lot of attention to nominal anchors. But there are large problems if fiscal policy is immobilized, particularly if it is thought that monetary policy can exclusively focus on nominal variables.

I have never been able to understand why some enthusiasts can discuss nominal GNP targeting for monetary policy without ever bringing up the question of how monetary policy does or does not mesh with budgetary policy. I am even a holdout for the old-fashioned view that central banks should be concerned with real as well as nominal targets. And I certainly am a holdout for the view that monetary and fiscal policies ought to be formulated in a coordinated way. The American economy, just like an automobile, cannot feasibly be divided up into separate parts, with one driver given control of the gas pedal and a second driver allocated the brakes. No doubt it would be an easier and more manageable world if monetary policy and fiscal policy could be compartmentalized so that the Federal Reserve could be told to worry exclusively about inflation, while the administration and Congress could exclusively worry about real growth and employment. But, alas, the world is not that simple. The actions of the Federal Reserve influence real growth and jobs, not only prices. Fiscal actions influence inflation as well as real growth. It is therefore no "solution" to the problems of economic policy to tell the Federal Reserve to pay attention exclusively to nominal variables while the administration and Congress worry about output and jobs. That is especially true if the Federal Reserve and the administration have differing preferences about what the national objectives ought to be!

International surveillance through nominal GNP targeting.   Essentially the same objections apply to the idea of countries jointly using nominal GNP targeting. There is no good reason to focus just on one variable in the international context either. The case for using a common intermediate-target variable as the focus of cooperation across countries is no more persuasive than the case for using a surrogate intermediate target domestically.[9]

An Evolutionary "First-Best" Vision

Frankel's paper argues for international cooperation beginning "on a small scale" and then having it "grow as the degree of political consensus grows." This incremental approach strikes me as politically sound, and I share with Frankel the conviction that progress is likely to come in this evolutionary way. Frankel infers, however, that this "epsilon-small by epsilon-small" approach supports his proposal for nominal income targeting. I do not see that inference as compelling. On the contrary, I believe that incremental progress is equally consistent with other visions of how international cooperation might proceed.

My own alternative, first-best vision would have the following elements. Each of the national governments participating in the process would submit projections of the baseline outlook (either with own-country policies unchanged, or incorporating policy changes that have already been decided upon). Each projection would preferably be derived from some analytical framework ("model") that tries to be internally consistent. An individual government would concentrate most on projecting the key macroeconomic variables pertaining to its own economy. But each government would also be free to submit projections for other economies if it chose to do so. An international institution that provides the secretariat for "surveillance" (extensive monitoring of the process) would also provide its own baseline projections of the outlook for each major country or region. One may think of the IMF World Economic Outlook and the OECD Economic Outlook exercises as nascent prototypes of such surveillance.

Which variables—"indicators"—would be focused upon in these projections? In principle, a variety would be projected and evaluated, not merely one or two. Equally important, the actual instruments and the ultimate-target variables of national policies would both feature prominently in the projections. In no sense would the exercise focus only on intermediate, indicator variables.

Then, in addition to the baseline projections, the exercise would typically consider "what if" simulations. Such simulations would examine what would be the consequences if this or that policy instrument were to be changed. Similarly, the questions would be asked: What if such and such a nonpolicy shock were to occur? Changes resulting from these hypothetical policy and nonpolicy alterations would be measured relative to the baseline outlook. Such "what if" scenarios would be prepared, at a minimum, by the international secretariat. Ideally, national governments would also be interested in preparing their own "what if" simulations, for changes in their own policy instruments especially, but even for changes in other governments' policy instruments and for various nonpolicy shocks. (Differences in preferred models would of course lead to differences in the answers to the "what if" questions.)

At periodic meetings of policymakers and/or their deputies, the discussions would examine both the baseline-outlook projections and the "what if" scenarios. No less important, the discussions would involve frank exchanges of information on what individual governments' goals were. Efforts would be made to classify differences in baseline projections and "what if" scenarios according to whether they were due to differences in goals, differences in preferred models, or differences in assumptions about nonpolicy shocks.

The international secretariat would play, and would be acknowledged as playing, a key analytical role. In particular, the secretariat would catalyze a systematic comparison of the prior meetings' ex ante projections with new information about how the ex post outcome was turning out. And the secretariat would try to use judiciously chosen, "what if" scenarios to catalyze mutually supportive changes in policies.

A rudimentary variant of the preceding vision of intergovernmental cooperation does not seem to me beyond reach at the present time. Efforts along these lines might be amenable to evolutionary strengthening no less than Frankel's nominal income targeting. Indeed, on days when I am feeling optimistic, I even think that the last few years of G-7 discussions have been hesitantly groping in this direction.

To be sure, on my pessimistic days, I fear that actual discussions in G-7 meetings have focused primarily on "exchange rate cooperation" and have *not* been edging toward this vision of what could happen. The Louvre Accord of February 1987, if one can accept the account of it by Funabashi (1988), suggests an example of poorly conceived cooperation not consistent with the first-best vision.[10]

Having disagreed with Frankel on several points, I want to agree strongly with him on questions of more public disclosure of projections, targets, and intentions for using policy instruments. Surely it ought to be possible for the G-7 finance ministers to authorize a somewhat fuller and more candid description of what the surveillance process is at the current time and how they might see it evolving in future years!

Economists' Public Discussions of Intergovernmental Cooperation

To conclude, I want to put forward a proposal of my own, for better balance in what we economists say in public about the subject of international "cooperation" and "coordination" of national economic policies.

An unfortunate dynamic seems to have crept into our public debates. Broad conclusions about the merits and demerits of intergovernmental cooperation have been polarized. For example, Jeff Frankel has tended to emphasize the negative aspects and the potential for harm. Martin Feldstein has gone especially far in that direction. The opposite leaning, emphasizing the positive aspects and the potential for benefits, has been characteristic of others—for example, Jacob Frenkel and his co-authors in recent papers. I, too, have tended to stress the positive aspect.

As Bill Branson and Stanley Fischer also observed at the conference itself, perhaps economists just relish arguing with each other, particularly about intergovernmental cooperation and coordination. Yet my proposal is that we should be more on our guard against this polarizing tendency. Little is served by exaggerating our analytical disagreements, especially in discussions before nonspecialized audiences who are not familiar with all the caveats to the polarized positions. In fact, I believe, there is less dispersion of views among us than the wider public has been led to believe. Why not let that situation shine through in public discussions?

Notes

1. The original version of Frankel's paper was entitled "A Modest Proposal for International Nominal Targeting (INT)," resembling the title of Jonathan Swift's 1729 famous satire ("A modest proposal for preventing the children of poor people in Ireland from being a burden to their parents or country . . .''). Accordingly, the original version of my comments began with some observations about the witting or unwitting following of J. Frankel in J. Swift's footsteps. Because Frankel subsequently altered his title, I have deleted my original opening remarks.

2. I use "cooperation" to refer to the entire range of activities through which national governments might collaborate; "coordination" refers to the more ambitious forms of cooperation in which governments mutually adjust their behavior after bargaining consultations. For discussion, see Bryant (1987) or Horne and Masson (1988).

3. Note that the bulk of section 3.2, despite its title of "Overcoming Obstacles," is really about the obstacles, not about overcoming them.

4. The only models suggesting that fiscal expansions depreciate the own-country currency and/or have negative effects on foreign real activity are known to be defective (in particular, because they fail to allow adequately for capital mobility). For further discussion, see Bryant et al. (1988, ch. 3) and Bryant, Helliwell, and Hooper (1989).

5. For a fiscal action, the effects from income/absorption changes and expenditure switching both work in the same direction on the current balance of the originating country, and also on output in foreign countries. The total effect is the sum of both gross effects. In contrast, for a monetary action, the income/absorption and the expenditure-switching effects work in opposite directions, suggesting that the total effect—a net sum of two gross effects with differing signs—could be small.

6. In all bargains that can be reached, each party expects to gain: his own model predicts that gains will occur. In "strong" bargains, each party expects to gain according to the *other* party's model as well as his own. In contrast, in a "weak" bargain, one or both of the parties will be disappointed if the other party's model proves to be correct. Frankel's discussion of the argument made by Holtham and Hughes Hallett is not persuasive to me, but I do not have space to rebut Frankel's position here.

7. Frankel emphasizes the need for policymakers to be able to monitor "performance" of the surrogate-target variable. But he fails to stress that nominal GNP has

terrible characteristics from this perspective: how can policymakers tell whether changes in countries' nominal GNPs are due to policy actions or to unexpected nonpolicy shocks?

8. My comments here summarize an argument I have made carefully elsewhere (Bryant 1980, 1983).

9. Frankel would prefer to use total nominal domestic demand rather than nominal GNP if his general approach could be adopted internationally. On this point, he is unambiguously right. For the reasons he summarizes, if national governments were to go down his second-best road, they should do so by focusing on total domestic demand, not GNP.

10. In passing, note that Frankel gives a minor nod in the direction of the first-best vision by admitting that "epsilon-small" evolutionary cooperation could take the form I have outlined. But he then, unconvincingly, goes back to his theme that a long list of indicators is a bad thing and that incrementalism requires focusing on a single variable, nominal GNP.

References

Bryant, Ralph C. 1980. *Money and monetary policy in interdependent nations.* Washington, DC: Brookings Institution.

_____. 1983. *Controlling money: The federal reserve and its critics.* Washington, DC: Brookings Institution.

_____. 1987. Intergovernmental coordination of economic policies: An interim stocktaking. In P. B. Kenen, ed., *International monetary cooperation: Essays in honor of Henry C. Wallich.* Essays in International Finance no. 169 (December). Princeton: International Finance Section, Princeton University.

Bryant, Ralph C., John F. Helliwell, and Peter Hooper. 1989. Domestic and cross-border consequences of U.S. macroeconomic policies. Brookings Discussion Paper in International Economics no. 68 (January). Washington, DC: Brookings Institution; also circulated as Federal Reserve Board Discussion Paper in International Finance no. 344 (March 1989).

Bryant, Ralph C., Dale W. Henderson, Gerald Holtham, Peter Hooper, and Steven A. Symansky, eds. 1988. *Empirical Macroeconomics for Interdependent Economies.* Washington, DC: Brookings Institution.

Feldstein, Martin. 1988. Thinking about international economic coordination. *Journal of Economic Perspectives* 2 (Spring): 3–13.

Frankel, Jeffrey A., and Katherine Rockett. 1988. International macroeconomic policy coordination when policymakers do not agree on the true model, *American Economic Review,* 78, no. 3 (June): 318–40.

Funabashi, Yoichi. 1988. *Managing the dollar: From the Plaza to the Louvre.* Washington, DC: Institute for International Economics, May.

Ghosh, Atish R., and Paul R. Masson. 1988a. International policy coordination in a world with model uncertainty. *IMF Staff Papers* 35 (June).

_____. 1988b. Model uncertainty, learning, and the gains from coordination. Typescript (rev. December).

Holtham, Gerald, and Andrew Hughes Hallett. 1987. International policy coordination and model uncertainty. In R. Bryant and R. Portes, eds., *Global macroeconomics: Policy conflict and cooperation.* London: Macmillan.

Horne, Jocelyn, and Paul R. Masson. 1988. Scope and limits of international economic cooperation and policy coordination. *IMF Staff Papers,* 35 (June).

Comment   Douglas D. Purvis

Jeffrey Frankel's paper presents a number of interesting and challenging analytical points and opinions on the potential for international coordination of macroeconomic policies. It has not triggered an especially cogent response from me, but rather a number of somewhat disconnected thoughts on the subject. This response is due partly to the nature of the views presented in his paper—which I found difficult to understand as a coherent package. But my response also reflects my own admitted ambivalence on the issue. To pursue the not entirely semantic point raised in the first session at this conference, I support international *cooperation* broadly conceived, but—for reasons similar to those already put forward by Stanley Fischer and Martin Feldstein in earlier sessions of this conference, and indeed in a number of Jeff Frankel's own writings on the subject—I remain skeptical about the benefits of tighter forms of international policy *coordination*.

In what follows, I will use the term *cooperation* to describe the ongoing informal processes involving consultation and the exchange of information, while reserving the term *coordination* to describe more explicit attempts to design and implement economic policies at the international level. Of course, there is nothing that rules out cooperation leading to policies that differ in important ways from those that would have been followed in the absence of cooperation, but the key difference is that policy changes are not formally negotiated in some international forum.

My own ambivalence on the issue of coordination stood me in good stead as I tried to digest Frankel's proposal. One particularly unsettling aspect of his paper is that it devotes a great deal of space to presenting a persuasive discussion of the obstacles to successful international coordination of policies, and then goes on to develop a case for international nominal targeting (INT) as a strategic first step towards international policy coordination. The immediate question that arises is: what if one found both arguments convincing? How could one reconcile a negative perspective on "full coordination" with a case for taking the first step toward that goal? Frankel's paper does not address this question, in part because it is completely silent about what the ultimate goal of "full coordination" actually looks like. In that respect, I am reminded of the immortal words of that great American philosopher, Yogi Berra: "If you don't know where you are going, you might end up somewhere else."

Before discussing some of the specifics of Frankel's paper, I want to note an irony in the literature on policy coordination. Interest in policy coordination is often motivated by the observation that the flexible exchange rate system has somehow failed. Some of the evidence that is often adduced in support of this

Douglas D. Purvis is Professor and Head, Department of Economics at Queen's University and a member of the board of directors of the National Bureau of Economic Research.

view is that national macroeconomic policies are not nearly as independent as the standard theory predicts, and that business cycles remain closely synchronized internationally. Yet most proposals for coordination reinforce both of these outcomes! Of course, what is missing in my statement of the "irony" is that, in the absence of coordination, the outcome is achieved in conjunction with excessive exchange rate variability, while coordination attempts to limit such variability; in this regard I wish Frankel had not been so brief in his discussion in section 3.3, "Policy Independence and Exchange Rate Flexibility." The brevity of that section also undermines Frankel's discussion of the "Hosomi Fund"; the case for such a fund is not established, nor does there appear a serious discussion of how such a fund would actually operate or what it might reasonably be expected to achieve.

I now take up a number of specific questions raised by Frankel's proposal.

Absence of Consideration of the Monetary/Fiscal Mix

In developing his case for INT, Frankel explicitly sets aside questions of the monetary/fiscal mix, choosing instead to "address problems concerning the overall degree of expansion of macroeconomic policies, whether monetary and fiscal policies are too tight or too loose, rather than the proper mix of the two." I believe that this strategy is unfortunate for two related reasons.

First, the strategy ignores the different incentives that are created for policy reactions in one country by the choice of policy mix in its trading partners. Thus if Frankel's proposal for INT were adopted, *how* the United States achieved its nominal income target would strongly influence how the OECD countries would wish to react in order to achieve their targets. It is impossible for me to imagine the determination and implementation of acceptable targets proceeding without consideration of the policy mix.

Second, Frankel ultimately hangs his INT proposal on the issue of whether one views the shortcoming of the Nash noncooperative equilibrium as being one of either insufficient or excessive contraction. However, except for the inflation credibility issue—which in any event strictly applies only to monetary policy—the issue is perhaps better phrased in terms of excessive or insufficient short-term reaction of policy to disturbances rather than in terms of the average- or medium-term stance of the policy. Thus the "shortcomings" are perhaps better viewed in terms of the nature of the international spillovers created by domestic policy actions. If a particular policy has beggar-thy-neighbor effects on its trading partners, then that policy will tend to be used excessively in the absence of cooperation, while if a policy has beneficial effects on its trading partners, it will be used insufficiently. Whether these mean policy will be too contractionary or too inflationary depends upon the specifics of the situation, including the nature of the appropriate model, on the relevant history of the economies (i.e., on the state of the business cycle), and on the nature of the shocks hitting the system. Had the question been posed in this manner, the monetary/fiscal mix would have been a central issue, since the nature of the spillovers created by the two policies can be quite different, as can the appropriate domestic response of each to any particular shock.

These points are illustrated clearly by the experience of the OECD countries in the early 1980s. It can be argued that the sharp monetary contraction in the United States was essentially beggar-thy-neighbor in its effects on the other OECD countries, serving primarily to "export" U.S. inflation via real appreciation. Those countries reacted to their increased inflation by adopting tight monetary policies; the business cycle was harmonized not because the effects of the U.S. disinflation were generalized but because the U.S. policy was mimicked by her major trading partners. Clearly the international repercussions would have been dramatically different had the U.S. achieved the same nominal income using fiscal contraction! (This is taken up in detail in my paper "Public Sector Deficits, International Capital Movements and the Domestic Economy: The Medium-Term is the Message," *Canadian Journal of Economics* 18, no. 4 [November 1985].)

Further, I would also suggest that not distinguishing between monetary and fiscal policies may bias the case for nominal income targeting; if, for example, the paper had focused on monetary policy, a good case could have been made for targeting only the inflation rate rather than nominal income.

The Perceived Obstacles to "Full" Coordination

Section 3.2, a major section of Frankel's paper, is called "Overcoming Obstacles to Coordinated Expansion or Contraction." In fact, the title of the section is highly misleading as most of the discussion is devoted to showing how powerful the obstacles are and gives little attention to the issue of how to overcome them. The discussion is thoughtful and persuasive; in many places one is surprised at how "operational" the perspective is. But lurking just beneath the surface is the macroeconomic F-word; what is presented is a compelling case against "fine-tuning." I, for one, am convinced of the case, and indeed much of my suspicion of proposals for international policy coordination arises from the belief that most proposals involve thinly disguised fine-tuning and hence are doomed to the failures that have rewarded virtually all previous such efforts.

Other than reiterating my basic concerns about where Frankel's proposal is taking us, I have only a couple of minor comments on this section; in the spirit of cooperation if not coordination, I leave the discussion of the implications and interpretation of the results of the empirical international modeling exercises to Ralph Bryant.

First, the discussion of model uncertainty might be dismissed (perhaps wrongly) by many readers as "quibbling" about details while at the same time masking more fundamental disagreements. One obvious example is the "two solitudes" that have characterized American official positions and those of most other countries about the "twin deficits." A related issue is the controversy that surrounds the neo-Ricardian proposition that deficits do not matter; as Stanley Fischer reminded us in the opening discussion, this controversy is central to most other branches of modern macroeconomics but is conspicuously absent from discussion at this conference.

Second, I worry that in some circumstances the international cooperation process sometimes leads to too much convergence. Officials sometimes fall into the trap of too readily accepting superficial and politically convenient explanations of important events. The "party line" is easy to repeat or let go unchallenged, and this can impede proper analysis and response to important problems.

A third reaction I have is to Frankel's discussion of the G-7 "indicators" exercise. One can interpret the indicators as simply putting some structure on the cooperative process of consultation and information exchange. Alternatively, one can think of the list as a series of targets which govern the coordination of policies and by which policy is judged after the fact. Frankel's discussion tends to the latter interpretation, and as a result the G-7 exercise gets failing grades as an exercise in coordination. I am more sympathetic to the former interpretation, and I think in that light the G-7 exercise can be rated more positively as an exercise in cooperation. Certainly Frankel's identification of indicators with targets colors his whole discussion of the post-Tokyo G-7 activities.

Finally, despite the attention given to the technical issues, it becomes clear that the most serious obstacle to international coordination—indeed the only one that appears ultimately to matter—is the perceived loss of national sovereignty. It is for this reason that Frankel proposes a "gradual" evolution toward coordination starting with the INT; the argument is that the perceived loss of sovereignty from such a modest initiative will be small while the gains will provide the basis for gradually expanding the degree of coordination. My view is that, if I were to accept the ultimate objective of "full coordination," I would worry that the gradual approach would be too risky. The initial gains (both perceived and actual) would be too small, while the perceived loss of sovereignty would be so large as to undermine domestic political support for the exercise. In many countries the finance minister returning home to announce and defend a target for domestic nominal income growth negotiated with officials and politicians from other countries is simply unacceptable.

Two Circumstances Where Cooperation Is Essential

Two circumstances (not identified by Frankel), where cooperation if not in fact coordination might be justified, warrant attention.

The first is when one country, for whatever reason, changes its medium-term objectives and thus initiates a dramatic change in policies. This could happen for example in response to changes in domestic political or economic circumstances. But whatever the cause, the change will have far-reaching implications for the country's trading partners, and in turn their reaction will have important implications for world economic performance. As a result, this is an occasion where extensive consultation and information exchange might have a big payoff. Further gains will be possible if the consultative process gives the policy initiative credibility both with the other governments and with domestic agents; in the best of all worlds, the credibility will be further enhanced by the policy reactions of the other countries. Again the international experience with the sharp disinflation initiated in the United States in the early 1980s serves to illustrate this point. In my view, the other OECD countries reacted to the American initiative in a manner that had unfortunate consequences for the world economy; more extensive cooperation might have mitigated some of the output loss and unemployment that arose from the worldwide monetary contraction.

The second is in the event of international crises, financial and otherwise. The joint response of the major OECD countries in the face of the worldwide stock market crash of October 1987 is widely recognized to have mitigated the repercussions of that crash. It seems clear that the lines of communication that had been established over the previous few years—in the summit process, in G-5, G-7 and G-10 meetings, and through the forums at the IMF and the OECD—were important in facilitating the cooperation required for that response. Similarly, the eleventh-hour negotiations that led to successful negotiation of the Canada–U.S. Free Trade Agreement were heavily dependent on the close working relationship that had evolved between Canadian Minister of Finance Michael Wilson and U.S. Treasury Secretary James Baker, a relationship that was built up in the G-7 process.

These two circumstances are relevant in that many commentators think that in the next few months the world economy will experience one or the other. The election of a new U.S. president in late 1988 will usher in a new era in the international economy, and a common view is that the new president will have to alter the medium-term stance of U.S. fiscal policy by addressing the federal deficit, or that world financial markets will become unstable. In either case, substantial international cooperation would be in order, and at least the lines of communication are open.

Concluding Remarks

How then to evaluate Jeffrey Frankel's proposal. If one were somehow forced to accept some form of coordination, then I think that Frankel's INT is an attractive option. For example, I feel much more comfortable with it than I do with those proposals that set out explicitly to directly limit exchange rate variations, especially real exchange rate variations. But I also recall Yogi Berra's admonition noted earlier, and I would feel more comfortable with Frankel's proposal for INT if it represented the actual ultimate desired form of coordination rather than simply the first step toward some vague fuller form of coordination.

4   Equilibrium Exchange Rates

Paul R. Krugman

In the three years since the Plaza Accord the central bankers and finance ministers of the large industrial nations have come to a consensus in favor of exchange rate management. For better or for worse, it is now taken as a matter of course that the G-5 countries will at any given time form a collective view about the appropriate levels of nominal exchange rates, and make at least some effort to stabilize actual rates in the vicinity of those appropriate rates. Admittedly, what we have at the moment are "soft, quiet" rather than "loud, hard" target zones—that is, the zones are not publicly announced, nor is there great determination to defend them in the face of strong market pressures. That means that the zones are still a long way from a restoration of fixed rates. Yet in a muted form the de facto target-zone regime of the late 1980s does pose many of the traditional difficulties of any regime in which governments actively attempt to set the exchange rate.

The most basic of these difficulties is that of objective: what are the appropriate target exchange rates? At the time of the Plaza Accord, there was general agreement that the dollar needed to go lower (although only a few months before the U.S. administration had been claiming the strong dollar as a sign of successful economic policies). The question since has been where to stop. In a long-established fixed rate system, historical parities provide a natural focal point for policy coordination, and the problem of assessing equilibrium rates arises only when parity adjustment forces itself on reluctant policymakers. In the present situation, however, the effort to stabilize exchange rates requires making a judgement about appropriate levels more or less from scratch.

Paul R. Krugman is professor of economics at the Massachusetts Institute of Technology and a research associate of the National Bureau of Economic Research.

The purpose of this paper is to discuss the issues raised in an effort to determine equilibrium exchange rates that may be appropriate targets for coordinated policies. I do not here attempt to address the question of whether it makes sense to have exchange rate targets at all, which would bring a number of additional issues into the picture; of course to the extent that equilibrium rates are found to be either hard to assess or unstable, this helps load the scales against trying to fix rates. The main focus, however, is on the hypothetical situation of a group of policymakers, such as the G-5 ministers, who have decided for better or worse to try to stabilize currencies around some agreed central rates. What considerations should enter into their choice of central rates? What problems of assessment should they be concerned about, and what methods are most likely to give reasonable answers?

The paper is in four parts. The first addresses the broad conceptual issue of what is meant by an equilibrium rate, and the reasons why target rates might differ from the current market rates on the eve of monetary agreement. The second part examines the extent to which equilibrium rates may be expected to show long-run trends; this issue is important both because an exchange rate regime needs somehow to accommodate such trends and because secular trends in equilibrium rates complicate the problem of guessing at the right rates during a transition to greater exchange rate stability. The third part examines the role of exchange rates in the process of narrowing international current account balances, reviewing and (I hope) settling some disputes that have arisen over the respective roles of fiscal and exchange rate adjustment in this process. The final part of the paper addresses the practical issues of assessment: how do we make a good guess at equilibrium exchange rates, and where might we go wrong?

4.1   The Meaning of Equilibrium Exchange Rates

The idea that one ought to attempt to calculate an equilibrium real exchange rate—with the implicit view that this rate may be different from the actual current rate—is itself controversial. In the years prior to the Plaza, then-Undersecretary Beryl Sprinkel repeatedly asserted that the equilibrium exchange rate is whatever the actual market rate is at this moment. His statement was of course true in the sense that the exchange market is pretty much continuously clearing. What advocates of some deliberate policy toward the exchange rate believe is not that there is literal disequilibrium in the market, but something more complex.

Briefly put, when we talk of the "equilibrium exchange rate" as something different from the current rate, we usually mean two things. First is that the equilibrium *real* exchange rate at some time in the future will be foreseeably different from today's real exchange rate. Second is that policy toward the *nominal* exchange rate can somehow facilitate the adjustment toward this future real exchange rate. Thus the question of whether it makes sense to calculate equilibrium real exchange rates as a basis for policy breaks into two subquestions: are there predictable and analyzable sources of real exchange rate shifts, and can nominal exchange rate policy facilitate such shifts?

4.1.1   Sources of Shifts in the Equilibrium Real Exchange Rate

Real Shocks

There is universal agreement on the principle that real events can change equilibrium real exchange rates, which are after all relative prices like any others. The sources of dispute are how large and how frequent such shocks are.

One possible source of shifts in equilibrium real exchange rates is the presence of secular trends due to differences in rates of technological change, differences in product mix, and so on. The potential presence of secular trends in the real exchange rate is of crucial importance and is given separate treatment below.

Aside from such long-run trends, the major source of real shocks to equilibrium exchange rates seems likely to be commodity-price shocks. For the G-5 countries, which are all primarily exporters of manufactures, such shocks cannot have the same importance that they do for primary exporters, but differences in resource position may mean that equilibrium rates are affected significantly nonetheless. In particular, a fall in the price of oil should presumably lower the equilibrium real exchange rate of self-sufficient Britain, while raising that of import-dependent Japan.

Capital Flows

A more controversial source of shifts in equilibrium real exchange rates is shifts in international capital flows.

Suppose that for some reason a country is the temporary recipient of substantial capital inflows. This might be because of an investment boom generated by technological change or resource discoveries, because of changes in tax laws, or because of a bulge in government deficits. Whatever the source, the capital inflows will normally be spent domestically to some important extent, raising the demand for nontraded goods produced domestically and also (perhaps) raising the relative price of a country's goods on world markets. To the extent that the capital flows are predictably temporary, there will be a prospective decline in the equilibrium real exchange rate. The relevance of this example to the U.S. case is of course obvious.

Why is this controversial? There are serious problems in deciding which capital flows are transitory and likely to trail off in the near future, and which are going to be long-term features of the landscape. For example, is Japan's current account surplus a temporary bulge, to be followed by a return to the much more modest surpluses of the pre-1980 period, or is Japan going to be a twentieth-century equivalent of nineteenth-century Britain, consistently exporting several percentage points of GNP in capital for decades to come? A case can be made for either view. Also, economists can legitimately disagree about the substitutability of traded goods produced in different countries, and about the substitution between traded and nontraded goods within each country, leading to uncertainty about how large a real exchange rate change is needed to accommodate a given capital flow.

In addition to these legitimate controversies, however, there is also considerable sheer confusion about the relationship between real exchange rates and capital flows, the result of a failure by many economists to understand the meaning of the saving-investment identity. Like the long-run trend in exchange rates, this is a topic that requires further discussion and is given a section of its own.

Nominal Shocks

Most policymakers and many economists believe that real exchange rates can be temporarily pushed away from their long-run equilibrium values by nominal shocks, such as changes in monetary policy or, for that matter, pegging of nominal exchange rates at levels that imply disequilibrium real exchange rates at current price levels. Perhaps the most famous example in theory is the Dornbusch (1976) model, in which a monetary expansion leads temporarily to a large nominal depreciation that both exceeds and precedes the subsequent price increase. During the adjustment implied by the Dornbusch model, we would see a depreciation and then a subsequent appreciation of the real exchange rate.

The view that nominal shocks produce temporary disequilibrium real exchange rates depends on the belief that nominal prices are at least somewhat sticky in terms of domestic currency (more on this below). Aside from direct testing of this proposition, however, there is also the question of whether such nominal sources of real exchange rate movements are important in practice. An implication of nominal stickiness models of real exchange rate fluctuations is that such fluctuations should be temporary; the Dornbusch model, for example, is often taken to imply that the real exchange rate should follow a first-order autoregressive process. Yet a number of studies have been unable to reject the hypothesis that in the floating rate period real exchange rates have followed a random walk. This result is often taken as evidence that whatever the possible role of nominal shocks, in practice real exchange rate movements must represent primarily more-or-less permanent real shocks.

While appealing, this argument is wrong. In fact, the failure to find clear evidence of autoregression of real rates in the floating rate period does not demonstrate that nominal shocks are unimportant as sources of real exchange rate fluctuations. Instead, it should be viewed as a demonstration of the difficulty of discovering evidence of structural characteristics of the economy using theory-free time series methods. Quite strong autoregression in economic terms might well produce a time series that cannot be rejected as a random walk without many years of data; and the evidence is beginning to show that this is precisely what has happened with data on the real exchange rate.

A full-fledged treatment of this issue has been produced recently by Huizinga (1987). It may be useful, however, to have a semiformal treatment that makes the point to those (like myself) who are less than fully versed in the time series methods. (This exposition closely follows Frankel 1989.)

Consider, then, a situation in which the real exchange rate, measured as a deviation from its long-run equilibrium level, follows a process

(1) $x_t = bx_{t-1} + e_t,$ $0 < b < 1,$

where e is an i.i.d. random variable with variance s^2. We may pose the "random walk" question as follows: how much data would we need to reject the hypothesis $b = 1$?

A crude approach to this would be to simply estimate b using ordinary least squares, and apply a t-test. It is by now familiar that this is not quite right, since under the null hypothesis that $b = 0$ the assumption of boundedness for the right-hand-side variable is not valid. Even though this is not the right test, however, it is illuminating (at least to me) to see what we can expect by way of standard errors on b when the true value is something less than one.

In a regression with only one independent variable, the true variance of the estimate of b is

$$\text{var}(b) = s^2/[N \, \text{var}(x)],$$

where N is the number of observations. In turn, the variance of x generated by the process described is $s^2/(1 - b^2)$. Thus it turns out that the variance of the estimate is independent of the volatility of the shocks generating exchange rate fluctuations; it is simply equal to

$$(1 - b^2)/N.$$

Now consider what a fairly high degree of price stickiness might imply. Suppose that we are working with annual data and that $b = 0.8$—that is, the "half-life" of a nominal shock is five years. This is not an unreasonable number if one tries substituting typical estimates of the slope of the Phillips curve into an IS-LM model. Then the variance of the estimate of b will be $0.36/N$.

In order to put the true b two standard deviations away from one, the variance of the estimate will need to be reduced to $(0.1)^2 = 0.01$. This will require thirty-six years of data! Thus it should be no surprise that the floating rate period has not yielded enough evidence to reject the hypothesis of no mean reversion.

Nor are very long time series necessarily the answer (although Jeffrey Frankel has found that with a very long time series on the real dollar-pound rate, strong mean reversion can in fact be confirmed; see Frankel 1989). In long series, any drift in the real exchange rate over time will be correlated with the lagged rate, and a regression of the form of equation (1) will end up largely telling us this; in effect, by omitting variables representing structural change, one will end up biasing the results in such a way as to miss the mean reversion.

It is somewhat ironic that, given the way the failure to reject a random walk has been used in doctrinal debate, a random walk will be harder to reject the stickier are prices, and hence the more slowly the real exchange rate reverts to its long-run equilibrium. In a way, therefore, it is arguable that the high degree of persistence in real exchange rates found since 1973 is in fact evidence that fairly inflexible prices are the rule, and that therefore nominal shocks in fact have very large effects on real exchange rates.

This brings us, however, to the question of price behavior. Sometimes debates over exchange rate theory and policy are seen as simply another round in the eternal struggle between equilibrium and sticky price theories of macroeconomics. This is not entirely right; some of the crucial issues are not contingent solely on one's view about how prices behave. However, the question of whether nominal rate changes help facilitate real exchange rate changes is crucial to the subject of this paper and needs some discussion.

4.1.2   Nominal and Real Exchange Rates

Most economists would now agree that in the long run the real exchange rate is a real phenomenon, not affected by nominal currency parities. How one gets to the long run, however, may depend very much on nominal parities. If one pegs the nominal exchange rate at a level that, given current price levels, does not produce the long-run real exchange rate, then that long-run rate must be established through some combination of inflation in the undervalued countries and deflation in the overvalued.

How costly is this process? Even if one believed in high flexibility of prices, one might prefer to adjust the exchange rate in order to preserve a greater degree of domestic price stability; this was essentially the position of Friedman (1953) in his classic defense of floating rates. However, the willingness of governments to defend nominal parities depends critically on their view about how much price rigidity there is in domestic currency. If prices were perfectly flexible, of course, wages and prices would move continuously and instantly to clear markets. Even if prices were not totally flexible, however, one could imagine a world in which residents of each country regarded themselves as part of a world economy, where national boundaries made little difference, and where workers and firms therefore tried to set prices and wages in a way that indexed them against exchange rate changes (as actually happens in "dollarized'' economies like that of Israel a few years back). In such a world, exchange rates would have little real significance, since a nominal exchange rate change would simply have the effect of producing some combination of inflation in the depreciating country and deflation in the appreciating country. The neutrality of nominal exchange rates is a key theme of ''global monetarists'' such as McKinnon (1984), McKinnon and Ohno (1986), and Mundell (1987), sometimes expressed in the slogan that the exchange rate is the relative price of two moneys, *not* the relative price of two goods or two kinds of labor.

In fact, however, the experience of floating rates in the 1980s—a period of relatively low inflation differentials among the major industrial countries—has given very clear evidence in favor of the view that prices are substantially rigid in domestic currency. Consider figures 4.1 and 4.2, which show the U.S. nominal exchange rate (actually an average index against other OECD countries) versus an index of U.S. relative unit labor costs (using the same weights) and an index of the price of U.S. exports compared with the export prices of the rest of the OECD. It turns out that the nominal exchange rate has very nearly been the relative price of two kinds of labor, and of two goods as well.

Why is this true? Without taking a long detour into the new microfoundations of Keynesian economics, we may state the basic point briefly. Whether because of menu costs or bounded rationality, firms do not constantly change their prices and wage offers in response to changes in demand, nor do they index their prices optimally. Instead, they fix prices in nominal terms for fairly

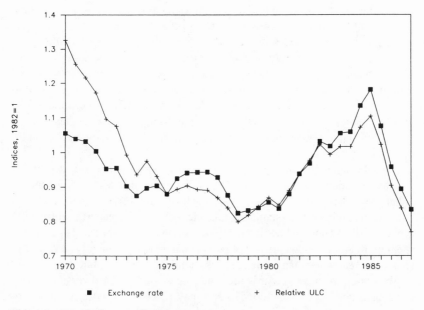

Fig. 4.1 Nominal vs. real exchange rate

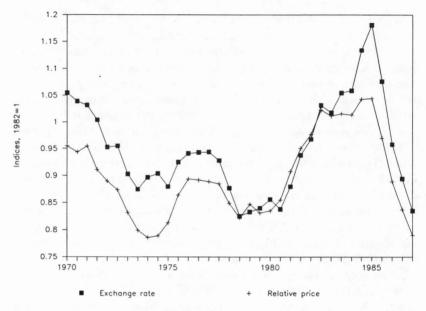

Fig. 4.2   Nominal vs. real exchange rate

long periods—and the overlapping pricing decisions of thousands of price-setters create substantial inertia in the overall level of wages and prices.

The important addendum for international economics is that when prices are set in nominal terms, they are set in terms of domestic currency. In principle, this needn't happen. Prices in the Federal Republic of Germany could be set in dollars, or prices in Italy in ecu; the medium of exchange and the unit of account functions of money can be, and sometimes are, separated. In advanced countries, however, prices are sufficiently predictable that there is no need to turn to a foreign currency for a usable standard, unlike the situation in hyperinflation countries. And the fact is that domestic currency has a much more predictable purchasing power for residents of every advanced country than any foreign currency.

The only major objection to this evidence that makes any sense is the argument that the causation is actually running the other way—that what really happens is that real exchange rates are moving around for real reasons, and that the attempt of monetary authorities to stabilize domestic price levels creates the correlation between real and nominal rates. This view is often buttressed by an appeal to the apparent random-walk character of real exchange rates, which is taken as evidence that real rather than nominal shocks dominate exchange rate movements.

We have seen, however, that the evidence against mean reversion in real exchange rates is not well founded and may indeed be used as evidence of more, not less, price rigidity. There is also a question of plausibility. What were the real shocks that raised the equilibrium relative price of U.S. labor by

15 percent from the first half of 1984 to the first half of 1985, then drove it down by 20 percent over the following year?

There is also a further piece of evidence of the importance of nominal exchange rates. This is the way that changes in the exchange regime are strikingly reflected in changes in the behavior of real exchange rates. Suppose that one believed that real exchange rates were a real phenomenon, not affected by nominal rates. Then there would be no particular reason why a change in the exchange rate regime should alter the behavior of real exchange rates. In particular, one would expect real exchange rates to be no more variable under floating rates than under fixed.

Figure 4.3, which is borrowed from Rudiger Dornbusch and Alberto Giovannini, shows monthly changes in the real exchange rate (using wholesale prices as deflators) between the U.S. and Germany from 1960 to 1986. That is, the first half of this figure shows the experience under fixed rates, the second half under floating rates. The variance of monthly changes in this real exchange rate was fifteen times as large in the second half of the sample as in the first.

In sum, then, there is at this point overwhelming evidence that nominal exchange rate changes do in the short run produce real exchange rate changes, and that the effects on the real exchange rate are quite persistent. The implication of this for the discussion of exchange rate policy is clear. First, if policymakers know where the equilibrium real exchange rate is headed, they can greatly facilitate adjustment by allowing or inducing nominal rates to move in that direction. Second, getting nominal rates wrong can be very costly because it may take a long time for the equilibrium real rates to get themselves established.

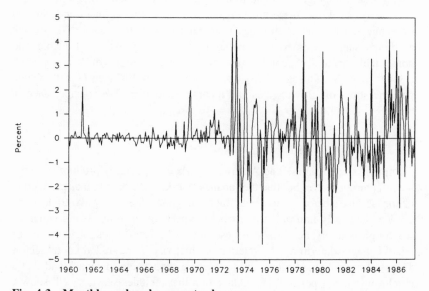

Fig. 4.3 Monthly real exchange rate changes

4.2   Long-run Trends in Equilibrium Real Exchange Rates

Even though the evidence is now pretty clear that there is a strong element of mean reversion in real exchange rate behavior, long-run secular trends in equilibrium real rates still pose crucial problems for exchange rate stabilization. These problems are of two kinds. First, even a functioning system can be ripped apart if the secular trends run too quickly. Suppose, for example, that we could correctly estimate the sustainable dollar-yen rate at the present instant to be 130, and that we are prepared to adjust the central parity in line with relative inflation. We will still find ourselves in trouble if there is a secular appreciation of the equilibrium real yen that raises the equilibrium yen, even after correcting for differential inflation, to ninety within five years. Arguably it was the secular decline in the equilibrium real dollar that really broke up Bretton Woods: the overvaluation of the dollar in 1971 owed little to a faster U.S. inflation rate since 1960, and much to a decline in the real dollar compatible with international equilibrium.

Even more important than the question of drift in the future equilibrium rate is the problem of getting the rates right to start with. By any historical standard, the real yen looks extremely high right now. Yet Japan continues to run huge current account surpluses. What most econometric evidence suggests is that the explanation lies in a rapid secular upward trend in the equilibrium real yen. If correct, this interpretation tells us that the pace of secular change has been rapid enough to make the usual indicators of competitiveness useless over only an eight-year period.

It is important, then, to get at the determinants of long-run trends in equilibrium real exchange rates and to have some idea of their likely future path.

Broadly speaking, there are two major theories of secular trends in real exchange rates. First is the theory associated with Balassa (1964), which attributes such trends to differential productivity growth in tradable and nontradable sectors. Second is the alternative, more Keynesian approach associated with Johnson (1958) and Houthakker and Magee (1969), which puts the stress on growth rates and income elasticities. We consider each in turn.

4.2.1   Tradables versus Nontradables

Suppose that Japanese and American workers are equally productive in the manufacturing sector, but that the Japanese workers are only half as productive in the service sector. Since manufactured goods are generally traded and services generally nontraded, we would expect, other things being equal, to see rough equality between Japanese and U.S. wage rates, that is, to see relative wages determined by relative productivity in the traded goods sector. This will mean that services will be twice as expensive in Japan, and that a purchasing power parity (PPP) calculation that includes services will show a apparently overvalued yen. More to the point, if Japanese productivity growth continues to be concentrated in manufacturing to a greater extent than is the case for the United States, there will be a secular drift in the equilibrium real exchange rate if services are included in the deflators.

This is the essence of the differential productivity argument for trends in equilibrium real exchange rates. It was introduced by Kravis and Balassa both to explain trends in real exchange rates and to explain absolute differences in the cost of living across countries at a point in time. Marston (1987) has shown that interpretation of movements in the real exchange rate between the United States and Japan in the 1973–83 period must be heavily qualified by this Kravis-Balassa effect because Japanese productivity growth was so heavily concentrated in traded goods industries.

While the tradable-nontradable approach to trends in equilibrium real exchange rates identifies an important reason for secular trends, it is not a complete story. The reason is that changes in the relative price of tradables and nontradables would be the only source of real exchange rate changes only if PPP held over time for traded goods. As we have seen, however, in figure 4.2, there are large short-run swings in the relative prices even of exportables. Admittedly, it is possible to conceive of models in which large deviations from PPP for traded goods occur in the short run yet the law of one price for tradables holds in the long run; indeed, we will describe such a model below. Yet this need not be the case if countries in fact produce different mixes of goods. In practice there are several cases in which PPP for traded goods seems to be clearly violated in the long run. The United States has appeared to need significantly lower relative export prices in the late 1970s and 1980s in order to balance its trade than it needed in the late 1960s. Japan, on the other side, has a very strong currency by historical standards even when traded goods prices rather than more aggregated indices are used as the basis for the calculation, yet it continues to run large current surpluses.

To think about the role of shifts in traded goods PPP, it is necessary to shift to an alternative approach, one that emphasizes the imperfect substitution among exportables from different industrial countries.

4.2.2   Income Elasticities and Secular Trends

Although much theoretical literature in international economics is set in a general equilibrium framework with fairly complex production structures and many relative prices, the workhorse of practical trade balance analysis is still, as it was a generation ago, the partial equilibrium analysis of trade flows that are assumed to depend on real income and a single relative price. This framework can be defended as a pretty close approximation to a more carefully specified framework in which expenditure as well as income enters into import demand; in any case, since this framework is still the way most practical analysis is done, it will be used as the starting point here without much apology.

Consider, then, a two-country world in which we define y, y^* as domestic and foreign real output, p, p^* as the prices in local currency of these outputs, and e as the price of foreign currency in terms of domestic. Define $r = ep^*/p$ as the real exchange rate, which is in this case the price of foreign relative to domestic goods. Then the standard trade balance model may be written as follows. Export volume depends on foreign output and the relative price of domestic goods:

$$(2) \qquad\qquad x = x(y^*, r).$$

Import volume depends on domestic income and the relative price of imports:

$$(3) \qquad\qquad m = m(y, r).$$

The trade balance (in domestic currency) may be written

$$(4) \qquad\qquad B = px - ep^*m = p(x - rm),$$

so that the trade balance in terms of domestic output is simply

$$(5) \qquad\qquad b = x - rm.$$

Now it was pointed out in the 1950s by Johnson (1958) that if the framework given by equations (2)–(5) is a reasonable description of trade balance determination, then economic growth is likely to require secular changes in real exchange rates. To see why, define the following. Let z_x = income elasticity of demand for exports; z_m = income elasticity of demand for imports; e_x = price elasticity of demand for exports; e_m = price elasticity of demand for imports; y' = rate of growth of domestic output, that is, $(dy/dt)/y$; $y^{*\prime}$ = rate of growth of foreign output; and r' = rate of real depreciation.

Now differentiate equation (4). We have

$$(6) \qquad db/dt = x(z_x y^{*\prime} + e_x r') - rm[z_m y' + (1 - e_m)r']$$

Suppose that initially $b = 0$, so that $x = rm$. Then in order to keep a zero trade balance, we must have

$$(7) \qquad\qquad z^x y^{*\prime} - z^m y' + (e^x + e^m - 1)r' = 0.$$

This implies a trend in the real exchange rate of

$$(8) \qquad\qquad r' = (z_m y' - z_x y^{*\prime})/(e_x + e_m - 1)$$

Equation (8) immediately identifies two reasons why there may be a trend in the equilibrium exchange rate: either countries may face different elasticities of import and export demand, or they may have different long term rates of growth. More generally, there will be a trend in the real exchange rate unless

(9) $z_x/z_m = y'/y^{*'}$,

which we would a priori imagine to be unlikely.

Econometric estimates of trade equations along the lines of equations (2) and (3) generally find two things. First, price elasticities are fairly small. While a great deal of effort has gone into trying to push up price elasticity estimates, on the presumption that they are understated due to mismeasurement or long lags, standard estimates remain in the range 1–2. This implies that goods produced in different countries are quite imperfect substitutes, so that differences in growth rates or in income elasticities can produce large secular trends in relative prices. Second, there is indeed a wide spread of estimated income elasticities. Tables 4.1 and 4.4 present two sets of estimates of income elasticities: the Houthakker-Magee estimates from 1969 and a more recent set from Krugman (1988a). What is clear is that there is a very wide range of results.

So we might expect to find that strong trends in equilibrium real exchange rates even when only traded goods are considered will be the norm rather than the exception. However, inspection of very long time series shows that this is less true than one might expect. For example, Frankel (1989) has computed the real (CPI) exchange rate between Britain and the United States since 1870. Instead of a gradual secular drift, the series gives the definite impression of a persistent mean reversion, which leaves the real exchange rate little changed over more than a century.

Why does long-run PPP work as well as it does? The immediate answer is a systematic association between relative growth rates and apparent income elasticities, which I have called the "45-degree rule." The deeper explanation of the 45-degree rule is a more debatable issue.

4.2.3 The 45-Degree Rule

In 1969 Houthakker and Magee published a paper that remains a benchmark for comparative estimation of trade equations across a large number of countries. Their main conclusion was that there were large differences among countries in their relative income elasticities—specifically, that Japan faced the highly favorable combination of a high-income elasticity of demand for its exports and a low-income elasticity of import demand, while the United States and the United Kingdom faced the reverse. While Houthakker and Magee did of course notice that Japan was the fastest growing country in their sample, while the United States and the United Kingdom were the slowest, they did not explicitly consider the possibility that the differences in underlying growth rates were somehow systematically related to the differences in estimated income elasticities. Yet it is difficult to escape this conclusion. Table 4.1 presents the Houthakker-Magee income elasticity results for industrial countries, together with the growth rates of those countries over the period

Table 4.1   Income Elasticities and Growth Rates in the 1950s and 1960s

| Country | Income Elasticity | | | Growth rate, 1955–65 |
	Imports	Exports	Ratio	
United Kingdom	1.66	0.86	0.52	2.82
United States	1.51	0.99	0.66	3.46
Belgium	1.94	1.83	0.94	3.77
Sweden	1.42	1.76	1.24	4.18
Norway	1.40	1.59	1.36	4.41
Switzerland	1.81	1.47	0.81	4.66
Canada	1.20	1.41	1.18	4.66
Netherlands	1.89	1.88	0.99	4.67
Denmark	1.31	1.69	1.29	4.74
Italy	2.19	2.95	1.35	5.40
France	1.66	1.53	0.92	5.62
Germany	1.80	2.08	1.56	6.21
Japan	1.23	3.55	2.89	9.40

Source: Income elasticities from Houthakker and Magee (1969); growth rates from *International Financial Statistics.*

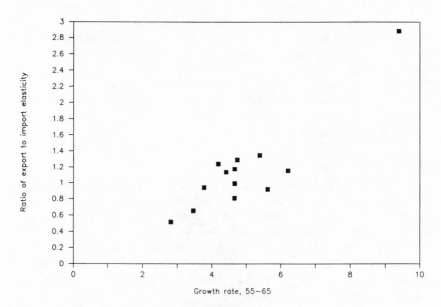

Fig. 4.4   Growth vs. elasticity ration, 1955–1965

1955–65. The relationship is striking; it becomes even more so when the ratio z_x/z_m is graphed against y', a plot shown in figure 4.4.

Basically, what the Houthakker-Magee results show is that equation (9) holds—that is, the ratio of income elasticities over their estimation period was such as to allow countries to have very different growth rates without strong trends in equilibrium real exchange rates. This may be confirmed more formally, by regressing the natural logarithm of the Houthakker-Magee elasticity ratio on the national growth rates:

$$\ln(z_x/z_m) = -1.81 + 1.210 \ln(y'),$$

$$(0.0208)$$

$$R^2 = 0.754, \text{ SEE} = 0.211.$$

In this regression we see that on average, if country A grew twice as rapidly as country B over the period 1955–65, then country A turned out to have an estimated ratio of export to import elasticities that was twice that of country B.

The result of this systematic relationship between growth rates and income elasticities was to make relative PPP hold much better than one would have expected if one assumed that income elasticities were identical, or distributed randomly. One might have expected Japan to need to have rapidly falling relative export prices in order to accommodate its extremely rapid economic growth—but the combination of high export elasticity and low import elasticity took care of that. One might have expected the United Kingdom to receive compensation for its low growth rate by a secular appreciation of its real exchange rate—but the combination of low export elasticity and high import elasticity deprived it of that benefit.

A similar though less clear-cut relationship between growth rates and income elasticities is apparent in more recent data. (The reason the result is less clear is probably that the spread of growth rates has narrowed.) Tables 4.2 and 4.3 report the results of a set of standard export and import equations estimated for industrial countries on annual data for the period 1971–86. The dependent variables are X = manufactures exports in 1982 prices and M = manufactures imports in 1982 prices. The explanatory variables are Y = GNP in constant prices; Y^* = foreign GNP in constant prices, calculated as a geometric average of GNP in fourteen industrial countries, weighted by their 1978 shares of the exporting country's exports; RXP = OECD index of relative export prices of manufactures; and RMP = relative price of manufactures imports, calculated as ratio of manufactures import unit value to GNP deflator.

All data are from OECD *Economic Outlook*. All equations were estimated in log-linear form; where severe serial correlation was evident, a correction was made.

By and large, these estimates look fairly decent; taken one at a time, they might suggest the need for more careful cleaning of data, addition of some extra variables, etc., but they would not discourage a researcher from using the income and price elasticity framework. The major exception is the United Kingdom, whose import equation refuses to make sense; I have not been able to resolve this puzzle, and will drop the United Kingdom from subsequent discussion.

Table 4.2   Estimates of Export Equations, 1971–1986[a]

Country	Coefficients on			SEE	R^2	D-W	ρ
	Y^*	RXP	RXP(-1)				
Austria	3.05	-0.56	-0.04	0.03	0.992	2.11	—
	(0.10)	(0.42)	(0.42)				
Belgium	1.24	0.39	-0.58	0.02	0.971	2.18	—
	(0.13)	(0.16)	(0.14)				
Canada	2.87	0.62	0.18	0.02	0.996	1.96	—
	(0.09)	(0.20)	(0.18)				
Germany	2.15	-0.32	-0.23	0.03	0.987	2.11	—
	(0.09)	(0.23)	(0.21)				
United Kingdom	1.30	0.00	-0.54	0.03	0.963	2.01	—
	(0.08)	(0.14)	(0.13)				
Italy	2.41	0.08	-0.31	0.04	0.982	1.61	—
	(0.11)	(0.19)	(0.20)				
Japan	1.65	-0.35	-0.53	0.06	0.978	2.19	0.81
	(0.80)	(0.18)	(0.21)				
Netherlands	3.86	-0.56	-0.20	0.03	0.980	1.46	0.94
	(0.66)	(0.22)	(0.29)				
United States	1.70	-0.44	-0.98	0.04	0.976	2.10	—
	(0.08)	(0.16)	(0.16)				

[a]All equations estimated on annual data, 1971–86. Standard errors.

Table 4.3   Estimates of Import Equations, 1971–1986

Country	Coefficients on			SEE	R^2	D-W	ρ
	Y	RMP	RMP(-1)				
Austria	2.94	-0.14	0.41	0.04	0.979	1.74	0.41
	(0.99)	(0.43)	(0.75)				
Belgium	1.99	-0.39	0.14	0.03	0.975	1.62	—
	(0.10)	(0.16)	(0.15)				
Canada	1.66	-0.79	-0.66	0.07	0.916	1.66	0.40
	(0.27)	(0.51)	(0.51)				
Germany	2.83	-0.33	0.24	0.03	0.988	1.24	0.54
	(0.26)	(0.20)	(0.26)				
United Kingdom	-0.20	1.03	-0.04	0.01	0.999	1.95	0.95
	(0.09)	(0.05)	(0.04)				
Italy	3.65	-0.51	-0.17	0.04	0.981	1.69	—
	(0.37)	(0.20)	(0.14)				
Japan	0.80	0.03	-0.45	0.12	0.928	1.51	—
	(1.19)	(0.29)	(0.38)				
Netherlands	2.66	-0.11	-0.11	0.02	0.987	2.13	0.79
	(0.46)	(0.14)	(0.19)				
United States	1.31	0.11	-1.04	0.08	0.957	1.62	—
	(0.44)	(0.34)	(0.36)				

What we may note, however, is that there is still, as in the Houthakker-Magee (1969) results, a systematic tendency for high-growth countries to face favorable income elasticities. Table 4.4 presents a summary of estimated income elasticities, their ratios, and growth rates (calculated by fitting trends to domestic and foreign GNP). When these results are plotted in figure 4.5, the result is less striking than for the Houthakker-Magee data in figure 4.4—partly because the spread of growth rates is smaller—but the upward-sloping relationship is still apparent. On average the 45-degree rule continues to hold, although with much less confidence:

$$\ln(z_x/z_m) = -0.00 + 1.029 \ln (y'/y^*),$$
$$(0.609)$$
$$R^2 = 0.322, \text{SEE} = 0.401.$$

Perhaps a more illuminating test is to look at the way in which estimates changed from the earlier period to the later period. In the 1950s and 1960s, as Houthakker and Magee (1969) noted, Japan was the country with highly favorable income elasticities, while the United States and the United Kingdom were the countries disfavored. In the 1970s and 1980s there was a general convergence of growth rates. European growth rates declined more than those of the United States, so that the United States grew almost as rapidly as its trading partners; Japan, though still fast growing, was not as far out of line as before. If there is some systematic reason why income elasticities seem to match relative growth rates, we should expect to find a decline in Japan's z_x/z_m ratio and a rise in that of the United States. And indeed we do find this: according to the estimates made here, Japan's ratio of elasticities, while still high, is lower in my estimates than in the Houthakker-Magee results, while the United States actually is estimated to have a z_x/z_m ratio greater than one.

Table 4.4   **Income Elasticities and Growth Rates, 1970–1986**

Country	Growth Rate of GNP			Income Elasticity		
	Domestic	Foreign	Ratio	Exports	Imports	Ratio
United States	2.49	2.91	0.86	1.70	1.31	1.30
Netherlands	1.96	2.17	0.90	3.86	2.66	1.45
Germany	2.10	2.23	0.94	2.15	2.83	0.76
Belgium	2.15	2.19	0.98	1.24	1.99	0.62
Italy	2.56	2.37	1.08	2.41	3.65	0.66
Austria	2.63	2.08	1.26	3.06	2.60	1.18
Canada	3.59	2.55	1.41	2.87	1.66	1.73
Japan	4.15	2.37	1.75	1.65	0.80	2.06

Source: Tables 4.2 and 4.3.

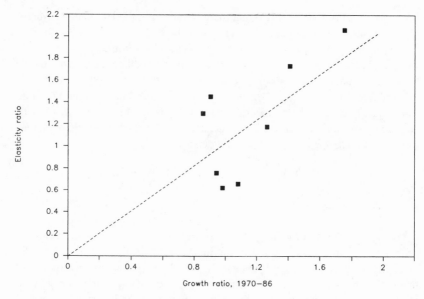

Fig. 4.5   Growth vs. elasticity ratio, 1970–1986

Clearly something is going on here. It seems unlikely that the systematic association of growth rates and income elasticities is a pure coincidence. So our next step is to turn to potential explanations.

4.2.4   Why Does PPP Work So Well in the Long Run?

There is a basic puzzle in relating short-run and long-run real exchange rate behavior. In the short run, PPP can be decisively rejected: both direct evidence on relative price behavior, as in Figure 4.2, and examination of econometric trade equations clearly demonstrate that goods produced in different countries are very imperfect substitutes. Yet in the long run, PPP works fairly well; this is reconciled with the low price elasticities of trade equations by the 45-degree rule, which systematically relates income elasticities to relative growth rates.

The obvious candidate for an explanation of the 45-degree rule lies in supply-side effects. In Krugman (1988a) it is argued that conventional supply-side effects arising simply from outward shifts of supply curves, or even more complex effects arising from biased growth, cannot explain the kind of result that we see in the data. Instead, it is necessary to appeal to more exotic stories. Specifically, the 45-degree rule can be explained if we argue that specialization among industrial countries is primarily due to increasing returns rather than comparative advantage; in this case goods *currently* produced by the industrial countries might be quite poor substitutes, but rough equality of (say) unit labor costs is enforced in the long run by the possibility that growing economies can widen the range of goods that they produce.

The story runs as follows. Fast growing countries expand their share of world markets, not by reducing the relative prices of their goods, but by expanding the range of goods that they produce as their economies grow. What we measure as exports and imports are not really fixed sets of goods, but instead aggregates whose definitions change over time as more goods are added to the list. What we call "Japanese exports" is a meaningful aggregate facing a downward sloping demand curve at any point in time; but as the Japanese economy grows over time, the definition of that aggregate changes in such a way as to make the apparent demand curve shift outward. The result is to produce apparently favorable income elasticities that allow the country to expand its economy without the need for a secular real depreciation.

Krugman (1988a) offers as an illustrative example the case of trade between Dixit-Stiglitz–type economies that grow at different rates. The relative prices of representative goods produced in each country will remain unchanged, so all differences in export and import growth rates would be attributed by a conventional econometric analysis to income elasticity differences. It is straightforward to show that in this case econometric estimates will show precisely a 45-degree rule.

Admittedly, this suggested link between new trade theory, with its emphasis on noncomparative advantage specialization, and long-run real exchange rate behavior, is speculative. (I of course have a particular stake in its validity.) It does, however, have the virtue of providing a theoretical rationale for the deep-seated feeling of many international economists that PPP, however grossly violated it is in the short run, has substantially more validity in the very long run.

4.3 Exchange Rates and the Adjustment Process

We have seen that long-run secular trends in equilibrium exchange rates are probably less prevalent than one might have thought a priori, and that thus in the long run PPP may be a better guide than evidence of low price elasticities would have led one to conclude. However, much policy must still be made for the short and medium run, where an assurance that things will work out over a span of decades is not much help. Also, real shocks and secular trends still do shift equilibrium real exchange rates, so that the problem of adjusting to an appropriate real rate is still an issue.

Thus even given the long-run results suggested in the previous section, it remains important to ask the traditional question of the role of exchange rates in the adjustment process. Suppose that a country has a current account imbalance that it believes to be undesirable and unsustainable. What role can or should the exchange rate play in adjusting this imbalance?

This is actually a straightforward question, one which economists have understood well since the 1950s. However, recently the issue has become confused again. The reasons for this are puzzling; some economists have fallen into the trap of confusing accounting identities with behavioral descriptions, while others seem to have become so preoccupied with the subtleties of intertemporal models that they have lost touch with the basics. In any case, it seems necessary to restate the nature of the useful role that exchange rate adjustment can play in balance of payments adjustment.

4.3.1   Expenditure-switching versus Expenditure-reducing

The main source of confusion in the discussion of balance of payments adjustment has always been the fact that a country's balance of payments depends on at least two variables, and that a country with a balance of payments concern always has at least one other objective. The minimal situation is that of a country whose current account depends on both the level of domestic demand and the real exchange rate, and which cares both about the current account and the level of domestic employment.

Figure 4.6 reproduces the familiar diagrammatic exposition introduced by Swan (1963). On the axes are real domestic demand ("absorption") and the real exchange rate (measured here so that a rise represents a higher relative price for domestic goods). The line XX represents combinations of demand and the real exchange rate such that the current account is at some level regarded as desirable and/or sustainable; this is "external balance." The line II represents points where domestic resources are fully employed; this is "internal balance." The line XX is downward sloping because a rise in domestic demand, other things equal, will increase imports and siphon off exports; it must therefore be offset by a real depreciation to keep the current account unchanged. The line II is upward sloping because an increase in domestic demand will raise the demand for domestic output, unless a real appreciation shifts demand away from domestic goods. Each zone off the lines

Real exchange rate

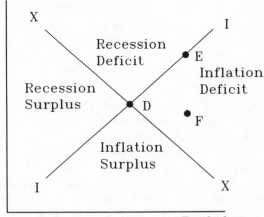

Real domestic demand

Fig. 4.6

is characterized by a particular sort of disequilibrium. For example, points to the right of the equilibrium point E are characterized by over-full employment and hence inflationary pressure, together with a balance of payments deficit.

The rough characterization of the United States with an overvalued dollar was that it was at a point like D: on the internal balance line, because unemployment was fairly close to the level regarded as compatible with price stability, but with an unsustainable current account deficit. To correct such a problem requires both a real depreciation and a reduction in domestic demand. Either alone leads to difficulties: a reduction in demand alone, that is, a move left from D, would improve the trade problem but lead to increased unemployment. A real depreciation without any fall in demand, that is, a move down from D, would improve the trade problem but threaten inflation (this may be in the process of happening). Thus real depreciation and demand reduction are necessary complements.

This seems a straightforward and sensible enough analysis. Why has it come under attack? A number of writers, including most particularly McKinnon (1984), Mundell (1987), and the editorial staff of the *Wall Street Journal,* have argued that real depreciation is either unnecessary or impossible to achieve through nominal depreciation. Although this view is a regression from an understanding that one thought had been achieved and reopens an issue that ought to have been closed, it is influential and apparently persuasive enough to warrant some discussion.

4.3.2   Is Real Exchange Rate Adjustment Necessary?

The main focus of the attack on the need for real exchange rate adjustment is on the savings-investment identity, $X - M = S - I$. This says that the current account deficit is necessarily identical to the gap between savings and investment. The conclusion that many seem to have drawn is that this means that trade problems are purely financial problems, that an increase in savings will translate into a reduce external deficit without any need for real exchange rates to change. Indeed, McKinnon has repeatedly asserted that real exchange rate changes are necessary only in a world with limited capital mobility; once there is free movement of capital, changes in the savings-investment balance are reflected directly in trade, without the need to consider price elasticities.

It should be immediately apparent what is wrong with this argument; it neglects the question of what goods expenditure falls on. Figure 4.6 is entirely consistent with the savings-investment identity, but it adds the additional information that a fall in domestic demand will fall at least partly on domestic goods, leading to an excess supply that must be offset by a fall in these goods' relative price. Ultimately trade flows reflect real demands for real goods and services, and no amount of emphasis on the financial side should be allowed to gloss over that basic truth.

Now there is a more sophisticated argument about why real exchange rate changes *might* not be necessary, one that actually goes back to the Keynes-Ohlin debate over the transfer problem. Suppose that the United States reduces its real expenditure by 100 billion constant dollars. By the world budget identity, other countries must increase their expenditure correspondingly. In principle other countries could increase their demand for U.S. goods and services by enough to compensate for the reduced domestic demand, even at a constant real exchange rate. In this case no real depreciation would be necessary.

Is this likely? The question is precisely that which arises in the classic transfer problem: how does the marginal propensity of U.S. residents to spend on U.S. goods compare with that of foreign residents? In a perfectly integrated world inhabited by people with identical homothetic preferences, these marginal propensities would be the same. In the real world, which remains very imperfectly integrated, there is no reasonable doubt that U.S. residents spend a much higher fraction of any marginal change in spending on U.S. goods.

Tautologically, the answer may be regarded as the product of two terms: the share of imports in expenditure and the elasticity of imports with respect to expenditure.

First, we ask what share of U.S. expenditure falls on foreign goods. One might be inclined to answer with the share of imports in GNP, or in GNP plus the trade deficit (to take account of the fact that expenditure currently exceeds income): that is, about 11 percent. This is not a very large number given the alarms being raised about international competition in the United States, but it is in any case the wrong number; it is too large by a factor of perhaps two. On average, U.S. residents probably spend only 5 or 6 percent of their income on imports. The reason is that something like half of U.S. imports are intermediate goods. The spending on these goods is presumably related to U.S. output rather than expenditure; this makes an important difference, as we will see, and this needs to be kept separate.

Next, we poll the econometricians for an elasticity. Import demand is generally estimated to rise more than proportionally to whatever activity variable the econometrician puts in, for fairly obvious reasons: goods, which are traded more than services, respond more to cyclical fluctuations in spending, and capacity constraints cause some of an increase in demand to spill over into imports. However, the typical elasticity of imports with respect to spending or income is usually around 2 and rarely more than 3.

Putting these together, we find that a generous estimate of the share of a marginal dollar spent on imports will still be less than 20 cents. Taking a round number, then, let us suppose that U.S. residents spend 80 percent of a marginal dollar on U.S. goods. What about foreign residents?

Here we note that the United States is less than a third of the world market economy. Thus even in normal times, when U.S. trade is roughly balanced, U.S. exports constitute only about 5 percent of the income of the rest of the world, and less of their final expenditure. Again a generous estimate might be that foreign residents will spend 10 cents of a marginal dollar on U.S. goods.

Thus a minimal estimate is that U.S. residents spend eight times as high a share of a marginal increase in spending on U.S. goods than do foreigners. This disparity is no doubt smaller than it ever was—but in an important sense we are still closer to a world in which all of a spending shift falls on domestic goods than we are to one in which spending is fully internationalized.

Now return to our assumed case, in which U.S. residents reduce their expenditure by $100 billion, while foreign residents correspondingly increase their expenditure by the same amount. The results are illustrated in table 4.5.

Case A in table 4.5 shows what happens, all else equal, if U.S. spending falls by $100 billion and rest of world (RoW) spending rises by the same amount. The key point is that, as we have argued, U.S. residents have a much higher marginal propensity to spend on U.S. goods than RoW residents. When U.S. spending falls by $100 billion, U.S. spending on imports falls by only $20 billion, while domestic demand for U.S. goods falls by $80 billion. The increase in RoW spending provides a new source of demand for U.S. exports, but not nearly enough: out of the $100 billion rise in RoW spending, only $10 billion falls on U.S. products. The result, then, is to produce a $70 billion excess supply of U.S. goods and a $70 billion excess demand for RoW goods.

How are we to make the redistribution of world expenditure effective? Somehow the world needs to be persuaded to *switch* $70 billion of spending from RoW goods to U.S. goods. The only nonprotectionist way to do this is to make U.S. goods relatively cheaper. That is, we need real depreciation of the United States against the rest of the world.

The reason why this real depreciation is needed is precisely that world markets for goods and services are imperfectly integrated, so that residents of each country have a much higher propensity to spend on their own products than foreigners have to spend on that country's products. So the microeconomic fact of an imperfectly integrated world market has the macroeconomic implication that real exchange rate changes are an essential part of the balance of payments adjustment process.

Because of the imperfect integration of world markets for goods and services, then, current account adjustment does require real exchange rate adjustment. However, it is not necessary that this occur through a nominal depreciation of the dollar. Instead of dollar decline, we could achieve the same

Table 4.5   **Reducing a Trade Imbalance**

Case	Total Spending	Spending on U.S. Products	Spending on RoW Products
A:			
U.S.	− 100	− 80	− 20
RoW	+ 100	+ 10	+ 90
B:			
U.S.	− 100	− 80	− 20
RoW	+ 800	+ 80	+ 720

result through a combination of deflation in the United States and inflation abroad. The need for real exchange rate adjustment is only a case for nominal exchange rate flexibility if relative prices and wages are more easily altered through exchange rate changes than through differential price level movements. But it was shown earlier in this paper that substantial stickiness of prices and wages in domestic currency is in fact a major feature of the world economy. Because there is in fact inertia to nominal prices, it is easier to reduce the relative price of U.S. labor and output via a dollar depreciation than via U.S. deflation. Thus the case for real exchange rate changes in the adjustment process is also a case for nominal exchange rate changes to facilitate this adjustment.

4.3.3   The Role of Growth in Surplus Countries

In the numerical illustration in part A of table 4.5, it is assumed that the fall in U.S. expenditure is matched by only an equal rise in RoW expenditure. Many in the United States have argued, however, that growth in surplus countries—which means a rise in RoW expenditure over and above the fall in U.S. expenditure, whether they realize it or not—should take the place of exchange rate adjustment. This is a point that is correct conceptually, but there just isn't much in it as a practical matter. I want to return to table 4.5, part B, in order to see why.

Let us pose the following question: How much would foreign expenditure have to rise in order to allow the United States to cut expenditure by $100 billion and convert all of that cut into a trade balance improvement, without the need for a real depreciation to induce a switch of expenditure to U.S. goods? The answer is shown in part B. Since the fall in U.S. expenditure reduces the demand for U.S. goods by $80 billion, and we are assuming that only 10 percent of a marginal increase in RoW spending falls on U.S. goods, expenditure in the rest of the world must rise by $800 billion. In this way the total spending on U.S. goods is left unchanged, with the decline in domestic demand offset by an equal increase in export demand.

Unfortunately, there is a side consequence: the total expenditure on RoW goods rises by $700 billion—$720 billion increase in domestic demand minus the $20 billion fall in U.S. exports. Thus the alternative to U.S. depreciation offered here will work only if there is at least $700 billion of usable excess capacity in the rest of the world. At current exchange rates, the GNP of market economies outside the United States is about $9 trillion, so this means that to improve the U.S. trade position by $100 billion using foreign growth as an alternative to real depreciation would require that we find room for an increase of almost 8 percent in RoW GNP. If we were to try to deal with the whole U.S. trade deficit in this way, the needed foreign growth would be more like 12 percent.

The problem should be immediately obvious—there isn't that much excess capacity in the surplus countries. Indeed, the IMF has estimated that none of industrial countries with current account surpluses have a usable excess capacity of more than 2 percent of GNP. This result may perhaps be challenged, but what matters is what the policymakers in the surplus countries believe; and the fact is that the authorities in the Federal Republic of Germany, in particular, regard themselves as having only small room for expansion at best. So the possibility of substituting growth in surplus countries for real exchange rate adjustment, while correct in principle, is only a minor issue in the current context.

4.4 Problems of Assessment

The expenditure-switching versus expenditure-reducing framework described in the previous section would offer a straightforward guide to exchange rate policy if there were neither structural change that shifted equilibrium exchange rates, nor lags in the effects of exchange rates on trade. Unfortunately, in reality both structural change and lags are key issues. Arguably, both have become even more serious issues in the 1980s than before. As a result, the assessment of equilibrium exchange rates remains a difficult and problematic exercise.

4.4.1 Does the Dollar Need to Fall Further?

As it happens, the current perplexity over the appropriate adjustment of the U.S. dollar provides a nice example of how uncertainty about lags and structural change interact to make determination of appropriate exchange rate policy very difficult. Suppose that we apply figure 4.6 to U.S. experience during the 1980s.

Suppose that there were neither structural change nor lags in the effects of the exchange rate. Then we would be able to draw internal and external balance schedules for the United States. In 1980, the United States was near most estimates of the NAIRU, and running a slight current surplus; thus the economy was at a point like D. By 1985, a massive expansion in domestic demand had been matched by a large dollar appreciation; economic recovery had raised employment back to a level approaching some estimates of the full employment level, so that the economy appeared to be at a point like E, on the internal balance line but with an external deficit.

Now as figure 4.6 shows, what has happened since 1985 is that the United States has experienced a substantial real depreciation that, depending on one's measure, has either brought the real exchange rate back to its 1980 level or brought it well below that level, without a corresponding fall in real demand relative to output. So the current situation ought to be represented by a point like F. In the absence of structural change or lags, we would expect to find a combination of persistence of the external deficit to at least some extent and inflationary pressure in the domestic economy.

To some extent this has happened. The U.S. trade deficit has declined considerably in volume terms, and somewhat in dollar terms, while unemployment has fallen to levels that are somewhat below earlier estimates of the NAIRU. However, both the negative and positive effects of the real depreciation have been smaller than widely expected. To make the point, consider that constant dollar real expenditure in the United States currently exceeds constant-dollar output by approximately four percent. Suppose that in 1980 one had suddenly increased real expenditure in the United States by 4 percent. One would have expected this to have a substantial negative effect on the external balance, but not to be reflected almost one-for-one in the external deficit. One would also have expected a severe overheating of the domestic economy. The point is that the external deficit is larger—that the dollar's real depreciation has had less effect—than figure 4.6 alone would suggest.

Why should this be? Unfortunately there are two possible explanations. One is that the XX and II schedules have shifted in such a way as to reduce the equilibrium exchange rate; in effect, the declining dollar has been chasing a moving target. The other is that there are long lags in the effect of dollar decline, perhaps longer than in the past. The first explanation suggests that the dollar needs to decline substantially from its current level; the second, that what is needed is more patience.

The case for a decline in the equilibrium dollar has been advanced by a number of economists. It rests on the observation that at least four elements of the world environment have changed in ways that reduce the U.S. net export position at any given real exchange rate. These are: a) the continued relative decline of the U.S. advantage in technology over advanced rivals, which deprives the United States of the ability to sell goods at a premium; b) the debt crisis, which has reduced LDC imports from the world at large but disproportionately from the United States; c) slow growth in Europe, which has also depressed demand for U.S. exports; and d) the shift of the United States into net debtor status, which has eliminated the former U.S. surplus in investment income.

Added to these factors is the possible role of "hysteresis" in trade: U.S. firms may have lost markets during the period of the strong dollar which it is not worth their while to recapture even with a return of the dollar to its original level.

By placing maximum weight on all of these factors, it is possible to make a case that the U.S. dollar needs as much as a 20 or even 30 percent depreciation below its 1980 level to be consistent with restoration of external balance.

On the other side, however, is the argument that such large shifts from PPP are rare historically, and that in time the United States should not have to depreciate its currency to a level that makes production costs radically lower than those in other advanced countries. This argument implies that what we are seeing is long lags in adjustment, and that given time there will be substantial further narrowing of the U.S. trade imbalance even at the current value of the dollar.

Ideally, econometric estimates of trade equations would identify lags. However, in practice this is difficult. Furthermore, there are some reasons to believe that the lags themselves may have changed. That is, lags in exchange rate responses may have become longer in recent years.

4.4.2   Uncertainty and Lags in the Impact of Exchange Rates

A striking feature of the period since 1985 has been the determination of non–U.S. firms in holding on to markets gained during the period 1980–85, despite a radical worsening of their relative cost position. U.S. firms also seem to have been reluctant to take advantage of the weaker dollar to attempt to regain lost markets. And multinational firms, wherever they are based, have been reluctant to reverse their location decisions from the strong dollar period.

One explanation of this lack of response to the weak dollar is that firms do not regard the current exchange rate as permanent, that they expect the dollar to return to levels of a few years ago. A broader explanation, however, which need not be specific to the dollar, is that uncertainty per se makes firms reluctant to respond to the exchange rate, and hence increases the lags in trade responses to the exchange rate. This point has been emphasized in recent theoretical work by Dixit (1988) and is emphasized in a practical context by Krugman (1988b).

The point may be made by considering a simple hypothetical example. Consider a hypothetical Japanese firm that has lost its cost advantage over U.S. rivals as the result of the strong yen. At the current exchange rate—say 120 yen to the dollar—it is losing money on its U.S. sales. This firm is not especially optimistic; it hopes that the yen may return to 140, which would make it profitable again, but regards it as equally likely that the yen will rise to 100, greatly increasing its losses. If that were the whole story, the firm would simply exit immediately. However, the firm has invested heavily in building its U.S. market position, and it knows that if it abandons that position now it will not be worth trying to regain it even if the yen does fall.

Table 4.6 shows some hypothetical numbers for this Japanese firm. We suppose that, at the current rate of 120 yen, it is losing money at an annual rate of $100 million. If the yen goes back to 140, it will be able to make $100

Table 4.6   **Payoffs to a Firm Delaying Exit**

Value of Yen	Initial Year Loss	PDV of Later Years
100	− 100	0
140	− 100	900

million annually; if the yen rises to 100, it will lose $300 million per year if it still tries to hand on. Also, we suppose that the firm discounts future earnings at an annual rate of 10 percent.

The expected returns to this firm from sales in the U.S. market are clearly negative. However, the firm does not have to choose between leaving the U.S. market now and staying forever; its immediate choice is whether to exit now or wait a year, then choose again. And we can show that despite current losses the firm should hang in there for one more year.

Table 4.6 shows the returns to the firm if it chooses not to drop out and to wait instead for a year before making its decision. In the first year the firm loses $100 million. In the second year it drops out if the yen goes to 100, but stays in if it falls to 140. In this latter case, it will earn $100 million per year thereafter, with a present value discounted to the first year of $900 million. The overall expected present value to the firm of this wait-and-see strategy is therefore the average between what happens if the yen goes to 100 or to 140: $350 million.

By contrast, if the firm immediately drops out it makes nothing and loses nothing.

Clearly, in an expected value sense, the firm is better off holding on and hoping for better times even though it is losing money at the current exchange rate, and *even though it regards an adverse movement in the rate as being as likely as a favorable movement*. Of course, if the firm regarded a return to 140 as more likely than a rise to 100, the case for remaining in the market in the face of losses would be even stronger.

Uncertainty, then, makes firms cautious about exiting from hard-won market positions. Similar examples will show that a U.S. firm will be hesitant about taking advantage of low costs to break into a market, and for that matter will make multinational firms hesitant about relocating production.

4.5   Conclusions

Experience and analysis have taught us a great deal about how a system of flexible exchange rates works. Unfortunately, we still do not know enough to give clear and simple advice in all circumstances to central bankers and finance ministers. In particular, the current situation is one in which an intelligent appreciation of what we know about equilibrium exchange rates leads to a definite "don't know" in response to questions about where to go from here.

What we do know are three things, in particular. First, nominal exchange rates matter. There is now overwhelming evidence for stickiness of prices in domestic currency, and the persistence of real exchange rate fluctuations is more likely evidence for slow price adjustment than it is for the prevalence of real shocks. Second, in the very long run, PPP works better than one might expect, possibly because of supply-side effects involving scale economies and product differentiation. Third, despite this, in the medium term the combination of strong distribution effects and fairly low price elasticities makes exchange rate changes an essential part of the adjustment process.

The source of current perplexity is the difficulty of untangling different sources of change. Are the disappointing results of dollar depreciation due to structural changes or simply stretched-out lags? This is the key issue; at least by focusing on it we have a better chance of getting the right policy.

References

Balassa, Bela. 1964. The purchasing power parity doctrine: A reappraisal. *Journal of Political Economy* 72: 584–96.

Dixit, Avinash. 1988. Entry and exit decisions of a firm facing a fluctuating exchange rate. Mimeograph.

Dornbusch, Rudiger. 1976. Expectations and exchange rate dynamics. *Journal of Political Economy.*

Frankel, J. 1989. Quantifying international capital mobility. Paper presented at the NBER Conference on Saving, Maui, January 6–7.

Friedman, M. 1953. The case for flexible exchange rates. In *Essays in Positive Economics.* Chicago: University of Chicago Press.

Houthakker, H., and S. Magee. 1969. Income and price elasticities in world trade. *Review of Economics and Statistics* 51:111–25.

Huizinga, J. 1987. An empirical investigation of the long run behavior of real exchange rates. Paper presented at Carnegie-Rochester Conference.

Johnson, H. 1958. *International trade and economic growth: Studies in pure theory.* London: Allen and Unwin.

Krugman, P. 1988a. Differences in income elasticities and secular trends in real exchange rates. Paper presented at International Seminar on Macroeconomics, Tokyo, June.

———. 1988b. *Exchange Rate Instability.* Cambridge, MA: MIT Press.

Marston, R. 1987. Real exchange rates and productivity growth in the United States and Japan. In S. Arndt, ed., *Real-Financial Linkages in the Open Economy.* Washington, DC: American Enterprise Institute.

McKinnon, R. 1984. *An International Standard for Monetary Stabilization.* Washington, DC: Institute for International Economics.

McKinnon, R., and K. Ohno. 1986. Getting the exchange rate right: Insular versus open economies. Paper presented at American Economic Association meeting, New Orleans, December.

Mundell, R. 1987. A new deal on exchange rates. Paper presented at a MITI symposium, Tokyo, January.

Swan, T. 1963. Longer-run problems of the balance of payments. In H. W. Arndt and W. M. Corden, eds., *The Australian Economy: A Volume of Readings.* Melbourne: Cheshire Press.

Comment   C. Fred Bergsten

Paul Krugman has provided an outstanding analysis of how exchange rate changes contribute to the international adjustment process. His paper offers a

C. Fred Bergsten is the director of the Institute for International Economics.

number of useful insights both for our intellectual understanding of the issue and for the continuing debate over exchange-rate policy.

In particular, Krugman underlines and reinforces the traditional view that currency changes can, and indeed must, play a central role in restoring and maintaining sustainable combinations of internal and external balance. As he notes, some observers have become disillusioned with the pace and magnitude of the decline in the external deficit of the United States (and the corresponding surpluses in Japan and Germany) despite the sizable fall of the dollar since early 1985. He cites a number of considerations to help explain this result and could have added several more.

First, most models show that the American current account deficit was headed toward annual levels of $300–$400 billion when the dollar was at its peak in early 1985.[1] Halting the deterioration at less than $150 billion in 1987, and subsequently cutting it by at least $20 billion in nominal terms (and by much more in real terms), has thus been a considerable achievement.

Second, most analyses fail to take full account of the implications for achieving equilibrium of large initial imbalances. In the case of the United States, merchandise exports were only 60 percent as large as merchandise imports when the deficit peaked in 1987. Hence exports had to grow almost twice as fast as imports simply to avoid further increases in the deficit. The gap was even more dramatic in the case of the bilateral United States–Japan imbalance because Japanese exports were almost three times greater than American exports in 1987.

Third, many analyses fail to distinguish between real and nominal responses to currency changes and to the wide disparity between them. Cline remedies this problem and suggests that, for the United States, an improvement of $100 billion in the nominal current account balance will require an adjustment of almost $200 billion in real terms.[2] Indeed, the U.S. deficit by the first quarter of 1989 had been cut by about 43 percent in real terms from its peak in the third quarter of 1986. The observed "sluggishness" of the response of the nominal deficit to a lower dollar thus masks much more substantial volume gains, which of course are of primary significance for the key variables in the real economy—growth, production, employment—and thus probably trade policy, though not for the financing of the imbalance.

Fourth, despite repeated international commitments to decisively reduce the budget deficit and despite the existence of the Gramm-Rudman-Hollings legislation, the United States failed at least through 1988 to complement dollar depreciation with adequate cutbacks in the growth of domestic demand. Domestic demand in fact continued to grow as rapidly, or more rapidly, than productive capacity. Supply constraints reportedly limited the expansion of exports in a number of sectors.[3]

Moreover, once the economy reached full employment and full capacity utilization by around the middle of 1988 (if not earlier), resources would have been available for additional reduction in the external imbalance only at the cost of a further acceleration of inflation. The Federal Reserve thus responded by tightening monetary policy, inter alia halting the depreciation of the dollar and in fact pushing it back up.

This fifth point—uncertainty on the part of the private sector concerning the future course of the exchange rate itself—is raised by Krugman but deserves even greater emphasis. Many American exporters, when asked why they have failed to expand productive capacity to satisfy both domestic and rising foreign demand, reply that they have no confidence that the exchange rate of the dollar would still be at a level permitting them to remain competitive internationally by the time the new capacity would come on stream.

Hysteresis thus has a critical time dimension. Krugman and others have argued that currencies probably need to overshoot to persuade firms to reenter export (and import-competing) markets. In addition, these firms may require assurances that exchange rates which permit them to compete will remain in place for some time. Indeed, there is presumably a tradeoff between the magnitude of the needed depreciation and its expected duration.

This suggests the need for systemic reform, to install and maintain an exchange rate regime that will offer such assurances. Here Krugman, despite calling for broad target zones in his widely praised Robbins lectures,[4] concludes with surprising agnosticism that "we still do not know enough to give clear and simple advice in all circumstances to central bankers and finance ministers" and "what we know about equilibrium exchange rates leads to a definite 'don't know' in response to questions about where to go from here."

Fortunately, the situation is not nearly so hopeless. Krugman has in fact slightly (but crucially) misspecified the problem: it is not whether economists can advise officials what to do "in all circumstances" but whether we can with some confidence offer them a system which promises to perform more effectively than either pure floating or the loose "reference ranges" installed with the Louvre Accord of February 1987.[5]

On this more modest criterion, there is growing evidence for the superiority of a system of target zones. Such a regime has been developed in detail, and simulated against recent history, by Williamson and Miller (1987).[6] Both Branson and Frankel, in their presentations to this conference, indicate that the Williamson-Miller "blueprint" performs better than any of the proposed alternatives (or the status quo).[7] As noted, Krugman has previously endorsed such an approach (and rightly stresses in his present paper the high costs of permitting wrong nominal rates to persist).

Such a system rests explicitly on the view that the exchange rate is an intermediate target, to be used to achieve and maintain current account positions that are agreed internationally to be sustainable in economic, financial, and policy (e.g., anti-protection) terms. Krugman's "most basic of these [exchange-rate] difficulties" should thus be restated: the hardest task, both intellectually and politically, will be to agree on targets for external and internal balance. It should then be an easier task to agree on currency zones that will help produce such outcomes, satisfying Krugman's dictum that policymakers can greatly facilitate adjustment by inducing nominal rates to move toward equilibrium once they know where equilibrium lies. Such a regime of course rejects the utility of purchasing power parity calculations for any practical purpose, for the reasons brilliantly developed in the paper, thus rendering even the yen zone (over which Krugman puzzles) susceptible to successful targeting.

Installing such zones in practice is a much trickier matter, however. The recent efforts of the Group of Seven to stabilize flexible exchange rates reveal that they are willing to try only "around current levels."[8] The authorities have been unable to find a technique to simultaneously alter levels and stabilize, as they could under fixed exchange rate regimes past (Bretton Woods) and present (European Monetary System), and there are admittedly great uncertainties as to whether such efforts could succeed within a context that continued to permit considerable rate flexibility. Hence any lasting monetary reform will probably have to be a two-step process, addressed initially to *establishing* equilibrium rates by completing the realignment begun in 1985 (perhaps through a "second Plaza agreement"[9]) and subsequently moving to a system of target zones to *maintain* equilibrium for the longer run.

Notes

1. Marris (1987, 86) foresaw a deficit of $320 billion by 1990 with further increases thereafter. Simulations with the Federal Reserve's Helkie-Hooper model show a deficit of over $400 billion by 1992 if the real exchange rate of the dollar had remained at its first-quarter 1985 level; see Cline (1989, 33).
2. See Cline (1989, ch. 6, especially 269–70).
3. A detailed proposal for linking the external and internal components of a U.S. adjustment strategy can be found in Bergsten (1988, especially ch. 4 and 5).
4. See Krugman (1988, especially 104–6).
5. See Funabashi (1988, especially ch. 8).
6. See Williamson and Miller (1987).
7. See also Currie and Wren-Lewis (1989, especially 199–200).
8. See Funabashi (1988, 183–86).
9. See Bergsten (1989).

References

Bergsten, C. Fred. 1988. *America in the world economy: A strategy for the 1990s.* Washington, DC: Institute for International Economics, November.
———. 1989. U.S. priority objectives for the Paris Summit: A "Second Plaza Agreement" and the Uruguay Round. Statement before the Joint Economic Committee, U.S. Congress, July 6.
Cline, William R. 1989. *United States external adjustment and the world economy.* Washington, DC: Institute for International Economics, March.
Currie, David, and Simon Wren-Lewis. 1989. A comparison of alternative regimes for international macropolicy coordination. In Marcus Miller, Barry Eichengreen, and Richard Portes, eds., *Blueprints for exchange rate management.* London: Academic Press.

Funabashi, Yoichi. 1988. *Managing the dollar: From the Plaza to the Louvre.* Washington, DC: Institute for International Economics, May.

Krugman, Paul. 1988. *Exchange rate instability.* Cambridge, MA: MIT Press.

Marris, Stephen. 1987. *Deficits and the dollar: The world economy at risk.* Washington, DC: Institute for International Economics, rev. August.

Williamson, John, and Marcus H. Miller. 1987. *Targets and indicators: A blueprint for the international coordination of economic policy.* Washington, DC: Institute for International Economics, September.

Comment   Michael Mussa

It is a pleasure, once again, to comment on a stimulating paper by Paul Krugman. The last time I had such an opportunity was at a conference held in Grand Teton National Park in August 1985. On that occasion, I noted that the view of the Teton Range across Jackson Lake provided an appropriate setting in which to discuss the recent turbulent behavior of exchange rates. In light of recent official efforts to stabilize exchange rates, I rather suspect that Jacob Frenkel, now the Research Director and Economic Counsellor at the IMF, concluded that the tidelands of South Carolina would provide more suitable inspiration for today's discussion of exchange rate policy.

Just before lunch, Paul mentioned that he intended to take a walk and have a look at some of the local alligators. He didn't make clear whether he was seeking solace, or merely planning to get in a little practice for this afternoon's session. In fact, I agree with many of the points that Paul makes in his paper. In particular, in the last paper I wrote before joining the Council of Economic Advisers (see Mussa 1986), I attempted to document one of the key points that Paul discusses—real exchange rates have been much more volatile under the floating exchange rate regime that has prevailed since 1973 than under the Bretton Woods system of fixed exchange rates. As Paul emphasizes, this increased volatility of real exchange rates is closely associated with the increased volatility of nominal exchange rates and with the continued apparent sluggishness in the adjustment of national price levels. However, despite "the new micro-foundations of Keynesian economics," I am not as certain as Paul that we have a completely satisfactory understanding of the degree of price level inertia that appears to be associated with the large real exchange rate movements of the 1980s.

After summarizing the evidence that nominal exchange rate changes produce shorter-term but highly persistent changes in real exchange rates, Paul states two implications of this phenomenon for exchange rate policy. "First, if policymakers know where the equilibrium real exchange rate is headed, they

Michael Mussa is the William H. Abbott Professor of International Business at the Graduate School of Business, University of Chicago, and a research associate of the National Bureau of Economic Research.

can greatly facilitate adjustment by allowing or inducing nominal rates to move in that direction. Second, getting nominal rates wrong can be very costly because it may take a long time for the equilibrium real rates to get themselves established.'' These statements suggest that Paul supports a quite activist role for exchange rate management as a tool of economic policy. However, the analysis in the remaining two-thirds of Paul's paper leads him to a far more cautious conclusion. "Unfortunately, we still do not know enough to give clear and simple advice in all circumstances to central bankers and finance ministers. In particular, the current situation is one in which an intelligent appreciation of what we know about equilibrium exchange rates leads to a definite 'don't know' in response to questions about where to go from here.''

I share the conclusion that Paul reaches at the end of his paper, and I would like to suggest some further reasons for a cautious attitude toward the usefulness of exchange rate management.

Most importantly, in my judgement, much of the support for an activist policy of exchange rate management directed at reducing movements in real exchange rates is based on misconceptions concerning the causes and consequences of the major swing in the real foreign exchange value of the U.S. dollar during the 1980s. Certainly strong real appreciation of the U.S. dollar between the summer of 1980 and early 1985 created, or contributed to, a number of important economic problems, many of which have not been fully corrected by the subsequent depreciation of the dollar. These problems include the large and persistent U.S. trade deficit, the difficulties experienced by many tradable goods industries in the United States, and the protectionist sentiments that these difficulties have helped to engender. However, the existence of these important problems does not establish that most of the appreciation and subsequent depreciation of the U.S. dollar during the 1980s was either avoidable or undesirable, given other events that were occurring in the world economy.

The tightening of U.S. monetary policy from late 1980 through the summer of 1982 was surely needed to bring down the U.S. inflation rate and restore confidence in the future conduct of U.S. monetary policy. Real appreciation of the U.S. dollar above what many economists believe to be its equilibrium path was an essentially inevitable consequence of this monetary policy. Further appreciation of the dollar in 1983 and 1984 probably reflected (among other things) the extremely strong recovery of the U.S. economy from the recession of 1981–82, together with continued success in keeping the inflation rate moderate. The appreciation of the dollar during this period surely helped to contain the inflationary pressures that probably would otherwise have accompanied this very rapid economic recovery. Also, the appreciation of the dollar and the associated growth of the U.S. trade deficit helped to spread some of the force of the rapid growth of domestic demand in the U.S. economy to other countries where growth of domestic demand remained very sluggish. Even with the moderating effects of dollar appreciation and a growing trade deficit, the Federal Reserve became sufficiently concerned with the threat of a resurgence of inflation, that monetary policy was tightened again between April and November of 1984. In view of the enormous costs of bringing down inflation in 1981–82, it is difficult to criticize the Federal Reserve for seeking to preserve its victory over inflation, even though the effect of monetary tightening in 1984 was almost surely to push the dollar further away from its longer-run equilibrium value.

The downward movement of the dollar from February 1985 through 1987 can be fairly characterized as a movement toward long-run equilibrium. Exchange rate management probably played a useful but subsidiary role in this exchange rate adjustment. The Plaza Agreement may have helped to accelerate dollar depreciation in the autumn of 1985 and in 1986. However, that process was already ongoing for six months before Plaza. The Louvre Accord and subsequent efforts at exchange rate stabilization may have contributed to greater stability of exchange rates since early 1987. However, in my judgement, the tightening of U.S. monetary policy because of concerns about renewed inflation and the evidence of improvement in the U.S. trade balance were probably far more important than exchange rate management in ending, and even partially reversing, the process of dollar depreciation.

In any event, the key development during the period of dollar depreciation since early 1985 is the absence of a "hard landing." Despite two years of precipitous decline in the foreign-exchange value of the dollar, and despite the worldwide stock market crash of October 1987, economic expansion continues in the United States and in most other industrial countries. Indeed, the improvement in the U.S. real trade balance since late 1986 (one of the desired effects of dollar depreciation) has clearly helped to keep the U.S. expansion going, despite a slower rate of growth of domestic demand in the United States. Recently, inflationary pressures may have picked up somewhat in the United States, but the U.S. inflation rate remains quite moderate in comparison with dire predictions of the consequences of dollar depreciation, and in spite of a relatively low unemployment rate. Of course, because of the recent tightening of monetary policy, or for other reasons, the U.S. economy could enter a recession in 1989 or 1990. However, such a recession would not be unusual given the postwar history of U.S. business cycles. Thus, all things considered, the U.S. economy and the world economy do not appear to have suffered substantial damage from the correction in the foreign-exchange value of the dollar since early 1985.

It is certainly possible that an active policy of exchange rate management or, more importantly, a better mix of monetary and fiscal policy could have avoided some of the appreciation of the dollar between 1980 and early 1985. And, surely, cheering the dollar up at the end of its long period of appreciation was not a wise endeavor. However, the experience of the 1980s raises grave doubts about the feasibility and desirability of a policy that always seeks to drive the exchange rate toward some estimate of the value that would yield trade or current account balance. Sometimes it may be necessary or desirable to allow the exchange rate to move away from their longer-run equilibrium values, in order to accommodate powerful forces at work in the world economy, or in order to provide latitude for economic policy to pursue objectives more important than the rapid achievement of current account equilibrium.

This general reason for caution about policies' exchange rate management has considerable current relevance. Recognizing that we really don't know how much more, if at all, the dollar needs to depreciate, suppose, for the sake of argument, that we knew that the dollar had to depreciate 25 percent in real terms. It remains highly questionable whether exchange rate policy should seek an immediate depreciation of 25 percent, or indeed any immediate depreciation. With the U.S. production relatively close to capacity, and with some evidence of increased inflationary pressures, monetary policy has appropriately been tightened. The effect has probably been to strengthen the dollar in foreign-exchange markets. An effort to drive the dollar down by easing of monetary policy would be a mistake so long as the threat of resurgence of inflation remains serious. An effort to drive the dollar down through other means (except possibly a tightening of fiscal policy) could also be counterproductive. It could easily contribute to inflationary pressures that would lead to further monetary tightening. Thus, even if longer-run considerations suggest a substantially lower dollar, it may not be desirable to move in that direction immediately.

Conversely, suppose that we knew that the dollar was now at its long-run equilibrium value. Suppose further that the Federal Reserve has overdone its monetary tightening, and the U.S. economy is about to fall into recession (with other industrial nations continuing to expand). In a recession, U.S. interest rates are likely to fall substantially unless this is vigorously resisted by the Federal Reserve. Lower U.S. interest rates probably mean sharp declines in the dollar. In this recession scenario, it would not make sense to tighten monetary policy in order to hold the exchange rate. Other efforts at exchange rate management might well prove ineffective. Thus, it is not difficult to conceive of situations in which the desirable policy is to allow an exchange rate to move away from its long-run equilibrium value.

Another reason for caution in policies of exchange rate management is that we really don't know what represents a sustainable level of the current account balance in the medium term. Paul touches on this point early in his paper, but I believe that it deserves more emphasis. Suppose that we have already seen most of the favorable effect on the U.S. trade balance of dollar depreciation since early 1985. Suppose further that the U.S. will grow at about the same rate as other industrial countries and that conventional estimates of income and relative price elasticities of exports and imports are correct. If the United States needs to achieve a zero current account balance by the middle 1990s, then the standard calculations indicate the need for a substantial (20 to 30 percent) further decline in the real foreign exchange value of the dollar. However, if the United States and the rest of the world can live with a U.S. current account deficit of 1.5 percent of U.S. GNP (one-half of the current level), then the implied magnitude of required dollar depreciation under the standard assumptions is cut in half. A measured current account deficit of 1.5 percent of GNP might correspond to an actual deficit of only 1 percent of GNP. With such a deficit in the middle 1990s, the ratio of U.S. net external liabilities to U.S. GNP would stabilize at around 15 to 20 percent, well below the ratios for a number of other industrial countries. Thus, a measured current account deficit equal to 1.5 percent of GNP is not a totally unreasonable assumption on which to base estimates of the need for further exchange rate adjustment.

If further significant improvement in the U.S. trade balance is still in the pipeline from past dollar depreciation, then little further depreciation may be needed to reach a current account deficit equal to 1.5 percent of U.S. GNP. More improvement still in the pipeline means not only less work to be done by further depreciation, it also means that relative price elasticities are probably larger than previous estimates and, hence, more effectiveness from each unit of depreciation. Pushing on all of these fronts, taking account of the many excellent points in Paul's paper, it is possible to construct a plausible case that no further real depreciation of the dollar may be needed to reach a sustainable current account position in the medium term.

This possibility, and the analysis that underlies it, justifies the caution that Paul urges in giving advice to policymakers about "where we go from here" with respect to the foreign-exchange value of the dollar. However, I would also emphasize that, allowing for substantial uncertainty, the best available evidence still points to the likely need for some further real dollar depreciation in the medium term. By making this point, with suitable cautions and qualifications, we may help to guard against the danger that a "don't know" response to the question of where the exchange rate needs to move will be used to justify a policy of pegging the exchange rate where it is now. For exchange rate policy, I believe that the most important conclusion is Paul Krugman's final conclusion, "in the medium term . . . exchange rate changes [are] an essential part of the adjustment process."

Reference

Mussa, M. 1986. The nominal exchange rate regime and the behavior of real exchange rates. Carnegie-Rochester Conference Series, v. 25, ed. Karl Brunner and Allan Meltzer, 117–213. Amsterdam: North-Holland.

5 The Effectiveness of Foreign-Exchange Intervention: Recent Experience, 1985–1988

Maurice Obstfeld

But ultimately there are limits to what can be achieved by a pure intervention policy. The monetary crises under the Bretton Woods system showed that powerful market trends cannot be suppressed through exchange market interventions by central banks, and more recent monetary history has reaffirmed this.

Deutsche Bundesbank (1982, 25)

5.1 Introduction

In a report published in July 1985, economic policymakers from ten industrial countries reviewed the performance of floating exchange rates to date and concluded that "the key elements of the current international monetary system require no major institutional change."[1] Within three months, however, finance ministers and central bank governors from five of the largest industrial countries announced their readiness for concerted action to reduce the U.S. dollar's foreign-exchange value. The Group of Five's announcement, made at the Plaza Hotel in New York on Sunday, September 22, initiated a series of international accords centered around the management of key dollar exchange rates.[2] Understandings concerning joint intervention in foreign-exchange markets have figured prominently in these accords, which thus represent a clear modification of the U.S. distaste for intervention that prevailed during the first half of the Reagan administration.

Maurice Obstfeld is professor of economics at the University of California, Berkeley, and a research associate of the National Bureau of Economic Research.

The author is very grateful to Susan Collins and Jeffrey Miron for help in assembling data. Useful comments and suggestions were made by David Backus, Kathryn Dominguez, Martin Feldstein, John Flemming, Kenneth Froot, Hans Genberg, Michael Klein, Michael Leahy, and Shuntaro Namba. All errors and opinions are, however, the responsibility of the author alone. Generous financial support was provided by the John M. Olin Foundation and the National Science Foundation.

This paper focuses on the practice and effects of foreign-exchange intervention during the years 1985–88 by the three largest industrial economies, the Federal Republic of Germany, Japan, and the United States. A wide variety of economic policy tools—monetary, fiscal, and commercial, to name just three—can be used to influence exchange rates. To isolate the "pure" effects of intervention on exchange rates, the discussion below distinguishes between sterilized interventions, whose monetary effects are neutralized by offsetting domestic liquidity measures, and nonsterilized interventions, which alter money supplies and therefore involve the joint exercise of monetary policy and exchange market policy. If effective in achieving significant and sustained exchange rate changes, sterilized intervention could give governments an additional policy tool helpful in resolving conflicts between the monetary policies appropriate for internal balance and those appropriate for external balance.

In June 1982, participants at the Versailles Economic Summit commissioned an official Working Group on Exchange Market Intervention to study the efficacy of government interventions in exchange markets. The Working Group's April 1983 report concluded that sterilized intervention is a relatively weak instrument of exchange-rate policy, with little apparent effectiveness beyond the very short run. This finding is in accord with the statement by the Bundesbank given above, as well as with academic research on the subject, which reaches conclusions that are at least as negative.[3] In the months since the Plaza meeting, however, a substantial realignment of industrial country currency values has been achieved and exchange market intervention (much of it sterilized) has been conducted on a scale not seen since the early 1970s. A fresh look at intervention experience may yield new conclusions, conclusions relevant for evaluating the recent experience of international policy coordination and the prospects for its future success.

The paper is organized as follows. Section 5.2 reviews the recent evolution of key macroeconomic fundamentals, other than intervention, that are likely to have influenced exchange rates. This narrative sets out the macroeconomic context in which intervention has been conducted, and also provides information needed for assessing the independent role of intervention in currency market developments.

Section 5.3 then sets out the mechanics of both sterilized and nonsterilized intervention, emphasizing the effects on asset supplies of alternative intervention strategies. Portfolio-balance theories of effective sterilized intervention are reviewed in this section, which also presents some econometric evidence on foreign currency risk premiums.

Section 5.4 considers an alternative to the portfolio-balance rationale for sterilized intervention, the "signaling" theory. According to this view, official portfolio shifts between nonmoney assets can influence exchange rates, independently of any resulting need for private portfolio rebalancing, by credibly signaling future policy intentions or information not widely appreciated by the market. A simple but limited model of effective signaling, driven by the government's concern about capital losses on its net assets, is outlined and evaluated. Alternative signaling models driven by asymmetric information also receive brief attention.

Section 5.5 reports approximate data on foreign-exchange interventions carried out since the first half of the 1980s, and evaluates the likelihood that portfolio effects associated with those interventions have had a major influence on exchange rates. The conclusion reached is that monetary and fiscal policies, and not intervention per se, have been the main policy determinants of exchange rates in recent years. Pure intervention seems to have played an effective signaling role, in the sense of speeding desired exchange rate movements or impeding undesired ones, when promptly backed up by other, more substantive policy adjustments. But the portfolio effects of pure intervention have generally been elusive enough that intervention cannot be regarded as a macroeconomic policy tool in its own right, with an impact somehow independent of short-term decisions on monetary and fiscal policy. Even in 1987, when massive sterilized interventions were carried out by Germany and Japan, any associated portfolio effects failed to stop sharp appreciations of both the mark and the yen against the dollar. Recent experience does not justify the view that sterilized intervention offers much help in resolving open-economy policy dilemmas.

5.2 After the Strong Dollar: Macroeconomic Adjustment in the Federal Republic of Germany, Japan, and the United States

The dollar reached its most recent peak in the first quarter of 1985 amid a pattern of large and growing external imbalances in the main industrial countries.[4] By 1987, the current account deficit of the United States stood at $154 billion, or 3.4 percent of U.S. gross national product; the current-account surplus of Japan was $87 billion, or 3.6 percent of GNP; and that of Germany was $45 billion, or 4.0 percent of GNP.[5] The size and persistence of these imbalances is unprecedented in the postwar period; to reduce them to sustainable levels, without compromising the goal of noninflationary growth, was the immediate objective of the international policy coordination efforts mounted in the second half of the 1980s.

5.2.1 The Evolution of Cooperative Exchange Rate Management

A substantial realignment of the principal currencies' real exchange rates appeared to be a precondition for a return to a sustainable configuration of current accounts. Between December 1978 and February 1985, the dollar had appreciated (in nominal terms) by 45 percent against the German mark and by 25 percent against the Japanese yen; by the end of August 1985, having depreciated from February levels by 19.4 percent against the mark and by

9.4 percent against the yen, the dollar seemed set on the necessary downward adjustment path.[6] (See figs. 5.1 and 5.2, which show bilateral nominal exchange rates from the end of 1978 and from the start of 1985, respectively.) A sharp dollar upswing in the first week of September 1985, occurring against a backdrop of rising protectionism in the U.S. Congress, was the catalyst for the Group of Five (G-5) Plaza announcement and the approach to exchange rate management it initiated.[7]

Significant milestones in the ongoing evolution of this approach include the following:

Plaza Agreement (September 22, 1985). Participants agreed that "exchange rates should better reflect fundamental economic conditions than has been the case," that "in view of the present and prospective changes in fundamentals, some further orderly appreciation of the main non-dollar currencies against the dollar is desirable," and that G-5 governments would "stand ready to cooperate more closely to encourage this when to do so would be helpful." Funabashi (1988) has given an account of the meeting based, in part, on interviews with unnamed participants. According to this account, an understanding was reached to conduct simultaneous sales of up to $18 billion, with the goal of

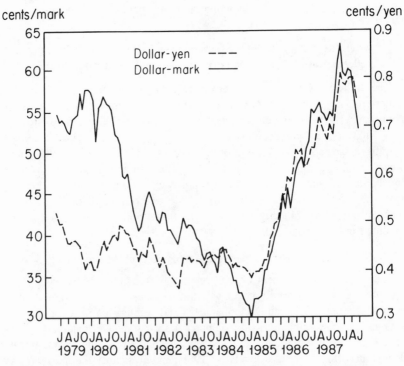

Fig. 5.1   Dollar-mark and dollar-yen nominal exchange rates, 1978–1988

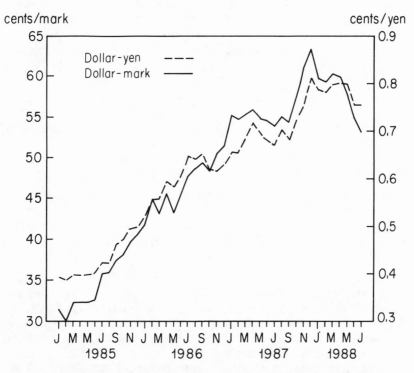

Fig. 5.2   Dollar-mark and dollar-yen nominal exchange rates, 1985–1988

lowering the dollar's value by 10 to 12 percent over a period of six weeks. The implications of this intervention for national monetary policies and interest rates—and, in particular, the question of sterilization—were apparently not discussed. Pledges on fiscal policy were made, however, including a U.S. pledge to pursue tax reform and government deficit reduction.

Coordinated interest rate reductions (March-April 1986). On March 6 and 7, the central banks of France, Germany, Japan, and the United States all lowered their discount rates, hoping to stimulate global growth without upsetting the exchange rate realignment process. On April 21 the monetary authorities of Japan and the United States both lowered their discount rates again.

Tokyo Summit (May 4–5, 1986). The Group of Seven heads of state set up the Group of Seven Finance Ministers to review the "mutual compatibility" of members' policies between the annual summit meetings. These multilateral surveillance exercises, to be conducted in cooperation with the International Monetary Fund, were to consider a number of "indicators" of economic performance, including exchange rates, international reserves, current account and trade balances, and fiscal deficits. The summit declaration seemed to back off a bit from the more vigorous interventionism of the Plaza announcement:

it recommended that "remedial efforts focus first and foremost on underlying policy fundamentals," and reaffirmed the 1983 Williamsburg Summit commitment "to intervene in exchange markets when to do so would be helpful."

First meeting of the G-7 finance ministers (September 27, 1986). A year after the Plaza Agreement, the G-7 finance ministers agreed that members should adopt macroeconomic policies to reduce external imbalances to sustainable levels "without further significant exchange rate adjustment." In other words, even though major effects of the exchange rate realignment on current accounts remained to be seen, realignment had proceeded far enough over the past year to allow countries to stabilize currency values. Nonetheless, between October 1986 and February 1987, the dollar depreciated roughly 13.0 percent further against the mark and 5.5 percent further against the yen. (See fig. 5.2.)

Louvre Accord (February 22, 1987). The G-7 finance ministers and central bank governors (except Italy) made their strongest statement yet on the need to hold nominal exchange rates near existing levels, but did not reveal to the public exact reference levels or allowable ranges of variation around them:

> The Ministers and Governors agreed that the substantial exchange rate changes since the Plaza Agreement will increasingly contribute to reducing external imbalances and have now brought their currencies within ranges broadly consistent with underlying economic fundamentals, given the policy commitments summarized in this statement. Further substantial exchange rate shifts among their currencies could damage growth and adjustment prospects in their countries. In current circumstances, therefore, they agreed to cooperate closely to foster stability of exchange rates around current levels.

The published "policy commitments" included a German promise of tax cuts, Japanese assurances of fiscal stimulus and tax reform, and a U.S. pledge to cut the federal deficit to 2.3 percent of GNP in 1988. According to Funabashi (1988, 186–87), the participants also agreed to spend as much as $4 billion intervening over the period ending in April. Their goal, he reports, was to stabilize the mark and the yen within ±5 percent ranges of 1.8250 marks/dollar and 153.50 yen/dollar, respectively. Intervention would occur "on a voluntary basis" within a ±2.5 percent band of these central rates, was "expected to intensify" between the 2.5 and 5 percent limits, and would be supplemented by mandatory "consultation on policy adjustment" at the 5 percent limit. A 7 percent appreciation of the yen relative to its Louvre parity was, however, ratified at a G-7 meeting in April 1987, where it was agreed, once again, that "around current levels" member currencies "are within ranges broadly consistent with economic fundamentals and the basic policy intentions outlined at the Louvre meeting." A similar favorable assessment of the appropriateness of current exchange rate levels was offered by the G-7 after their September 26, 1987 meeting. This last announcement, however, followed nearly six months of relative stability of mutual G-7 exchange rates.

The G-7 response to the stock market crash (December 22, 1987). After the stock market collapse of October 19, 1987, the dollar depreciated sharply against foreign currencies. The subsequent G-7 communiqué refrained from any direct pronouncement on the appropriateness of current exchange rate levels. A warning to the foreign-exchange markets was, however, issued:

> The Ministers and Governors agreed that either excessive fluctuation of exchange rates, a further decline of the dollar, or a rise in the dollar to an extent that becomes destabilizing to the adjustment process could be counterproductive by damaging growth prospects in the world economy. They re-emphasized their common interest in more stable exchange rates among their currencies and agreed to continue to cooperate closely in monitoring and implementing policies to strengthen underlying economic fundamentals to foster stability of exchange rates. In addition, they agreed to cooperate closely on exchange markets.

(This warning was repeated, in almost identical words, after the April 1988 G-7 meeting.) The communiqué praised the period of exchange rate stability from the Louvre to the September G-7 meeting, as well as "the basic objectives and economic policy directions agreed in the Louvre Accord. . . ." Policy pledges included greater fiscal stimulus in Germany, continued stimulus in Japan, and further fiscal consolidation in the United States.[8] This G-7 declaration followed disappointing news on the U.S. trade deficit in the first half of December; the declaration, perhaps because of its vagueness, did nothing to dispel the ensuing selling pressure on the dollar, which only abated in early January after concerted intervention.[9]

Toronto Summit (June 19–21, 1988). After another, nearly six months of relative exchange rate stability, the seven heads of state repeated the now familiar ban on further dollar depreciation or "destabilizing" appreciation. Around the same time, however, positive news on the U.S. foreign deficit, rising dollar interest rates, and official remarks seemingly favorable to the possibility of some dollar appreciation set off a two-month slide of the mark and yen against the dollar.

G-7 Berlin statement (September 24, 1988). In the wake of the previous summer's dollar appreciation, the participants endorsed exchange rate stability in general terms but did not repeat their earlier formula, which had labeled as "counterproductive" any significant change in the dollar's value. After the G-7 meeting, however, individual statements by the G-5 foreign ministers expressed satisfaction with the prevailing levels of exchange rates. Their assessment contradicted that of the IMF's managing director, who, in widely publicized remarks, deplored the dollar's appreciation since the Toronto Summit.

5.2.2 Exchange Rate Fundamentals: Monetary Policies

In evaluating the role played by pure intervention in recent years, it is useful to have some perspective on the behavior of other fundamental determinants of exchange rates, and on the ability of these fundamentals to explain exchange market developments. Because of the close link between intervention and monetary policy, a natural focus is an account of money-market conditions in Germany, Japan, and the United States. In recent years, the often erratic behavior of money demand and of individual monetary aggregates has made it perilous to use any one as an indicator of the stance of monetary policy. Some inferences about monetary tightness can, however, be based on the behavior of short-term nominal interest rates. In sticky price exchange rate models, these rates tend to fall (rise) in the short run, reinforcing the home currency's depreciation (appreciation), when monetary policy is expansionary (contractionary) or when the money demand function shifts downward (upward).[10] The peril in relying even on short-term nominal interest rates as indicators of monetary ease is, of course, that these rates are influenced by other factors, notably the price level and output. It is therefore advisable to consider additional relevant information, when it is available, in assessing the stance of monetary policy.

Figure 5.3 shows short-term nominal interest rates on mark, yen, and dollar deposits since 1978; interest differentials (dollar less mark and dollar less yen) are shown in figure 5.4. The figures suggest that the foundation for the

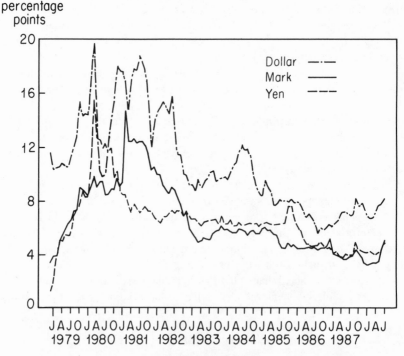

Fig. 5.3   Nominal short-term interest rate levels for dollar, mark, and yen assets, 1978–1988

downward trend of the dollar after the first quarter of 1985 was a falling trend in dollar interest rates from a local peak reached early in the summer of 1984. As dollar interest fell through the late spring of 1985, yen and mark interest fluctuated in narrow ranges. Accordingly, the interest differential in favor of dollars dropped precipitously over the period. Apparently behind this drop was a sharp shift in U.S. monetary policy: as dollar interest rates began to fall, M2 growth, which had been in the lower portion of its 6–9 percent 1984 target range, jumped sufficiently to finish the year around the top.[11] In addition, the Federal Reserve made ½ percent cuts in its discount rate in November and December of 1984. In subsequent testimony before Congress, Federal Reserve Chairman Paul Volcker included the disruptive effects of the dollar's continuing strength among the factors that motivated this easing of monetary policy.[12]

The effects of looser money did not show up immediately in exchange markets; indeed, during the fall of 1984, the dollar appreciated against the mark and yen, and then jumped upward between December 1984 and February 1985 as the pace of U.S. interest rate reduction slowed and (in February) temporarily reversed. The dollar began to decline from its peak, however, as a renewed narrowing of the interest differentials favoring dollars began in

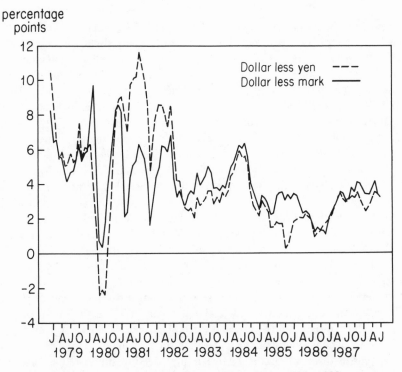

Fig. 5.4   Nominal short-term interest rate differentials, 1978–1988

March. Fueling this development was U.S. M2 growth around the top of its range, another ½ percent discount rate cut in May, and progress on the Gramm-Rudman-Hollings deficit reduction legislation, which President Reagan signed at the end of 1985. Falling interest rates in Germany probably slowed, but did not prevent, the dollar's very sharp depreciation against the mark.

A firming of U.S. interest rates in the summer of 1985 helped set the stage for the September dollar rally that preceded the Plaza announcement. The announcement was not accompanied by an immediate change in international interest differentials; however, it occasioned an immediate fall in the dollar, even before any official intervention occurred. The exchange markets' response represented, in part, a reassessment of the likely permanence of the expansionary monetary tack pursued by the Federal Reserve in previous months. As an official U.S. account put it:

> In part, the exchange market reaction reflected the fact that the announcement was unexpected. More importantly, market participants noted that the initiative had come from the United States and viewed it as a change in the U.S. government's previously perceived attitude of accepting or even welcoming the strong dollar. In addition, the agreement was interpreted as eliminating the likelihood that the Federal Reserve would tighten reserve conditions in response to rapid U.S. monetary growth.[13]

Faced with selling pressure on the yen, the Bank of Japan pushed yen interest sharply higher in October; mark interest rates rose only slightly in that month. Over the course of 1986, dollar interest first rose, then declined, and then rose relative to yen interest, while falling more or less steadily relative to mark interest. The dollar's depreciation against the yen from end-September 1985 to end-December 1986, 36.4 percent, was about the same as its depreciation against the mark, 37.6 percent, in contrast to the dollar's greater fall vis-à-vis the mark in the months before the Plaza Agreement. During this period, U.S. M2 growth remained strong; in addition to the coordinated discount-rate cuts mentioned above, which brought the U.S. rate down to 6.5 percent by the end of April, the Federal Reserve carried out two unilateral ½ percent cuts in July and August.

Already by mid-1986, some policymakers in the United States, notably Chairman Volcker, and many abroad, worried that further dollar depreciation might have adverse effects on U.S. inflation and on the world economy. In September, the G-7 issued the above-mentioned declaration that current exchange rate levels were broadly consistent with "fundamentals." On October 31, 1986, U.S. Treasury Secretary James A. Baker and Japanese Finance Minister Kiichi Miyazawa reiterated that "the exchange rate realignment achieved between the yen and the dollar since the Plaza Agreement is now broadly consistent with the underlying fundamentals. . . ." The Bank of Japan cut its discount rate, and Miyazawa pledged to stimulate the Japanese economy further through tax reform and additional public spending.[14] In November, short-term dollar interest rates began to edge upward.

Disappointing news on the U.S. trade balance, disappointing implementation of the Japanese fiscal undertakings in the Baker-Miyazawa accord, and hints from U.S. officials that the dollar might need to depreciate further led to a renewed bout of dollar weakness in December and January. On January 21, Baker and Miyazawa issued a second communiqué characterizing the dollar-yen rate as "broadly consistent with fundamentals," despite a dollar depreciation against the yen of close to 6 percent since the earlier Baker-Miyazawa declaration.[15] In later attempts to relieve the upward pressure on their currencies, the Bundesbank and the Bank of Japan lowered their discount rates, reinforcing an ongoing widening of the dollar's interest advantage. The Bundesbank's action followed a year in which, partly as a result of interventions connected with European Monetary System (EMS) pressures and partly as a result of dollar interventions, the central bank money stock had finished far above the top of its target range. (The mark was revalued within the EMS on January 12, 1987.) The Louvre Accord, the first concerted attempt to stabilize currency values since the dollar turnaround of early 1985, was announced on February 22, 1987.

The Louvre Accord resulted in a period, about eight months long, of approximate stability for the main industrial country exchange rates. This broad stabilization was achieved despite continuing pressure for further dollar depreciation due, in part, to the persistence of a large U.S. current account deficit. The dollar-mark exchange rate basically remained within a 5 percent band during this period, while the dollar-yen rate fluctuated within a 10 percent band. The dollar exchange rates of the pound sterling, the French franc, the Canadian dollar, and the lira were also unusually stable.

It seems apparent in retrospect that the relative exchange rate stability that followed the Louvre meeting was enforced with the help of restrictive monetary policy in the United States and relatively expansionary policies in Germany and Japan. Short-term mark and yen interest rates moved downward after the Louvre, remaining near, and mostly below, 4 percent until September 1987. Germany's central bank money stock was allowed to overshoot its 1987 target growth range of 3–6 percent by a considerable margin; as a result, German M1 and M3 both grew at exceptionally rapid rates over the year. Japan's money supply—whether measured as M1 or as M2 plus the stock of certificates of deposit—grew at its fastest rate of the decade (in both cases well above 10 percent per year). In the United States, meanwhile, short-term interest rates moved to a higher range and the growth rate of M2 was held below the bottom of its target interval;[16] in early September the Federal Reserve raised its discount rate from 5.5 to 6 percent.

Interest rate increases in all three countries, and a widening of the U.S.-foreign short-term interest differential, preceded the stock market crash of October 19, 1987. This generalized rise in interest rates is sometimes identified as a catalyst of the crash. The stock market plunge was immediately followed by a worldwide *fall* in interest rates as investors shifted from stocks into bonds and as central banks acted to head off any incipient liquidity crisis; in the process, the interest differential in favor of dollars declined. By the end of 1987, the dollar had registered another decisive external decline, shattering the lower limit specified by the Louvre Accord. The dollar's fall was heavily influenced by adverse U.S. trade news, and it occurred in spite of an interest rate reduction in Japan and an even deeper reduction in Europe. The December G-7 meeting, as noted earlier, reaffirmed the goal of exchange rate stability and warned against further dollar depreciation, to no great immediate effect.

After the dollar, buttressed by favorable trade news and more intervention, recovered some of its losses in January, the currency's exchange rates against the yen and the mark remained in relatively narrow bands through the middle of June—another period, nearly six months long, of approximate stability. A new phase of dollar appreciation began after mid-June, sparked, as noted above, by evidence of U.S. trade balance improvement, firming dollar interest rates, and official intimations that some dollar appreciation might now be tolerated. The surprising magnitude and duration of the dollar's summer-time rise raised the worrisome possibility that progress in external adjustment might be slowed or even reversed. By September, however, the dollar upswing had moderated with the aid of sharply higher short-term interest rates in Germany.

5.2.3   Exchange Rate Fundamentals: Government and Private Demand

A brief look at events impinging more directly than monetary policy on output markets will complete this survey of macroeconomic developments in the recent period of exchange rate realignment. Table 5.1 reports data on central-government fiscal deficits (general-government deficits are given in parentheses) and real domestic demand growth in the three largest economies.[17]

Important changes in fiscal positions are evident in the data. Over the course of the early 1980s, U.S. government deficits—central and general alike—rose sharply relative to GNP; starting in 1986, a leveling off and possible reversal of this trend appears. Both Germany and Japan, however, display declining deficit ratios over the early 1980s. In the German case, this downward trend seems to end in 1985–86, while in the Japanese case, the trend continues through the time of this writing.

In retrospect, the stabilizing of the American and German fiscal deficit ratios around the mid-1980s stands out as a key factor behind the dollar-mark realignment that began late in the first quarter of 1985. Although Japan's fiscal deficits have continued to decline throughout the 1980s, U.S. fiscal consolidation has contributed to dollar-yen realignment as well. Before 1985, market participants may have expected the then-divergent trends in national fiscal positions to continue for some time; these expectations would have contributed, in turn, to the dollar's appreciation against the mark and yen. Thus, the

Table 5.1   **Fiscal Policy and Domestic Demand in Japan, the Federal Republic of Germany, and the United States, 1980–1988**

	Germany	Japan	United States
	Central (General) Government Fiscal Balance (% of nominal GNP/GDP)		
1980	−1.9 (−2.9)	−6.2 (−4.4)	−2.3 (−1.3)
1981	−2.5 (−3.7)	−5.9 (−3.8)	−2.4 (−1.0)
1982	−2.4 (−3.3)	−5.9 (−3.6)	−4.1 (−3.5)
1983	−1.9 (−2.5)	−5.6 (−3.7)	−5.6 (−3.8)
1984	−1.6 (−1.9)	−4.7 (−2.1)	−5.1 (−2.8)
1985	−1.3 (−1.1)	−3.9 (−0.8)	−5.3 (−3.3)
1986	−1.2 (−1.3)	−3.4 (−0.9)	−4.8 (−3.4)
1987	−1.4 (−1.8)	−2.7 (0.6)	−3.4 (−2.3)
1988	−1.7 (−2.0)	−2.1 (1.1)	−3.3 (−1.8)
	Annual Growth of Total Real Domestic Demand (%)		
1980	1.1	0.8	−1.8
1981	−2.7	2.1	2.2
1982	−2.0	2.8	−1.9
1983	2.3	1.8	5.1
1984	2.0	3.8	8.7
1985	0.8	4.0	3.8
1986	3.6	4.1	3.7
1987	3.1	5.2	3.0
1988	3.5	7.7	3.0

Source: IMF, *World Economic Outlook* (October 1988 and April 1989): tables A13, A17, and A2 in both issues.

impact of fiscal policy on exchange rates in the late 1980s should not be judged by the sizes of *actual* fiscal adjustments alone. To the extent that fiscal policy actions from 1985 on signaled changes in the trends of the decade's first half, they would have been accompanied by changes in *expected future* deficit ratios that have an effect on exchange rates independent of current fiscal moves. Branson (1988) has insisted on the importance of such expectations effects in arguing that the anticipated enactment of the Gramm-Rudman-Hollings legislation contributed to the dollar's 1985 depreciation.

Lacking the benefits of hindsight, market participants were able to discern changes in national fiscal trends only over time. A growing perception that American and German fiscal trends had been altered probably contributed to steady downward pressure on the dollar relative to the mark and yen in 1986 and 1987.

Given the likely importance of fiscal policy expectations, little can be gained from attempts to correlate even year-to-year movements in currency values with ex post changes in fiscal stance. Possibly, more can be learned from divergent movements in real domestic demand, which are less likely than fiscal deficit changes to have been associated with large shifts in long-term expectations. It is difficult in practice, however, to disentangle the ''pure'' exchange rate effect of a demand shift—which alters the terms of trade at constant money price levels—from the expectations about future monetary policy reactions that the shift creates. Thus, an acceleration of demand growth in the United States can cause nominal dollar appreciation for two reasons: it signals the possible need for a rise in the relative price of U.S. traded goods, and, if the economy is running near full capacity, it also raises the likelihood that the Federal Reserve will restrict monetary growth in the future.

Since 1985, cumulative demand growth has been strongest in Japan; from 1986, demand growth has been comparable in the United States and Germany. Overall demand factors are therefore likely contributors to the yen's appreciation against both the dollar and the mark over the 1985–88 period. The very high rate of U.S. demand growth in 1984 (8.7 percent) is noteworthy. A plausible hypothesis is that the buoyant business environment associated with this exceptional growth, perhaps coupled with expectations that monetary tightness would be needed later to discourage inflation, kept the dollar high in 1984 and early 1985 even after U.S. monetary policy loosened.

5.3   Sterilized Intervention as a Policy Instrument

After 1985, monetary policies in the three main industrial countries have operated in a setting of relatively inflexible fiscal policies, first to amplify the dollar's real depreciation in the hope of hastening current account adjustment, then to stabilize currencies at levels supposedly consistent with external equilibrium in the long run. At the same time, each country has used monetary means to pursue the additional domestic goal of growth with low inflation. In a world of N countries and N policy tools (the individual countries' monetary policies), it is only by accident that N domestic objectives and $N - 1$ exchange rate targets can simultaneously be attained in the short run. Unless $N - 1$ additional policy instruments are available, conflicts between internal and external balance are bound to arise, as they have done continually in recent years.

Sterilized foreign-exchange intervention furnishes $N - 1$ additional policy tools with the potential to be useful complements to monetary policies. These $N - 1$ additional tools are pure changes in the *relative* stocks of national currency bonds held in private portfolios. A major difficulty in evaluating intervention is to identify empirically the channels, if any, through which intervention has significant, lasting effects on exchange rates.

5.3.1   The Mechanics of Intervention and Sterilization

Official intervention in the foreign-exchange market has the direct effect of altering the balance sheet of the central bank, and possibly of other government agencies. U.S. intervention, for example, is carried out by both the Federal Reserve and by the Exchange Stabilization Fund (ESF) of the U.S. Treasury.

When foreign-exchange intervention is not sterilized, it can affect exchange rates by changing the stock of high-powered (or base) money, a change that leads to adjustments in broader monetary aggregates, in interest rates, and in market expectations about future price level inflation. A stylized balance sheet for the German Bundesbank would show its net asset holdings—consisting of net foreign assets (NFA) and net domestic assets (NDA)—equal to its monetary liabilities, the German monetary base (B):[18]

$$NFA + NDA = B.$$

A nonsterilized Bundesbank purchase of a $1 million bank deposit at DM 2 per dollar, say, alters the central bank's balance sheet by raising NFA (on the asset side) and B (on the liability side), both by DM 2 million. The corresponding change in the private sector's balance sheet is the mirror image of this one: a DM 2 million rise in German high-powered money holdings, and a DM 2 million decline in holdings of dollar deposits.

The Bundesbank could sterilize this intervention's expansionary effect on the monetary base through several types of offsetting operation, for example, a DM 2 million open market sale of mark-denominated domestic government securities. This additional operation would reduce the Bundesbank's net domestic assets and its monetary liabilities, both by DM 2 million. Taken together, the two Bundesbank actions—intervention plus sterilization—would leave the public with unchanged holdings of high-powered money, but with a higher stock of interest-bearing mark assets and a correspondingly lower stock of interest-bearing dollar assets. In this sense, sterilized intervention is a "pure" change in the relative stocks of national currency bonds held by the public, that is, a change that is not accompanied by a change in the monetary base.[19]

As noted above, sterilized interventions can take many forms. Consider, for example, a hypothetical forward exchange market intervention in which the Bundesbank sells three-month forward marks for forward dollars. This operation is essentially the same as the sterilized intervention just described, in that it increases the net stock of mark bonds held by the private sector (the private sector's net claims on future delivery of marks), decreases the net stock of dollar bonds, but does not change the German base.[20] Operations by non–central bank government agencies, such as the U.S. ESF, are automatically sterilized if the balances drawn on for intervention purposes are held in the private banking system, say, or in the form of government securities purchased and sold in the open market. If some of these balances are held at central banks, however, the agencies' interventions may have monetary effects.

Certain central bank transactions are automatically sterilized, after some time lag. Imagine that the Bundesbank lends DM 1 million to the Bank of France for intramarginal franc purchases under the EMS very short-term financing facility. At an exchange rate of Ffr 3.5 per mark, say, these transactions change the two central banks' balance sheets as follows:

Balance Sheet of the Bundesbank

Change in Net Assets	Change in Monetary Liabilities
ΔNFA $= +$ DM 1 million	ΔB $= +$ DM 1 million

Balance Sheet of the Bank of France

Change in Net Assets	Change in Monetary Liabilities
ΔNFA $= -$ Ffr 3.5 million	ΔB $= -$ Ffr 3.5 million

As a result of this coordinated intervention, there is a symmetric monetary adjustment (absent immediate sterilization), because Germany's high-powered money stock rises as France's falls. Under EMS rules, however, the increase in German money may be automatically sterilized if, after the statutory three and a half months, the Bundesbank requests repayment of its loan in marks. Since repayment leaves the French central bank's *net* foreign assets the same—a liability to the Bundesbank is settled through an equal depletion of mark reserves—the French monetary base can remain at its lower level. The German base falls, however, if the Bank of France discharges its debt to the Bundesbank by drawing on French official holdings of marketable mark securities:

Balance Sheet of the Bundesbank

Change in Net Assets	Change in Monetary Liabilities
ΔNFA $= -$ DM 1 million	ΔB $= -$ DM 1 million

In effect, the Bank of France automatically sterilizes the increase in the German base when it repays its loan using marketable mark reserves; the initial symmetry of the intervention unwinds. Such automatic sterilization would not occur if France repaid Germany in dollars or, say, in European Currency Units.[21]

5.3.2   International Portfolio Balance and Exchange Rates

Since sterilized intervention operates by changing the currency denomination of bonds held by the public, such changes must affect asset market equilibrium if any exchange rate change is to result. As a matter of theory, the link between government asset swaps and equilibrium is not immediate: a government exchange of foreign for domestic assets with domestic residents may wash out if private agents fully capitalize, as part of their own wealth, all future net taxes levied by the government. In this extreme case of Ricardian equivalence between debt issue and taxes, the government cannot systematically affect the relevant "outside" bond supplies, that is the net supply of claims on governments that the public must hold. The evidence on Ricardian equivalence is ambiguous, so in what follows, I will assume that government asset operations do indeed move outside asset supplies in the intended directions, though not necessarily on a one-for-one basis.[22]

How should changes in outside supplies of national currency debt affect asset markets? Portfolio-balance theories of exchange rate determination link relative expected nominal rates of return on bonds of different currency denomination to outside asset supplies. According to these theories, a wealth owner cares about the riskiness of a portfolio as well as the expected return that it offers. Since bonds of different currency denomination are perfect substitutes for risk averters only under very unlikely circumstances, a change in outside asset supplies generally alters the risk characteristics of the market portfolio and thus requires an equilibrating adjustment in currencies' relative expected returns.

More precisely, let R_t be the one-period risk-free nominal interest rate on domestic currency, R_t^* the corresponding rate on foreign currency, S_t the (spot) price of foreign currency in terms of domestic, and $E_t(\cdot)$ a conditional expectation, given information as of date t. Then the domestic currency payoff on a domestic currency bond held for one period is $1 + R_t$, while the expected domestic currency payoff on the same investment in a one-period foreign bond is $(1 + R_t^*)E_t(S_{t+1})/S_t$. The portfolio-balance view posits that the return differential or (relative) *risk premium* on foreign currency,

$$(1) \qquad (1 + R_t^*)E_t(S_{t+1})/S_t - (1 + R_t) \equiv \rho_t,$$

is a function of the outside supplies of assets denominated in domestic and foreign currency. An implication is that changes in outside asset supplies, such as those caused by sterilized intervention, can alter asset market prices, including exchange rates. The general presumption is that, all else equal, an increase in the stock of domestic currency debt that the public must hold will raise the domestic currency interest rate, lower the foreign currency interest rate, and depreciate the domestic currency in the foreign-exchange market (see Branson and Henderson 1985). As note 22 above warns, however, the exchange rate effect of a sterilized intervention is impossible to evaluate in *general* equilibrium without a complete model of how future macroeconomic policies of all kinds adjust to keep the government within its intertemporal budget constraint.

There is a large body of evidence contradicting the hypothesis that ρ_t in equation (1) is identically zero, or even constant over time; Hodrick (1987) presents a thorough review of this evidence and of its interpretation by various authors. The risk premium ρ_t could be identically zero if investors were risk neutral (and certain other conditions held); in this case, bonds differing in currency of denomination would be perfect substitutes, implying that changes in their relative outside supplies do not necessarily call for equilibrating changes in relative asset returns. Under perfect substitution, there is no meaningful distinction (leaving aside the incentive effects to be discussed in sec. 5.4) between monetary changes brought about by transactions in foreign-exchange markets and changes of equal magnitude brought about by measures such as open market trades of domestic securities. The condition $\rho_t \equiv 0$ is often called the uncovered interest parity condition.[23]

The statement that uncovered interest parity fails to hold is not the same as the statement that sterilized intervention is effective in moving exchange rates.[24] The latter statement would be supported, however, by econometric evidence that government debt supplies play a systematic role in determining ρ_t. Evidence of this sort has not, however, been forthcoming. Define

$$v_{t+1} \equiv (1 + R_t^*) [S_{t+1} - E_t(S_{t+1})]/S_t,$$

so that v_{t+1} is uncorrelated with time-t information. Most studies proceed by regressing

$$(2) \qquad (1 + R_t^*)S_{t+1}/S_t - (1 + R_t) = \rho_t + v_{t+1},$$

on time-t government debt supplies, which are assumed to be correlated with the relevant outside asset supplies. Hodrick (1987, 119–28) documents the failure of such tests to produce significant evidence that asset supplies affect risk premiums.

Some of the tests discussed by Hodrick impose added structure on the problem of relating the ex post excess return, equation (2), to outside asset supplies by assuming that international investors are mean-variance optimizers. The resulting capital asset pricing model (CAPM) implies that the coefficient in the regression equation depends on the degree of investor risk aversion and the covariance matrix of unexpected asset returns, which is assumed not to change over time. Evidence that the covariance matrix does indeed change over time (see Cumby and Obstfeld 1984) has led some researchers to postulate explicitly time-varying covariance matrices in estimation. Engel and Rodrigues (1987), Giovannini and Jorion (1989), and Mark (1988) take this approach; the first two papers find evidence against versions of the CAPM with time-varying covariances, while the last is more favorable. It seems fair to say, however, that none of these models can explain more than a small fraction of the volatility in the ex post excess return defined by equation (2). Allowing for time-varying covariances in the CAPM does little if anything to support the view that shifts in outside asset supplies, per se, have significant exchange rate effects.[25]

5.3.3 Consumption-Based Asset Pricing Models

An alternative approach to modeling the risk premium views consumption risk as a major determinant of asset returns. On this view, the mechanisms that might underlie any effects of sterilized intervention are somewhat less direct than those driving portfolio-balance models. Presumably, sterilized intervention could affect exchange rates by altering the composition of private wealth, and thereby altering the covariance of wealth, and hence of consumption, with the returns on various currencies.

The consumption-based theory builds on the intertemporal efficiency condition for an individual who derives utility $u(c_t)$ from consuming c_t in period t, has a subjective discount factor β, and faces the home price level P_t in addition to home and foreign nominal interest rates R_t and R_t^* and a nominal price of foreign currency S_t. The efficiency condition is

$$(3) \qquad E_t(S_{t+1}/S_t) - \frac{1 + R_t}{1 + R_t^*} = - \frac{\mathrm{cov}_t(Q_{t+1}, S_{t+1}/S_t)}{E_t(Q_{t+1})},$$

where

$$Q_{t+1} \equiv \beta u'(c_{t+1})/P_{t+1} \div u'(c_t)/P_t$$

and $\mathrm{cov}_t(\cdot)$ is a conditional covariance.[26] The term on the right-hand side of equation (3) is (up to a discount factor) the risk premium ρ_t defined in equation (1); if it is identically zero, equation (3) becomes the uncovered interest parity condition

$$(4) \qquad \frac{1 + R_t}{1 + R_t^*} = E_t(S_{t+1}/S_t).$$

As noted earlier, condition (4) has been tested extensively, for example, by testing whether the interest factor ratio is an unbiased predictor of future spot rate changes. Table 5.2 presents estimates of the equation

$$S_{t+1}/S_t = a + b(1 + R_t)/(1 + R_t^*) + \epsilon_{t+1},$$

Table 5.2   Tests Based on $S_{t+1}/S_t = a + b(1 + R_t)/(1 + R_t^*) + \epsilon_{t+1}$

Currency	a	b	$Q(18)$	F-stat	Significance
Mark	2.383	-1.364	15.76	1.036	0.363
	(1.742)	(1.726)			
Yen	4.013	-2.967	19.43	6.333	0.004
	(1.152)	(1.141)			
Pound	2.289	-1.304	32.74	3.165	0.052
	(0.935)	(0.939)			

Note: Quarterly data, three-month interest rates. Exchange and interest rates are end-of-quarter quotations. Sample period for yen is 76:2 to 86:3; for other currencies, 75:2 to 86:3. The Q-statistic tests for serial correlation at lags up to 18 and is distributed $\chi^2(18)$ if equation errors are white noise. The F-statistic tests the null hypothesis $a = 0$, $b = 1$. Its significance is the probability of finding the estimated coefficients under the null.

along with F-tests of the null hypothesis of unbiasedness, $a = 0$, $b = 1$. (The time interval is three months, and the data are nonoverlapping.) Included are results for the exchange rates of the mark, the yen, and the pound sterling against the dollar. The results are rather negative, and indicate that interest rate differences have tended to mispredict the direction of subsequent exchange rate change in recent years.

To assess the possibility that the results of table 5.2 are explained by a time-varying consumption-based risk premium, it is useful to write equation (3) in a form that is comparable to equation (4). This can be done by observing that $E_t(Q_{t+1}) = (1 + R_t)^{-1}$, which implies

$$(5) \qquad \frac{1 + R_t}{1 + R_t^*} = E_t[(S_{t+1}/S_t)Q_{t+1}(1 + R_t)].$$

Equation (5) shows how depreciation, adjusted for consumption risk, is related to the international interest differential. The prediction of this equation is that the ordinary least-squares regression $(S_{t+1}/S_t)Q_{t+1}(1 + R_t) = a + b(1 + R_t)/(1 + R_t^*) + \mu_{t+1}$ should yield estimated coefficients of $a = 0$ and $b = 1$; table 5.3 reports the results of empirical tests. For the purpose of these tests, it was assumed that (1) utility is separable in consumption of services, nondurables, and durables; (2) the utility derived from any consumption category can be measured by a function that is isoelastic with elasticity 2 (so that $u'[c]$ is a constant times c^{-2}); and (3) $\beta = 0.985$ (per quarter).[27]

Table 5.3   **Tests Based on $(S_{t+1}/S_t) Q_{t+1}(1+R_t)=a+b(1+R_t)/(1+R_t^*)+\mu_{t+1}$**

Currency	a	b	$Q(18)$	F-stat	Significance
		Consumption Data: Services			
Mark	−0.347	1.325	14.97	1.992	0.148
	(1.855)	(1.837)			
Yen	2.585	−1.567	15.81	2.571	0.089
	(1.208)	(1.196)			
Pound	0.963	0.014	30.73	2.699	0.078
	(1.071)	(1.076)			
		Consumption Data: Nondurables			
Mark	0.804	0.193	14.40	0.792	0.459
	(1.817)	(1.780)			
Yen	3.069	−2.037	17.80	2.542	0.091
	(1.365)	(1.352)			
Pound	1.421	−0.438	16.39	1.464	0.242
	(1.131)	(1.136)			

Note: See footnote to table 5.2. The appendix describes the consumption data underlying the results reported above.

While the results of table 5.3 do make the consumption-based model look marginally better than the simple uncovered interest parity model, they do not justify a large shift in priors. Figure 5.5 illustrates why the consumption-based model cannot go very far in explaining the risk premium; it compares the ex post values of the right-hand sides of equations (4) and (5), using data for the first regression reported in table 5.3. (This is a completely representative picture, however.) The correlation between these two variables is extremely high: price levels are not very variable compared with exchange rates, and except at implausibly high levels of risk aversion, aggregate consumption variability is insufficient to help much in explaining excess returns in the foreign-exchange market.

Hodrick (1987) reviews a largely negative body of evidence on consumption based international asset pricing models.[28] Slightly more favorable results have been reported recently by Cumby (1988), Hodrick (1989), and Obstfeld (1989a). Nonetheless, the low explanatory power of these models precludes any strong inferences about the validity of a portfolio-balance rationale for sterilized intervention. Perhaps the point to take home is that ex post exchange rate variability is so high relative to that of other variables in all of the models reviewed that only the weakest conclusions can be drawn from the econometric record.

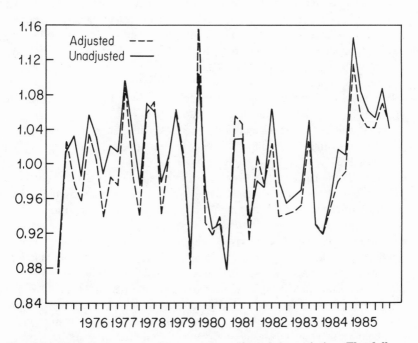

Fig. 5.5 Depreciation versus consumption-adjusted depreciation: The dollar-mark exchange rate, 1975–1986

5.4   Intervention as a Signal to Exchange Markets

The failure of risk models to explain the apparent deviations from uncovered interest parity has led some researchers to conclude that participants in exchange markets ignore easily available information about exchange rates and make biased exchange rate forecasts.[29] Other researchers interpret the negative results as evidence of weaknesses in the econometric methods and the empirical risk models that have been applied.[30]

Members of both schools agree, however, that there is a channel through which sterilized intervention can move exchange rates even when bonds of different currency denomination are perfect substitutes. That channel is the new information about economic conditions and future economic policies that the volume and direction of intervention may signal to the market independently of any other current policy changes. Marston (1988) provides an interesting comparative discussion of two episodes—the Carter administration's dollar support operations of late 1978, and the Plaza declaration—in which sterilized intervention accompanied explicit policy announcements aimed at changing the course of exchange markets.

Notice that the *signaling effect* of intervention might not be detectable by means of econometric tests such as those discussed in section 5.3 because forward-rate forecast errors can be uncorrelated with lagged intervention despite being correlated with contemporaneous intervention. This correlation pattern could occur if, for example, currency-denominated bonds were perfect substitutes, expectations were rational, and sterilized intervention helped significantly in predicting future monetary policies. While the results of section 5.3 thus allow no direct inferences about the signaling effect, alternative econometric tests of signaling can be designed. In a study covering the period 1977–81, Dominguez (1988) provides empirical support for the proposition that Federal Reserve intervention has at times communicated information useful for predicting future monetary policies.[31] Humpage (1988), who uses a different methodology, cites evidence suggesting a signaling effect over the recent period from August 1984 to August 1987.

It must be emphasized, however, that if intervention affects exchange rates *only* through the signals it sends, then it is not a macroeconomic policy instrument in the same sense that monetary and fiscal policies are. Intervention may alter the way that monetary policy announcements affect the exchange rate, for example, but it derives its power in this case entirely from its ability to influence market perceptions or expectations about other economic factors.

Consideration of episodes such as those described by Marston (1988) raises three fundamental (and closely connected) questions about the hypothesis that sterilized intervention affects exchange rates through a signaling mechanism. First, what information is contained in interventions that is not contained in the verbal policy announcements that frequently complement intervention and sometimes substitute for it? Second, why should sterilized foreign-exchange intervention, rather than other reallocations of the government's asset port-folio, be particularly effective in signaling official intentions or information? For example, would it not be equally effective to signal that currency depreciation is desired through open market sales of domestic bonds that are subsequently "sterilized" by an offsetting increase in commercial banks' rediscount quotas? Third, what, if anything, assures the market that the signals sterilized intervention conveys are credible? In other words, are there costs that discourage governments from sending deceptive signals in attempts to obtain short-term advantages?

An obvious advantage of foreign-exchange intervention as a signaling device is that it can be deployed rapidly and around the clock, with immediate impact in the markets where exchange rates are set. The difficulties one faces in taking the analysis of intervention signals beyond this observation were well summarized by Tobin (1971, 408) in a discussion of the role of discount rate changes in monetary management:

> For many students of central bank policy the psychology of the announcement is the most important and perhaps the only important aspect of the discount rate. Unfortunately there is little of a systematic character that can be said about it. Will the public conclude from the announcement of a fall in the discount rate that predictions of recession are now confirmed by the expert economic intelligence of the central bank, and therefore regard the an-nouncement as a deflationary portent? Or will the market judge that the authorities have thus indicated their resolute intention of preventing deflation, arresting and reversing the recession, and accordingly interpret the announce-ment as an inflationary sign? What do the authorities themselves regard as the likely psychological effects of their announcements? Clearly it is easy to become enmeshed in a game of infinite regress between the central bank and the market.

In the decades since this passage first was published, some progress has been made in systematically modeling the announcement effects of sterilized interven-tion. It is fair to say, however, that the models put forward so far are not close to representing the full range of government concerns that motivate intervention.

One reason sterilized intervention may send more informative and more credible signals than announcements or other public debt management policies centers on the effect of unanticipated exchange rate changes on the govern-ment's net worth. (Mussa 1981 discusses the relevance of this effect.) For example, a government that buys foreign exchange on a sterilized basis—thereby going long in foreign currency and short in domestic—will lose more money than it otherwise would have lost if its own currency subsequently appreciates by a percentage amount greater than the nominal interest differ-ential. Public finance considerations thus lend credibility to a government that uses sterilized purchases of foreign exchange to signal a future depreciation of the domestic currency; conversely, sterilized sales of foreign currency may communicate a credible signal that policies to appreciate the domestic currency will be pursued. The expectations created when a policy authority "puts its money where its mouth is" in this way can move exchange rates even under perfect asset substitutability.

As an illustration, suppose that the U.S. Treasury's ESF decides to intervene in marks to support the dollar's exchange rate against the German currency. A hypothetical possibility is that the ESF draws on a mark credit line with the Bundesbank (borrowing DM 10 million, say) and purchases dollar securities on the open market (say, $5 million in U.S. Treasury bills at an exchange rate of DM 2 per dollar). The effect on the U.S. government's balance sheet is:

Balance Sheet of the U.S. Government

Change in Assets	Change in Liabilities
+ $5 million	+ DM 10 million

This intervention has no effect on the U.S. monetary base. Although its monetary effects in the United States are therefore sterilized, the intervention does alter U.S. incentives: having gone long in dollars and short in marks, the Treasury is now more vulnerable to an unanticipated rise in the mark's dollar price. Foreign-exchange traders may therefore view the Treasury's action as a signal that American policies consistent with dollar appreciation are in store.[32]

In November 1978, the announcement that the U.S. Treasury would sell "Carter bonds" denominated in nondollar currencies may initially have altered market forecasts by appearing to reduce the U.S. government's incentive to inflate. (The rapid unwinding of the initial favorable market response to the Carter package illustrates the perils of intervention signals that are not backed up promptly by concrete policy changes.) Similarly, recent proposals that the U.S. government borrow yen rather than dollars, put forward by the *Economist* magazine and others, build on the idea of stabilizing currency markets by reducing the U.S. temptation to default partially on external dollar debts through an inflation of dollar prices.

The foregoing ideas can be formalized in the context of recent research on dynamic optimal taxation. Work by Lucas and Stokey (1983), Persson, Persson, and Svensson (1987), Calvo and Obstfeld (1990), and Obstfeld (1989c) has shown how government debt management policies, such as changes in the maturity structure of government debt or in the mix between real and nominal public liabilities, can enhance the credibility (technically speaking, the dynamic consistency) of optimal government plans. More generally, alternative debt strategies can alter the economy's equilibrium path, even when the expectations theory of the term structure holds and the Fisher equation links the own returns on real and nominal bonds.

The basic setup assumed in this literature is one in which the government must finance expenditures and debt repayments via distorting taxes, including the inflation tax on monetary balances. Since the real present value of its debt repayments depends on policies, potential asset revaluations affect the net marginal benefit to the government of any contemplated policy change. Realizing this linkage, the public uses government portfolio shifts, which change marginal government incentives, to predict future policy shifts. As a result, government asset swaps such as sterilized intervention, which might appear pointless at first glance, can alter expectations systematically, and can be analyzed by methods analogous to those that have been used to analyze the expectational effects of other types of official portfolio shift.

As suggested above, a government that buys home currency bonds and sells foreign bonds may reduce its own future incentives to create surprise inflation, and thereby lead traders to infer that the home currency will be stronger in the future than they had previously believed. Given current money supplies, the sterilized sale of foreign currency will thus cause a spot appreciation of the home currency. Bohn (1988) develops a model of the type described above to examine the incentive effects of government operations in foreign exchange.[33]

Such models could be useful in understanding the apparently stronger effects of *concerted,* as opposed to unilateral, intervention. If the Japanese authorities coordinate their dollar purchases with official American sales of yen, the Japanese government's gains from yen appreciation, and the U.S. government's gains from dollar depreciation, *both* decline. The positive effect on the dollar's value would be smaller if Japan intervened alone and the American government's incentives didn't change.

How powerful in practice are the budgetary incentives underlying these ideas? In testimony before Congress shortly after the Plaza Agreement, Stephen H. Axilrod, then Federal Reserve Staff Director for Monetary and Financial Policy, felt it necessary to comment on the budgetary implications of recent U.S. purchases of foreign currencies. After pointing out that lower interest earnings on those investments might be offset by an appreciation of foreign currencies against the dollar, he concluded that any net effect "would be very small absolutely and relative to Treasury receipts."[34] Economic theory implies, however, that the cost to the government of foreign exchange losses should be measured as the product of the amount of the loss and a shadow price reflecting the difficulty the government would encounter in replacing the lost resources. A government that is already running a large deficit will view a given loss as more costly than would a government with a balanced budget.

This is not to say that public sector losses on exchange markets have not been large in some years. Germany lost more than DM 9 billion on its reserves in 1987 as a result of the dollar's depreciation (see table 5.6, below). This loss had a substantial impact on the country's public sector deficit and caused the German government considerable domestic embarrassment.

Interesting as they are, the public finance models are quite specialized; they capture only one aspect of government behavior and probably not the most important one. In reality, governments pursue many goals not present in these models, such as high employment, and respond to purely political events, such as sectoral pressures for protection. Furthermore, the observability assumptions of these models, which require full public knowledge of government preferences, constraints, and information, are inadequate for addressing some issues.

Stein (1989) presents a simple incomplete information model in which the market cannot directly observe the authorities' utility trade-off between an exchange rate target and a domestic policy target. Uncertainty over official preferences prevents the market from accurately forecasting future monetary policy. Because of the temptation to manipulate the *current* exchange rate through a time-inconsistent policy, the authorities cannot credibly announce the future level of the money supply. Surprisingly, however, the authorities can credibly communicate some of their private information to the market, and in a way that favorably affects the current exchange rate. Specifically, the authorities can credibly announce a *range* of future exchange rate targets, even though the announcement of any precise policy target is not credible. Aside from rationalizing the recent G-7 practice of indicating only broad target ranges for exchange rates, Stein's model suggests that intervention itself could provide a noisy but credible message about policymakers' private information.

Intervention may be costly for a government, as noted earlier, with costs that depend on the private information the government has. While such signaling costs play no role in Stein's analysis, they may allow the market to use observed interventions for more precise inferences about that data available to the authorities. Asymmetric information thus provides an additional mechanism through which intervention costs can lend credence to intervention signals.

Uncertainty has additional implications for intervention that any realistic analysis must recognize. Policymakers have imperfect information about market fundamentals; for example, they usually are unable to observe directly shifts in comparative advantage or the location of new international investment opportunities. By "testing the market" through intervention, authorities may gain a better idea of whether particular exchange rate movements represent transitory factors that ought to be offset—such as erroneous rumors about future policies—or permanent developments that it would be unwise to resist through monetary adjustments. Government agencies may well lose money in carrying out such exploratory intervention operations, but at least part of this cost can be viewed as a price paid for insight into market conditions. Generally, individual market actors will also gain information by observing the effects of official interventions.

Economics is still far from a full account of the signals conveyed by intervention or of the factors that might make those signals believable. In analyzing the signaling effects of intervention, practical analysis currently has no choice but to rely on an informal weighing of the myriad factors entering government preferences and information sets and influencing government constraints.

5.5   Recent Foreign-Exchange Intervention: An Assessment

Earlier sections of this paper documented the macroeconomic adjustments that accompanied the dollar's decline from its peak in early 1985, and reviewed the theory and econometric evidence concerning the use of sterilized intervention as an additional instrument of macroeconomic policy alongside conventional monetary and fiscal policy. The econometric evidence is consistent with the 1983 finding of the Working Group on Exchange Market Intervention, cited in the introduction, that the portfolio effects of sterilized intervention are weak except, possibly, in the very short run. As the Working Group also recognized, however, the signaling effect of exchange market intervention is of potential importance. Unfortunately, it is difficult, except within models too stylized to be immediately useful to policymakers, to design signals to the exchange market that are credible and therefore effective.

Intervention, often sterilized and often concerted, has nonetheless loomed large in recent currency experience, so it is important to ask whether and through what channels intervention aided in promoting the 1985–88 realignment. In this section I try to answer this question by examining the timing and magnitudes of interventions by the three largest industrial countries. The message in the data appears to be that monetary and fiscal actions, rather than sterilized interventions, have been the dominant policy determinants of the broad exchange rate movements of recent years. On several occasions, however, intervention seems to have been effective in signaling to exchange markets the major governments' resolve to adjust other macroeconomic policies, if necessary, to achieve exchange-rate goals. On other occasions, authorities have been convinced by exchange market pressures to modify these goals rather than to make fully accommodating monetary or fiscal changes. Sterilized intervention has not helped governments resolve conflicts between internal and external balance in any fundamental way.

5.5.1   Intervention Data for the United States, the Federal Republic of Germany, and Japan, 1985–88

Table 5.4 reports the dollar value of net U.S. open market purchases of foreign currencies, both by the Federal Reserve and the ESF. For reasons to be discussed in a moment, these data do not completely capture quarterly changes in the U.S. official foreign asset position, which might be more relevant for assessing the portfolio effects of intervention. Given its small size relative to the global supply of dollar assets, however, the most interesting

Table 5.4   **United States: Open Market Purchases of Foreign Exchange**

	Quarterly Purchase			
	1	2	3	4
1985	0.7	0.0	0.2	3.1
1986	0.0	0.0	0.0	0.0
1987	−1.5	−3.4	0.3	−3.9
1988	−1.0	2.4*	2.1**	—

Source: Data for 1985–87 from IMF, *World Economic Outlook* (April 1988): table 22; 1988 data from *Federal Reserve Bulletin* (April 1988, July 1988, October 1988, and February 1989).
Note: Purchases (+) and sales (−) in billions of U.S. dollars.
*Includes intervention purchases of foreign exchange during July.
**August and September only.

aspect of U.S. intervention is its possible signaling effect, which is well captured by the data on market transactions reported in table 5.4.

Table 5.5 reports changes in the dollar values of German and Japanese foreign-exchange reserves. The numbers in table 5.5 include, along with changes in central-bank reserve holdings, changes in the net foreign claims of other government agencies that intervene in financial markets. Also included

Table 5.5   **The Federal Republic of Germany and Japan: Increase in Dollar Value of Foreign Exchange Reserves**

Yearly Quarter	Germany	Japan
1985		
1	−2.9	0.2
2	2.3	0.9
3	3.1	−0.3
4	1.5	−0.8
1986		
1	0.8	1.2
2	−0.9	5.9
3	4.3	7.5
4	2.6	0.7
1987		
1	8.2	15.8
2	2.3	10.5
3	1.5	2.8
4	15.0	8.9
1988		
1	−5.7	3.2
2	−7.8	2.4
3	−6.7	3.1
4	0.6	6.1

Source: IMF, *World Economic Outlook* (April 1988): table 23; and IMF, *International Financial Statistics* (March 1989): line 1d.*d.*
Note: In billions of U.S. dollars.

are fluctuations in the dollar value of existing nondollar reserves that are induced entirely by exchange rate changes; but despite this valuation discrepancy, the numbers in table 5.5 are reasonably well correlated with the dollar value of actual foreign-exchange acquisitions by the two countries' authorities. Because of German EMS interventions, the reported series is significantly more reliable as an indicator of dollar acquisitions for Japan than for Germany.

The intervention series probably most useful in assessing the pressure of intervention on domestic financial markets is the domestic currency value of official foreign asset acquisitions—essentially, the balance of payments in domestic currency. This variable captures the incipient addition to domestic base money resulting from intervention. Table 5.6 reports quarterly data on the mark value of Bundesbank acquisitions of reserve assets. Capital gains on existing reserves, which are excluded from the acquisition data, appear in the second column.[35] Such capital gains do not put direct pressure on domestic financial markets, but they can have significant consequences for the government's finances.

Some caveats applying to all of the data are in order. Even in the absence of valuation changes, the figures in tables 5.5 and 5.6 may differ considerably from outright official purchases of foreign exchange in the open market.

Table 5.6   **The Federal Republic of Germany: Bundesbank Foreign Asset Acquisitions and Capital Gains**

Yearly Quarter	Asset Acquisitions	Capital Gains
1985		
1	−12.6	4.2
2	6.0	−2.7
3	5.7	−2.3
4	2.8	−2.3
1986		
1	2.2	−1.0
2	−8.1	1.1
3	8.9	−1.0
4	3.0	−2.2
1987		
1	14.2	−0.1
2	5.8	−0.3
3	−1.5	0.1
4	22.7	−9.1
1988		
1	−2.9	−0.1
2	−10.0	1.1
3	−22.3	1.9
4	0.6	−0.7

Note: Acquisitions and gains (+) in billions of marks.

Source: *Monthly Report of the Deutsche Bundesbank* (April 1989): table IX.1. For a more precise description of "capital gains," see footnote 6 to table IX.1. Asset acquisitions are "Change in the Bundesbank's net external assets" (from table IX.1) less capital gains.

Interest earnings on the Bundesbank's dollar assets, for example, when reinvested in dollars, swell the bank's net foreign assets, even though no transaction in the foreign-exchange market is directly involved. As argued by Adams and Henderson (1983), however, such reinvestment is correctly thought of as intervention, since the German government could have used dollar interest earnings to reduce the flow of mark-denominated government debt into private portfolios, simultaneously leaving more dollar bonds for the private market to hold. There are, in addition, some problems of measurement related to off-balance-sheet items, end-of-quarter "window dressing" of balance sheets, and so on.

5.5.2   Intervention and the Exchange Markets

An informal review of tables 5.4–5.6 in the light of the narrative of section 5.2 provides a vantage from which to evaluate recent intervention experience.

Pre-Plaza period (January–September 1985). Table 5.6 shows that the Bundesbank intervened heavily in the first quarter of 1985 to stop the dollar's rise to its peak; the United States intervened at the same time, but on a much smaller scale. The Bundesbank sterilized its intervention—in the Bundesbank's published monetary survey, the reduction in central bank money due to foreign-exchange flows in the first quarter of 1985 (DM 12.2 billion) is accompanied by an unusually large domestic open-market purchase under repurchase agreement (DM 12.1 billion). Short-term mark interest rates showed only a temporary and relatively small increase in this quarter.[36] In the two subsequent quarters, the German authorities purchased dollars as the dollar depreciated, and took advantage of the mark's relative strength to lower interest rates in the face of a weak domestic economy. Japan's foreign reserves (measured in dollars) show a net rise over these two quarters (table 5.5); the United States, for the most part, stayed on the sidelines (table 5.4). All told, the period shows no sustained, coordinated attempt to drive the dollar down through intervention.

Plaza to Louvre (September 1985–February 1987). In the last quarter of 1985 the United States and Japan, backing up the Plaza Agreement, both intervened to push the dollar down. Germany also carried out open market dollar sales, but once nonmarket transactions are taken into account, its foreign reserves show a net *increase* for the quarter (tables 5.5 and 5.6). Intervention clearly did little to promote the dollar's depreciation over 1986; U.S. activity was insignificant, and Japan bought dollars to counteract yen appreciation. Indeed, by the second half of 1986, the Bundesbank had joined Japan in trying to brake the dollar's fall through dollar purchases, but the resulting interventions were allowed to have no substantial effect on interest rates in either country and were ineffective.[37] Only after Germany and Japan decisively lowered interest rates in January 1987, and the United States intervened at month's end, did the dollar stabilize briefly; from end-October 1986 to end-January 1987, the dollar price of marks had risen by 14.3 percent and that of yen by 5.9 percent. The Bundesbank has summarized the experience of intervention in the months before the Louvre accord as follows:

> These [intervention] efforts were in vain, not least because statements by U.S. officials repeatedly aroused the impression on the markets that the U.S. authorities wanted the dollar to depreciate further. Moreover, until then [late January 1987] the Americans hardly participated in the operations to support their currency. Nor did the Federal Reserve counteract the downward trend in the dollar through monetary policy measures, despite the risks to price stability which it clearly perceived.[38]

Evidently, pure intervention by Japan and Germany had little effect compared with concrete monetary policy actions, favorable news on the U.S. trade balance, a pointedly visible reentry of the United States into the foreign-exchange market, and a more straightforward American acknowledgment that the time for dollar stabilization had come.[39]

From the Louvre to the crash (February–October 1987). After the Louvre Accord, the yen appreciated substantially in spite of heavy Japanese dollar purchases in the first half of 1987 (table 5.5). (Germany's sizable intervention in the first quarter of 1987 was motivated largely by an EMS realignment episode.) On March 11, the United States bought $30 million in marks to counteract heavy private sales of the German currency. Pressure on the mark rapidly subsided, but then the yen began to appreciate. Between March 23 and April 6, the Federal Reserve intervened daily and purchased a total of $3.0 billion with yen; between April 7 and 17, the Federal Reserve intervened on three occasions, buying $532 million.[40] These operations marked the first major U.S. intervention in foreign-exchange markets since the Plaza period in late 1985, but intervention now aimed at supporting the dollar, not bringing it down. The Bundesbank and other European central banks also participated in these dollar support operations. Pressure on the yen eased only after the dollar-yen interest differential widened substantially (see fig. 5.4), and industrial country exchange rates remained roughly stable until the worldwide stock market crash in October. As noted above, this stability owed much to monetary policies.

From the crash to the Toronto Summit (October 1987–June 1988). Concerted official purchases of dollars began at the end of October and continued through January. All three countries intervened heavily to support the dollar, and as a result of these and earlier operations, the overall increases in German and Japanese foreign reserves over 1987 are remarkably large. In spite of this heavy intervention, the dollar depreciated by 16.2 percent against the mark, and by 18.5 percent against the yen, between end-September and end-December 1987, before partially recovering and stabilizing in the last part of January 1988. From then until mid-June, the dollar-mark and dollar-yen exchange rates fluctuated within relatively narrow ranges. The United States conducted moderate dollar support operations in March and April of 1988, while Japan intervened more heavily to discourage yen appreciation. Germany, however, allowed its reserves to fall during the period, presumably to help counteract a perceived weakness of the mark. Short-term mark interest rates also drifted upward after the end of January. Until the second half of June, however, the interest differential favoring dollar over mark assets increased.

Toronto to Berlin (June–September 1988). Several developments, already reviewed above, led to a sharp appreciation of the dollar in June. The U.S. began intervening to discourage the dollar's rise on June 27; foreign-exchange operations by the U.S. and foreign authorities, sometimes on a large scale, continued through the summer. (Japan's dollar reserves rose in this period despite the dollar's strength, but the Bundesbank sold DM 22.3 billion in reserves in the third quarter of 1988 alone.) By early September the dollar appeared once again to have stabilized; but from end-May to end-August, the U.S. currency had appreciated by 7.9 percent against the mark and by 7.2 percent against the yen, despite forceful intervention efforts by the Federal Reserve and foreign central banks.

5.5.3   How Effective Has Intervention Been?

International currency experience since 1985 lends little support to the idea that sterilized intervention has been an important determinant of exchange rates. Anecdotal as well as econometric evidence suggests that intervention has been useful as a device for signaling to exchange markets official views on currency values. The signals sent by intervention have been effective, however, only when they have been backed up by the prompt adjustment of monetary policies, or when events such as unexpected trade balance news have coincidentally altered market sentiment. Concerted intervention operations have naturally been the most convincing, since international agreement on exchange rate objectives ensures that national authorities will not act at cross-purposes, as they did around the end of 1986.

Except possibly in 1987 and 1988, the scale of intervention was simply too small to have had significant portfolio effects. Between the Plaza Agreement on September 22 and the end of October 1985, the G-10 countries as a group sold around $7 billion in the market, hardly enough to make a major difference to global asset supplies.[41] The Plaza Agreement seems, however, to have sent an important signal that derived some of its credibility from the rapid progress of protectionist legislation through the U.S. Congress. Despite the dollar's fall, protectionist pressures remained strong over the next three years, and these may have *reduced* the credibility of later attempts to stabilize exchange rates in the face of slow trade balance adjustment.

Intervention totals for 1987–88 are much higher than for 1985 or 1986, but even so, the intervention provided at best a partial brake on exchange market pressures. Germany's official external asset acquisitions in 1987 were DM 41.2 billion (table 5.6), equal to roughly one-third of its year-end currency stock. Most of this reserve inflow was sterilized through domestic open market operations, however, and Germany's stock of high-powered central bank money rose by only DM 15.5 billion in 1987. In 1986, when reserve inflows were much lower, central bank money rose by DM 13.1 billion. How large were the effects of this DM 41.2 billion inflow on the supply of mark-denominated bonds? The IMF estimates that the net stock of German general government debt was 21.8 percent of GNP, or DM 440.4 billion, in 1987. The year's reserve inflow thus represented 9.4 percent of Germany's net public debt—a large number, but not large enough to prevent a sharp mark appreciation against the dollar.[42] It is doubtful that sterilized interventions on this scale could be the norm in a viable target-zone system. As noted above, the interventions had an adverse effect on Germany's public finances serious enough to spark political debate.

Japan, too, sterilized much of the massive reserve inflow it experienced as a result of its own 1987 interventions. Foreign assets of the Japanese monetary authorities increased by ¥ 5.1 trillion in that year, yet high-powered money rose by only ¥ 2.8 trillion, compared with a rise of ¥ 2.4 trillion in 1986.[43] IMF estimates put Japan's 1987 net general government debt at 21.7 percent of GNP, or ¥ 74.8 trillion.[44] So Japan's ¥ 5.1 trillion 1987 reserve increase amounted to 6.8 percent of the net public debt. (And this figure understates the effect on yen-denominated asset supplies because it includes yen capital losses on official Japanese foreign reserves, suffered as a result of the dollar's 1987 depreciation.) Although too large and costly to become a way of life for the Japanese government, the intervention of 1987 still did not prevent a substantial yen appreciation over the course of that year.

Shifting fiscal trends contributed to the dollar's fall from its peak of early 1985, but it is monetary policy that has been the more important instrument of medium-term exchange rate management. On several occasions, officials chose to adjust their exchange rate objectives in the face of market pressure, rather than compromise domestic policy goals. Substantial departures from internationally agreed exchange rate targets occurred, in spite of heavy intervention, in the three months after the Louvre Accord, in the three months following the October 1987 stock market crash, and in the summer of 1988.

Outcomes such as those described above could occur in a world where the portfolio effects of sterilized intervention are very potent: it is at least a logical possibility that the mark and yen would have appreciated far more against the dollar than they did in 1987 had the massive interventions of that year not been carried out. To settle the question definitively, economists would need a generally acceptable structural exchange rate model in which a counterfactual scenario with no intervention could be simulated. After many fruitless attempts to pin down econometrically significant portfolio effects due to intervention, however, it seems more reasonable to take governments' repeated failures to keep exchange rates within agreed ranges at face value: portfolio effects either are absent or are so small and uncertain that only unacceptably high intervention levels would have succeeded in maintaining exchange rate targets.[45] The limited econometric evidence on the most recent experience appears to support this face-value interpretation. For example, Humpage's (1988) study of daily data on intervention and exchange rates concludes that "frequent or otherwise systematic intervention that does not provide new information to the market will not affect exchange rates," and that beyond any signaling effect, "exchange-market intervention has no apparent influence on day-to-day exchange-rate movements" (15).

With a reliably significant and sustained portfolio effect on exchange markets, sterilized intervention could ease international policy cooperation by giving each country an additional policy instrument that might help it attain external as well as internal targets. In the absence of this additional instrument, however, authorities inevitably encounter dilemmas as a result of attempts to gear monetary policy to exchange rate stabilization alone. A nominal exchange rate fixed by monetary means provides an efficient automatic offset to purely monetary disturbances, but a monetary policy that steadies the nominal exchange rate when real exchange rate adjustment is still necessary can be counterproductive. It causes some combination of unnecessary deflation at home and inflation abroad when a real depreciation of home currency is needed, and it causes some combination of unnecessary inflation at home and deflation abroad when real appreciation is needed.[46] The "black Monday" of October 1987 has often been attributed to fears that the Federal Reserve would raise interest rates further to keep the dollar within its Louvre limits, despite the apparent incompatibility of the prevailing real exchange rate with external balance.[47] Had the Federal Reserve taken this course, the real dollar depreciation that occurred after the stock-market crash would have been brought about, not by a relatively painless fall in the dollar's nominal value, but by a recession originating in the United States.

Appendix

The following data were used in the econometric work of section 5.3 and in constructing figures 5.1–5.5.

Nominal interest rates (R, R*): Three-month Eurocurrency rates, observed at month's end, from Data Resources, Inc. (DRI).

Spot exchange rates (S): End-of-month observations from OECD, *Main Economic Indicators,* various issues.

Real per capita U.S. consumption (c) and price level (P): Separate seasonally unadjusted series on nominal consumption of services and of nondurables were deflated by seasonally unadjusted price indexes for consumption of services and of nondurables, then divided by seasonally unadjusted data on the civilian noninstitutional population of the United States. The resulting per capita real consumption data were deseasonalized by log-linear regression. Population data from *Economic Report of the President,* February 1988, and from U.S. Department of Labor, Bureau of Labor Statistics, *Employment and Earnings.* Consumption and price data from DRI.

Notes

1. See "Report of the Deputies: The Functioning of the International Monetary System," Supplement on the Group of Ten Deputies' Report, *IMF Survey* (July 1985): 2–14.

2. The Group of Five (G-5) countries are France, the Federal Republic of Germany, Japan, the United Kingdom, and the United States. The Group of Seven (G-7) consists of the G-5 plus Canada and Italy; the Group of Ten (G-10), of the G-7 plus Belgium, the Netherlands, and Sweden.

3. A recent survey of research on sterilized intervention is found in Weber (1986). The conclusions of Federal Reserve participants in the Versailles Working Group are summarized by Henderson and Sampson (1983).

4. Throughout this paper, a currency is said, synonymously, to appreciate, rise, strengthen, or increase in value against a foreign currency when its price in terms of the foreign currency rises. When that price falls, the currency is said to depreciate, fall, weaken, or decline in value against the foreign currency.

5. IMF, *World Economic Outlook* (April 1989): table A31.

6. The cited changes are based on end-of-month exchange rates, expressed as dollars per foreign currency unit. Between December 1978 and August 1985, the U.S. price level had risen by a greater percentage than Japan's or Germany's had, so even a complete reversal of the nominal exchange rate movements up to February 1985 would not have restored the *real* exchange rates prevailing at the period's start.

7. The dollar's September surge is not visible in the end-of-month data plotted in figures 5.1 and 5.2.

8. See "Group of Seven Countries Agrees to Intensify Policy Coordination," *IMF Survey* (11 January 1988): 8–10; and "Ministers Stress Exchange Rate Stability, Oppose Global Debt-Forgiveness Plans," *IMF Survey* (18 April 1988): 116. Earlier communiqués are reproduced in full in Funabashi (1988).

9. The important role of trade balance reports in explaining recent exchange rate behavior does not contradict the asset market theory of exchange rates. It is *unanticipated* trade balance movements and trade balance data *revisions* that have had the greatest effects on currencies because such surprises change market assessments of the long-run real and nominal exchange rates consistent with external balance. For a formal model, see Mussa (1979). The effects on current exchange rates of shifts in expected long-run equilibrium exchange rates often are amplified by anticipated policy responses to the news. For example, a market belief that the Federal Reserve is likely to ease monetary policy following an unexpectedly negative trade balance report increases the dollar's tendency to depreciate immediately afterward.

10. See, for example, Dornbusch (1976). In Dornbusch's model, monetary expansion could cause an immediate *rise* in the short-term nominal interest rate if output were to respond immediately and strongly to monetary expansion. This possibility does not seem very relevant to the three main industrial countries. Central bankers seem confident of their ability to lower short-term interest rates in the short run, and some formal econometric tests (such as tests based on money announcements) support their view.

11. See IMF, *World Economic Outlook* (April 1988): 63, chart 19.

12. Volcker's February 20, 1985, testimony before the Senate Committee on Banking, Housing, and Urban Affairs is reproduced in *Federal Reserve Bulletin* 71 (April 1985): 211–21.

13. See "Treasury and Federal Reserve Foreign Exchange Operations: Interim Report," *Federal Reserve Bulletin* 72 (February 1986): 110.

14. Funabashi (1988, 274–75).

15. Funabashi (1988, 161–63) suggests that Japanese authorities manipulated the Tokyo foreign-exchange market to bring about the yen depreciation that occurred between the conclusion of the first Baker-Miyazawa deal in September 1986 and its announcement a month later.

16. IMF, *World Economic Outlook* (April 1988): 63, chart 19. The money growth rates cited in this paragraph are changes in annual averages (table A14, 125). Since the October 1987 stock market crash caused some easing of monetary policies, a measure of money growth more relevant for assessing the domestic policy impact of the Louvre Agreement may be the growth rate of money for the year ending in September 1987. (A year-long interval is chosen to correct for money-supply seasonality.) From end-September 1986 through the same time in 1987, growth rates of Japan's monetary aggregates and of German M1 are not very different from the figures cited; growth of German M3 is 6.4 percent, which is, however, higher than the upper limit for 1988 M3 growth (6 percent) set by the Bundesbank in January of that year.

17. Domestic demand is the sum of domestic consumption and investment demand, both private and public. Domestic demand growth rather than output growth is reported because the former variable is a more direct measure of pressure on the exchange rate. In the Mundell-Fleming model, for example, an increase in domestic demand can cause the home currency to appreciate even though output does not change. (See Mundell 1968; a more recent analytical discussion of the effects of demand factors on real and nominal exchange rates is in Obstfeld 1985.) The movements in government deficits reported above, though not cyclically or inflation adjusted, are broadly consistent (in recent years) with changes in the IMF's fiscal impulse measures.

18. Central bank net worth is ignored for simplicity of exposition. See Adams and Henderson (1983) for a more detailed discussion of intervention practices. Kenen (1988, ch. 5) discusses some asymmetries in current intervention arrangements.

19. My discussion draws a perhaps artificially sharp distinction between "money" and "bonds," and lumps all interest-bearing assets together under the latter category. As a practical matter, financial authorities have available a rich menu of financial operations, across liquidity categories, maturities, and currencies. I judge an intervention to be sterilized when it has no effect on the monetary base, defined as the stock of reservable central bank liabilities, including currency; and I exclude from the definition of "bonds" any interest-bearing reserves of the domestic banking system held at the central bank.

20. I leave maturity issues aside for the purpose of this example.

21. For simplicity, this example has abstracted entirely from interest payments. Of course, the intervention's effects would be reversed entirely if the Bank of France went to the open market to purchase the needed marks with high-powered francs.

22. Pure intervention has no effect on exchange rates in a Ricardian setting for the same reason that private firms' decisions on the currency of denomination of their borrowing may have no effect. (See Froot, ch. 8 in this volume.) Stockman (1979) and Obstfeld (1982) discuss the relation between Ricardian equivalence and intervention effects. As illustrated in those papers, and as stressed more recently by Backus and Kehoe (1989), the analysis of intervention cannot be conducted independently of an analysis of the resulting effects on the government's intertemporal budget constraint.

Thus, if pure intervention disturbs asset market equilibrium because taxes are distorting, the effect of intervention would depend heavily on which taxes (if any) need to be adjusted afterward to ensure government solvency. In principle, it is easy to imagine that a given intervention could have a wide variety of effects, depending on how its budgetary impact is accommodated. (The same point naturally applies to the evaluation of any other policy.) Section 5.4 below discusses the linkage between intervention and government budget constraints from the perspective of policy credibility.

23. Engel and Flood (1985, 314) argue that "certain types of sterilized intervention can be effective in temporarily altering exchange rates, even in the presence of uncovered interest parity." They give as an example a (nonsterilized) sale of foreign bonds by the central bank, accompanied by a temporary rise in monetary transfer payments that holds the money supply constant and simultaneously raises private net wealth at the initial money price level. A key feature of this policy package is, however, the *fiscal policy* change that accompanies the central bank's foreign-exchange intervention. It is not surprising that a fiscal change accompanied by a nonsterilized intervention disturbs equilibrium, even when the money supply remains constant as a result of the combined policy actions.

24. The implication of Ricardian equivalence, that the government does not change outside asset supplies when it conducts sterilized intervention, has already been mentioned. Backus and Kehoe (1989), in a non-Ricardian model with risk-averse investors, present other examples of sterilized interventions that have no effects. Suppose that the dollar-mark rate will be $\$S(\omega)$ per mark next period if the state of nature ω occurs, and imagine two bonds with respective payoffs of DM 1 and $\$S(\omega)$ in state ω, and with a common payoff of zero in other states. These securities are perfect substitutes because they have the same payoff in every state of nature; intervention operations that change their relative supplies thus have no effects, in spite of the fact that the bonds' face values differ in currency of denomination. Backus and Kehoe present further examples, all of which involve operations in securities which are perfect substitutes (despite private risk aversion) because of their identical state-contingent payoffs. These examples are of limited practical relevance for evaluating sterilized intervention, since the securities traded in reality do not have identical payoffs across states of nature, and therefore are not generally perfect substitutes for investors.

25. The work just reviewed relies on some version of the ARCH specification proposed by Engle (1982) to model time variation in covariances. Pagan and Hong (1988) question the adequacy of the ARCH specification on empirical grounds.

26. See Hodrick (1987) for a derivation.

27. Consumption of durables is not considered in the tests for reasons outlined by Grossman and Laroque (1990). Because of the deseasonalization I performed in constructing the consumption-adjusted depreciation series used in table 5.3, the reported standard errors are subject to a (hopefully minor) asymptotic inconsistency. See the appendix for a description of the seasonal adjustment procedure used.

28. For some additional negative evidence, see Kaminsky and Peruga (1987).

29. Froot and Frankel (1989) suggest this as one possible explanation (among others) for the results of their study of survey data on exchange rate expectations.

30. One type of econometric problem, which arises when large infrequent interventions can disturb the data-generating process, is the "peso problem." (See Lewis 1988 and Obstfeld 1989b for discussions.) Peso problems are clearly of potential relevance in analyzing recent exchange market data.

31. Dominguez shows that in the period from the Federal Reserve's monetary-targeting shift in October 1979 until the following spring, there is a significant positive relationship between money surprises (defined as Federal Reserve money announcements less Money Market Survey forecasts) and official U.S. purchases of foreign currencies carried out in the interval between forecast and announcement. Her

interpretation is that the Federal Reserve used intervention to signal information about monetary policy not reflected in the prior market forecast.

32. The intervention does raise Germany's monetary base by DM 10 million (assuming the Bundesbank doesn't sterilize), but the currency composition of the Bundesbank's balance sheet is not changed.

33. Backus and Kehoe (1989) also mention the possible strategic effects of sterilized intervention, but do not suggest a particular model. Bohn's account stresses that a nationalistic government will be motivated not only by its own budgetary needs but by its potential ability to alter the net real foreign asset position of the domestic *private* sector. For example, if domestic nationals have a net foreign debt denominated in home currency, the government has an added incentive to inflate. The welfare effects of policy-induced wealth redistributions from foreigners to domestic residents are likely to be large compared with the costs of tax distortions (which determine the welfare value of wealth transfers from the domestic public to the government). If bonds are perfect substitutes, however, individual portfolio composition is indeterminate in equilibrium, as is the direction of the wealth redistribution associated with an exchange rate change. In this setting, the government might well lack sufficient information to calculate the effect on net foreign wealth various actions. Even if U.S. Treasury bonds were initially placed with Japanese investors, say, there is nothing to prevent the original buyers from quickly selling the bonds to Americans in the secondary market and investing the proceeds in, say, sterling. Watson et al. (1986, 39) note that "it is not possible to obtain information on the ownership of new or outstanding international bonds."

34. *Federal Reserve Bulletin* (January 1986): 17.

35. The coverage of table 5.6 is potentially broader than that of table 5.5 because table 5.5 excludes foreign assets other than those classified by the IMF as foreign-exchange reserves, for example, SDRs and the IMF reserve position. Notice that the capital gains reported in table 5.6 are changes in the mark (not dollar) value of reserves; in some quarters, these data measure capital gains inexactly because they include SDR allocations.

36. See *Monthly Report of the Deutsche Bundesbank* (December 1986): table I.3.

37. On Bundesbank dollar purchases over 1986, see *Report of the Deutsche Bundesbank for the Year 1987*, 29.

38. *Report of the Deutsche Bundesbank for the Year 1986*, 63.

39. The U.S. intervention, however, amounted to a mere $50 million in yen sold on January 28, 1987 (*Federal Reserve Bulletin* [May 1987]: 333). This intervention was intended to underscore the second Baker-Miyazawa statement, issued January 21 (see above).

40. See *Federal Reserve Bulletin* (July 1987): 553–55.

41. See *Federal Reserve Bulletin* (February 1986): 112. As noted earlier, this figure may overstate the true extent of intervention because it omits such factors as interest earnings on dollar reserves. Feldstein (1986) argues that the intervention that followed the Plaza Agreement had little effect on exchange rates.

42. See *Monthly Report of the Deutsche Bundesbank* (April 1989): table I.3; IMF, *World Economic Outlook* (April 1989): table 22. To assess the intervention's effect on relative bond supplies, the entire foreign reserve inflow (and not just the sterilized portion) is counted as an addition to the stock of outstanding mark debt, because monetary-base growth not brought about by foreign asset purchases would otherwise have been brought about by purchases of mark assets.

43. See IMF, *International Financial Statistics* (October 1988), lines 11 and 14. As noted below, the dollar depreciated over 1987, so the ¥ 5.1 billion figure understates the expansionary pressure on Japan's money supply: it includes the negative effect of

capital losses on official dollar reserves measured in yen. Such capital losses do not directly reduce the high-powered money supply.

44. See IMF, *World Economic Outlook* (April 1989): table 22.

45. If intervention has some small but reliable portfolio effect, why don't governments exploit it to the maximum extent to hit exchange rate targets? In principle, nothing prevents governments from taking unlimited open positions in foreign exchange. Surely part of the answer is that governments themselves regard the effects of intervention as being unreliable. If a government is not confident that it can control the exchange rate by intervening, a large open foreign-exchange position would seriously restrict other macroeconomic policy choices by placing budgetary stability at risk. In addition, governments wish to keep the option of changing exchange rate targets.

46. The responses of alternative exchange rate regimes to various shocks are analyzed in Obstfeld (1985). Controls on cross-border capital movements are a possible way out of the dilemma of instrument insufficiency, but it is fanciful to think that a reversal of the trend toward more global financial markets is fully enforceable or, at the moment, politically feasible.

47. See, for example, Feldstein (1988).

References

Adams, Donald B., and Dale W. Henderson. 1983. *Definition and measurement of exchange market intervention*. Staff Study no. 126 (September). Washington, DC: Board of Governors of the Federal Reserve System.

Backus, David K., and Patrick J. Kehoe. 1989. On the denomination of government debt: A critique of the portfolio balance approach. *Journal of Monetary Economics* 23 (May): 359–76.

Bohn, Henning. 1988. Time consistency of monetary policy in the open economy. Wharton School, University of Pennsylvania, September. Typescript.

Branson, William H. 1988. Sources of misalignment in the 1980s. In Richard C. Marston, ed., *Misalignment of exchange rates: Effects on trade and industry*. Chicago: University of Chicago Press.

Branson, William H., and Dale W. Henderson. 1985. The specification and influence of asset markets. In Ronald W. Jones and Peter B. Kenen, eds., *Handbook of international economics*, vol. 2. Amsterdam: North-Holland.

Calvo, Guillermo A., and Maurice Obstfeld. 1990. Time consistency of fiscal and monetary policy: A comment. *Econometrica* 58 (September). In press.

Cumby, Robert E. 1988. Is it risk? Explaining deviations from uncovered interest parity. *Journal of Monetary Economics* 22 (September): 279–99.

Cumby, Robert E., and Maurice Obstfeld. 1984. International interest rate and price level linkages under flexible exchange rates: A review of recent evidence. In John F. O. Bilson and Richard C. Marston, eds., *Exchange rate theory and practice*. Chicago: University of Chicago Press.

Deutsche Bundesbank. 1982. *The Deutsche Bundesbank: Its monetary policy instruments and functions*. Deutsche Bundesbank Special Series no. 7 (October).

Dominguez, Kathryn M. 1988. The informational role of official foreign exchange intervention operations: An empirical investigation. Harvard University. Typescript.

Dornbusch, Rudiger. 1976. Expectations and exchange rate dynamics. *Journal of Political Economy* 84 (December): 1161–76.

Engel, Charles M., and Robert P. Flood. 1985. Exchange rate dynamics, sticky prices, and the current account. *Journal of Money, Credit and Banking* 17 (August): 312–27.

Engel, Charles M., and Anthony P. Rodrigues. 1987. Tests of international CAPM with time-varying covariances. NBER Working Paper no. 2303, July. Cambridge, MA: National Bureau of Economic Research.

Engle, Robert F. 1982. Autoregressive conditional heteroscedasticity with estimates of the variance of United Kingdom inflation. *Econometrica* 50 (July): 987–1007.

Feldstein, Martin S. 1986. New evidence on the effects of exchange rate intervention. NBER Working Paper no. 2052, October. Cambridge, MA: National Bureau of Economic Research.

———. 1988. Distinguished lecture on economics in government: Thinking about international economic coordination. *Journal of Economic Perspectives* 2 (Spring): 3–13.

Froot, Kenneth A., and Jeffrey A. Frankel. 1989. Forward discount bias: Is it an exchange risk premium? *Quarterly Journal of Economics* 104 (February): 139–61.

Funabashi, Yoichi. 1988. *Managing the dollar: From the Plaza to the Louvre.* Washington, DC: Institute for International Economics, May.

Giovannini, Alberto, and Philippe Jorion. 1989. The time-variation of risk and return in the foreign exchange and stock markets. *Journal of Finance* 44, no. 2 (June): 307–25.

Grossman, Sanford J., and Guy Laroque. 1990. Asset pricing and optimal portfolio choice in the presence of illiquid durable consumption goods. *Econometrica* 58 (January): 25–51.

Henderson, Dale W., and Stephanie Sampson. 1983. Intervention in foreign exchange markets: A summary of ten staff studies. *Federal Reserve Bulletin* 69 (November): 830–36.

Hodrick, Robert J. 1987. *The empirical evidence on the efficiency of forward and futures foreign exchange markets.* Fundamentals of Pure and Applied Economics no. 24. Chur, Switzerland: Harwood Academic Publishers.

———. 1989. U.S. international capital flows: Perspectives from rational maximizing models. In Karl Brunner and Allan H. Meltzer, eds., *Carnegie-Rochester Conference Series on Public Policy* 30: 231–88. Amsterdam: North-Holland Publishing Company.

Humpage, Owen F. 1988. Intervention and the dollar's decline. *Federal Reserve Bank of Cleveland Economic Review* 24 (Quarter 2): 2–16.

Kaminsky, Graciela L., and Rodrigo Peruga. 1987. Risk premium and the foreign exchange market. University of California–San Diego. Typescript.

Kenen, Peter B. 1988. *Managing exchange rates.* London: Routledge.

Lewis, Karen K. 1988. The persistence of the 'peso problem' when policy is noisy. *Journal of International Money and Finance* 7 (March): 5–21.

Lucas, Robert E., Jr., and Nancy L. Stokey. 1983. Optimal fiscal and monetary policy in an economy without capital. *Journal of Monetary Economics* 12 (July): 55–93.

Mark, Nelson C. 1988. Time varying betas and risk premia in the pricing of forward foreign exchange contracts. *Journal of Financial Economics* 22 (December): 335–54.

Marston, Richard C. 1988. Exchange rate policy reconsidered. In Martin Feldstein, ed., *International economic cooperation.* Chicago: University of Chicago Press.

Mundell, Robert A. 1968. *International economics.* New York: Macmillan.

Mussa, Michael. 1979. The role of the trade balance in exchange rate dynamics. University of Chicago. Typescript.

———. 1981. *The role of official intervention.* Occasional Paper no. 6. New York: Group of 30.

Obstfeld, Maurice. 1982. The capitalization of income streams and the effects of open market policy under fixed exchange rates. *Journal of Monetary Economics* 9 (January): 87–98.
———. 1985. Floating exchange rates: Experience and prospects. *Brookings Papers on Economic Activity* 2: 369–450.
———. 1989a. How integrated are world capital markets? Some new tests. In Guillermo A. Calvo et al., eds., *Debt, stabilization and development: Essays in memory of Carlos Diaz Alejandro*. Oxford: Basil Blackwell.
———. 1989b. Commentary (on Richard A. Meese, Empirical assessment of foreign currency risk premiums). In Courtenay C. Stone, ed., *Financial risk: Theory, evidence and implications*. Boston, MA: Kluwer Academic.
———. 1989c. Dynamic seigniorage theory: An exploration. NBER Working Paper no. 2869 (February). Cambridge, MA: National Bureau of Economic Research.
Pagan, A., and Y. Hong. 1988. Non-parametric estimation and the risk premium. Working Paper no. 135 (May). Rochester Center for Economic Research.
Persson, Mats, Torsten Persson, and Lars E. O. Svensson. 1987. Time consistency of fiscal and monetary policy. *Econometrica* 55 (November): 1419–31.
Stein, Jeremy C. 1989. Cheap talk and the Fed: A theory of imprecise policy announcements. *American Economic Review* 79 (March): 32–42.
Stockman, Alan C. 1979. Monetary control and sterilization under pegged exchange rates. University of Rochester. Typescript.
Tobin, James. 1971. An essay on the principles of debt management. In *Essays in economics*, vol. 1, *Macroeconomics*, 378–455. Chicago: Markham Publ. Co.
Watson, Maxwell, et al. 1986. *International capital markets: Developments and prospects*. Washington, DC: International Monetary Fund, December.
Weber, Warren E. 1986. Do sterilized interventions affect exchange rates? *Federal Reserve Bank of Minneapolis Quarterly Review* 10 (Summer): 14–23.

Comment   J. S. Flemming

Maurice Obstfeld's survey is thorough in its treatment of intervention by the G-3 countries, and in its discussion of their changing attitudes toward intervention during the period since the Versailles Summit of June 1982—from which the Jurgensen group emerged. He looks at the theory of and econometric tests of effectiveness, as well as at the historical narrative, and concludes that (sterilized) intervention is not a very effective supplement to monetary and fiscal policies affecting exchange rates—a judicious conclusion from which I would not wish to dissent. I do however have six comments.

1. In section 5.2.1 attention is drawn to the fact that, although in September 1986 G-7 finance ministers saw no need for "further significant exchange rate adjustment," within six months the dollar had fallen 5–15 percent.

One strand running through the whole process of bringing the dollar down to earth has been a disjunction between the implication of ex ante statements ("the present rate is about right") and action when the rate changes (very little)

J. S. Flemming is an Executive Director of the Bank of England.

and satisfaction is again expressed at the new level. Despite all the talk of credible commitment to published (monetary) targets, the aim seems to be to prevent interest rate differentials reflecting exchange adjustments which are (at least with hindsight) recognized as (having been) necessary.

Given the implications for the U.S. bond market of the interest rate rise required in early 1985, had the subsequent decline in the dollar been anticipated, ambivalence may have been warranted. The strategy was certainly successful; as time passes, however, one would expect the trick to be more difficult to repeat and the attempt to be perceived to become more costly.

2. In his discussion of sterilization, Obstfeld refers to the sharpness of the distinction between "money" and "bonds," where the latter includes all interest-bearing assets. In the first half of the period under review, we in the United Kingdom used a technique of debt management to control a broad monetary aggregate (including interest-bearing ["bond"?] elements) which almost certainly worked by twisting the yield curve. We had a great deal of inconclusive discussion of the exchange rate effect of this policy of "over-funding." Could one say something about the differing degrees of substitutability at different maturities and infer from that the direction of exchange rate pressure generated by the policy?

3. Obstfeld mentions the possibility of bonds in different currencies being perfect substitutes. That would imply not only that overfunding did not affect the exchange rate but also that it could not have affected the growth of the money supply either—which is rejected by our evidence.

In any case, I find the hypothesis profoundly unattractive for its implications that portfolios of a heterogeneous population will typically be undiversified and liable to jump from one corner to another.

4. As far as models of this area are concerned, Obstfeld mentions the failure of the consumption-based CAPM, despite its theoretical attractions. There are a number of possible reasons for this. A paper by Attanasio and Weber (UCL 87–33) suggests that the use of aggregate rather than cohort consumption data may be to blame.

5. Obstfeld discusses at some length a rational signaling effect related to the effects of the portfolio shift of sterilized intervention on the cost to the authorities of subsequent exchange rate changes. This is ingenious stuff but not, I think, very convincing especially given the secrecy of most central banks about their operations and the untimeliness and obscurity of most of their accounting statements. The restriction to fully rational models precludes another role, related to that of signaling, which is dear to the hearts of many central bankers.

The failure of economists to model exchange rates, the remarkable performance of the random-walk model (see Charles Goodhart's 1987 inaugural lecture) the extent of chartist influence on traders, and the documented failure of traders to follow the advice even of in-house economists, together with the observed volatility of exchange rates, all suggest the possibility of "giving the market a lead.'' With no other rocks to cling to, might evidence that the authorities were prepared to ''defend'' a rate increase its plausibility in market eyes at least when the chosen rate fell within the zone of the market's apparent indeterminacy? The testing of this suggestion is made more difficult by the tendency of authorities to attempt from time to time to defend the indefensible.

6. Although I have said that I would not dissent from Obstfeld's conclusion about the effectiveness of intervention, I am less happy with his apparent rejection of any kind of nominal exchange rate targeting when real exchange rate adjustment is necessary. In an economy with a rapidly changing financial structure, velocity of any monetary aggregate may become even less stable than PPP-type relationships. Nominal exchange rate targets or management do not mean fixity. Other people's inflation rates (at least in the aggregate) are fairly easy to forecast. Thus a target path for the domestic price level can be combined with a target path for the real exchange rate and converted into a target path for the nominal rate. Nor do I believe that confusion on these issues could account for the stock market crash of last October. The incompatibility of prevailing rates with prevailing hopes meant something had to give—but not that it had to be, or naturally could be, resolved by a crash.

Reference

Goodhart, C. 1987. The foreign exchange market: A random walk with a dragging anchor. London School of Economics. Typescript.

Comment   Hans Genberg

Obstfeld's paper reviews and reexamines the evidence on the effectiveness of official interventions in the foreign-exchange markets that has become available since the 1983 study of the Versailles Working Group. The rationale for the undertaking is that we have observed such interventions on a much larger scale in the past four to five years than before. Therefore, recent data ought to be particularly useful for detecting any exchange rate response to these interventions.

The main points of the paper can be summarized by four statements: First, based on a review of exchange rate behavior and macroeconomic policy since late 1984, the conclusion is reached that the major movements in exchange rates since that time can be explained by economic fundamentals. Second, an examination of the available empirical evidence suggests that sterilized interventions do not influence exchange rate movements, at least as far as

Hans Genberg is professor of economics at the Graduate Institute of International Studies in Switzerland.

channels that operate via portfolio-balance effects are concerned. Third, data show that interventions have been large and frequent in recent years, and that most of them have been sterilized. Fourth, the fact that substantial amounts of foreign exchange have been used for sterilized intervention in spite of the evidence that such interventions have no effect on the exchange rate represents a puzzle. Assuming that governments also believe that interventions do not influence exchange rates, why do they engage in them? Obstfeld suggests that one possibility might be that interventions operate via signaling effects rather than through portfolio-balance channels.

As this brief synopsis suggests, the paper contains a nice blend of factual information (about exchange rate movements, interventions in the foreign-exchange markets, and macroeconomic policies in general), theory, and empirical evidence. I have no major disagreement with Obstfeld about his interpretation of the facts or of the empirical evidence, nor about the theoretical possibility of signaling effects. In my comments I will first elaborate on the points raised in the paper. I then raise some doubts about the desirability of using intervention and exchange rate announcements as a way to signal other policy changes. I conclude by arguing that we do not yet seem to have a satisfactory explanation of why central banks engage in sterilized interventions in view of the evidence showing that they are largely ineffective as an instrument for exchange rate management. Before proceeding I would like to draw attention to the fact that Obstfeld tells a convincing story about exchange rate movements since 1984 based on the evolution of monetary and fiscal policies. There is no need to refer to such elusive concepts as unwinding of speculative bubbles, and consequently one common argument for exchange rate targeting as a policy goal is undermined.

The data presented in figure 5.5 of the paper indicate why econometric evidence on the effectiveness of sterilized interventions is not likely to detect any links between exchange rate movements and relative asset stocks as in the portfolio-balance models. These data show that ex post yield differentials can be as large as $10-15$ percentage points on a quarterly basis (mainly due to exchange rate effects). Suppose that the portfolio-balance model were correct in predicting that changes in asset stocks resulting from sterilized interventions do require changes in ex ante yields. Suppose further that, for the modification in asset stocks actually achieved by interventions, the required variation in yields is on the order of $2-3$ percentage points on an annual basis. In this case one should not expect interventions to be able to account for more than between 2 and 5 percent of observed ex post yield differentials. Other sources of exchange rate fluctuations are evidently so large that they swamp any reasonable portfolio-balance effects of sterilized interventions.

Why then do central banks engage in these types of interventions to such a large extent? Obstfeld suggests one possibility, namely that the authorities use interventions as a signal of future changes in monetary, fiscal, and trade policies that ultimately will move the exchange rate in the desired direction. Currencies will reflect the information contained in the signals immediately as market participants act on these signals. A number of questions are raised by this view of the role of interventions: Why, for instance, is a mere statement of the reorientation of the fundamental policies not sufficient to provide the signal? Also, does signaling intervention provide an extra policy instrument, and is signaling a reliable way to influence markets?

To deal with some of these questions, Obstfeld outlines a theory that is basically a version of the "putting the money where your mouth is" argument. By buying foreign assets to prevent an appreciation of the domestic currency, the central bank creates incentives for itself to pursue monetary and fiscal policies that are consistent with the intervention. The reason is that such policies would prevent capital losses on the acquired foreign assets. But creating the incentive to pursue a specific set of policies is presumably not enough. It is also necessary actually to carry out these policies. Otherwise the effect of the initial announcement is reversed and the credibility of future announcements endangered. So to be effective, an announced exchange rate target must be followed by the required adjustment in economic policies. Intervening in the foreign-exchange market to bolster credibility does not alter this fact. As already noted, such intervention "only" makes it costlier (in terms of capital losses on foreign-exchange holdings) for central banks to deviate from the required policies. But as table 5.6 in the paper illustrates, central banks appear not to be greatly influenced by such incentives since they seem to have lost substantial amounts of money on their intervention activities. The quantitative importance of the incentive effects of interventions is thus questionable.

What this discussion shows me is, first of all, that signals by means of policy announcements and interventions in the foreign-exchange market are no substitutes for genuine changes in economic policies. There are no additional degrees of freedom to be had this way. Furthermore, it is questionable how much additional mileage the authorities can get from interventions compared with straightforward policy announcements relating to basic macroeconomic policies. Add to this the danger that signals stated in terms of desired exchange rate movements are not always easy to interpret and may therefore constitute a source of uncertainty in the economy, and we end up, in my judgement, with a rather weak case for the use of sterilized interventions as a tool for exchange rate management.

If this assessment is correct, the question remains why there has been so much sterilized intervention in the foreign-exchange markets. I can think of two possible reasons, neither of which is entirely satisfactory. One is that the authorities are really concerned only with very short term exchange rate fluctuations, and that interventions do have an effect on these. The main problem with this explanation is that governments have not provided a rationale for adopting such a short-term perspective.

The other reason is that governments want to be seen as "doing something" about exchange rate misalignments and volatility, but they are unwilling to alter underlying policies. Interventions in the foreign-exchange market constitute a placebo for public opinion. The difficulty here, of course, is that the private sector may not be fooled indefinitely by such a placebo.

This then leaves me with the impression that we do not yet have an entirely satisfactory explanation for the reasons behind central banks' interventions in the foreign-exchange markets. Obstfeld's thorough and comprehensive paper has provided a definitive assessment of the effects of interventions. A further analysis of the reasons that motivate governments to conduct these policies should be next on the research agenda in this field.

Comment   Shuntaro Namba

We have experienced dramatic volatility in foreign-exchange markets especially after the so-called Plaza Agreement. On the other hand, the importance of international policy coordination among the major industrialized countries has been reaffirmed and put into practice. Under these circumstances, Professor Maurice Obstfeld's paper is a valuable attempt to evaluate the recent effects of foreign-exchange intervention.

The paper is well-balanced in its contents, containing both theoretical analyses and detailed case studies based upon recent developments in the foreign-exchange market. Also, it is an excellent survey, summarizing the theoretical and empirical studies on the effectiveness of intervention.

I would like to note one important point first. The effects of a certain limited amount of foreign-exchange intervention will depend largely on the outstanding net asset holdings of the private sector and their currency composition. For example, it is a well-known fact that large-scale current account imbalance has been persistent between the United States and Japan at present. As a result, the outstanding net asset holdings of the private sector have also been subject to change in their value and contents. In order empirically to evaluate the effects of intervention, we need to pay the closest attention to this aspect.

Fundamental Views on Intervention

The most significant finding of Obstfeld's paper—one based both on empirical analyses and on recent experience—is summarized in section 5.1 as follows: "The conclusion reached is that monetary and fiscal policies, and not intervention per se, have been the main policy determinants of exchange rates in recent years."

This is harmonious with our view of intervention as a policy measure. We recognize that intervention is a measure which can be flexibly adopted to prevent erratic movements in the exchange rate caused by abrupt changes of market sentiments, without committing ourselves to set certain market levels.

According to our knowledge of economic theories, real foreign-exchange rates can be determined by the following four factors: (1) the purchasing power

Shuntaro Namba is the Chief of Research Division II of the Institute for Monetary and Economic Studies, Bank of Japan.

parity based on relative price levels among countries; (2) real interest rate differentials; (3) risk premiums based on accumulated current account imbalances or other related factors; and (4) market expectations.

Monetary and fiscal policy management will influence these four factors. On the other hand, effects that are drawn only from sterilized intervention are not clear, or else are rather limited.

Consequently, we aim at preventing excessive volatility in foreign-exchange markets by controlling the market determinants, especially real interest differentials and accumulated current account imbalances, through internationally coordinated monetary and fiscal policy management.

Effects of Intervention

In Obstfeld's paper, the effects of intervention are evaluated as follows: nonsterilized interventions are regarded as effective, while according to empirical analyses, sterilized interventions have limited effect. Obstfeld states "the portfolio effects of pure intervention have generally been elusive enough that intervention cannot be regarded as a macroeconomic policy tool in its own right" (sec. 5.1).

When interventions are nonsterilized, for example in cases when the Japanese monetary authority buys dollars and sells yen, high-powered money in the economy will increase, reflecting the rise in foreign reserves; this increase will then result in lower interest rates and an expanded money supply. Therefore, in addition to the rise in dollar demand due to interventions, lower interest rates and deteriorating balances of payments caused by easier monetary conditions will eventually cause high dollar/low yen ratios.

The effectiveness of nonsterilized intervention is broadly recognized in academic circles, and we also support this view. However, I would like to add another point: we cannot be certain in advance whether or not the intervention is going to be sterilized. For example, in the case of a policy of intervention in buying the dollar, we determine the volume of money which should be absorbed in the money market in consideration of the overall monetary situation. In other words, we cannot conduct monetary policy presupposing the effectiveness of the nonsterilized intervention.

A sterilized intervention can work effectively through the following two channels: (1) if it changes the amount of foreign-currency–denominated bonds and of home-currency–denominated bonds, and then changes risk premiums arising from foreign-exchange volatility; and (2) if it influences market participants' expectations.

Generally, the effectiveness of sterilized interventions depends largely on the conditions of the foreign-exchange market. Two aspects of those market conditions are considered below.

Substitutability between Domestic-Currency– and Foreign-Currency–Denominated Assets

How many changes in the foreign-exchange rate are needed to absorb changes in the private sector's foreign-currency–denominated positions? If the market is risk neutral and the substitutability of assets between currencies is perfect, then the risk premium will be zero. In that case, changes in foreign-currency–denominated positions will be absorbed in the market without affecting the foreign-exchange rate (therefore, the first channel for a sterilized intervention does not work).

On the other hand, if the market is risk-averse and the substitutability between domestic and foreign currencies is not perfect, changes in foreign-currency positions will result in an increase or decrease in risk premiums. These changes cannot be absorbed without changes in the foreign-exchange rate (so, the first channel does work).

Market Efficiency

Do the foreign-exchange rates effectively reflect various sources of market information, such as interest rates, rates of inflation, price levels, balances of payments, and each government's policy stance?

If the market is completely efficient, official interventions cannot change investors' expectations since investors are already well informed about the market (therefore, the second channel does not work).

So, intervention will be perfectly ineffective when (a) the substitutability between foreign-currency– and home-currency–denominated assets is perfect and (b) the market is completely efficient at the same time. However, according to the various empirical analyses conducted to date, there seems to be some truth to the claim that the current foreign-exchange market is in no such condition. However, it is not clear whether this is because of the imperfectness of the substitutability between assets, or because of the inefficiency of the market.

In either case, we cannot determine a priori whether these two channels would work. Future developments of empirical studies in this field are awaited.

In section 5.3, Obstfeld also presents econometric analyses of the existence of risk premiums and discusses whether or not they can change. He summarizes: "There is a large body of evidence contradicting the hypothesis that ρ_t in equation (1) [the risk premium] is identically zero, or even constant over time."(sec. 5.3.2)

We confirmed through our econometric analyses that intervention can affect risk premiums and that, consequently, sterilized interventions can have some effect. At the same time, however, we get the result that the effects of a certain limited amount of intervention are decreasing recently (see below).

In section 5.4, Obstfeld indicates that sterilized intervention can affect the foreign-exchange market through the so-called "signaling effect," through which information on future policy stances of the monetary authority is conveyed.

Obstfeld also points out that sterilized intervention has the signaling effect since markets can learn from the monetary authority's move to avoid the estimated loss in its foreign-currency–denominated assets caused by exchange rate fluctuations. This is quite an interesting point, since the idea is related to the "profitability criterion" concerning the effectiveness of intervention.

Concerted intervention is often regarded as more effective than unilateral intervention. One reason for this is that the monetary authorities of involved countries sometimes offer a kind of collateral as a pledge of exchange rate stability. Therefore, the signaling effects of concerted intervention have a higher credibility to the market than those of unilateral intervention.

Also, the foreign-exchange market is counted as the most efficient one among all financial markets as it fairly quickly reacts to all information on the policy stances of various governments and monetary authorities. So, in addition to the signaling effect that Obstfeld pointed out, I would like to add that an unanticipated intervention also plays an important role in conveying a signaling effect in a fairly efficient market.

Our Recent Econometric Result

Recently, Mitsuhiro Fukao, a member of the staff of our institute, estimated an equation of real foreign-exchange rates explained by real interest rate differentials between the United States and Japan and risk premium factors. The regression was conducted through the period from the first quarter of 1973 to the end of 1987.

$$e_t = \alpha + \beta_t \left(r_t^{\,j} - r_t^{\,u} \right) + \gamma_t \left(M^{jj} B_t^{\,j} + M^{jg} B_t^{\,g} \right) + \epsilon_t \,,$$

where e_t is the real exchange rate of yen against the dollar (dollar/yen, indexed); $r^{\,j}$ and $r^{\,u}$ are the long-term real interest rates for Japan and the United States, respectively; M^{jj} is the variance for rates of change in yen-dollar real exchange rates as compared to the previous term (unchanged throughout the observed period); M^{jg} is the covariance between rates of change in yen-dollar real exchange rates and those in mark-dollar real exchange rates as compared to the previous term (unchanged throughout the observed period); B^j and B^g are accumulated current account imbalances for Japan and for the total of all EMS participant countries, respectively (standardized by the total of nominal GNP for major countries); α is a constant; β_t is the coefficient for real interest rates; and γ_t is the coefficient for accumulated current account imbalances.

This equation is basically the same as Obstfeld's equation (1). Here, γ_t $(M^{jj} B_t^{\,j} + M^{jg} B_t^{\,g})$ is the risk premium. For this regression, Fukao used the Kalman filter which allows the coefficients β_t and γ_t to vary during the observed period.

The result of the estimation is as follows: while real interest rate coefficient (β_t) increased largely, risk premium coefficient (γ_t) has decreased but not reached zero in this regression period.

This reflects the financial globalization in which real interest rate differentials become as important as a real foreign-exchange determinant. Also the effects of the change of the risk premium explained by the change in the external net asset are seen to have decreased.

From this empirical result, we can get the following implications concerning the effectiveness of sterilized intervention: risk premium factors are apparent ($\gamma_t \neq 0$); therefore, sterilized intervention can be effective to some degree. But the effects of sterilized intervention recently have been weakened.

According to our estimation, if an additional $10 billion of sterilized intervention had been conducted, it would have changed the yen rate from the actual level by 7.7 percent in the fourth quarter of 1974 and by 1.7 percent in the last quarter of 1987.

6 Can the European Monetary System be Copied Outside Europe? Lessons from Ten Years of Monetary Policy Coordination in Europe

Francesco Giavazzi and Alberto Giovannini

6.1 Introduction

The European Monetary System (EMS), greeted with considerable skepticism in 1978, is now enjoying remarkable popularity. The causes of this shift in public opinion are plausibly to be found in the history of the international monetary system during two periods: from 1971 to 1978, and from 1979 to the present. In Europe, the period following the collapse of the Bretton Woods system was characterized by several attempts to limit exchange rate fluctuations, represented by experiments with the "snake." These experiments proved to be a failure for the large "romance" countries: France and Italy. France made two attempts and Italy one attempt to join the snake, which were definitely abandoned in, respectively, 1976 and 1973. The Belgian franc, the Dutch guilder, and the Deutsche mark, by contrast, entered the snake in 1972 and never left it until the start of the EMS.

The failed attempts of France and Italy, and the suspicion that the new technical features that characterized the EMS were more like gimmickry than substantial reforms, justified the skepticism of observers in 1978. On the other hand, during the most recent decade, events in the world financial markets have renewed dissatisfaction with flexible exchange rates. The unprecedented swings of the nominal and real dollar exchange rate, associated with a dramatic worsening of the U.S. current account balance, and the new position of the United States as the largest debtor in the world economy, have led many

Francesco Giavazzi is a professor of Economics at the University of Bologna and a research associate of the NBER. Alberto Giovannini is an associate professor at the Graduate School of Business, Columbia University, and a faculty research fellow of the NBER.

The authors thank Reiko Nakamura for able research assistance. Support from the Smith Richardson Foundation is gratefully acknowledged. This research is part of NBER's research program in International Studies. The opinions expressed are those of the authors and do not represent the views of the National Bureau of Economic Research.

observers to believe that there is something inherently unstable about flexible exchange rates, and that it would be desirable to reform the international monetary system. All the leading proposals for world monetary reform advocate, in one form or another, the limitation of exchange rate flexibility.

In stark contrast with the gyrations of the dollar, European currencies and intra-European competitiveness indices have kept relatively stable over the past ten years[1]; at the same time, inflation rates and inflation rate differentials across Europe have been dramatically reduced. Hence the shift in public opinion and the renewed interest in the EMS. In this paper we discuss some aspects of the EMS experience in an attempt to answer the question of whether the EMS can be copied outside Europe.

This paper is organized around two main questions. The first is: why is the aversion to exchange rate fluctuations stronger in Europe than elsewhere? European countries are highly integrated and have built institutions—the Common Market for agricultural products in particular—that are dependent upon exchange rate stability. European exchange rate stability is justified by a much broader and more important trend toward economic unification, which in part transcends purely economic motivations. In section 6.2 we discuss the economic and historical justifications for limiting exchange rate flexibility in Europe, and in section 6.3 we review the workings of the EMS exchange rate arrangements.

The second question is: how does the EMS hold together? What are the macroeconomic benefits from belonging to the system?[2] It is often said that joining the EMS has helped high-inflation countries like France and Italy to disinflate. Theoretical models suggest that such an arrangement is desirable for the inflation-prone countries when the nominal exchange rate target is more credible than money stock targets or interest rate targets. However, there is no accepted explanation of why nominal exchange rate targets are more credible. The explanation we propose is based on the claim that the EMS exchange rate targets are a part of a broader agreement that includes the Common Market and the other community institutions. Abandoning the EMS targets is equivalent to abandoning this larger system. An additional complication is that, in the EMS, the country exporting its reputation as an ''inflation fighter'' tends to suffer higher inflation than it would otherwise. The disinflation which occurred after the start of the EMS and the stabilization of the Federal Republic of Germany's real effective exchange rate are discussed in sections 6.4 and 6.5.

The achievement of monetary convergence, which can be credited in part to the EMS, has been reached at the expense of divergent fiscal performances. In section 6.6 we discuss the effects of the EMS on the fiscal performances of the countries that joined it. In section 6.7 we offer a few concluding remarks.

6.2   Why Did Europeans Set Up the EMS?

The coordination of macroeconomic policies has a long tradition in Europe: it dates back at least to the 1950s when six European countries signed the

Treaty of Rome. The immediate effect of the treaty was the establishment of a customs union and of a common market for cereals—later extended to all agricultural products. But its intentions were much more ambitious. The treaty lays down a set of principles for the conduct of macroeconomic policy among its members: mutual consultations in the area of short-run macroeconomic policy; the commitment to "regard exchange rate policy as a matter of common interest"; and the possibility of mutual assistance to overcome balance of payments crises. The Monetary Committee of the European Communities dates back to 1958: its role was to promote the coordination of monetary policies, and it was formed by two representatives from each country, one from the treasury, the other from the central bank.

Behind these early steps for policy coordination in Europe lies the special European aversion for exchange rate fluctuations. This aversion is motivated by three factors. The first is rooted in Europe's recent history. In the 1920s and 1930s many European countries sought to defend themselves against external shocks through competitive exchange rate depreciations. Many in Europe today hold those policies responsible for the disruption of international trade and economic activity and the ensuing collapse of European democracies.[3] The experience of the 1920s and 1930s is important to an understanding of the postwar quest for exchange rate stability which led to the Bretton Woods system.

Openness is the second explanation for the European distaste for exchange rate fluctuations. The EEC as a whole is not a particularly open region—no more for example than the United States or Japan. In 1987 the share of imports in GDP was 12.3 percent in the EEC, 10.1 percent in the United States, and 11.4 percent in Japan. Therefore there is no particular reason why Europeans should worry about the fluctuations of the ECU relative to the dollar or the yen—no more at least than Americans and Japanese worry about fluctuations of their own currencies. But what is special in the EEC is that the region is not a common currency area. Individual countries have different currencies and are also much more open than the region as a whole. Even before the creation of the customs union, the share of imports in GDP was as high as 40 percent in Belgium and the Netherlands, 16 percent in Germany. The trade creation and trade diversion effects of the union rapidly raised these figures: now they are around 60–70 percent in the small northern countries, and 25–30 percent in Germany, France, Italy, and the United Kingdom. Openness however is mostly an intra-European affair: thus, to the extent that exchange rate fluctuations pose problems for an economy, it is the fluctuation of intra-EEC exchange rates that Europeans view as worrisome.

The third explanation for the European aversion to exchange rate fluctuations lies in the very institutions set up with the Treaty of Rome, and in the common agricultural market in particular. As we shall now explain, the survival of the common agricultural market depends upon the stability of intra-European exchange rates. Consider French and German grains for example: they are almost perfect substitutes. Thus, the "Law of One Price" for cereals should hold exactly. However, input prices in agriculture—labor costs in particular—do not follow the "Law of One Price": exchange rate realignments could thus produce large shifts in the profitability of the farming sector across Europe and induce swings in agricultural trade in the region. The problem is aggravated by the fact that across European agricultural markets the "Law of One Price" rules *by law*. This is so because the European Commission regulates the cereals market by setting an EEC-wide price for each product. The price is set in ECUs and translated in local currencies at the ongoing exchange rate.

Europeans, at least since the 1960s, have agonized over the difficulty of running a common market in a region that does not use a common currency. The rules of Bretton Woods permitted excursions of up to 3 percent between any two European currencies.[4] Such excursions were big enough to interfere with the functioning of the cereals market. The problem precipitated in 1969 with the August devaluation of the French franc and the October revaluation of the Deutsche mark. The response to the realignments was the temporary suspension of the free cereals market. France prevented a jump of cereals prices on the home market by converting the common ECU price at an artificial exchange rate—one that did not reflect the devaluation. Germany avoided being flooded with French cereals by imposing a tariff on imports and granting an export subsidy to its own farmers. After the fall of Bretton Woods, responding to realignments with the introduction of tariffs and subsidies became common practice. By 1974 a German farmer exporting butter to Italy received a subsidy equal to 28.3 percent of the price; if the butter was shipped the other way, a corresponding tax was levied on the Italian exporter.

Beyond infringing upon the basic principle on which the EEC was set up, the tariffs and subsidies introduced to cope with realignments have also been costly for the EEC budget for two reasons. The first is that it proved easier to remove the tariffs by letting agricultural prices rise in the devaluing country than to remove the subsidies by cutting prices in the revaluing country. Therefore the revenue from the tariffs did not match the expenditure on the subsidies. The persistence of export subsidies in strong-currency countries aggravated Europe's chronic overproduction of food. By the mid-1970s two-thirds of the financial resources available to the EEC were absorbed by the cost of running the agricultural market—leaving very little room for action in other areas.

Exchange rate stability then became a vital issue for the EEC, and it was thus natural that the Commission would become a strong supporter of schemes designed to limit intra-European exchange rate fluctuations. The problem has not disappeared in the EMS. The "agri-monetary" consequences of a realignment are an important item in the negotiations, as documented by the realignment communiqués that always carefully spell out the provisions for agricultural markets—the timing of price adjustments, etc.

For many years, the common agricultural policy has been the only important activity of the EEC and the main reason for its existence. In the early 1970s the agricultural market absorbed 90 percent of the total EEC budget; in 1985 the figure was still as high as 73 percent. It is unlikely that the EEC would still be here had it failed to keep the common agricultural market alive. Over the years the operation of the agricultural market has provided the testing ground for cooperation in other areas. The EEC is now moving in new directions. The planned liberalization of 1992 is its first major initiative outside of agriculture: if successful it will reduce the importance of agriculture among the activities of the EEC and enhance the EEC's role in the coordination of economic policies across Europe. To some extent the evolution of the EEC has been possible because this institution survived the difficulties of operating the cereals market. Exchange rate stability has thus been an important condition for institutional developments in Europe.

Trying to understand the EMS without considering the grounds for the particular European aversion to exchange rate fluctuations would be misleading. For the countries that belong to the EMS, leaving the system is a step that many would associate with the abandonment of other areas of European cooperation as well. On some crucial occasions, the link between the EMS and other institutions of European cooperation has been instrumental in forcing policy shifts that, in turn, have made the survival of the exchange rate system possible.

6.3   The EMS Is an (Imperfect) Greater Deutsche Mark Area

Ten years of operation of the EMS provide an important case study to those who are interested in designing new forms of international monetary policy coordination. In any fixed exchange rate regime, the task of running monetary policy is not explicitly assigned to any one country. Supporters of the hypothesis that international monetary policy coordination is feasible claim that, in commodity standard systems like the gold standard or the Bretton Woods regime, the establishment of nominal parities in terms of an external numeraire forces all countries to pursue the nominal target in a symmetric fashion. This mechanism, it is claimed, imposes a sort of implicit coordination of monetary policies. In a fiat currency system like the EMS, systematic cooperation by monetary authorities could help to define common monetary targets to be pursued jointly by all countries.

Are the use of an external numeraire—like gold in the earlier fixed exchange rate regimes—or the institution of consultation bodies—like the EEC Monetary Committee and the Committee of Central Bank Governors—effective enough measures to induce international monetary policy cooperation? The evidence from the EMS suggests a negative answer to that question. The EMS, like the gold standard and the Bretton Woods system, is characterized by a "center" country—the Federal Republic of Germany—whose central bank pursues its own monetary targets independently of the policies pursued by the other members.[5] The other countries, which have—to a significant extent—

converged to Germany's monetary policies, have maintained limited independence by the systematic use of capital controls and the adoption of periodic exchange rate devaluations.

The strongest evidence in support of the hypothesis that the EMS actually worked as some imperfect Greater Deutsche Mark Area comes from the study of interest rates: West German interest rates are unaffected by most intra-EMS shocks, like the expectations of parity realignments, while interest rates denominated in the other currencies suffer the full impact of intra-EMS portfolio disturbances. Countries like Italy and France have sheltered their economies from the wide fluctuations in interest rates that have been observed in the (unregulated) Euromarkets by imposing capital controls. This situation, as Giovannini (1989) shows, is similar to that of the gold standard and the Bretton Woods period, when countries other than Great Britain and the United States, respectively, sought to defend their policies from the influence of the "center" country by imposing various forms of regulatory hurdles on the international transmission of monetary policies.[6]

6.4   Macroeconomic Effects: Inflation

One of the most dramatic changes in the economies of the EMS member countries since 1979 has been the decrease in the rate of inflation. Table 6.1 compares inflation rates of various European countries at the start of the EMS with the present. The table suggests both a significant convergence of European inflation rates toward the West German levels, and a general decrease of inflation, which is not limited to the countries belonging to the EMS. Since we concluded in the preceding section that Germany's monetary policy has been at the center of the EMS, and since West German authorities built a wide reputation as "inflation fighters" in the post–World War II period, the natural question raised by this experience is whether the structure and working of the EMS, and in particular the central role played by the West

Table 6.1   The European Disinflation

	1978	1987
Belgium	4.3	2.1
Denmark	9.9	4.6
France	9.5	3.3
West Germany	4.3	2.1
Ireland	10.5	2.9
Italy	13.9	5.5
Netherlands	5.4	−1.0
United Kingdom	11.3	4.0

Note: GDP deflator: annual growth, percent.
Source: European Economy.

German monetary authorities, have played any role in the disinflation experience of countries as different as Denmark, France, and Italy. In this section we review the argument that pegging the exchange rate can help a country in the disinflation effort, and we present the evidence for a number of EMS countries and a country outside the EMS, the United Kingdom. The theoretical model points to the problem of the credibility of the exchange rate target and the costs of the exchange rate union for the center country—the Federal Republic of Germany. In our empirical analysis we attempt to measure both the credibility of intra-European exchange rate targets and the size, timing, and effects of shifts in the expectations after 1979.

6.4.1 Breaking the Inflation Inertia: The Role of Expectations

One fundamental feature of the inflationary process in modern industrial economies appears to be its persistence, a phenomenon that has been linked to the mechanics of wage and price setting. Firms and unions—for a number of reasons that we do not need to explore here[7]—find it more convenient to set prices and wages much less frequently than the rate of arrival of economic news. Therefore wages and prices are crucially affected by workers' and firms' expectations. Workers and firms are concerned, for example, to preserve the purchasing power of their income, and incorporate in their output prices their forecasts of the future evolution of the general price level. Indirectly, wage and price setters concerned about the evolution of the general price level need to forecast the stance of monetary policy.

The special nature of wage and price setting therefore creates a problem of coordination between the central bank and the public. The central bank might want to use monetary policy to steer the economy toward a higher output path, but the public, anticipating future expansionary policies, can sterilize them fully by incorporating in their current pricing decisions the expectation of future monetary expansion and higher inflation. This process, by itself, generates inflation and tends to force the monetary authority to accommodate the higher rate of growth of prices, in order to avoid a severe recession. Hence in equilibrium there is higher inflation, and less output growth, than initially desired by both the public and the monetary authorities. This is the inflationary bias of monetary policy in the presence of price and wage inertia, first described and analyzed by Barro and Gordon (1983).

The coordination problem of monetary policy and sluggish prices and wages is also at the core of the issue of disinflation. Bringing inflation down requires a change in inflationary expectations on the part of price setters. How can the monetary authorities "convince" price setters that an announced contraction will be lasting and credible? The reputation that a central bank needs to bring down inflation can be obtained in two ways. The first, and more painful method for society as a whole, is by showing that, even in the worst of a depression, the announced monetary targets are not reneged. The initial monetary contraction after the announcement of a disinflation plan generates a recession, since it is imposed in an economy where inflation and money growth expectations are high. The slower the response of private sector expectations to the monetary contraction, the longer and harsher the recession, because the very fact that the monetary authority sticks to the announced contractionary path comes to private agents as a surprise.

Alternatively, the monetary authority could avoid going through this prolonged "initiation" period by seeking a way to influence expectations with some institutional reform. The institutional reform of interest for us is a change in the exchange rate regime. How can the transition from flexible to fixed exchange rates bring about an improvement in the output-inflation tradeoff and facilitate the disinflation effort? Under fixed exchange rates, a central bank tends to loosen control of the domestic supply of money, since the changes in international reserves needed to support the exchange rate parity produce changes in the domestic supply of money which, in principle, the monetary authority cannot influence.

Now, suppose a country decides to passively peg its exchange rate to another country, whose monetary authority enjoys the reputation of being an inflation-buster. By "passive peg" we mean that the first country's monetary authority, after announcing the exchange rate parity, simply accommodates the second country's monetary policies, without any attempt to directly influence their choice of targets. What happens to the inflation expectations of the private sector? Wage and price setters need to evaluate the credibility of this institutional reform, that is they need to determine the likelihood that the announced exchange rate targets will be pursued consistently. If, and only if, the exchange rate target is a credible one, expectations will adjust and the process of disinflation will be facilitated.

In practice, the EMS has not completely eliminated inflation differentials. Countries with higher inflation rates have resorted to periodic exchange rate realignments to recover the losses in competitiveness caused by persisting inflation differentials and fixed exchange rates. The disruptions caused by speculators' expectations of these exchange rate realignments have been limited—as we stressed above—through the systematic use of capital controls. Even when exchange rates are periodically realigned, though, pegging to a low inflation country can improve the output-inflation tradeoff. This happens because the terms-of-trade fluctuations that occur during the intervals when exchange rates are not changed provide a strong enough deterrent to central banks not to deviate from the center country's monetary policies as much as they would under a pure floating rate regime. With periodic realignments, however, the center country's output-inflation tradeoff is affected as well. During the intervals when exchange rates are kept fixed, the center country's terms of trade worsen because the partner's inflation rate is higher than its own. As a consequence, the center country's output-inflation tradeoff also worsens: the inflation buster exports reputation and imports inflation.

In summary, the argument that pegging to Germany has helped high-inflation countries in the disinflation efforts of the 1980s rests crucially on the assumption that exchange rate targets are more credible than monetary targets. In the next section we try to measure the effects of the EMS on inflation expectations and the short-run output-inflation tradeoff among member countries, and we confront the issue of the credibility of exchange-rate targets.

6.4.2   Measuring the Shifts in Expectations

Our discussion in the previous section suggests that one important macro-economic benefit of the EMS for countries other than the Federal Republic of Germany could have been associated with a shift in inflationary expectations originating from the public's awareness that, in a fixed exchange rate regime like the EMS, monetary policy is run, by and large, by the Bundesbank. In order to assess the empirical relevance of these effects, we need to measure the shifts of expectations. Consider the dynamics of wages and prices. As we argued above, private agents (firms and unions) set prices and wages by forming expectations on future macroeconomic variables, like the overall rate of inflation. These expectations are necessarily a function of agents' available information, reflected in current and past realization of all relevant macro-economic variables. If a monetary reform like the EMS is put in place, private agents who believe that the reform will actually change monetary policies in the way described above, have to reevaluate the methods they use to extrapolate from past macroeconomic variables the expectations about future inflation and economic activity. Hence the shift in expectations, and its effect on the inflationary process, will be reflected in a shift of statistical equations relating wages and prices to available information. In this section we study the process of disinflation in Denmark, France, the Federal Republic of Germany, Ireland, Italy, and, for comparison, the United Kingdom, by comparing how the relation between price and wage inflation and output has shifted after the start of the EMS. We are concerned with both the timing of the shifts and their magnitude.

We estimate a (quarterly) system of three equations specifying the dynamics of CPI inflation, wage inflation, and output growth, which we measure using industrial production indices. Each equation includes on the right-hand side a time trend, seasonal dummy variables, four lags of wage inflation, CPI inflation and industrial production growth, and dummy variables representing country-specific events that the model cannot explain.[8] We also include four lags of M1 growth rates, as well as changes in the relative price of imported intermediate and final goods. This last set of variables is assumed to be determined outside of the system: while innovations in wage and price inflation are plausibly correlated with money growth and changes in relative prices of intermediate and final goods, these variables are assumed to affect inflation and output growth only with a one-quarter lag.[9]

The first question we address is whether there is evidence of a significant shift in these statistical equations after 1979. A test of the stability of the parameter estimates was performed for each equation and each country, using as a cutting point the first quarter of 1979.[10] The results of the test indicate the presence of a structural shift only in the case of France: in no other country are the shifts of wage-price dynamics after 1979 statistically significant. While this evidence goes against the hypothesis that the EMS has been associated with a shift in expectations, the negative result is very likely to be caused by the low power of the parameter stability tests we employ.

The next question we address regards the timing and the direction of the shifts in the inflation processes. Using parameter estimates obtained over the 1960–79 sample, and the actual realizations of the forcing variables (money growth and relative prices of intermediate and final goods), we compute dynamic simulations of wage and price inflation and output growth. Table 6.2 reports the timing and the direction of estimated shifts in inflation and output dynamics obtained from the simulations. For every country we show the date when the simulated paths of inflation and output growth start diverging in a persistent way from the actual paths, and the sign of the divergence. The words "higher" and "lower" reported in parenthesis under each date indicate that the actual realizations of the variables were respectively higher and lower than their simulated values.

Table 6.2 shows a number of impressive regularities. First, for all countries except Germany, and possibly Denmark, actual and simulated inflation and output paths start diverging later than the beginning of the EMS. Second, simulations for output growth tend to be less clearcut than simulations for inflation. And third, the directions of the divergences are opposite for Germany and the other countries in the table. In Germany actual inflation after 1979 is higher than its simulated value, and output growth is lower. The opposite results of Germany and the other countries are consistent with the model of imported reputation. The delayed shifts in the output-inflation tradeoffs for most countries, which occur well after the start of the EMS, and the very similar pattern followed by U.K. inflation and output, raise the question of the

Table 6.2   The Timing and Direction of the Shift in Expectations

	Denmark	France	Germany	Ireland	Italy	United Kingdom
Price inflation	80:1	83:2	79:2	82:3	85:1	81:3
(direction)	(lower)	(lower)	(higher)	(lower)	(lower)	(lower)
Wage inflation	80:2	83:2	79:2	80:2	85:1	81:1
(direction)	(lower)	(lower)	(higher)	(lower)	(lower)	(lower)
Output growth	80:3	none	79:2	none	none	none
(direction)	(higher)		(lower)			

Note: The words "higher" and "lower" indicate that the actual realization of the variables are respectively higher and lower than their simulated values. The word "more" indicates that no systematic divergence between actual and simulated values can be detected. In the case of Italy, the divergence between actual and simulated variables occurs close to the end of the simulation period.

nature of the shift in expectation, and of the role played by the reform of the exchange rate regime.

Further evidence on the effects of the exchange rate reform on expectations is reported in figures 6.1–6.3, which depict the Euro–interest rate differentials between three-month krone, franc, and lira deposits and deutsche mark deposits. Interest rate differentials contain both expectations of exchange rates and risk premiums. The presumption is that, if exchange rate targets were perfectly credible, both components of the interest rate differentials would tend to zero: expected changes in exchange rates would disappear, and the substitutability between Eurodeposits denominated in francs, marks, lire, and kroner—which is presumably inversely related to risk premiums—would increase. The figures, by contrast, show that interest rate differentials are not stabilized after 1979. In particular, the years 1982 and 1983 are associated with a crisis of confidence in the EMS, as shown by the large increases in interest rate differentials.

In summary, the evidence from the simulation of the output-inflation model suggests a delayed response in expectations, while interest rate differentials indicate that expectations and risk premiums did not decrease after the start of the EMS. Is this evidence consistent with the theory? The failure of interest rate differentials to disappear is clearly not enough to dismiss the imported credibility model. Although higher interest rates on lira, franc, and krone deposits most likely indicate that private agents attached a positive probability

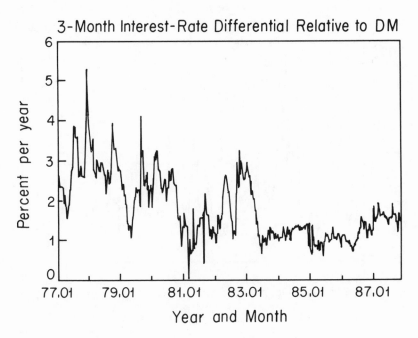

Fig. 6.1 Danish kroner

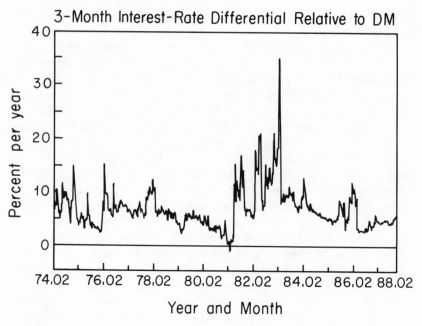

Fig. 6.2   French franc

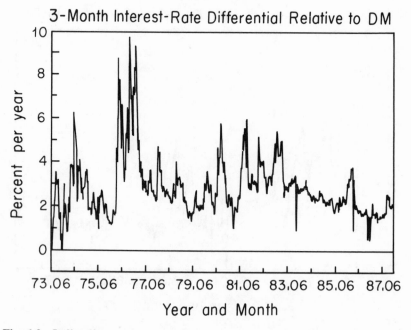

Fig. 6.3   Italian lira

to devaluations of these currencies relative to the deutsche mark, European countries were subject to the effects of the unprecedented dollar appreciation in the early 1980s and the second oil shock: the exchange rate mechanism might have limited the expected devaluations relative to a pure floating regime. Hence, while the forward exchange rate data seem to be inconclusive on the issue of the credibility of the exchange rate targets, there is no prima facie inconsistency between the simulation results and the behavior of forward premiums.

Finally, we turn to the analysis of the magnitudes of the shifts in the output-inflation tradeoffs. Table 6.3 reports changes in inflation and cumulative output growth that have occurred in European countries since 1979, and compares them with simulations of the same magnitudes obtained from the model described above. Contrast, for example, the experiences of Germany, Ireland, and Italy. According to our simulations, every percentage point of inflation reduction since 1979 would have afforded Germany 10.7 percent growth: by contrast, the output growth for every point of inflation reduction was only 4.10. In the case of Ireland and Italy, our simulations predict that every point of inflation reduction could have afforded those countries 4.10 and 0.67 percent growth, respectively. But in reality, real growth for every point of inflation reduction was higher in both cases: 6.94 percent in Ireland and 2.18 percent in Italy. Similarly, our simulations predicted a fall in output by 1.34 percent for every percentage point reduction of inflation in Denmark, whereas in fact output has increased by 10.6 percent for every percentage point reduction of inflation. These comparisons vividly illustrate the estimated effects of shifts in expectations and their uneven distribution among Germany and the European partners.

It is however puzzling that price and wage expectations seem to have adjusted with a lag. One possible interpretation of this puzzle is that the effects of the EMS on expectations were not as direct as predicted by the Barro-Gordon (1983) model. The experience in France, Italy, and Ireland and our estimates of the timing of the shifts in expectations, suggest that the shifts in expectations were prompted by shifts in domestic policies.

In Italy we estimate a shift in expectations in the first quarter of 1985, in the aftermath of a government decree which had set a ceiling on wage

Table 6.3   **The Shift in the Output-Inflation Tradeoff**

	Denmark	France	Germany	Ireland	Italy	United Kingdom
End of the simulations	84:4	85:4	86:4	88:1	86:4	87:1
Change in inflation	− 1.83	− 4.86	− 3.37	− 9.72	− 8.38	− 6.23
Predicted change in inflation	− 2.57	6.78	− 5.51	− 8.57	− 12.87	6.63
Cumulative change in output	19.43	5.06	13.82	39.84	18.30	12.10
Predicted cumulative change in output	− 3.45	26.18	58.95	59.60	8.25	9.98

indexation. That decree had been challenged by the unions and was eventually ratified by a national referendum in June 1984.

In Ireland there was a major turnaround in economic policies in the summer of 1982, marked by an announcement of tighter guidelines for monetary policy, a decision not to devalue the central parity of the punt in the February and June 1982 EMS realignments, and a decision to freeze pay increases in the public sector.[11]

In France, the turnaround in macroeconomic policies occurred in March 1983, after the expansionary experiment of the first Mitterrand government had produced a large current account deficit (3.5 percent of GDP) and a speculative attack on the franc. The government accompanied the EMS exchange realignment with a freeze in budgetary expenses, an increase in income taxes, and a dramatic tightening of credit.[12]

What was the linkage between these policies and the EMS constraint? In the case of Ireland and France the linkage is apparent. In particular, French authorities justified the unpopular policies as a necessary step to ensure EMS membership and linked the membership in the EMS to the participation in the EEC.[13] In the case of Italy, we were unable to find any important reference to the EMS in the government pronouncements after the decree on wage indexation, but we cannot exclude the possibility that the external constraint might have motivated that unpopular policy. In conclusion, EMS membership might have helped countries other than Germany in their disinflation efforts only to the extent that they provided a justification for unpopular policies vis-à-vis the domestic public, which could have helped to strengthen the credibility of the exchange rate targets.

6.5   The "European Alliance"

The view of the EMS as a system designed to enhance the credibility of inflation-prone countries leaves us with a puzzle. What incentives does the Federal Republic of Germany have to belong to such a system? The imported credibility model suggests that the center country may be the loser in an agreement in which it provides the nominal anchor that helps its partners to disinflate. If the decision to peg to a stable currency produced an instantaneous adjustment of expectations, the center country would be unaffected by the decisions of others to peg to its currency. But if learning takes time and disinflation is a dynamic process, during the transition the terms of trade of the center country worsen, and so does its output-inflation tradeoff. These effects are obviously smaller the larger the center country is relative to its partners: the United States was not concerned when Grenada or Belize decided to peg to the dollar. But even if we consider Germany and the Netherlands a de facto monetary union and we sum their economic size, the joint GDP of the two countries (one thousand billion ECUs in 1985) is still only two-thirds of the joint GDP of the other members of the EMS. The EMS area also accounts for some 30 percent of total German and Dutch trade.

The empirical results described in section 6.4.2 seem to confirm that Germany's output-inflation tradeoff has worsened since the start of the EMS. The evidence would thus justify the initial reluctance of the Deutsche Bundesbank to join the system. It remains to be explained, however, why German policymakers have tried, since the late 1960s, to avoid an uncoordinated response of European countries to the fall of Bretton Woods. As it became clear that the Bretton Woods system was approaching its final days, German policymakers became increasingly worried that other European currencies might not be able to follow the appreciation of the deutsche mark vis-à-vis the dollar: they were preoccupied by the idea that the realignment of intra-European parities would disrupt the European customs union as well as the common agricultural market—two institutions that they considered important to the German economy.[14]

In this section we look for evidence of Germany's incentives to stay in the EMS by analyzing the behavior of Germany's terms of trade from the Bretton Woods era to the 1980s. The terms-of-trade index we use is the real effective exchange rate of the deutsche mark built using relative wholesale prices and the IMF Multilateral Exchange Rate Model (MERM) weights that are designed to measure a country's competitiveness relative to its trading partners. We are interested in finding out whether the EMS has stabilized Germany's terms of trade relative to previous periods.

The definition of ''stability,'' however, is ambiguous. One possibility is to look at the variability of unanticipated changes in the real effective exchange rate. This measure however eliminates most of the low-frequency components of the series. Indeed, it could be argued that those low-frequency components are worthy of special attention. Williamson (1983) suggests that while exchange rate *volatility* (measured by the standard deviation of unanticipated exchange rate changes) might have a negative impact on trade and welfare, exchange rate *misalignment* (that is prolonged deviations of the exchange rate from some fundamental level) is likely to bring about the largest costs.[15] Table 6.4 reports the simplest possible measure of the variability of the real effective exchange rate: its standard deviation. The data are monthly, from 1960 to 1985. The volatility of the effective real rate increases dramatically after the end of Bretton Woods, but stabilizes in the EMS. The second column in the table suggests why this might have happened. We construct the real effective exchange rate of the deutsche mark vis-à-vis its EMS partners and compute the correlation between the index of ''global'' competitiveness and that of Germany's competitiveness inside the EMS. In the 1960s and 1970s the correlation between the two indices is very high, indicating that the French franc, the lira, and the other EMS currencies did not follow the deutsche mark—particularly at the time of its large appreciation vis-à-vis the dollar after the collapse of Bretton Woods. The phenomenon reverses after 1979: the correlation between the global and the intra-EMS indices becomes negative, indicating that the EMS has limited the effects of the fluctuations of the dollar/DM rate on Germany's competitiveness. Similar computations for the

Table 6.4   Federal Republic of Germany's Terms-of-Trade

Year: Month	Standard Error of Real Effective Exchange Rate (global index)	Correlation between Global and Intra-EEC Indices of Competitiveness
1960:1–1971:8	0.041	0.824
1960:1–1979:1	0.127	0.911
1960:1–1985:12	0.124	0.620
1979:2–1985:12	0.114	−0.033

Sources: IMF, International Financial Statistics. Real exchange rates are constructed using wholesale prices. Effective exchange rate weights are the IMF-MERM weights for 1977, normalized to account for Germany's competitiveness vis-à-vis its eight major trading partners— in the case of the global index—and its four major EMS partners—in the case of the intra-EMS index. Weights are as follows. Global index: Belgium, 0.0588; France, 0.2106; Italy 0.151; Japan, 0.152; Netherlands, 0.074; Switzerland, 0.043; United Kingdom, 0.058; United States, 0.262. Intra-EMS index: Belgium, 0.121; France, 0.416; Italy, 0.311; Netherlands, 0.152.

other EMS countries show that the phenomenon documented in table 6.4 is specific to Germany. Belgium for example offers a mirror image of the German experience: the correlation between the global and the intra-EMS indices increases after 1979. Given that Belgium is one of Germany's major trading partners, this has stabilized Germany's real exchange rate. The cost for Belgium has been an increase in the volatility of the real effective exchange rate.

The evidence on Germany's terms of trade seems to support the "European Alliance" view of the EMS: the system has protected Germany from the effects of dollar fluctuations. In the early 1970s, at the time of the first dollar collapse, Germany appreciated both vis-à-vis the dollar and vis-à-vis its European partners: the result was a large swing in the country's terms of trade. After the dollar fall of 1985 the EMS currencies followed the deutsche mark much closer and attenuated the impact on Germany's terms of trade. The comparison between the two periods clearly shows the extent to which the EMS has stabilized Germany's overall competitiveness. From November 1969 to March 1973 the deutsche mark appreciated 25 percent vis-à-vis the dollar; this was accompanied by an 18.6 percent worsening of Germany's overall competitiveness. During the period from January 1985 to December 1987, the deutsche mark appreciation was similar—27 percent—but this time it was accompanied by a loss of competitiveness only half as large—9 percent.

6.6   Fiscal Implications of Monetary Convergence

Our discussion of the European disinflation has so far neglected the fiscal implications of monetary convergence. The important interactions between inflation and the financing of budget deficits open up an additional set of issues concerning the economic effects of the EMS and the prospects of financial markets liberalization planned for 1992. What has been the effect of the convergence of inflation rates on the government debt in the high-inflation countries? There are two channels through which a disinflation affects the budget. The first is direct: a monetary contraction reduces the portion of the budget deficit that can be financed by printing money. The second channel stems from the rise in real interest rates and the fall in output associated with the disinflation. When the gap between the real rate and the growth rate widens, debt starts to grow. The larger a country's initial stock of public debt—as a percent of GDP—the more serious will be the impact on the budget of any increase in the real rate and of any reduction in the rate of growth.

All these problems are particularly important in Europe because high debt levels and dependence on money financing were the norm in many countries before the start of the EMS. Table 6.5 shows the fiscal situation of Ireland, Italy, Denmark, and Belgium before the start of the EMS. We concentrate on these countries, neglecting France, Germany, and the Netherlands, because the latter were characterized by neither high debt levels nor significant money financing—and it is not surprising that the first four countries eventually developed a fiscal problem. In 1978 none of these countries, with the possible exception of Belgium, could be characterized as facing a dramatic fiscal problem. Ireland and Italy had a high debt ratio and a primary deficit that exceeded the revenue from money financing, but real rates were well below the growth rate of income, and the ratio of debt to GDP was stable. Denmark had a small primary surplus and a large revenue from money financing: the sum of the two was more than enough to service the debt, even at high real rates. Belgium is the only country where debt was growing.

To analyze the effects of inflation convergence on debt and deficits, we need to isolate the components of government deficits and of debt dynamics. We study the government budget constraint:

$$(1) \qquad B_t - B_{t-1} = (1 + i_{t-1})B_{t-1} + (C_t - C_{t-1}) + D_t.$$

Table 6.5   **Fiscal Conditions at the Start of the EMS (as percent of 1978 GDP)**

	Debt Level	Money Financing	Money Financing Plus Primary Surplus	r	$(r - n)$
Belgium	0.65	0.0	−2.0	3.0	0.0
Ireland	0.82	1.8	−3.5	−0.6	−7.8
Italy	0.51	2.2	−2.2	−2.4	−5.1
Denmark	0.18	3.4	+5.2	5.5	4.0

Note: Debt level is the stock of public debt on the market, that is, total debt net of debt held by the central bank. Money financing corresponds to the public sector borrowing requirement financed by the central bank. Primary surplus is the budget deficit net of interest. The ex post short-term real rate of interest is r, and n is the growth rate of GDP at constant prices.

Sources: The fiscal variables for Ireland and Italy are from the local central bank *Bulletins*. For Belgium and Denmark, debt levels are from Chouraqui et al. (1986); money financing and the debt held by the central bank are computed from line 12a of *International Financial Statistics*. Interest rates and growth rates for all countries are from *European Economy*.

The increase in the stock of government debt, B, equals the capitalized value of last period's debt, less the increase in credit to the government by the central bank $(C_t - C_{t-1})$, plus the noninterest (or primary) budget deficit. B_t and C_t denote stocks of credit at the end of period t, and i_t is the interest rate on government borrowing from the end of period $t - 1$ to the end of period t. Dividing both sides of the equation by nominal income at time t, Y_t, and applying the usual approximations, we obtain:

$$(2) \qquad b_t - b_{t-1} = (r_{t-1} - n_{t-1})b_{t-1} + d_t - (c_t - c_{t-1})$$
$$- (\pi_t + n_{t-1})c_{t-1},$$

where lowercase letters denote the corresponding variables in uppercase letters expressed as percent of GNP. Equation (2) says that the increase in government debt is higher, the higher the real interest burden on the existing stock of debt—measured by the real interest rate in excess of the rate of growth of the economy—and the higher the primary deficit. An alternative means of financing deficits is represented by the last two terms on the right-hand side of equation (2): the increase of credit to the government by the central bank (in percent of GNP), seigniorage, and the inflation tax. Seigniorage is represented by $(c_t - c_{t-1})$ and $n_{t-1}c_{t-1}$, that is, the noninflationary growth of the total stock of credit from the central bank. The inflation tax (in percent of GNP) is $\pi_t c_{t-1}$.

In the steady state, barring nonneutralities of the tax system, the only fiscal consequence of a slowdown in the rate of inflation is the change in seigniorage revenue and in the inflation tax. If the economy is along the efficient portion of the revenue curve, both seigniorage and the inflation tax fall. Thus a country that prior to the disinflation relied on seigniorage and on the inflation tax as sources of revenue must sooner or later correct its primary deficit. If the country could simply jump from the high- to the low-inflation steady state and the fiscal correction occurred simultaneously with the jump in inflation, the debt level would be unaffected by the change in monetary regime. But if the country postpones the fiscal correction, debt grows: the longer the postponement, the larger becomes the change in the primary deficit required to stabilize the debt because in the meantime the stock of the debt has grown.

The response of European fiscal authorities to the revenue loss induced by the disinflation was uneven. Denmark and Ireland swiftly turned the primary deficit into a large surplus; Italy waited. Thus arises the question of what is the cost of waiting. How quickly does the required change in the primary deficit grow if you delay the fiscal correction? Figure 6.4 helps to answer this question. On the vertical and on the horizontal axis we have, respectively, the primary deficit and the debt level. The two downward sloping schedules describe steady states in which the ratio of public debt to GDP is constant. They are drawn for two different levels of $(\pi + n)c$, the steady-state revenue from money financing in equation (2). Money financing is higher along the

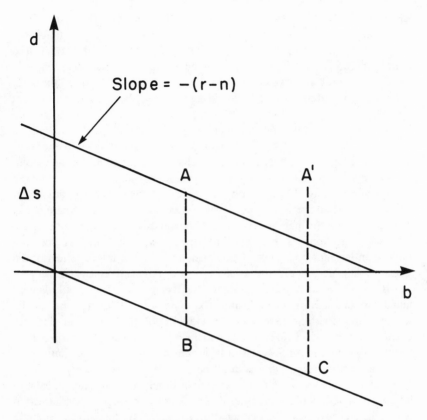

Fig. 6.4   The effects of delaying fiscal adjustment

upper schedule than it is along the lower one. The slope of the two schedules is $-(r - n)$: if the interest rate is above the growth rate of income a higher debt level requires a smaller primary deficit. As $(r - n)$ becomes smaller, the schedules flatten out since the cost of sustaining higher debt levels also becomes smaller.

Consider now a country starting off from a point such as A, and assume that inflation jumps to zero, so that it loses all the revenue from the inflation tax. If the fiscal authorities correct the budget immediately, the country simply moves from A to B at an unchanged stock of debt. But if the fiscal correction is delayed, the economy starts drifting from A toward a point such as A'. How fast does the required fiscal correction grow? The difference between the budget correction required in A and in A' is $(r - n)$ times the increase in the stock of debt: that is, the required fiscal correction grows at $(r - n)$.

Suppose a country starts off with a 75 percent ratio of public debt to GDP and a primary deficit equal to 2 percent of GDP. Assume that prior to the disinflation, money financing brought into the coffers of the treasury 3.5

percent of GDP each year, and that $(r - n)$ is equal to 0.02. If the fiscal correction is done immediately, it must fully offset the loss in money financing: if this falls to zero, the primary deficit must move from a 2 percent deficit to a surplus of 1.5 percent.[16] If the fiscal correction does not take place, ten years later the debt level will have grown from 50 to 90 percent of GDP, but the fiscal correction required to stabilize it will have grown only from 1.5 to 1.8 percent of GDP.

This simple example suggests that, if policymakers' public support is negatively affected by a fiscal contraction, there is a strong incentive to wait. A delay in fiscal adjustment increases the chances of reelection of the current government. Come tomorrow, the fiscal contraction—and the accompanying loss of consensus—will be only slightly higher. Waiting can be very attractive.

The output response to the monetary contraction and to the turnaround in fiscal policy has further effects on the dynamics of the stabilization. As discussed in section 6.3, the decision to peg to a stable currency does not produce an instantaneous shift in expectations: thus, the impact effect of the central bank's decision to embark on a new monetary path, consistent with the peg, is an increase in real interest rates. The rise in interest rates will depress output, so that during the transition $(r - n)$ will be higher: this is the secondary burden of the disinflation. In addition, lower output will reduce tax revenues and add a cyclical component to the primary deficit. If, on top of this, the primary deficit is abruptly cut, it is unclear whether the simple jump from A to B described in figure 6.4 is at all possible.

In Table 6.6 we show the results of simple simulations designed to capture the dynamics of debt in the presence of a response to the monetary contraction by output, real rates, and the budget. Rows 1, 2, and 3 illustrate the example discussed above. Rows 2 and 3 correspond, respectively, to the instantaneous

Table 6.6   Disinflation, Debt, and the Budget

Simulation	Debt	Monetary Financing	Budget Surplus Required for Debt Stabilization
1. Initial conditions	0.75	0.035	−0.020
2. Instantaneous fiscal correction	0.75	0.0	0.015
3. Fiscal correction after 10 years	0.91	0.0	0.018
4. Fiscal correction after 10 years with $(r - n)$ effect	1.07	0.0	0.021
5. Fiscal correction after 10 years with $(r - n)$ and cyclical effects	1.20	0.0	0.024

Note: In all simulations the steady-state value of $(r - n)$ is 0.02. In cases 2 and 3 the stabilization has no effect on real variables. In case 4 output falls and real rates rise during the disinflation, but there are no cyclical effects on the budget. The path of $(r - n)$ is: year 1: 0.07; year 2: 0.07; year 3: 0.05; year 4: 0.04; year 5: 0.03; and year 6: 0.02. In case 5 $(r - n)$ rises and the recession raises the budget deficit. The paths of $(r - n)$ and of the cyclical component of the budget are $(r - n,$ cycl.): year 1: 0.07, 0.035; year 2: 0.07, 0.035; year 3: 0.05, 0.020; year 4: 0.04, 0.010; year 5: 0.03, 0.005; year 6: 0.02, 0.0.

fiscal correction and to the case when the correction comes ten years later. The simulation reported in row 4 allows for a temporary increase in $(r - n)$, which jumps from 2 to 3 percent at the outset of the disinflation and then gradually falls back to 2 percent.[17] The fiscal correction occurs, as in case shown in row 3 after ten years. Row 5 extends the example by including the effect of the recession on the budget. The recession is assumed to worsen the budget by an amount equal to 3.5 percent of GDP in the first year, which gradually returns to zero in six years.

The results of these simulations suggest that the effects of the monetary convergence on the government debt of some EMS members has been sizable and could make the fiscal situation of countries like Italy and Ireland more and more difficult to manage. Such convergence is however necessary to achieve a sustainable elimination of inflation rate differentials.

6.7 Concluding Remarks

In this paper we have reviewed the experience of the EMS to identify the lessons that this experiment in monetary coordination could provide to those who are considering a reform of the international monetary system.

Clearly, an institution like the EMS would not work outside of Europe, for a number of reasons. First, the incentives that countries have to belong to the EMS—the high degree of integration of European economies, and the more comprehensive design of institutional integration, of which the EMS is just an element and which lends credibility to the EMS exchange rate targets—are not present, say, among the United States, Europe, and Japan. Second, the operation of monetary policies has not been linked to the exchange rate constraint by all countries: the Federal Republic of Germany appears to have pursued its own monetary targets without attempting to accommodate international influences, while the other countries have either followed Germany's policies, or changed exchange rates, or imposed capital controls. The striking similarity between the EMS and previous experiences of fixed exchange rates suggests that the institution of fixed rates cannot, per se, induce international monetary policy cooperation. Finally, the differences in the use of the inflation tax among European countries and the divergent behavior of government debt after 1979 indicate that the pursuit of monetary convergence among countries with different fiscal structures might entail substantial fiscal reforms.

Notes

1. An important exception is the United Kingdom which remained outside the EMS.
2. Ideally this question should be answered by integrating the analysis of the informational benefits of a common currency (or fixed exchange rates) with the analysis of the macroeconomic effects of alternative exchange rate regimes. Unfortunately, the

current models of money are still ill-suited for such an ambitious task. Hence we concentrate here on the macroeconomic aspects.

3. The memory of these events is kept alive by the Nurske's illuminating account of the effects of the exchange rate policies of the 1920s. See Nurske (1944).

4. The rules set 1 percent margins around the dollar parity of each currency, thus in principle permitting bilateral excursions of up to 4 percent. European countries however had agreed to maintain their dollar parities within smaller margins: 0.75 percent.

5. See Giovannini (1989) for a historical comparison of the gold standard, Bretton Woods, and the EMS, a formal statement of the "asymmetry" hypothesis, and an analysis of the empirical evidence.

6. In the form of changes in regulations affecting the gold market and of controls on international capital flows.

7. See, for example, Blanchard (1988) and Rotemberg (1988) for excellent surveys.

8. The dummies are the following: for all countries, from 1971:3 to the end of the sample, fall of the fixed rates regime; for Italy, 69:2–70:1 *Autumno Caldo*, 73:3–74:1 price freeze; for France, 63:4–64:4, 69:1–70:4, 74:1–74:4, 77:1–77:4, 82:3–83:4 wage and price controls; 68:2–68:3 "May 1968;" for the United Kingdom, 67:4 sterling devaluation, 73:4–74:4 wage controls.

9. The estimates are obtained assuming that superneutrality holds, that is, the sum of the coefficients of nominal variables is equal to 1 in the equations explaining wage and price inflation, and is zero in the equation explaining output growth. These constraints were not rejected in the largest majority of cases.

10. In Giavazzi and Giovannini (1989) we report a more detailed analysis of the model and all the statistical results. Detailed statistics for Ireland, which do not appear there, are available from us on request.

11. Dornbusch (1988).

12. Sachs and Wyplosz (1986).

13. Sachs and Wyplosz (1986).

14. For an account of the German position in those years see Emminger (1977) and Kloten (1978).

15. Recent research by Krugman and Baldwin (1987), Baldwin and Krugman (1986), Dixit (1987), and especially Krugman (1988) provides the first attempt at formalizing the linkage between the uncertainty and slow mean-reversion in exchange rate movements and the speed of adjustment of intersectoral factor movements and investment.

16. In reality, even if inflation falls to zero, not all money financing will be lost. At $\pi = 0$ money financing is equal to nc.

17. The precise figures are shown at the bottom of table 6.6.

References

Baldwin, R., and P. Krugman. 1986. Persistent trade effects of large exchange rate shocks. Cambridge, MA: MIT. Mimeograph.

Barro, R. J., and D. Gordon. 1983. A positive theory of monetary policy in a natural rate model. *Journal of Political Economy* 91:589–610.

Blanchard, O. J. 1988. Why money affects output. Cambridge, MA: MIT. Manuscript.

Chouraqui, J. C., B. Jones, and R. B. Montador. 1986. Public debt in a medium-term perspective. *OECD Economic Studies* 7 (Autumn).

Dixit, A. 1987. Entry and exit decisions of firms under fluctuating real exchange rates. Princeton: Princeton University. Mimeograph.

Dornbusch, R. 1988. Ireland's failed stabilization. Cambridge, MA: MIT. Manuscript.

Emminger, O. 1977. The D-mark in the conflict between internal and external equilibrium, 1948–1975. *Essays in International Finance* no. 122. Princeton: International Finance Section, Princeton University.

Giavazzi, F., and A. Giovannini. 1989. *Limiting exchange rate flexibility: The European monetary system.* Cambridge, MA: MIT Press.

Giovannini, A. 1989. How do fixed-exchange-rates regimes work?: The evidence from the Gold Standard, Bretton Woods and the EMS. In B. Eichengreen, M. Miller, and R. Portes, eds., *Blueprints for exchange rate management.* New York: Academic Press.

Kloten, N. 1978. Germany's monetary and financial policy and the European Economic Community. In W. L. Kohl and G. Basevi, eds., *West Germany: A European and global power.* Lexington, MA: Lexington Books.

Krugman, P. 1988. Deindustrialization, reindustrialization, and the real exchange rate. Cambridge, MA: MIT. Mimeograph.

Krugman, P., and R. Baldwin. 1987. The persistence of the U.S. trade deficit. *Brookings Papers on Economic Activity* 2:1–55.

Nurske, R. 1944. *International currency experience.* Geneva: League of Nations.

Rotemberg, J. J. 1987. The new Keynesian microfoundations. In Stanley Fischer, ed., *NBER Macroeconomics Annual 1987,* 116–69. Cambridge, MA: MIT Press.

Sachs, J., and C. Wyplosz. 1986. The economic consequences of President Mitterand. *Economic Policy* 2:261–313.

Williamson, J. 1983. *The exchange rate system.* Washington, DC: Institute for International Economics.

Comment   Richard C. Marston

This paper is the latest of several influential studies of the European Monetary System by Giavazzi and Giovannini. It addresses two questions: Why does Europe have a stronger aversion to exchange rate fluctuations than elsewhere, and what incentives are there for countries to participate in the system? Let me begin with the latter question.

Giavazzi and Giovannini analyze the potential role of the EMS in establishing credible anti-inflation policies in countries like France or Italy. Drawing on earlier work by Barro and Gordon (1983), they argue that such countries have found it difficult to establish credible anti-inflation policies because there are incentives for a central bank to depart from such policies once the private sector has come to believe in them. Throughout the past few decades, however, the Bundesbank has established a sound reputation for inflation fighting. The EMS offers countries like France an opportunity to gain credibility for their inflation policies by tying their monetary policy to that of the Bundesbank.

Richard C. Marston is James R. F. Guy Professor of Finance and Economics at the Wharton School of the University of Pennsylvania and a research associate at the National Bureau of Economic Research.

This motivation for the EMS is certainly important, but as the authors point out, doubts about the credibility of the exchange rate pegs may undermine the credibility of the inflation policy. Since the EMS was founded in 1979, in fact, there have been eleven realignments of parity values. France and Italy alone have realigned on five occasions each. During many of those realignment periods, forward exchange premiums for the franc and lira have soared, thus showing how little credibility the existing pegs enjoyed. But despite so many realignments, it may still be the case that the EMS imparted an anti-inflationary bias to each country's monetary policy, lowering inflation below what it might have been without the EMS.

Giavazzi and Giovannini decide to investigate this issue empirically, and so they provide several different types of evidence concerning changes in inflation. The first is in their table 6.1 where they show a sharp reduction in inflation rates for the EMS countries in 1987 compared with 1978. I made similar calculations for the United States and Japan. These are shown in table C6.1. Japan's experience is remarkably similar to that of the Netherlands, and the U.S. experience is similar to that of Belgium, the Federal Republic of Germany, and Denmark. So there may be *worldwide* factors rather than just EMS-wide factors at work in lowering inflation.

The authors also set out to estimate nonstructural equations for inflation to determine whether there was a shift in behavior after 1979. Their results indicate that only France experienced a structural shift that was statistically significant, and that shift occurred not in 1979 but in 1983 when the Mitterrand government changed its policies. They point out that the test has low explanatory power, so they also conduct postsample simulations to see whether their equations estimated for the pre-EMS period track the EMS period itself. Their table 6.2 is quite interesting in that it shows a symmetrical pattern of inflation effects. Germany experienced a higher inflation than predicted, and the other countries (including a floating country, the United Kingdom), a lower inflation rate than predicted. This evidence suggests that the Bundesbank has perhaps compromised its inflation policy in trying to maintain fixed rates with the EMS. However, there is no evidence that the shifts in the equations are statistically significant. Second, there is no comparison with non-EMS countries (except the United Kingdom) to see whether this shift is just

Table C6.1   Disinflation Outside of the EMS

	1978	1987
United States	7.4	3.0
Japan	4.8	-0.3

Source: International Monetary Fund, *International Financial Statistics.*
Note: GNP deflator: annual growth, percent.

coincident with the EMS rather than being caused by it. As the authors would be the first to admit, it is not enough to compare pre-EMS and post-EMS periods and attribute all economic changes in Europe to the EMS.

I would like to expand on this point by citing recent studies by Ungerer et al. (1986) and Collins (1988). Ungerer et al. estimated equations explaining inflation rates in EMS and non-EMS countries by inverting money demand functions. That study concluded that there was a structural shift in the inflation equations for Europe in the period after the EMS was founded. Collins reestimated the equations and tested for both an EMS effect and a general post-1979 effect common to all countries in the sample. She showed that the only significant effect was due to a post-1979 shift variable common to all countries, EMS and non-EMS alike. Her paper again emphasizes the danger in attributing lower inflation in the EMS to the EMS when lower inflation characterizes countries outside the EMS as well.

There is a third issue that should be raised regarding the inflation equations estimated by Giavazzi and Giovannini. The tests for structural shifts in these equations are based on simulations using the *actual* values of money growth experienced over the period. But in the Barro-Gordon (1983) model, it is the entire equilibrium between the government and the private sector that is affected by the credibility of the inflation policy. If the government were able to precommit to a different inflation policy, we might find structural changes in the money growth process itself. The rate of growth would presumably shift, but so also might any feedback mechanism that determines the response of the money supply to other variables. This possibility may be worth exploring.

Giavazzi and Giovannini also ask whether there are any costs to an anti-inflation policy in Europe. The authors provide an interesting analysis of the effects of lower inflation on fiscal revenues, calculating the potential revenue loss due to the removal of the inflation tax from money balances. The authors, however, do not ask whether it is possible to expand the tax base (i.e., reserve money) by raising reserve requirements. I assume that they dismissed this policy action because of its distortionary effects on the banking sector (encouraging as it would the growth of near-money substitutes free of the tax). They do ask how costly it would be for a country to postpone fiscal adjustment after lowering inflation, and they reach the surprising conclusion that postponement for as long as ten years would raise the required tax burden only marginally.

The authors discuss at length why Europeans place so much emphasis on exchange rate stability. The dependence of EMS countries on trade with one another is an important part of the story. In the case of France, for example, over 40 percent of French trade is with other EMS countries. Fixed rates within the EMS help to stabilize the relative prices of goods originating in other EMS countries, and thus may help to stabilize *effective* exchange rates.

Trade patterns, however, are only one part of the story. It's equally important to know the predominant source of the economic disturbances affecting a country. Contrast the French trade pattern with the pattern of Canada where over 80 percent of Canadian trade is with the United States. Canada thus is more than twice as dependent on trade with its closest trading partner as is France with all of its EMS trading partners. Yet Canada has allowed its exchange rate vis-à-vis the U.S. dollar to vary quite substantially over time. The reason may be that Canada wants to insulate itself from disturbances originating in its main trading partner. In the case of the EMS, it's natural to ask why there isn't a similar concern about disturbances originating in one or more EMS countries affecting the rest of the EMS.

One of the main motivations for setting up the EMS in 1979 was to create a "zone of monetary stability" in Europe, shielding European countries from outside, not inside, disturbances. Many in Europe believed at the time that the main source of disturbances was the United States economy and dollar financial markets. (Marston 1985 analyzes the effects of such disturbances on EMS countries.) Experience with a widely fluctuating dollar in the 1980s could only have reinforced this belief. So it's not just the trade pattern itself, but the desire to insulate Europe from disturbances originating from the outside, which motivates the system.

But a system well-suited for the 1970s and 1980s may be less desirable in later years if the source of disturbances shifts. If disturbances originating in Europe assume increased importance (or if disturbances involving the dollar diminish in importance), the EMS may not seem so desirable, since fixing bilateral rates inhibits adjustment to European disturbances. In the United States or most other national economies, adjustment to disturbances between regions within the country can occur because there is sufficient internal factor mobility. A decline in demand for products from the rust-belt of the United States, for example, induces movement of labor to the sun-belt. Labor mobility in Europe, except among unskilled guest workers, is much less evident than in the United States. Even the coming of 1992 will not necessarily make French workers want to move to Frankfurt or British workers to Marseilles.

Perhaps this means that Europe needs to maintain some flexibility in its fixed exchange rate system to facilitate required changes in real exchange rates between European currencies. If this is true, then the movement to a common central bank may need to be reconsidered. A common central bank would solve the problem of credibility for an anti-inflation policy, since there would presumably be no way for individual governments to depart from the EMS norm. But the loss of the option to change parities may be undesirable in a Europe without other means of internal adjustment.

There are other issues raised by this paper which I have not had a chance to address. As in the case of their previous papers on the EMS, Giavazzi and Giovannini have provided numerous insights about how the EMS works and why it is so successful to date.

References

Barro, R., and D. Gordon. 1983. Rules, discretion, and reputation in a model of monetary policy. *Journal of Monetary Economics* (July): 101–21.

Collins, S. 1988. Inflation and the European Monetary System. In F. Giavazzi, S. Micossi, and M. Miller, eds., *The European Monetary System,* 112–36. Cambridge, England: Cambridge University Press.

Marston, R. 1985. Financial disturbances and the effects of an exchange rate union. In J. Bhandari, ed., *Exchange-rate management under uncertainty,* 272–91. Cambridge, MA: MIT Press.

Ungerer, H., O. Evans, T. Mayer, and P. Young. 1986. *The European Monetary System: Recent developments,* IMF Occasional Papers no. 48 (December).

Comment   Wolfgang Rieke

Giavazzi and Giovannini start with the question: "Why did Europeans set up the EMS?" (see sec. 6.2) We know the answers. President Giscard d'Estaing and Chancellor Schmidt felt strongly that Europe should be able to speak with a stronger voice and have an effective answer to the policy of benign neglect of the dollar pursued by the United States at the time. This argument may have weighed more heavily with Schmidt than with Giscard, given the persistent strength of the deutsche mark, but it met with the French desire for progress on the monetary integration front in Europe, a desire which had been frustrated earlier in the 1970s (Werner Plan). Both Giscard and Schmidt agreed that the European Economic Community was in dire need of a new initiative, and monetary integration appeared to offer the opportunity for it. They adhered to the fixed but adjustable rate philosophy which the Committee of Twenty (G-20) had agreed should be the basis of any reformed world monetary system when the committee wound up its work in 1974. Both Giscard and Schmidt were finance ministers of their countries at the time and as such involved in the reform exercise.

The economic arguments listed by the authors in their paper are well taken, historically and otherwise. The greater openness argument probably should come first, together with the fact that a large share of cross-border trade of all European countries is with each other, and it is in large part trade in goods and services with a high added value that is sensitive to exchange rate fluctuations. The producers of such tradable goods and services can be severely affected by exchange rate fluctuations, and they will not always be able to hedge these risks at reasonable costs. In their relations with third countries, trade in commodities weighs more heavily. As is well known, commodities are affected by price fluctuations of considerable magnitude that are largely unrelated to cost

Wolfgang Rieke is Head of the International Department of the Deutsche Bundesbank, Frankfurt, Federal Republic of Germany.

factors. Exchange rate variations are thus only one component of uncertainty with which trade in commodities has to cope.

The proponents of the EMS were confident that exchange rates could in fact be stabilized between countries that shared important objectives and were willing to pursue appropriate policies. Exchange rate stabilization vis-à-vis the most important international currency, the dollar, looked far less feasible. On the U.S. side, such attempts would indeed have been in conflict with the monetarist doctrine adopted by the Reagan administration. But even assuming that the United States, Japan, and Europe shared important objectives and pursued the appropriate policies, the huge potential for international capital flows would have made stabilization of dollar rates vis-à-vis major other currencies in the international money game difficult or impossible.

As noted by the authors the EEC's agricultural policy was an important factor in the actual operation of the EMS. For a time the EMS functioned on the hypothesis that decisions on exchange rates should not be affected by their possible implications for agricultural policy if they were considered necessary for macroeconomic reasons by all partners in the EMS. After all, agriculture accounts only for a small share of GNP. But this proved an illusion. The insistence on exchange rate fixity in the EMS today is in no small measure due to this factor.

In recent years, the credibility aspect has gained in importance insofar as the commitment to a fixed exchange rate (vis-à-vis the deutsche mark) has become a basic element of the anti-inflation policy of EMS countries. (The same is true of certain non-EMS participants, e.g., Austria, but also the United Kingdom, a participant in the EMS, but not in the ERM.) France feels strongly that resort to exchange rate adjustment to correct trade and payments imbalances would call into question the government's determination to deal effectively with the domestic causes of inflation and external competitiveness. As far as the current situation is concerned, it is also felt that a realignment could not be justified with reference to price and cost differentials which had been the agreed criterion for earlier exchange rate realignments. An urgent need is constantly seen for faster German economic growth to deal with intra-EMS imbalances. The recent acceleration of economic growth in the Federal Republic of Germany is thus most welcome, though it appears to owe as much to stronger demand growth outside Germany (and could well result in even larger payments imbalances) as to stronger domestic demand growth.

These considerations give rise to questions as to how the EMS is functioning and how it should function in the view of some of its partners. Giavazzi and Giovannini speak of the EMS as "an (imperfect) Greater Deutsche Mark Area." On the one hand, it is generally recognized that the key currency role of the deutsche mark and the monetary policy of the Bundesbank have provided the EMS with a reliable anchor of stability. The tricky $n - 1$ problem has thus been solved. But on the other hand, the German policy mix is said to impose a deflationary bias on the system. The argument appears to be contradictory. The stability orientation provided by the Federal Republic of Germany via the deutsche mark appears to be acceptable to the extent that it is necessary for the achievement of price stability within the whole EMS, allowing—at least for a time—other partners to rely on Germany to produce a "stability surplus" for export to them rather than rely on their own homemade stability. It is unacceptable to the extent that it impedes faster growth and external adjustment within the EEC and in relation to third countries.

The critics appear to be more confident than are the German authorities of Germany's ability to generate domestic demand growth that would be strong enough to reduce the current surplus without also giving free reign to stronger inflationary pressures. (I believe the same point is made by Paul Krugman in ch. 4 of this volume.) They also seem to be confident that Germany's partners could bring about the expenditure shifts needed to accommodate the external adjustment without adverse inflationary consequences, thus enabling them to rely more on homemade price stability. To the extent that exchange rates had already moved out of line, these countries would in fact have to be prepared to push their inflation rate below the German rate for awhile if exchange rate adjustment is to be avoided. One may well have doubts whether this is likely to occur.

The "Greater Deutsche Mark Area" argument does point to an asymmetry of rights and obligations. It is true that the Bundesbank enjoys full independence in its special area of responsibility and competence within Germany, partly for historical reasons. It also enjoys relative policy autonomy within the EMS, based on its economic weight and the accepted (rather than imposed) key currency role of the deutsche mark in that system. German interest rates are less affected than those of other countries by intra-EMS shocks. The monetary aggregates are relatively unaffected by intervention that is undertaken within the margins, the technique preferred by our partners in recent years. But this ignores that current account surpluses and capital inflows will affect the aggregates directly, forcing the Bundesbank to satisfy the additional liquidity needs of the banking system generated thereby. It can, of course, try to undo these effects by action on its interest rates, but this will take time to have its impact on the aggregates. And such action may well attract additional capital inflows and add to the surplus on current account, if the exchange rate is left unchanged.

The argument also ignores that the Bundesbank is exposed to outside shocks and that the deutsche mark is more exposed to currency competition are other currencies, given its preferred status as an international currency. This reduces its policy autonomy, sometimes in ways that are felt to cause difficulties within the EMS, though at times it will ease such difficulties and help maintain cohesion of exchange rates in the system. The bottom line is that the Bundesbank's policy autonomy is substantially circumscribed in today's integrated world economy and financial market environment.

If policy autonomy of the Bundesbank is not complete to begin with, why not share it more evenly with other partners so that common objectives can be formulated and pursued, with perhaps the same or greater beneficial effects as at present. Would common decision-making carry the same credibility? Given the still existing differences on major objectives, on available policy trade-offs and on instrument effectiveness, there seem to be reasons for caution. In Germany, common decision-making would cause considerable unease at this stage. It will only be overcome once the principle is firmly laid down that monetary stability is the sole or prime objective and responsibility of monetary policy, and that the central bank should enjoy a high degree of independence from the political authorities. At present, reference to the strong position of the Federal Republic of Germany and of the Bundesbank helps to calm domestic concerns that the EMS may be used as an instrument to undermine the stability of the deutsche mark.

The discussion about the inflation/growth trade-off leads the authors to ask: "What incentives does the Federal Republic of Germany have to belong to such a system?" My own inclination has been to look at this question in terms of costs and benefits. If Germany's closest trading partners (who are also its partners in a common effort that extends beyond the monetary and economic area) make greater efforts to achieve overall economic balance and monetary stability, it will be to Germany's benefit as well. What are these benefits? They are partly based on the belief that price stability will help to achieve sustained economic growth. Resource allocation will be positively affected if economic agents see less reason to allow for (uncertain) inflation in their decision-making. This view is supported by the observation that countries with high inflation do not generally have higher growth and less unemployment, though the causalities may be difficult to establish. Also, less homemade inflation in Germany's partner countries will reduce the potential for imported inflation and should reduce the need for exchange rate adjustment in its turn. (As argued earlier, exchange rate adjustment confronts the authorities with problems, e.g., in the area of agriculture.)

The reality is, of course, that some partners have relied on an overvalued currency to achieve greater price stability at home for longer than may be desirable on both sides. Germany can be expected to produce a "stability surplus" for export to others only so long as monetary stability in Germany itself is not put at risk. And there is a constant danger that the growing external imbalances which go with the efforts to avoid inflation differentials from growing will themselves become a source of tension.

The desire to protect German industry from the volatility of the dollar was a factor in setting up the EMS. Indeed, during the 1980s a major part of total German foreign trade was protected from the effects of massive dollar misalignment, though this did not eliminate all the negative effects, as the reaction of the economy to the subsequent dollar correction demonstrated. But if, as is presently the case, the exchange rate is virtually excluded as an adjustment instrument, and partner countries at the same time fail to apply effective domestic policies to deal with the causes of growing internal and external imbalances, then the price paid by the surplus country may become too high eventually.

To conclude, I agree with the authors that the EMS could not simply be copied at the global level for the very reasons cited by them. But this is not a final verdict against a future system based on world-scale fixed but adjustable rates, even though today and for the foreseeable future this kind of system seems unrealistic. Other options seem unattractive enough on various grounds to suggest that the fixed rate option cannot be discarded once and for all.

7   The Case for International Coordination of Financial Policy

David Folkerts-Landau

7.1 Introduction

The discussion of international policy coordination has so far largely been confined to issues relating to the coordination of monetary and fiscal policy. In this paper I will consider, in the light of recent developments in financial markets, the case for the international coordination of financial policy, that is, the coordination of regulatory and supervisory policies governing domestic and international financial transactions, markets, and institutions. It is generally recognized that the willingness of modern central banks to avoid liquidity crises in financial markets through the monetizing of eligible bank assets has to go hand in hand with appropriate bank supervisory and regulatory policies. Such policies are necessary to reduce the moral hazard facing banks with knowledge of the central bank intervention policy, that is to reduce the ability of banks to assume greater risk in anticipation of central bank assistance in the event depositors are unwilling to continue financing its loan portfolio. Since the market value of a failing bank's assets may not fully cover the amount of central bank assistance required to avoid a systemic liquidity crises, it is possible that, in the absence of an appropriate supervisory and regulatory policy, the public sector will assume private sector credit risk.

Recent developments in financial markets have greatly improved the ability of financial firms to transform the type and shift the location of financial transactions and balance sheets toward the less regulated activity and juris-

David Folkerts-Landau is the Deputy Division Chief of the Monetary Operations Division in the Central Banking Department of the International Monetary Fund.

The author has greatly benefited from comments by the discussant, Francesco Papadia, and also from suggestions by Morris Goldstein, Donald J. Mathieson, Michael Mussa, and Wolfgang Rieke. The views expressed are those of the author and do not necessarily represent those of the International Monetary Fund.

dictions, that is, to arbitrage regulatory differences. The redesign of financial transactions and redistribution of financial activity has generally induced financial authorities to liberalize regulatory constraints in the more stringently regulated activities and jurisdictions in order to ensure that financial activity will remain within their jurisdiction. We argue that such a noncooperative or competitive approach to financial policy will result in an international supervisory and regulatory structure that is on average insufficiently stringent. Under such a policy, banks can, therefore, be expected to take on a greater than optimal amount of credit and position risks, some of which will be borne by the public sector.[1] This is not to say that a competitive approach to the making of regulatory policies may not initially produce efficiency gains when starting from a financial system encumbered with historical restrictions on the domestic activities and on cross-border transactions. However, a persistent noncooperative approach to financial policy in the face of adaptive financial markets will ultimately result in an inefficiently large amount of private credit risk being shifted to the public sector through the mechanism of central bank liquidity assistance.

While the beneficial effects on macroeconomic performance of a stable financial structure with an efficient allocation of credit risk between the private and public sector are not always readily apparent and certainly are difficult to quantify, it is nevertheless widely believed that these effects are strong and immediate, as suggested in the following statement by Alan Greenspan, Chairman of the U.S. Federal Reserve Board:

> [there are] fundamental interdependencies between the macroeconomy and the financial markets that any policy maker—but especially one in the central bank—must recognize. For all the new techniques for shifting risk around the financial system, the ultimate safety and stability of that system depends on the stability of the economy on which it is based; and that economy cannot itself behave in a stable and predictable fashion if the markets in which claims on saving and capital are allocated are subject to waves of concern about key participants.[2]

In section 7.2 I review how the restructuring of financial markets has increased the ability of financial firms to arbitrage financial policies. A discussion of the optimality of the cooperative approach to financial policy follows in section 7.3, and I offer some conclusions in section 7.4.

7.2   The Dynamics of Financial Market Restructuring and the Ability to Arbitrage Financial Policy

7.2.1   Financial Sector Innovation and Regulatory Arbitrage

During the past fifteen years domestic and international financial activity denominated in the major currencies has undergone an unprecedented transformation which, although differing in detail, has been similar in its broad features in the major countries. Important aspects of these developments have been the innovation in financial instruments and techniques; the blurring of the segmentation of markets, types of firms, and instruments; the growth of off-balance sheet activity by banking firms; disintermediation from domestic banking systems into direct debt and offshore markets; globalization of the distribution of financial products and of some financial markets, together with an increased foreign presence in domestic markets; and a rapid growth in the volume of financial transactions supporting a given volume of the real transactions.[3] The driving force behind the innovations and the restructuring of private sector financial activity has been twofold: (1) the competitive response of financial intermediaries to greater opportunities for arbitraging regulatory and fiscal differences across domestic and international jurisdictions; and (2) the increased ability to exploit liquidity guarantees and implicit credit risk guarantees provided by financial authorities.[4] The greater opportunities to arbitrage existing differences in financial policies were created by the macroeconomic imbalances since the mid-1970s and by advances in communications and transactions technology. In particular, historically high inflation rates and correspondingly high nominal interest rates highlighted regulatory and fiscal cost differences between unevenly regulated financial activities, instruments, and jurisdictions. A reduction in the cost of data transfer and telecommunications reduced the cost of separating financial transactions from the underlying real transactions, thus fostering movement to less regulated jurisdictions. Some relaxation in capital controls increased the feasibility of moving financial transactions and balance sheets outside the home jurisdiction. The increased ability to exploit public sector guarantees occurred with financial innovations that facilitated growth in those off-balance sheet activities of banking firms that were designed to avoid capital requirements and achieve a higher risk-return point.

In the early 1970s, the regulatory and fiscal structures of the financial markets in the major industrialized countries were quite diverse in: (1) restrictions on yields on financial instruments; (2) regulations defining the permissible set of activities and instruments for financial intermediaries; and (3) fiscal and disclosure rules. For example, in the mid-1970s, interest rate ceilings were important constraints in France, Japan, and the United States, but were not present in the Federal Republic of Germany nor in the United Kingdom. Furthermore, banking firms were and still are prohibited from most securities market activities in the United States by the Glass-Steagall statute and in Japan by Article 65 of the Securities and Exchange Law, while German and Swiss universal banks are free from such restrictions. Some countries had antigambling statutes against financial futures.[5] Differences in the extent to which banking and commerce are integrated were also pronounced (see tables 7.1 and 7.2) across the major economies, as was the extent of integration of financial services and banking.

Table 7.1   Main Features of the Evolution of Financial Markets

	Switzerland 75	Switzerland 87	U.S. 75	U.S. 87	France 75	France 87	Germany 75	Germany 87	U.K. 75	U.K. 87	Canada 75	Canada 87	Italy 75	Italy 87
Type of financial market														
Banking system[a]	U	U	NU	NU	U	U	U	U	NU	U	NU	NU	NU	NU
Securitization of credit flows[b]	—	—	—	—	24.8	42.5	—	—	29.4	34.8	39.3	49.4	23.3	44.4
Secondary markets[c]	W	W	A	A	N	W	W	W	A	A	A	A	N	W
Domestic regulation														
Controls on interest rates[d]	N	N	Y	N	Y	M	N	N	N	N	N	N	Y	N
Controls on credit														
Nonselective[d]	N	N	M	N	Y	N	M	N	Y	N	N	N	Y	N
Selective	N	N	M	N	Y	M	M	M	N	N	N	N	Y	N
Controls on intermediaries' portfolios														
Other than precautionary[d]	N	N	N	N	Y	N	N	N	N	N	M	M	Y	N
External regulation														
Controls on portfolio investment[d]	N	N	N	N	Y	M	N	N	Y	N	N	N	Y	N
Controls on capital inflows[d]	Y	N	N	N	Y	Y	Y	Y	N	N	W	W	N	N
Access for foreign financial institutions[e]	E	E	E	E	E	E	E	E	E	E	N	E	R	E

Source: OECD Secretariat.

Note: 75 refers to 1975, the first year of the period studied; and 87 refers to 1987, the most recent year for which information is available.

[a]U = universal banking system, NU = nonuniversal banking system.

[b]Issues of securities as percent of total domestic credit flows.

[c]N = nonexistent; W = exist, but thin; and A = active.

[d]N = nonexistent; M = minor; and Y = important.

[e]N = not allowed or severely restricted; R = allowed with important restrictions (on branching, ownership, or other); E = allowed, subject to reciprocity and/or precautionary requirements.

Table 7.2   Predominant Form of Commerce-Banking and Financial Service Integration in the G-10 Countries

	Commercial Ownership of Banks	Bank Ownership of Commerce	Common Commerce Bank Holding Co.[a]	Generally Limited Integration Commerce-Banking[b]	Expanded Bank Powers[c]	Nonbank Subsidiary of Bank[d]	Financial Services-Bank Common Holding Company[e]	Degree of Integration of Banking and Securities Services[f]
Universal systems								
France			X		X			High
Germany		X			X			High
Italy				X	X			High
Netherlands				X	X			High
Switzerland				X	X			High
Blended systems								
Belgium			X	X		X		High
Canada				X		X		High[g]
Japan				X		X		Low
Sweden				X		X		High[g]
United Kingdom				X		X		High[g]
United States				X			X	Low

Source: Federal Reserve Bank of New York.

[a]The typical form of integration is for a single holding company to have significant ownership interests in both banks and commerce.

[b]In general, there are no controlling ownership affiliations between individual banks and commercial firms.

[c]Single "universal" banks directly provide all banking and securities services in-house.

[d]The typical form of integration is for banks to have wholly owned nonbank financial subsidiaries.

[e]A single holding company typically has significant ownership interests in both banks and nonbank financial firms.

[f]Either through expanded in-house powers or through institutional affiliations.

[g]Financial structure liberalization recently has increased the integration of banking and securities services.

In an environment of macroeconomic stability, the presence of capital and exchange controls, communication costs, as well as differences in legal and market conventions had made it costly to arbitrage these regulatory and fiscal differences by, for example, shifting financial activities to the unregulated Euromarkets. It was not until the late 1970s that macroeconomic disturbances, technological advances, and the removal of some capital controls combined to stimulate financial firms to exploit these differences. Nominal interest rates reached levels during the early 1980s that had not been experienced in most industrial countries since the post–World War II period and thereby precipitated a disintermediation from domestic banking systems, with deposit liabilities subject to interest rate ceilings, to the domestic direct debt markets, and to the Euromarkets. Bank liabilities were replaced with mutual funds, while bank assets were replaced with short-term securitized corporate claims, such as domestic commercial paper and Euro–commercial paper. Disintermediation initially was most important in the U.S. markets during the late 1970s, but took hold in nondollar markets by the mid-1980s. An important element in the disintermediation from banks to direct security markets has been the securitization of claims, and the introduction of asset-backed securities and noninvestment grade securities, which have significantly widened the credit risk spectrum (table 7.3). The securitization of claims has also spread to international lending, where syndicated loans have increasingly been displaced by issues of international bonds, note issuance facilities, and Euro–commercial paper.

The disintermediation from the banking sectors led to the growth of off-balance sheet bank transactions, most notably guarantees and short-term liquidity commitments, and fee-based activity rather than portfolio investment. An important source of innovation has been the possibility of off-balance-sheet financial activity which avoids capital charges. Loan guarantees, stand-bys, and letters of credit have become a significant source of revenue for banking organizations.[6] Perhaps the most outstanding example of a synthetic financial off-balance instrument is the currency and interest swap in which counterparties exchange obligations, for example, fix for floating interest

Table 7.3   **Issues of Securities in Domestic Credit Flows (as a percentage of market credit flows)**

	1970–72	1973–75	1976–78	1979–81	1983–85
United States	40.07	36.10	36.93	32.67	49.57
Japan	22.83	26.37	37.90	39.00	38.27
Germany	20.97	23.40	27.37	23.77	36.17
France	24.33	22.00	21.33	25.30	41.17
Italy	29.87	26.87	34.60	17.53	50.53
United Kingdom	17.43	13.63	27.67	28.80	34.80
Canada	45.07	30.03	34.87	36.83	51.97

Source: OECD, *Financial Statistics, Part 2* (Paris: 1987).

payments or dollar for sterling payments (table 7.4). Banks have been counterparties in the vast majority of swaps, the volume of which has grown from near zero in 1980 to $1 billion in 1988. Similarly, the writing of such contingent contracts as interest rate caps has provided banks with a source of revenue that did not until recently require capital commitment.[7] The side-stepping of the traditional balance sheet activities tended to preserve capital and lower regulatory compliance cost. It had the effect, however, of removing financial activity from the purview of bank regulators into less regulated activities and jurisdictions.

The sharp expansion of cross-border financial flows and the increased variability of nominal exchange rates that had accompanied the abandonment of the Bretton Woods system of fixed exchange rates led the way toward a rapid expansion of cross-border financial transactions. The level of activity in international financial markets was further stimulated by sectoral imbalances associated with increases in energy and commodity prices and the emergence of large fiscal imbalances in most industrialized countries which resulted in sharp increases in stocks of government bonds outstanding. For example, the recycling of the current account surpluses of the oil-exporting countries associated with the oil price increases of 1973 and 1979 was accomplished primarily by banking intermediaries.[8] During this period, most of the reserves accumulated by oil-exporting countries were initially held as deposits in banks in offshore financial markets and in the major industrialized countries, and lending from banks and other private creditors financed nearly half of the deficits of the nonoil developing countries.

The ability of financial institutions to exploit the opportunities presented by these macroeconomic conditions was influenced profoundly by innovations in telecommunications and data processing.[9] New developments in such areas as computer technology, computer software, and telecommunications permitted more rapid processing and transmission of information, completion of trans-actions, and less costly confirmation of payments. Such changes enlarged the set of markets in which financial institutions could provide intermediary services.

Table 7.4   Outstanding Swap Transactions by Currencies, December 31, 1987

Currency	Interest Rate Swaps		Currency Swaps	
	Millions of U.S. $	%	Millions of U.S. $	%
U.S. dollar	703,154	79.05	98,015	44.72
Japanese yen	59,988	6.74	37,025	16.89
Pound sterling	40,142	4.51	6,327	2.89
Deutsche mark	39,583	4.45	12,281	5.60
Other	46,662	5.25	65,542	29.90
Total	889,529	100.00	219,190	100.00

Source: International Swap Dealers Association, New York.

The gradual removal of capital controls in the major economies further increased the scope for cross-border regulatory and fiscal arbitrage. An early but significant step toward the liberalization of capital flows came with the removal of controls on capital outflows from the United States in 1974. The United Kingdom liberalized sterling cross-border transactions in 1979 by removing exchange controls to prevent capital outflows; their removal, along with the lifting of lending restrictions on banks (the so-called corset), opened the sterling banking and securities markets to foreign borrowers. The German authorities also have significantly reduced restrictions on capital inflows in the 1980s. Since the early 1980s, Japanese authorities have undertaken an extensive liberalization of cross-border financial activities. The number of foreign institutions allowed to borrow from Japanese banks, or to issue in the Japanese securities markets, has gradually been expanded. In addition, the Euroyen bond market was opened to foreign corporations in 1984. In the mid-1980s, the French authorities undertook an extensive liberalization of cross-border financial flows and reopened the Euro–French franc bond market. In this regard the integration of EEC financial markets through the removal of capital controls and the liberalization of restrictions on financial activities is one of the more significant developments in the recent history of world financial markets.

The lessening of capital controls, the growth of international trade and expansion of nonfinancial business across borders, and the disequilibria in international payments all acted as stimuli for financial institutions to expand into foreign markets. The number of foreign banking firms in the major industrial countries increased sharply and accounted for a considerably greater share of total bank assets (table 7.5). The introduction of foreign securities firms into domestic markets also proceeded at a rapid pace. Several stock exchanges (in Japan and the United Kingdom, for example) expanded their membership in 1986 and 1987 to include foreign firms. Moreover, the standardization of market practices such as bond ratings, settlement procedures, and codes of conduct have facilitated cross-border transactions.

While the main incentives to book bank transactions offshore were provided initially by domestic interest rate controls and reserve requirements, the growth of the Eurodollar bond market, on the other hand, has largely been due to the regulatory requirements of the U.S. Securities Act of 1933 and until recently the 30 percent withholding tax on interest payments made on U.S. domestic bonds. In excess of one third of all U.S. dollar bond issues are now underwritten in the Eurodollar market. Similarly, a cumbersome regulatory environment in the Japanese yen bond market and a withholding tax on domestic bonds stimulated the Euro-yen bond market. On the other hand, German, Swiss, and Dutch authorities insist that bonds denominated in these currencies be syndicated and underwritten, that is, anchored, domestically. However, in order to avoid the German turnover tax, nearly 60 percent of all secondary market turnover in German government bonds occurs in London together with about 50 percent of the turnover of corporate foreign deutsche

Table 7.5   **International Bank Assets by Nationality of Bank (in billions of dollars)**

Parent Country of Bank	December 1984		December 1986		December 1988	
	Amount	Share of total assets	Amount	Share of total assets	Amount	Share of total assets
France	200.7	8.9	276.1	8.1	384.1	8.4
Germany	143.2	6.4	270.0	7.9	353.8	7.7
Italy	90.6	4.0	145.1	4.3	201.2	4.4
Japan	517.9	23.0	1,117.7	32.8	1,756.4	38.2
Switzerland	82.9	3.7	152.0	4.5	238.6	5.2
U.K.	168.9	7.5	211.7	6.2	238.7	5.2
U.S	594.5	26.4	598.3	17.6	675.3	14.6
Other	450.7	20.1	635.4	18.6	749.8	16.3
Total	2,249.4	100.0	3,406.3	100.0	4,597.8	100.0

Source: Terrell, H., R. Dohner, and B. Lowrey, The U.S. and U.K. Activities of Japanese Banks: 1980–1988. Board of Governors of the Federal Reserve System, International Finance Discussion Papers, no. 361 (September 1989).

Note: Bank assets include claims of banking offices on nonlocal customers in foreign and domestic currencies and claims on local residents in foreign currencies.

mark bonds. Similarly, about 60 percent of the turnover in equity-related Swiss-franc bond issues takes place in London so as to avoid the turnover tax. A significant fraction of trading in equities of domestic European companies also takes place in London so as to avoid local turnover taxes, low liquidity, and inexperience of local traders. About 25 percent of total turnover in German equities takes place in London. Restrictions on short sales and the absence of domestic instruments also favor London. About one-third of total turnover in French equities takes place in London because of greater liquidity and lower transaction costs resulting from a fixed commission schedule for domestic trades. Another important incentive to issue and trade offshore is that the international clearing systems of Cedel and Euro-clear are faster and cheaper in settling trades than are many domestic clearing systems.

The prohibition on the underwriting and distribution of most securities issues by U.S. and Japanese banks has also acted as a strong incentive for banks to shift bond underwriting to London. Some countries, most notably the Federal Republic of Germany and Japan, had until recently local legal restriction on the use of financial futures. This has led to the use of interest rate futures contracts on foreign government securities on the London International Financial Futures Exchange and elsewhere.

The increasing ease of cross-border transactions, the growing volume of outstanding securities, and an increased foreign presence in domestic markets all have, contributed to the making of a global market in selected government securities. For these issues, the trading houses pass their bond book from London to New York to Tokyo to ensure continuous trading.

While money center or clearing banks, as suppliers of liquidity or lenders of last resort to nonbanks, are the main pillars supporting the domestic and international financial systems, it is the clearing and settling of payments among banks that transmits disturbances from one bank to another thus turning local financial disturbances into a systemic financial problem. These considerations have led financial authorities in the major countries, and particularly in the United States, to undertake an extensive program to strengthen payments systems. Efforts to reduce systemic risk through a reform of the wholesale payments systems are underway, most notably in the dollar system. These reforms of payments systems are aimed at preventing local operational, liquidity, and credit disturbances from disrupting the wholesale payments system. The reforms have, however, raised the regulatory cost of clearing payments through the traditional domestic clearance systems and led to the growth of offshore clearance and settlement systems.[10] Since offshore dollar arrangements ultimately must settle in the United States, either through Chips or Fedwire, significant disruptions in the offshore clearance and settlements system for foreign exchange and securities due to the failure of a participating institution, could well result in systemic liquidity problems in the United States and abroad. Offshore clearing of U.S. dollar payments for subsequent net settlement in the United States is thought to obscure and possibly increase the level of systemic risk in the U.S. large dollar payments system and in the international settlements process. Finally, offshore multilateral netting arrangements complicate the allocation of supervisory responsibilities. Formalized netting arrangements and offshore payments systems, that is, groupings of individual banks with interrelated credit and liquidity risks have shifted risks among participants, and it is unclear at what level a supervisor should examine credit, liquidity, and operational risks. Furthermore, while host country authorities of an offshore system will have an interest in supervising credit, liquidity, and operational risks, the home country of the multinational participants in the offshore system will also wish to supervise the offshore system to the extent that it affects the solvency and liquidity of home institutions. In addition the central bank responsible for the currency that is being cleared in the offshore system will have some supervisory interest in the system.

A number of broader policy issues have been raised by the proposals for different netting arrangements. In particular, it can be argued that organized netting systems are in effect monetary institutions or a monetary system. A shift away from the use of the central payments system toward the specialized netting system might amount to the decentralization of the major monetary mechanisms and thus undermine the integrity of key monetary aggregates. In essence, a netting group can arrive at the same financial position through netting without the large number of payment instructions and accompanying money flows to settle those instructions that would otherwise had been required. Thus netting could come to be a very close substitute for the function of money as a medium of exchange.

The development of multilateral clearing houses could also significantly alter the structure of interbank credit relationships. For example, several large over-the-counter markets such as the interbank foreign-exchange markets and the interbank swap market could move to organized exchanges, as is already the case with Eurodollar futures markets. In each case, net claims on the clearing organization would replace gross interbank credit exposure in the deposit markets. Under the 1987 Agreement on capital standards, bank claims on organized financial exchanges subject to daily margining have a zero-risk weight.

At a more fundamental level, one of the most important elements in the process of innovations has been the institutionalization of an "arbitrage mentality." For example, most of the prominent banking and investment banking firms have established arbitrage products departments with expensive human capital and equipment for the very purpose of undertaking regulatory, fiscal, and market arbitrage. Thus, the arbitraging of regulatory and fiscal structures has come to be viewed as a profit center.

7.2.2   The Financial Policy Response

The most important determinant of the financial policy response to financial innovations that attempt to arbitrage existing policies has been the desire by financial policy authorities to avoid major shifts of financial activity from one jurisdiction or market segment to another, either inside a country or to a foreign jurisdiction or unregulated market. Regulatory authorities have thus prevented a redistribution or loss of regulatory or fiscal control, by liberalizing regulatory or fiscal constraints in the high-cost jurisdictions, that is, by leveling the playing field around a lower common denominator. This approach is thus one of competition for "regulatory market share" by the regulators. In particular, the disintermediation from banking markets to securities markets or the shifting of financial transactions from onshore to offshore locations provided incentives for the deregulation of the adversely affected banking sector and some other domestic transactions.[11] This desire to avoid a sharp decline in the market share of the banking sector, for example, led to the gradual removal of interest rate restrictions on bank liabilities in the United States and Japan. It is likely that the growth of competition from the securities industry for traditional banking business will lead to the dismantling of some of the more onerous provisions of the Glass-Steagall Statute in the United States or Article 65 in Japan. The decline of U.S. banks in importance at the international league table is also likely to bring further pressure on banking regulators to amend financial policy toward banking.[12]

The response of regulatory agencies to structural changes in financial markets was strongly influenced by the extent to which the regulatory structure and its legislative oversight have been concentrated or specialized. The more specialized the regulatory structure, the more competition there has been among regulators, and the faster deregulation has taken place. In the United States, the regulatory structure was specialized not only by industries such as securities (Securities and Exchange Commission), banking (Federal Reserve, Federal Deposit Insurance Corporation, and the Comptroller of the Currency), and the futures markets (Commodity Futures Trading Commission), but also along geographic lines (federal and state) (tables 7.6 and 7.7). Moreover, the federal legislative oversight was lodged with several congressional committees. This dispersed system of regulatory agencies and legislative oversight at times created incentives for institutions to switch from one regulatory domain to another and for regulators to take actions to maintain the competitive positions of the institutions they regulated by reducing regulatory costs. In contrast, the financial systems of continental Europe tended to have one or two main supervisory agencies and a single legislative oversight. In such financial systems, financial firms had a more limited ability and incentive to shift their regulatory jurisdiction within the country by changing their product line, legal form, or domicile.

Loss of trading activity from the securities markets of some countries, for example, France, has led to a significant restructuring of the intermediary industry brought about largely by removing fixed commissions schedules in

Table 7.6   **Regulatory Segmentation and Functional Supervision for Banking and Securities Activities in the G-10 Countries**

	Regulatory Segmentation			Degree of Current or Planned Use of
G-10 Countries	One principal supervisor (one for both)	Two principal supervisors (one for each)	Multiple supervisors	Functional Supervision
Universal systems				
France	X[a]			Low[b]
Germany	X			Low[b]
Italy	X			Low[b]
Netherlands	X			Low[b]
Switzerland	X			Low[b]
Blended systems				
Belgium	X			Low
Canada		X		High
Japan		X		Limited
Sweden	X			Low
U.K.		X		High
U.S.			X	Limited

Source: Federal Reserve Bank of New York.

[a]The Banking Commission, the principal bank supervisor, shares responsibility for supervising and for securities activities of banks with the Stock Exchange Council.

[b]In the universal banking countries, banks are the principal providers of securities activities, so that the need to allocate supervisory responsibility has not spurred the development of functional supervision as it has in some blended system countries.

Table 7.7   **Consolidated Reporting and Capital Adequacy Requirements of Banks and Securities Firms in the G-10 Countries**

G-10 Countries	Extent of Consolidation of Banking Activities		Presence of Similar Consolidation Requirements for Banking and Securities Activities	
	Full	Partial	For most securities firms[a]	Only for bank-affiliated firms[b]
Universal systems				
France	X		X	
Germany		X	X	
Italy	X		X	
Netherlands	X		X	
Switzerland	X		X	
Blended systems				
Belgium	X			X
Canada	X			X
Japan		X		X
Sweden	X		X	
U.K.	X			X
U.S.	X			X

Source: New York Federal Reserve Bank.

[a]In universal banking system countries, banks are the principal providers of securities services.

[b]Securities activities conducted directly in-house by a bank (in countries in which banks are not the principal providers of securities services), by a bank's securities subsidiary, or by an affiliate of a bank holding company.

securities markets and by allowing foreign ownership. A desire to increase the efficiency of the financial system to remain competitive as an international financial center also motivated the fundamental restructuring of the U.K. financial system. The regulatory framework in Canada is also being restructured toward a universal banking system to reflect a growing penetration of financial intermediaries into each other's market. In order to bring Euromarket activities back into the domestic regulatory purview, some authorities have established international banking facilities, in particular Japan and the United States. Furthermore, some countries are changing their financial policy to induce offshore activity to return to domestic markets by liberalizing regulatory and fiscal restrictions. For example, the United States has recently permitted bonds to be converted from bearer (Eurobonds) to registered form and back after a ninety-day seasoning period, thus linking the Eurobond and domestic bond markets more closely. Similarly, German and Swiss financial authorities have tried to have turnover taxes abolished in order to induce trading activity to return the domestic market and to prevent further shifts of activity in primary and derivative instrument to London. Such efforts should receive new impetus from the introduction of a German public sector debt futures contract on the London International Financial Futures Exchange. The French stock exchange is also being restructured to avoid the further loss of French equity and based trading to London. Increased competition coming from de novo establishment of brokerage firms by foreign firms is undermining the long-standing monopoly of stock brokers over trading in France. A new stock market regulatory structure will safeguard investor protection and market transparency in Paris.

The effort of the EEC to establish, inter alia, a single financial market relies on some harmonization of national financial policies combined with home country control over financial policy. Efforts are underway to implement a sufficient degree of harmonization to obtain an EEC-wide agreement that will allow a financial institution to establish itself anywhere within the EEC and remain under the jurisdiction of its home country. Once the necessary harmonization of financial policy has been put in place, a bank or securities firm from, say, Spain would be allowed to conduct financial business in London while remaining entirely subject to Spanish financial policy. Since banks will be able to choose the jurisdiction under which they want to obtain a banking license, countries will have to adapt their regulatory structure to the least regulated jurisdiction if they wish to prevent a loss of financial activity.

It should be noted that while concern for longer-term shifts of financial transactions from one sector to another led to changes in policy by financial authorities, at times the initial policy response was motivated by attempts to avoid banking or liquidity crises. For example, with interest rate ceilings still in place in the 1970s, but with banks already relying on liability management, a credit tightening made it difficult for banks to refinance their liabilities, thus forcing them to sell off assets and borrow in Eurodollar markets. Such prospects tended to increase the pressure for removal of rate ceilings.

The above examples of the response of financial policy to financial innovations that are designed to arbitrage regulatory and fiscal cost in various markets were chosen to demonstrate that an important policy objective has been to prevent shifts of financial activities among sectors or to foreign locations. The main tool to accomplish this objective has been reform of the existing financial structure by reducing regulatory and fiscal costs to achieve a "level playing field."

Deregulation, in turn, has created incentives for further arbitrage and innovations. For example, the scope for regulatory arbitrage between domestic and offshore markets has also been extended by the gradual removal of capital controls and the increased financial flows associated with recent large-scale current account imbalances.[13] Furthermore, a greater presence of foreign financial intermediaries in domestic markets has served as a conduit for innovations and created competitive pressures.

7.2.3 The Role of Public Sector Guarantees

The changes in financial systems—innovations cum deregulation—discussed above have allowed financial firms, in particular banks, to shift activities to less regulated instruments or jurisdiction. Deregulation has greatly increased the access of intermediaries to financial instruments subject to greater market and liquidity risk. It has also increased competitiveness in financial systems through the removal of market segmentation, an increased reliance on market-determined interest rates, and an increased foreign presence. Such a new environment has produced a number of financial crises, which gradually have sharpened and extended the role of public sector guarantees of the financial system. If the ability by financial firms to assume greater risk had been met with a credible reduction of central bank support, then financial firms would have been disciplined by the markets away from assuming more risk. However, public sector liquidity guarantees and implicit solvency guarantees have increased in many instances over the past fifteen years. For example, the default of the Penn Central in 1970 on its commercial paper led to support measures by the Federal Reserve in the commercial paper market. In the spring of 1974, the 20th largest U.S. bank, the Franklin National, nearly failed, rendering it impossible for all but the ten largest banks to roll over their maturing CDs. This development was compounded by the use of short-term borrowings to finance real estate affiliates (REIT) of banks, which led to difficulties when an unexpected rise in interest rates occurred. Again intervention by the Federal Reserve avoided a major liquidity crisis. The failure of the Continental Illinois bank led to one of the most sweeping interventions by financial authorities, which, before it was over, established the policy that some banks are *too-large-to-fail*. Thus, such rescue operations generally defined a new more generous intervention policy of the financial authorities.

The extended role of financial authorities is being further defined by the LDC debt crisis, the U.S. savings and loan crisis, and the action during the October 1987 stock market adjustment. With regard to the LDC debt crisis, I have argued elsewhere[14] that the growth in bank lending to LDCs during the period 1973–82 was, in part, due to the de facto insurance of all bank deposit liabilities which makes it optimal for bank lenders to pursue high-risk lending opportunities. The U.S. savings and loan (S&L) crisis is an example of how deregulation of restrictions on the choice of assets, without curtailing the implicit or explicit cover of bank liabilities, is an inducement for banks near default to pursue a double-or-nothing strategy by undertaking a high-risk, high-return strategy. The contingent liability of the insurance fund has been estimated currently at $250 billion. The ongoing S&L rescue operation in the United States appears to be guided by two factors. The first is to protect and preserve the insurance fund and the second is to protect and preserve the existing banking structure.[15] Since the contingent claims far exceed the resources of the insurance fund, this policy effectively has committed the general resources of the federal government to secure deposit liabilities. The Continental Illinois rescue operation established that even depositors who are well outside of the statutory insurance limits, such as large foreign depositors, are de facto insured. In the case of Continental Illinois, only about $3.5 billion of deposits were insured. Evidence that a "too-big-to-fail" philosophy guides public sector support of banking can be found in testimony by FDIC Chairman William Seidman given in 1987 before the Senate Banking Committee

> Our experience to date in resolving several large failing bank cases suggests that the costs and dislocation of failing to fully protect certain bank depositors and creditors appear unacceptable. . . . Certainly the greatest threat to the sufficiency and viability of the deposit insurance fund is posed by the largest banks that might be considered "too-large-to-fail."

The result has been that the FDIC has given blanket assurances to the depositors and creditors in the three larger rescue cases it faced recently (Continental Illinois, First City, First Republic). An interpretation of the recent rescue actions by the FDIC as lender-of-last-resort activities is not appropriate since it consisted of lending on bad assets in support of an individual firm rather than in support of other banks that might be affected by the default, thus contradicting the Bagehot tenets. The possibilities of supporting the banks that are affected by a bank failure, instead of supporting the failed bank, by limiting deposit insurance to its statutory limit, was raised in Chairman Seidman's testimony in 1987 but was dismissed as impractical. Thus, it appears that the financial policy regarding failing banks is one of full support as long as the bank is too-big-to-fail. The extension of public sector support during the recent period of financial market restructuring seems to have been less obvious in countries other than the United States. But the perception that the financial authorities in these countries have similar views concerning too-big-to-fail firms is widespread.

7.3   The Argument for a Convergence and Cooperation of Financial Policy

In this section I first discuss the basic financial policy paradigm. Then I show that the dynamics of financial market restructuring as described above—arbitrage-driven innovations met with deregulation and increased guarantees by financial authorities—imply that a cooperative approach to the formulation and execution of financial policy dominates the competitive approach described above.

We take from the available evidence that unregulated banking systems without central bank liquidity support will be subject to periodic liquidity crises caused by a fundamental instability of the fractional reserve banking system. The ability to create currency through the open market purchase of securities or direct lending against eligible collateral has allowed central banks to guarantee the exchange rate between bank deposits and currency. In fact, during the period from 1793 to 1933 the United States experienced at least seventeen banking crises, while none have occurred since 1933, the beginning of active Federal Reserve intervention.[16] Thus the systemic financial instability in banking and payment systems was eliminated through the introduction of the central bank clearing house, where banks would hold their clearing balances, and which stood ready to convert bank deposit liabilities into currency, taking bank assets as collateral. However, in the absence of regulatory and supervisory restraints on the activities of banks, it is easy to see that, under a broad class of assumptions about the stochastic properties of the occurrence of liquidity crises, the central bank should expect to experience losses on the bank assets acquired in the course of providing liquidity. This is the case when the market value of the collateral is less than the amount of central bank assistance deemed necessary to prevent the failure of a bank from creating a systemic liquidity problem. While the monetary effects of the liquidity operation can be sterilized, the central bank's losses on acquired bank assets falls to the taxpayers. The public sector, therefore, assumes some of the credit risk of bank assets in return for an efficient banking system. Thus, as has occurred at various stages in the evolution of the payments and banking system, a certain amount of credit risk has been accepted, in this case by the central bank, as the cost of providing an efficient payment system. The taxpayer has assumed the credit risk inherent in bank assets that serve as collateral for central bank lending in return for an efficient payment system.

In order to reduce the credit risk incurred during liquidity operations, monetary authorities impose a regulatory and supervisory regime on financial systems (not only on banking systems) designed to reduce the expected losses on acquired bank assets to a desired level. Such a regulatory and supervisory regime typically involves the setting of capital requirements and position limits, as well as assesses the solvency of the bank through supervision and inspection of the bank's assets. However, the more restrictive the regulatory and supervisory regimes, the less efficient the financial system is in pricing savings and risk. Hence there exists a trade-off between the amount of credit risk assumed by the public sector and the efficiency of the financial system. Casual observation suggests that there exist significant differences in the willingness of the public sector in various countries to assume the credit risk of bank assets. For example, recent history suggests that the United States is willing to tolerate a significant amount of credit risk in the interest of a liberal financial system, whereas financial authorities in Germany appear willing to accept a less liberal financial system (e.g., the absence of well developed short-term money markets) in the interest of a lower credit risk for the public sector.

Two questions emerge from this approach:

(1) What is the nature of the trade-off between the amount of credit risk assumed by the public sector and the various regulatory and supervisory policies, given that the intervention policy of the central bank is fully anticipated? Do there exist stable equilibria?

(2) What is the efficient set of equilibria, that is, is it possible to identify supervisory and regulatory systems that have a least effect on the efficiency of the financial system for a desired level of credit risk?

In order to address these two questions, it is necessary to reexamine the role of the banking and payments system within modern financial systems. We argue that, in financial systems with well-developed capital and money markets, the main function of the large money center or clearing banks is the supply of liquidity to nonbanks, a function that is made possible through their access to central bank liquidity facilities. This specialization is shown to be a natural outgrowth of the banks' involvement in the payment system. We argue as well that wholesale payments systems transmit disturbances from one bank to another, thus turning local financial disturbances into systemic problems.

The interbank lending which arose out of the clearance of payments meant that large banks offered lines of credit to their correspondent banks and that such banks had to specialize in monitoring and managing interbank credit which frequently arose in the clearing process on short notice and without the safety of collateral. The need to develop the skill to evaluate continually the creditworthiness of correspondent banks led banks to specialize in a short-term liquidity-type of lending in support of providing efficient payment services to their depositors. Economies of scale then led clearing banks or money center banks to extend this expertise and become suppliers of liquidity to the nonbank sector. Such banks will, for example, extend lines of credit against a fee to issuers of short-term securitized debt instruments to ensure the holders that the security will be redeemed even in times of financial market disturbance. In addition, such banks will lend on short notice large amounts to finance securities dealers' inventory, provide funds for margin calls, and satisfy other needs for liquidity. The important point is that a group of large international banks, that is, money center or clearing banks, developed by specializing in the supply of liquidity necessary for the efficient operation of payments systems. This was clearly recognized, for example, by Corrigan (1986):

> The efficient working of a large modern economy clearly requires the presence of a stock of financial assets which are highly liquid and readily transferable, thereby facilitating the broad range of transactions needed to sustain the real and financial sectors of the economy. To be highly liquid, such assets must be available to the carrier at very short notice (a day or less) at par. To be readily transferable, ownership rights in such assets must be capable of being readily shifted to other economic agents, also at par and in a form in which they are acceptable by that other party.

The large clearing or money center banks have developed in response to this need for liquidity and have come to satisfy this need through the supply of liquid transaction balances either directly or indirectly through lines of credit. An examination of the balance sheets of large money center or clearing banks tends to support the view that the provision of liquidity is their major function. Other lending activity tends to be highly collateralized or actuarially priced. The narrow view of the role of money center or clearing banks allows stronger statements about the losses in efficiency due to regulatory restraints on banking activities. If money center or clearing banks possess no special advantage in term lending, then restrictions on their risk taking in this area are unlikely to reduce the efficiency of the financial intermediary system. On the other hand, restrictions on the ability of banks to provide liquidity to nonbanks would tend to reduce the efficiency of the financial sector. Thus the optimal type of financial regulation would seek to ensure an efficient pricing of liquidity supplied by banks.

Central bank liquidity assistance is optimal only as long as it is designed to avoid the externalities of the failure of a single or a few institutions. Such assistance should be designed to reduce systemic risk, that is, the risk that the failure of a single institution will cause a system-wide liquidity crisis. These considerations point toward the supervisory and regulatory policy that strengthens the ability of payment systems to withstand local operational, liquidity, and credit disturbances as reducing public sector credit risk without reducing efficiency. A consequence of the rapid growth of international trading in goods, services, and financial transactions and of the globalization of markets in twenty-four-hour trading is that the demand for international payment services is increasing rapidly. The international circulation of financial assets has created foreign markets for domestic assets, and large correspondent banks handle payments in currencies different from those of their countries of origin. Hence, netting schemes or international netting arrangements have been developed. This development has raised questions about whether market forces can produce an efficient and sound international payments system. Current initiatives have been undertaken so far by individual banks or small groups of banks, but in the presence of externalities, central bank cooperation might produce benefits. Systemic risk in netting arrange-ments ultimately derives from the credit extended in interbank settlement in the course of the settlement period. Many of these developments are inevitable due to the growth of a multicurrency reserve system in which various currency areas become overlapping. With the decline of the importance of the dollar, it is likely that in the future there will be no system that serves to anchor the one leading currency to the monetary bank supervision as lender-of-last-resort authority upon which that monetary and payment system are based. Thus clearing and settlement of foreign currency transactions have a supernational character. A third and new area of international central bank cooperation will have to be explored in addition to the area of monetary policy and bank supervision. The need for a collective involvement of national central banks in the functioning of the international payment system is brought into focus by the growth of private international netting schemes. The need expressed by the market for multilateral clearing houses for international transactions. Private cooperative arrangements without central bank involvement are unlikely to reduce systemic risk to acceptable levels, particularly the power to impose restrictions as well as provide liquidity occasionally required by members at closing time. The optimum solution among those that can realistically be achieved would require some kind of joint undertaking by the private and public sectors with a clear definition of rules and a strict definition of the scope of central bank activity.

It is easy to see that when financial innovation by financial firms is met by attempts of financial authorities to prevent shifts of financial activities across jurisdictions or to unregulated sectors, while at the same time extending financial guarantees, then the system can be expected to experience more financial crises, as financial firms are subject to more risk, and the authorities will be subject to a greater contingent liability. Thus, such a financial system, with a financial policy which we call competitive, may experience a greater than optimal number of crises, and may misallocate and misprice risk.

In order to narrow the scope for arbitrage, a cooperative approach to the formulation of financial policy among the main financial authorities would involve convergence of regulatory and fiscal features, as well as a convergence of central bank policy on liquidity guarantees. Such cooperation could generally be credibly entered into as it would involve a large number of rules which could not be abrogated easily, rather than the coordination of only one or two highly visible policy instruments.

7.4 Conclusion

The main conclusion of this paper is that the outcome of this uncoordinated restructuring process in financial markets—driven by regulatory and fiscal arbitrage by financial intermediaries and combined with competition for market share by financial authorities—can be inefficient and unstable and results in an inefficiently large amount of private credit risk being shifted to the public sector.[17] While innovations cum deregulation have greatly extended the scope for intermediaries to assume risk in the form of interest rate, currency, credit, market, and liquidity risk, this process has not been met by a greater cost to assume more risk. Such an increase in cost could have been brought about by a reduction in implicit or explicit liquidity and solvency guarantees extended to intermediaries by financial authorities.[18] Instead, in some notable instances such guarantees were significantly extended, thereby creating an even stronger incentive for banking intermediaries to assume more risk.[19] Hence the prevailing process of restructuring financial activities has led to perverse incentives regarding risk taking by financial intermediaries.

A corollary of the above argument is that competition for financial activity by financial authorities has not produced an optimal level of prudential regulation nor an optimal pricing and allocation of risk. As a result, the financial sector has been and may continue to be a source of instability. The U.S. S&L crisis, together with the failure of some individual banks, such as Continental Illinois, are the most visible examples. In addition, it can be argued, perhaps less obviously, that excessive risk taking in lending to developing countries, as well as the more recent financing of leveraged buy-outs is a direct consequence of the incentives for banking firms to leverage off public sector guarantees.[20]

A successful coordination of financial policy across jurisdictions can avoid creating incentives for intermediaries to assume excessive risk and can facilitate a desired level of prudential regulation. Through coordination of financial policy, it would be possible to arrive at a desired level of risk and financial guarantees. In this regard, the recently concluded Basle Agreement on risk-weighted capital standards for international banks is an outstanding example of a cooperative solution to a problem that had been created by a competitive approach to bank regulation.[21] Similarly, in recently inaugurated efforts to reduce payment system risk, U.S. authorities have tended to look for an international cooperative approach.

In order to proceed much further with the analysis and determine specific areas in which a convergence of policy would be most beneficial, it is first necessary to identify a desired structure of the financial system. In this regard, the hypothesis that large money center banks, that is, banks that are too large to fail, tend to have a comparative advantage in supplying liquidity to the financial system would suggest concentrating regulatory measures on risky activities not related to the liquidity supply function. Second, since the wholesale payments system transmits disturbances from one bank to other financial institutions the design of such systems and the control of risk here would tend to improve the trade-off between efficiency loss and the amount of credit risk assumed by the public sector.

An important problem in implementing a cooperative financial policy is the treatment of financial activity in jurisdictions that are not party to cooperative agreements when such activity is undertaken by affiliates of firms in jurisdictions that are party to cooperative agreements. One possible approach could be the strict exclusion of such affiliates from the guarantee cover and the timely and rigorous valuation, by supervisors, of the parents' claims on the affiliate. The task facing supervisors in valuing such claims would, in principle, appear to be no more difficult than that of valuing bank claims on domestic commercial firms.

The main implementation of the conclusions reached in this paper can be found in the Basle Agreement of the G-10 on the convergence of risk-based capital standards for international banks. In particular, the agreement—encompassing the definition of capital and risk weights for credit risk and some interest rate risk—was reached in direct response to the problems associated with a competitive financial policy. Some firms, most notably Japanese banks, already appear to have been forced to adjust their pricing in off-balance sheet activities, which according to the agreement require capital cover. There is much less progress in cooperating on the convergence of financial policy in securities markets.

In addition to the 1987 Basle Agreement on capital standards, agreement had been reached earlier, under the auspices of the Bank for International Settlements, on consolidated capital supervision and allocation of supervisory responsibilities between parent and host country supervisors. By 1987, consolidated supervision of foreign branches, as well as majority-owned subsidiaries for capital adequacy purposes, had been established among the G-5 and Switzerland (see table 7.7).

Table 7.8   Capital/Asset Ratios of Banks in Selected Industrial Countries, 1979–1988 (in percent)

	1979	1980	1981	1982	1983	1984	1985	1986	1987	1988
Canada[a]	3.2	3.0	3.5[b]	3.7	4.1	4.4	4.6	5.0	4.8	5.1
France[c]	2.3	2.1	2.0	2.2	2.4	2.7	3.7	4.5	4.9	5.4
Germany[d]	3.3	3.3	3.3	3.3	3.3	3.4	3.5	3.6	3.7	3.7
Japan[e]	5.1	5.3	5.3	5.0	5.2	5.2	4.8	4.8	4.8	4.9
Luxembourg[f]	—	3.5	3.5	3.5	3.6	3.8	4.0	4.1	4.1	4.1
Netherlands[g]	4.3	4.2	4.3	4.6	4.7	4.8	5.0	5.2	5.6	5.5
Switzerland[h]										
Largest five banks	7.6	7.6	7.4	7.3	7.1	7.1	7.8	7.8	7.9	8.0
All banks	7.6	7.6	7.5	7.5	7.3	7.4	7.8	7.9	8.0	8.0
United Kingdom										
Largest four banks[i]	7.2	6.9	6.5	6.4	6.7	6.3	7.9	8.4	8.2	8.8
All banks[j]	5.1	5.0	4.5	4.1	4.4	4.5	5.5	5.4	6.0	6.4
United States										
Nine money center banks[k]	4.5	4.5	4.6	4.9	5.4	6.2	6.8	7.3	8.2	9.2
Next 15 banks[k]	5.4	5.5	5.2	5.3	5.7	6.6	7.2	7.5	8.4	7.9
All country reporting banks[k,l]	5.3	5.4	5.4	5.6	5.9	6.5	6.9	7.2	7.9	8.1

Sources: Data provided by official sources and Fund staff estimates.

Note: Aggregate figures such as the ones in this table must be interpreted with caution, owing to differences across national groups of banks and over time in the accounting of bank assets and capital. In particular, provisioning practices vary considerably across these countries as do the definitions of capital. Therefore, cross-country comparisons may be less appropriate than developments over time within a single country.

[a]Ration of equity plus accumulated appropriations for contingencies (before 1981, accumulated appropriations for losses) to total assets (*Bank of Canada Review*).

[b]The changeover to consolidated reporting from November 1, 1981, had the statistical effect of increasing the aggregate capital/asset ratio by about 7 percent.

[c]Ratio of capital, reserves, general provisions, and subordinated debentures to total assets. Data exclude cooperative and mutual banks. This ratio is different from the official ratio of risk coverage where assets are assigned different weights depending on the quality of each category of them.

[d]Ratio of capital including published reserves to total assets. From December 1985, the Bundesbank data incorporate credit cooperatives (Deutsche Bundesbank, *Monthly Report*).

[e]Ratio of reserves for possible loan losses, specified reserves, share capital, legal reserves plus surplus, and profits and losses for the term to total assets (Bank of Japan, *Economic Statistics Monthly*).

[f]Ratio of capital resources (share capital, reserves excluding current-year profits, general provisions, and eligible subordinated loans) to total payables. Eligible subordinated loans are subject to prior authorization by the Institut Monétaire Luxembourgeois and may not exceed 50 percent of a bank's share capital and reserves. Data in the table are compiled on a nonconsolidated basis and as a weighted average of all banks (excluding foreign bank branches). An arithmetic mean for 1988 would show a ratio of 19.2 percent. Inclusion of current-year profits in banks' capital resources would result in a weighted average of 4.4 percent for 1988. Provisions for country risks, which are excluded from capital resources, have been moderately increased in the last year. The 1988 level of provision represents five times the level of 1982.

[g]Ratio of capital, disclosed free reserves, and subordinated loans to total assets. Eligible liabilities of business members of the agricultural credit institutions are not included (De Nederlandsche Bank, N.V., *Annual Report*).

[h]Ratio of capital plus published reserves, a part of hidden reserves, and certain subordinated loans to total assets (Swiss National Bank, Monthly Report).

[i]Ratio of share capital and reserves, plus minority interests and loan capital, to total assets (Bank of England).

[j]Ratio of capital and other funds (sterling and other currency liabilities) to total assets (Bank of England). Note that these figures include U.K. branches of foreign banks, which normally have little capital in the United Kingdom.

[k]Ratio of total capital (including equity, subordinated debentures, and reserves for loan losses) to total assets.

[l]Reporting banks are all banks that report their country exposure for publication in the *Country Exposure Lending Survey* of the Federal Financial Institutions Examination Council.

Table 7.9   **Equity Markets: Secondary Trading Values and Volumes, 1979–1988 (in billions of U.S. dollars)**

	Total World Trading Value	International Equity Markets			
		Trading Value	Percentage Change	Volume[a]	Percentage Change
1979	—	73.1	—	100.0	—
1980	—	120.4	64.7	135.7	35.7
1981	—	149.4	24.1	182.9	34.8
1982	—	151.6	1.5	175.3	−4.2
1983	—	272.0	79.4	265.7	51.6
1984	—	296.9	9.2	284.6	7.1
1985	—	385.2	29.7	276.5	−2.9
1986	7,024.6	800.8	107.9	402.8	45.7
1987	11,203.3	1,344.4	67.9	591.4	46.8
1988	10,638.2	1,212.6	−9.8	440.1	−25.6

Source: Salomon Brothers, *International Equity Flows–1989 Edition.*
[a]Index 1979 = 100.

Notes

1. In this paper I concentrate on central bank intervention to avoid systemic liquidity crises, but a mispriced deposit insurance scheme would present the same moral hazard problems.

2. See Greenspan (1988).

3. For a detailed description of developments in international financial markets, see Watson, Kincaid, and Folkerts-Landau (1987).

4. See Folkerts-Landau and Mathieson (1988), Kane (1983), and Silber (1983).

5. The antigambling statute in Illinois was superseded in 1974 to allow for trading in financial futures with cash settlement. See Miller (1986).

6. Standby letters of credit issued by the ten largest money center banks grew from 7.5 percent to 11.5 percent of total assets during 1981–85. Interest rate swaps grew from zero to 14 percent of total assets, on a national value, over the same period, while foreign exchange contracts rose to 105 percent of total assets by 1985.

7. Under the Basle Agreement on risk-weighted capital standards, such off-balance sheet transactions are now treated as balance sheet items.

8. See Folkerts-Landau (1985).

9. For a detailed discussion of the implications of these technological changes for financial markets, see Saunders and White (1986).

10. See *Report on Netting Schemes*. Basle, Switzerland: Bank for International Settlements, 1989.

11. A further motive for deregulating interest rate ceilings and restrictions on the investment choice of some financial intermediaries has been the need to finance fiscal deficits. A greater volume of government bonds outstanding acted as a stimulus to the development of secondary markets for debt securities with market-determined yields and presented an investment asset alternative to bank liabilities.

12. See Heller (1988) and Greenspan (1988).

13. Another example of an innovation made possible by deregulation are financial futures, the need for which increased with the spread of variable interest rates.

14. See Folkerts-Landau (1985).

15. See Golembe (1988).

16. See Schwartz (1988).

17. The contingent liability incurred by financial authorities through implicit or explicit guarantees to financial intermediaries should be added to expected fiscal deficits.

18. As described in section 7.3, the presence of guarantees covering the obligations of financial intermediaries is the main reason for regulatory restrictions on financial activities. Hence a reduction in such restrictions should be accompanied by a reduction in guarantees.

19. Since securities houses are increasingly thought to be protected by liquidity guarantees, this argument also applies here.

20. See Folkerts-Landau (1985).

21. In this instance, widely diverging capital standards had offered a competitive advantage to banks from some jurisdictions, most notably Japan (table 7.8), and some national regulators were reluctant to raise capital standards for fear of putting their banks at a further competitive disadvantage.

References

Corrigan, E. 1986. Financial market structure: A longer view. In Federal Reserve Bank of New York, *Annual Report*.

Corrigan, G. 1982. Are banks special? In Federal Reserve Bank of Minneapolis, *Annual Report*.

Cummings, C. M., and L. M. Seveet. 1987–88. Financial structure of the G-10 countries: How does the U.S. compare? In Federal Reserve Bank of New York, *Quarterly Review* (no. 4).

Diamond, D., and P. Dybvig. 1983. Bank runs, deposit insurance, and liquidity. *Journal of Political Economy*.

Eichengreen, B., and R. Portes. 1987. The analomy of financial crises. In R. Portes and A. Swoboda, *Threats to International Financial Stability*. Cambridge: Cambridge University Press.

Folkerts-Landau, D. 1985. The changing role of international bank lending in development finance. *IMF Staff Papers*.

Folkerts-Landau, D., and D. J. Mathieson. 1988. Innovation, institutional change, and regulatory response in international financial markets. In William S. Haraf and

Rose Marie Kushmeider, eds., *Restructuring banking and financial services in America,* 392–423. Washington, DC: American Enterprise Institute for Public Policy Research.

Golembe, C. 1988. *Financial reform and the handling of failed banks,* The Golembe Reports, vol. 4.

Goodfriend, M., and R. G. King. 1988. Financial deregulation, monetary policy and central banking. Washington, DC: American Enterprise Institute.

Greenspan, A. 1988. Innovation and regulation of banks in the 1990s. Remarks before the American Bankers Association, Honolulu.

Guttentag, J., and R. Herring. 1983a. *Disaster myopia in international banking.* Essays in International Finance no. 164, Princeton University. Princeton, NJ: Princeton University Press.

———. 1983b. *The lender of last resort function in an international context.* Essays in International Finance no. 151, Princeton University. Princeton, NJ: Princeton University Press.

Haberman, G. 1987. Capital requirements of commercial and investment banks: Contrasts in regulation. In Federal Reserve Bank of New York, *Quarterly Review.*

Heller, R. H. 1988. Reform and integration of world financial markets. Remarks at the Presidential Leadership Summit, Washington, DC.

International Financing Review, various issues.

Kane, E. 1983. Policy implications of structural changes in financial markets. *American Economic Review* 73 (no. 2).

———. 1987. How market forces influence the structure of financial regulations. Washington, DC: American Enterprise Institute. Typescript.

Kareken, J. 1986. Federal bank regulatory policy: A description and some observations. *Journal of Business* 59 (no. 1).

Miller, M. 1986. Financial innovation: The last twenty years and the next. *Journal of Financial and Quantitative Analysis* 21 (no. 4).

Saunders, A., and L. White, eds. 1986. *Technology and the regulation of financial markets.* Lexington, MA: Lexington Books.

Schwartz, Anna J. 1988. Financial stability and the federal safety net. In W. S. Haraf and R. M. Kuschmeider, eds. *Restructuring banking and financial services in America.* Washington, DC: American Enterprise Institute.

Silber, W. L. 1983. The process of financial innovation. *American Economic Review* 73 (no. 2).

Watson, M., R. Kincaid, and D. Folkerts-Landau. 1987. *International capital markets: Developments and prospects.* Washington, DC: International Monetary Fund.

Wojnilower, A. M. 1987. The central role of credit crunches in recent financial history. *Brookings Papers on Economic Activity* 2.

Comment   Francesco Papadia

Just to make clear to the reader how much I agree with the paper, and thus maybe spare him or her further reading of this comment, I want to put my main, but minor, disagreement at the beginning. This has to do with the use

Francesco Papadia is a director and head of the International Economy Section of the Research Department of the Banca d'Italia in Rome.

of the term "financial policy" for what I would rather call supervisory and regulatory policy. Of course, language is a convention and the author is careful to spell what he means by financial policy. Yet conventions are not irrelevant and not little confusion would arise if one decided that yes means no, and no means yes. The case here is less extreme, but financial policy evokes financing decisions for a firm or a government, not the admittedly heterogeneous set of activities which are commonly referred to as supervision and regulation of financial markets.

Having disposed of my main point of disagreement, I can now underline one of the merits of the paper: the illustration of the developments which increasingly allow financial firms to arbitrage regulations and liquidity support from regulatory authorities across geographical boundaries and sectors. The emphasis on this second aspect, that is, on the increasing ability of financial firms to shift business away from heavily regulated sectors, such as commercial banking, to less regulated ones is indeed an interesting feature of the paper, complementing the more usual remarks on arbitrage across jurisdictions. Also the explanation of the phenomenon given in the paper is convincing, stressing the increased opportunities flowing from technological advances, macroeconomic imbalances, and new financial products.

The only criticism I have of this aspect of the paper is that Folkerts-Landau does not pay much attention to what is probably the most extreme example of new opportunities for financial firms to arbitrage regulations and liquidity protection, namely the EEC single market to be achieved by 1992. The year 1992 has become the code word for a complex, yet simple, set of events. The simplicity lies in the fact that an integrated market will be created out of twelve segmented ones. The complexity lies in the fact that to achieve this result, a formidable number of institutional and behavioral changes are required.

As regards financial markets, a sizable chunk of 1992 will indeed occur in 1990. The twelve EEC countries have in fact decided that complete liberalization will take place by mid-1990, with provisional arrangements for Spain, Greece, Portugal, and Ireland. Complete liberalization means that all financial transactions will be allowed, including so-called monetary ones. Controls could be reimposed only by means of a safeguard clause for a maximum of six months.

The application to banks and other financial institutions of the general principle of allowing competition across borders, through the establishment of a minimum of harmonization and mutual recognition, implies that they will be allowed to operate in all member states of the EEC subject to the core harmonized provisions while complying with the rules of their country of origin. Thus, in principle, in every state there could be banks complying with twelve different regulatory and supervisory systems and this of course will affect competition. Unless customers are ultrarational and understand that different regulations imply different degrees of protection, for which they are somehow willing to pay, the result will be exactly, and to a very high degree, the one underlined in Folkerts-Landau's paper, that is, competition in laxity by supervisory authorities.

The main point of the paper is, in fact, that there is increasing competition between regulatory systems. Operators are increasingly able to "buy and sell" financial regulations, thus giving a specific example of a general phenomenon underlined a long time ago by Richard Cooper. This is putting pressure on regulators who see their "market share" decrease if they insist on tight regulation; the net result is a general loosening of regulations. The answer is increasing coordination of supervisory and regulatory policy.

All this is very neat in theory and relevant in practice. As often happens, however, it is not terribly neat in practice. Indeed, coordination of regulatory and supervisory policy can be either bad or good. The crucial difference is whether the regulations are economically justified or not. Schemes like emergency liquidity and deposit guarantees, for instance, could be needed because of information asymmetries, which make the confidence required to maintain banks in business potentially very volatile, or, as the author puts it, because "payments systems transmit disturbances from one bank to another, thus turning local financial disturbances into systemic problems." But such schemes induce banks to take extra risks, and therefore additional checks and regulations must control the quality of their assets. Alternatively, and some of the passages of the paper seem to support this view, authorities "bail out" banks and impose controls and regulations for some unclear and possibly not very good economic reasons.

The policy prescription is radically different depending on whether the regulations and the underlying schemes for providing emergency liquidity or deposit guarantees do or do not have to make up for a market failure. If they do, coordination of regulatory policy is obviously good; if they do not, the welfare effect of coordination is uncertain.

In fact, in the former case, coordination eliminates an avenue whereby financial institutions could increase the riskiness of their assets up to a point where the stabilization effect of liquidity protection or deposit guarantee would be completely offset. In the latter case, however, while the possibility to evade controls would clearly make any "bailing out activity" on the side of authorities more costly, it would also increase welfare by reducing economically unjustified restrictions. In addition, one would think that, in the long run, the very fact that bailing out activities were made more costly could make the authorities less prone to embark on them. In any event, it would certainly be a welfare-improving move to shun coordination while reducing regulations and "bailing out" activities.

The paper outlines the two possibilities but, reflecting the unfortunate fact that reality is not as clear-cut as one would wish, Folkerts-Landau does not really succeed in discriminating between the two, although he does harness relevant material for the purpose. This remains the task for further analysis.

A final sort of technical remark is that it cannot be literally true that there is "competition for market shares by financial authorities." The main point of the paper can be restated by saying that the possibility to arbitrage regulations across markets and sectors has transformed regulatory authorities from monopolists to monopolistic competitors. These are likely to maximize profits, or revenue, not market share. To see that the two maximization activities can yield drastically different results, imagine that the monopolistic firm applied a zero price and the regulatory authority applied zero control. They would thus maximize market share but realize zero revenue and zero control, hardly a desirable outcome. It is more reasonable that regulatory authorities maximize total control, which would be a function of market share and unitary control, that is, control per financial institution. This view is also more consistent with the empirical observation that supervisory authorities, while taking account of competition from other authorities, are surely not bringing their regulations to zero. Indeed, it appears that authorities from large countries, which are likely to be confronted with a steeper demand curve, because they are less exposed to competition from other authorities, tend to apply stricter regulations than those applied in small, and eventually tiny, countries.

8 Multinational Corporations, Exchange Rates, and Direct Investment

Kenneth A. Froot

Multinational corporations represent an enormous concentration of economic power in the United States and the rest of the world. U.S. multinationals themselves account for sales of $3.5 trillion and control assets of $4.2 trillion, which is almost 60 percent of total U.S. business assets. They occupy a dominant position in world trade. U.S. parents and their affiliates, for example, are associated with 79 percent of U.S. exports and 46 percent of U.S. imports; they alone account for about 18 percent of world trade.[1]

How might the presence of such large multinationals affect the behavior of the exchange rate? The typical business executive would probably find this question easier to answer than the economic theorist. The executive would probably point out that there has been a revolution in international financial markets over the last decade. Securitization, globalization, innovation, and deregulation have resulted in an explosion of new instruments and trading volume. The structure of multinationals' liabilities have changed dramatically, and today's investment projects are financed in ways that were difficult to imagine only a few years ago. The executive's view might be that the real-time fungibility of financial resources in today's hectic markets may, in the large, make exchange rates less manageable, more volatile, and increasingly unpredictable. He would probably add that the undisciplined behavior of the dollar during the 1980s has done nothing to assuage his concerns.

The source of these concerns probably lies more in the role of corporate financial innovations than in the role of "multi" nationals—companies which manage production facilities in more than one country. Naturally, multinationals

Kenneth A. Froot is Visiting Assistant Professor of Finance at Harvard University, Graduate School of Business, and a Faculty Research Fellow at the National Bureau of Economic Research.

The author thanks Geoff Carliner, Martin Feldstein, John Fleming, Jeff Frankel, Jim Hines, Paul Krugman, Lois Stekler, and Ray Vernon for helpful discussions, and Joe Mullally for excellent research assistance.

are major players in international financial markets by virtue of their size and global orientation. But most observers would agree that the impact of financial innovation would not disappear if all multinationals were suddenly restructured as wholly owned domestic corporations. Nevertheless, the prospect that currencies as well as a host of other financial variables are not well behaved is legitimate and worthy of more study.

In section 8.1 of this paper, we focus on the exchange rate effects of financial market innovations used by large corporations. We begin by showing that firms' choices of capital structure have no effects on exchange rates if capital markets are perfect. Thus, observers concerned that financial innovations have contributed to excessive exchange rate volatility must base their arguments on capital market imperfections. We consider several ways in which international capital markets may in fact be quite imperfect: incomplete integration, high costs of transacting, and irrationality on the part of investors.

We then argue there is no evidence that the kinds of financial innovations that firms have put to use for project financing make exchange rates more volatile or difficult to control. While there is mixed evidence on whether exchange rates are ''excessively'' volatile, firms' financial managers do not appear to be culpable. Indeed, the evidence that we do have suggests that, if anything, corporations trading at long investment horizons, rather than shorter speculative horizons, help to stabilize exchange rates. Policy proposals aimed at discouraging heavy trading and high volatility, such as ''Tobin'' and interest equalization taxes on foreign exchange transactions, do not usually distinguish between different motives for trading. To the extent that these taxes ignore such distinctions, they may be throwing the financial market innovation baby out with its bathwater.

The business executive's second answer to how multinationals affect exchange rates would be the economic theorist's first: through the return on real investments in different countries. There is, however, little literature on the effects of multinational investment on exchange rates. The reason is simple: the modern theory of the multinational as pioneered by Hymer (1976) and Kindleberger (1969) has no special implications for exchange rates or international capital flows. Under their ''economic-organizational'' view, firms engage in foreign direct investment (FDI) in order to internalize what would otherwise be market transactions. A host country firm may be more valuable under the control of the foreign parent than under anyone else because of imperfections in the goods or factor markets, economies of scale and scope, the difficulties in writing perfect licensing contracts, etc. Notice this interpretation of ownership and investment is completely agnostic on the way in which the host country assets are purchased. The capital need not flow in from the parents' home country or from investors anywhere abroad. It can be borrowed just as easily in the host country.

There is, however, an older, classical trade literature on multinationals which sought to explain foreign direct investment through international capital flows. Under this view—which Caves (1982) calls the ''capital-arbitrage'' explanation—multinationals act as a conduit for capital flows, and thus have a well-defined role in exchange rate determination. So it might be sensible to study the effect multinationals would have on exchange rates under this scenario. To the extent that the cost of capital is influenced by monetary policy, fiscal spending, and taxes, this view would lead to precise implications for domestic and international policy. Unfortunately, this view has several basic problems and has largely been discarded. It does not explain why foreign capital should flow into direct as opposed to portfolio investment. It also does not explain why rates of return are unequal in the first place, why the international capital market would ever be in disequilibrium.

Today, most international economists subscribe to Hymer's (1976) view of FDI, dismissing the empirical importance of the capital arbitrage view. We shall not argue here with the need to model foreign direct investment more as a problem in industrial organization than as a problem in international finance. Yet some recent research suggests a sense in which the older, capital arbitrage view of FDI may be realistic and of increasing importance from a policy perspective.

In the section 8.2 of this paper, we argue that technological progress, combined with multinationals' unique ability to move international capital, has made multinationals more important in determining international capital flows. Imperfections in capital markets which previously were regarded as small may now elicit large movements of capital. Changes in corporate taxation, in particular, may have substantial effects on both the level and composition of international capital flows, and to a more limited extent, the exchange rate. The new mobility of multinationals implies that subtle changes in incentives can significantly alter behavior.

These issues are particularly relevant for the United States, which is currently thought to be experiencing a large inflow of foreign direct investment. We look at evidence which suggests that incentives for direct investment by foreigners and incentives for foreign investment by domestics have been altered substantially by tax changes in the 1980s. The Tax Reform Act of 1986 (TRA), for example, may help explain the current surge in foreign FDI in the United States as well as the less well advertised (but equally significant) increase in U.S. FDI abroad. In terms of welfare effects, we cannot evaluate whether the 1986 TRA was a good thing. We can say, however, that given the current tax law, U.S. taxpayers benefit from the increase in foreign FDI, which effects a transfer of resources from foreign taxpayers to the U.S. Treasury.

We conclude in this section that the presence of astute and informed multinationals poses a new challenge to policymakers. We are rapidly leaving behind an era in which it was acceptable to design tax policy without regard for the effects of FDI incentive and currency value.

8.1   Multinational Financing and Exchange Rates

In this section we explore how financial innovation affects firms' financing decisions, and how these financing decisions in turn affect exchange rates.

In order to establish a way to think about this problem, we first examine the effects of financial market innovation under the assumption that capital markets are perfect. (We discuss below just what we mean by "perfect.") Under these conditions we show that Modigliani and Miller's (1958, hereafter MM) first proposition implies that changes in firms' capital structures should have no effect on exchange rates. We then discuss evidence which suggests that international markets are not perfect, and that the MM proposition fails. Specifically, we address the concerns of those observers who argue that financial innovations have had adverse effects on exchange rate volatility. We argue that the most important financial innovations for large firms are new markets for securitized corporate borrowing and security swaps. These facilitate trading at longer horizons. We then review, but find no evidence to support, the hypothesis that these particular innovations have tended to destabilize exchange rates.

MM's famous proposition 1 demonstrates the irrelevance of a firm's choice of debt and equity in a perfect capital market. The logic of their irrelevance proposition is, however, very general, and does not apply only to simple debt and equity instruments.[2] The proposition applies to *any* combination of financial instruments, no matter how complex. The basic intuition for irrelevance is very simple: a firm cannot change the *total* value of its securities by splitting its cash flows into different streams. The value of the whole is always equal to the sum of the values of the parts—the principle of value additivity. There is also a second, less obvious point in MM: the allocation of risk in the economy is independent of the firm's capital structure, so that asset prices like the exchange rate are not affected by alternative financing schemes.

To see the logic of this argument, consider an example in which financial innovations have made it possible for a firm to issue debt in different currencies. Specifically, consider an all-equity firm which can finance a fixed investment project with debt denominated either in dollars or in deutsche marks (DM). The market value in dollars of the firm's securities under dollar-debt finance is given by the market value of the equity plus the market value of the dollar debt $V_\$ = E_\$ + D_\$$. Suppose an investor purchases the equity in this firm, spending $E_\$ = V_\$ - D_\$$. He is then entitled to the profits from the investment project less the payments on the dollar debt. For simplicity, assume that the debt is sold to the rest of the world for $D_\$$ dollars. Figure 8.1a shows the balance sheets for the firm, the investor, and the rest of the world, respectively. The equity and debt are purchased out of liquid dollar assets, L_i and L_{RoW}, held initially by the investor and the rest of the world.

Now suppose that an identical firm decides to issue debt in DM rather than in dollars (perhaps even a different dollar amount of DM debt). The market value in dollars of the firm's securities is given by $V_{dm} = E_{dm} + D_{dm}$. Clearly, the cash flow generated by the firm's equity will generally be different under DM-debt financing than under dollar-debt financing: the payoffs from E_{dm} will not equal those of $E_\$$. Under DM-debt financing, for any

(a)

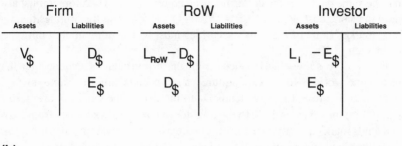

(b)

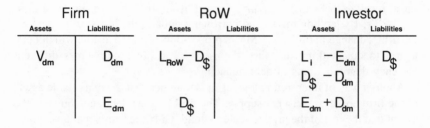

(c)

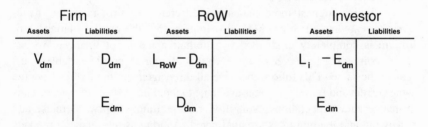

Fig. 8.1   Balance sheet implications of foreign-currency financing

given level of profits, an unanticipated appreciation of the mark relative to the dollar creates a windfall transfer to bondholders from shareholders. How does this particular capital structure affect the market value of the firm's securities and the equilibrium exchange rate?

To answer this, we assume that investors will pay the same amount of money for any two portfolios which provide exactly the same cash flow. If the investor purchases the equity only, he pays $E_{dm} = V_{dm} - D_{dm}$. This would entitle him to the firm's profits as before, but from those profits the payments on the DM-debt will be subtracted. To duplicate the payoffs from $E_\$$, the investor must also lend the equivalent of D_{dm} dollars in DM, while borrowing $D_\$$

dollars. For this portfolio he must pay $E_{dm} + D_{dm} - D_\$ = V_{dm} - D_\$$. Since this portfolio yields the firm's profits less the dollar-bond payments, it has the same payoff as the dollar-financed equity above. Therefore it must also have the same cost: $V_{dm} - D_\$ = E_\$ = V_\$ - D_\$$. But this implies that the total market value of the firm's securities must be the same under both types of financing, $V_{dm} = V_\$$.[3]

Figure 8.1b shows the balances from these transactions. Notice first that rest-of-the-world (RoW) expenditures and receipts are the same in both figures. In figure 8.1a, RoW lends $D_\$$ to the firm, whereas in figure 8.1b it lends $D_\$$ to the investor. In 8.1b the investor in turn borrows dollars from RoW and lends marks directly to the firm. The investor thereby duplicates the future cash flows and current expenditures he had in figure 8.1a. Since investors and RoW have the same expenditures and receipts as before, it follows that the firm must receive the same amount of cash from the sale of its securities: $V_{dm} = V_\$$. By lending marks and borrowing dollars, the investor has undone the firm's change in financing. MM's proposition 1, that investors will not pay a firm to do anything that they themselves can do, holds across different currency denominations of debt financing.

Another way of interpreting this result is to notice that the marketable assets of the firm are all in zero net supply. The firm is short debt and equity to the extent that the rest of the private sector is long. Only the firm's real investment projects, which generate the cash flow, are in positive net supply. Regardless of how this cash flow is partitioned, the sum of the value of the parts is equal to the value of the whole.

The figures suggest more than the indifference of firm managers to alternative capital structures. MM also implies that the capital market equilibrium is completely unaffected by alternative means of finance. We can see by comparing figures 8.1a and 8.1b that all real economic variables must remain the same. This follows because all three agents in the figures have the same current and future resources available to them in all states of nature. Thus exchange rate expectations, volatility, risk premiums, forward rates, and borrowing and lending rates are unaffected. As long as the financial markets are perfect, firm financing remains a veil, and has no implications for real economic variables.

In the discussion so far we have implicitly assumed that the investor prefers to purchase $E_\$$ over E_{dm}. In other words, he thinks that the added exchange rate exposure of $E_\$$ is worth paying for. There are two reasons why investors may not be willing to pay much for this exposure, why they may be approximately indifferent between $E_\$$ and E_{dm}.

First, if exchange rate risk is purely diversifiable then investors are not willing to pay to avoid it. There is, of course, a large empirical literature testing the diversifiability of exchange rate risk. While several studies have found that a number of variables, such as forward rates and past exchange rate changes, appear to have predictive power for exchange rate changes in excess of the forward discount, there is little positive evidence that this predictive power is attributable to an exchange risk premium.[4] Second, investors may be indifferent between $E_\$$ and E_{dm} even if exchange risk is not diversifiable as long as they already hold optimal amounts of currency risk. Investors might, for example, hold the stocks of foreign firms or hold foreign currency deposits directly. Once they have reached their optimal level of exchange rate exposure, investors' marginal utility of small changes in exposure is zero. Figure 8.1c shows the expenditures and receipts for all three agents when the firm issues DM-denominated debt which is then purchased by RoW. If both our investor and RoW already hold optimal levels of exchange rate exposure, then the value of the firm's securities will be the same in figure 8.1c as in 8.1a ($V_\$ = V_{dm}$). MM would therefore hold even if the debt swap depicted in figure 8.1b were ruled out.

Notice that investors could be satisfied with their exposure to exchange rates regardless of the size of the exchange risk premium. If risk premiums are large, then the first firms to provide diversification to investors would have been able to extract a substantially higher price for their securities, much like the innovative monopolist who is first to sell a new product. But as other firms move to fill the gap, the excess returns to financial innovation disappear. A firm which can diversify cheaply—due, for example, to low transactions costs—can gain by providing an unsatisfied clientele of shareholders with additional diversification. MM will fail, but this activity will make investors better diversified and world capital markets more integrated.

Before we go on to discuss the empirical shortcomings of MM, it is worth seeing more formally why asset valuations do not change as long as all clienteles are satisfied. Suppose that asset markets are efficient and investors are optimally diversified. Let the investor's utility be a function of his next-period consumption, $U = U(c)$. Suppose the investor, who holds N assets with real returns given by $r_1 \ldots r_N$, sells an amount of the ith asset equal to a share $d\omega_i$ of his total wealth, and uses the proceeds to purchase a share $d\omega_j$ of the jth asset, where $d\omega_i = -d\omega_j$. (To continue with the previous example, we might think of the investor selling a small amount of E_{dm} and using the proceeds to purchase $E_\$$ of an identical firm's stock.) Let investor consumption be current wealth times the gross return on the portfolio, $c = W\omega'\mathbf{r}$, where W is total wealth, ω is the $N \times 1$ vector of asset shares, and $\mathbf{r}$ is the $N \times 1$ vector of gross returns. The requirement that the investor has set his portfolio optimally implies

(1) $$E[U'(r_i - r_j)] = 0.$$

At the optimum, the expected marginal gain from a self-financing swap of one asset for another is zero.

It is easy to see that the capital market equilibrium remains efficient and that the consumption CAPM holds. As a result, the swap will not change asset prices. Suppose that r_j is the return on a portfolio of assets which is independent of consumption and the returns are normally distributed. Then equation (1) can be rewritten as:[5]

(2) $$E(r_i) - E(r_j) = \frac{E(U'')}{E(U')} \text{cov}(r_i,c).$$

Because equation (2) holds for any asset or portfolio, it must also hold for the world market portfolio, ω_m, the shares of each asset in the world portfolio:

(3) $$E(r_{m,i}) - E(r_j) = \frac{E(U'')}{E(U')} \text{cov}(r_{m,i},c),$$

where $r_{m,i}$ is the return on the world market portfolio, deflated by the ith investor's consumption price index. Combining equations (2) and (3) yields the standard consumption CAPM for the investor:

(4) $$E(r_i) - E(r_j) = \beta_i [E(r_{m,i}) - E(r_j)],$$

where

$$\beta_i = \frac{\text{cov}(r_i,c)}{\text{cov}(r_{m,i},c)}.$$

A similar equation would hold for RoW:

(5) $$E(r_{i,\text{RoW}}) - E(r_{j,\text{RoW}}) = \beta_{i,\text{RoW}}[E(r_{m,\text{RoW}}) - E(r_{j,\text{RoW}})],$$

where

$$\beta_{i,\text{RoW}} = \frac{\text{cov}(r_{i,\text{RoW}},c_{\text{RoW}})}{\text{cov}(r_{m,\text{RoW}},c_{\text{RoW}})}.$$

All securities continue to be priced by the same rule as they were before the swap. If the investor and RoW were initially not at an optimum, equations (4) and (5) would contain additional terms reflecting the swap of assets i and j (i.e., $[dU/d\omega_i]d\omega_i + [dU/d\omega_j]d\omega_j$), and then there would be a first-order effect on equilibrium prices. But as long as equation (1) holds for all investors, real required returns and the world capital market equilibrium are unaffected by the swap.

We have obviously made several strong assumptions to get these results, and we focus on these below. First, we assumed that international capital markets are integrated. By this we mean that all investors are informed of and have access to assets traded anywhere in the world. Second, we assumed that transactions costs are zero and that there are no taxes. And finally, we assumed that the multinational's choice of financing does not affect the value of its investment project, an assumption which we also relax below.

In spite of these unrealistic assumptions, the results above are very general. International asset pricing models are much more complicated than standard asset pricing models. They explicitly allow individuals in different countries to have different consumption baskets, and in any case, to use different numeraires to appraise real returns. Under these circumstances, the usual touchstone portfolios, such as the minimum-variance portfolio and the mean-variance efficient portfolio, are no longer very useful for describing the world capital market equilibrium, since different investors will define them differently. The usual separation theorems will fail. Yet, in spite of this kind of heterogeneity across investors, the above example and model continue to hold. Small changes in the financial structure do not alter the allocation of resources, and therefore, the world capital market equilibrium, no matter how complicated, remains unaffected.

8.1.1 Financial Innovation

Few economists would argue that the international capital market is perfect. Certainly, markets were far from perfect before the last decade's dramatic changes in the financial tools available to large firms. In this section we look briefly at how financial innovations affect firms' costs and choices of financing.[6] Our interest in these innovations is to see whether they have eliminated important market segmentation (by cutting transactions costs and reducing regulations and capital controls) and to identify new instruments corporations use to hedge risks and finance investments.

Twenty years ago corporations borrowed predominantly from banks, usually in domestic currency. Transactions costs were higher than they are today. International bond and currency markets were essentially undeveloped. The domestic capital markets of the largest developed countries (the U.S., Germany, France, Japan, and the U.K.) were largely separated from each other by a variety of capital controls.

The growth of the international currency market is a useful benchmark for the speed of financial innovation. Transactions costs have fallen to the point where on an average day the difference between the bid and ask rates in New York on the DM is about 0.05 percent! In 1973, the average bid/ask spread for the DM was slightly more than twice as large, 0.11 percent. Over $250 billion changes hands in currency markets around the world each day, roughly an order of magnitude greater than a decade ago. Indeed, some observers express concern that there may now be "too" much trade. Goodhart (1987) has found that only about 10 percent of daily trades in the foreign exchange market are between a bank and its customers, the remaining 90 percent are trades between banks.

A number of restrictions in the 1950s and 1960s on capital flows affecting multinationals stimulated the growth of the Eurobond market. Imposed in 1963, the U.S. interest equalization tax made it difficult for foreign affiliates of U.S. corporations and other foreign borrowers to issue debt in the U.S.

market. After having issued $14 billion of debt on U.S. markets at low rates from 1946–63, foreigners suddenly faced a cost-of-capital disadvantage in the U.S. market of 1 percentage point. In 1967 this was raised to 1.5 percentage points, and new restrictions on U.S. capital outflows were added.[7] The Eurobond market sprung up in London and Luxembourg as a response to these regulations. In addition to providing a means for avoiding the interest equalization tax, these bonds were more attractive to lenders than comparable U.S. domestic bonds because they did not have to be registered. Lenders therefore found it easy to avoid all taxes on their Eurobond earnings.

Volume grew quickly. Table 8.1 shows the growth of the international bond market, which includes both Eurobonds (bonds issued in a currency different from that of the jurisdiction of issue) and foreign bonds (bonds issued by a foreign source in the currency of the jurisdiction). Growth has been spectacular in every year except that following the oil shock in 1973, when the U.S. interest equalization tax was removed in an effort to assist in recycling petrodollars. This expansion of the international debt market is truly international, in that it is not limited to dollar-denominated borrowing. Table 8.1 also shows that while the denomination of most securities is still the dollar, the *share* of international borrowing in DM, yen, and the pound has grown as well. The DM and yen together have gone from 3 percent of international borrowing in 1981 to about 27 percent today.

Throughout the late 1970s, U.S. corporate borrowers had to be enticed to issue their debt on the international market instead of on the domestic market.

Table 8.1   New Issues in the International Bond Market (as a percentage of U.S. domestic bond issues)

	International Bond Issues			Currency of Eurobond Issues			
Year	Total	Foreign	International	U.S. Dollar	DM	Yen	Pound
1976	120.13	43.12	77.00	21.32	6.59	—	—
1977	110.49	34.31	76.18	27.11	12.04	—	0.52
1978	266.27	98.69	167.58	33.47	31.90	—	1.42
1979	239.16	84.25	154.90	39.86	18.74	—	1.10
1980	133.93	40.09	93.84	32.25	7.17	—	0.76
1981	194.53	55.95	138.58	55.56	3.61	—	1.41
1982	233.46	59.04	174.42	104.98	6.98	—	1.13
1983	210.37	56.18	154.19	108.59	7.19	—	3.63
1984	608.59	125.85	482.74	293.51	19.33	5.39	17.98
1985	544.96	84.98	459.98	265.35	26.32	18.09	16.72
1986	144.77	24.43	120.34	73.22	10.60	11.47	6.57
1987	101.47	21.06	80.41	32.45	8.87	13.22	8.58

Source: World Financial Markets, various issues; Economic Report of the President, 1988, table B-93; and *Financial Market Trends,* various issues. Data for 1987 are annualized from October for the foreign and international bond figures.

Perhaps as a consequence, the interest differential between Eurodollar and domestic dollar bonds was negative. As the market grew and borrowers became more familiar with the Eurobond market, the interest differential narrowed steadily toward zero. Kidwell, Marr, and Thompson (1985) study these interest differentials, finding them to be in the range of 70–140 basis points over the 1977–81 period and 30–60 basis points in 1983, the end of their sample.[8] Figure 8.2 shows the differential between dollar-denominated corporate bonds in the U.S. domestic and Eurobond markets. In 1984, the U.S. government lifted the 30 percent interest-withholding tax on the earnings of foreign investors. This granted U.S. domestic bonds the same U.S. tax status as Eurobonds, and may help explain the fall in the interest differential in 1985 and 1986.

Naturally, the fall in this interest differential could be a result of changes in required returns rather than improved financial integration. Evidence that these differentials are due to segmentation comes from a study by Kim and Stulz (1988). They argue that Eurobonds are imperfect substitutes for domestic bonds from the lenders' point of view. When Eurobonds first became popular, purchasers wanted to hold more than were initially available, and therefore bid up prices. Firms responded slowly to this unexpectedly strong demand. Because firms were able to raise capital relatively cheaply in this way, their stock prices increased when a Eurobond issue was announced. From 1979 to 1984 the savvy corporate CFO was able to raise the value of his or her firm by selling to an unsatisfied clientele of Eurobond purchasers. On this view,

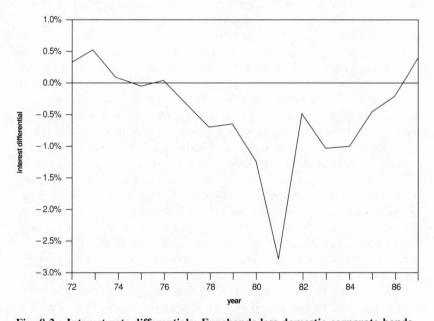

Fig. 8.2   Interest rate differentials: Eurobonds less domestic corporate bonds

MM failed, but only temporarily. As lenders became satisfied with the share of their portfolios devoted to Eurobonds, the differential fell. Today, CFOs cannot raise the value of their firm by issuing Eurobonds rather than domestic bonds; the clientele effects have disappeared.

Perhaps the strongest evidence that the Eurobond market was initially segmented comes from arbitrage activities that firms have been able to engineer. In the early 1980s, Exxon bought $175 million of 30-year zero coupon U.S. Treasury bonds, and sold an offsetting amount of Eurobonds for $200 million, earning an essentially riskless profit of $25 million. In early 1984, several other multinationals issued foreign DM bonds and used the proceeds to purchase German government securities called *Schuldschein*. PepsiCo, for example borrowed 250 million DM for ten years at 7.7 percent and then purchased 235 million DM in ten-year *Schuldschein* yielding 8.35 percent. The *Schuldschein* were placed in an irrevocable trust to cover interest payments and principal on the new PepsiCo debt. The deal, called a ''morning-to-midnight defeasance,'' locked in a riskless profit worth approximately $2 million. The company was not even required to record the bonds on its balance sheet. Soon after these deals were consummated, the interest differentials that made the arbitrage possible disappeared.[9]

To some extent, growth in international securitized borrowing has crowded out other sources of borrowing. As a result of ''securitization,'' traditional bank borrowing has fallen dramatically over the past decade. Even though many U.S. corporations view the Eurobond market as a financing substitute for the U.S. domestic market, domestic debt issuance has also grown at a rapid rate. Indeed, recent growth has been large relative to the growth of both GNP and equity financing, as shown in table 8.2.

Along with securitization and the fall in transactions costs has come an expanded set of debt instruments. While traditional fixed-rate debt still dominates, floating rate bonds and convertible bonds now account for almost 35 percent of total international issues. The growth of these instruments is shown in table 8.3. In addition, financial futures and options have grown quickly. While these instruments are redundant in that their payoffs can in theory be duplicated by trading other instruments, they have drastically reduced the costs of executing many trading strategies.

Perhaps the most important and newest instruments available to multinationals are currency and interest rate swaps. These have changed the international capital market in two respects. First, they allow the hedging of interest rate and exchange rate risk at horizons far longer than were previously possible on forward markets. Swaps therefore contribute to more efficient risk sharing. Second, swaps help reduce market segmentation. Swaps exploit the comparative advantage of one firm's ability to borrow more cheaply in one market compared with another firm, relative to both firm's borrowing costs in a second market. To the extent that these borrowing differentials are due to local market

Table 8.2   **Equity and Debt as a Fraction of GNP**

Year	Common Stock Issued	Bonds and Notes Issued
1970	0.69	2.86
1971	0.86	2.73
1972	0.88	2.11
1973	0.56	1.52
1974	0.27	2.14
1975	0.46	2.68
1976	0.47	2.37
1977	0.40	2.12
1978	0.34	0.91
1979	0.35	1.06
1980	0.71	1.63
1981	0.84	1.25
1982	0.75	1.41
1983	1.33	1.45
1984	1.77	0.59
1985	2.23	0.91
1986	1.31	3.81
1987	1.39	3.89

Source: Economic Report of the President, 1988, tables B-93 and B-1.

Table 8.3   **New Issues on the International Bond Market (in billions of dollars)**

Instruments	1982	1983	1984	1985	1986	1987
Fixed Rate	57.6	57.6	58.4	94.8	141.5	123.8
Floating Rate and CDs	15.3	13.8	38.2	58.7	51.2	10.7
Convertible	2.6	5.7	10.9	11.3	26.9	39.3
Other	—	—	—	5.4	6.2	3.5
Total	75.5	77.1	107.5	170.2	225.8	177.3

Source: Financial Market Trends, various issues.

differences in information or perception, swaps help reduce segmentation in the international capital market.

There is little data on swap volumes because swaps are an agreement between two parties and lack a clearinghouse mechanism and because current accounting standards treat swaps as off-balance-sheet transactions. Outstanding currency swaps grew from zero in 1982 to about $100 billion at the end of 1986. The outstanding volume of interest rate swaps is about three times larger.

8.1.2   Financial Innovations and Volatility

Many observers see financial innovations as reducing transactions costs, completing markets, improving international risk sharing, and pushing authorities toward financial liberalization.[10] Under this view, recent innovations are closing the gap between the real world and the idealized and frictionless capital market described in the examples above. The received wisdom is that innovations lubricate the market mechanism: they are all for the better.

Some observers, however, question whether this traditional response is correct. They ask whether easy access to trading has increased the volatility of exchange rates without adding to their information content. We now turn to these arguments, highlighting the particular ways that corporations have taken advantage of the revolution in international finance.

The long-held Keynesian view that asset prices do not move solely in response to changes in fundamentals has received new attention over the last decade. A number of studies have asked whether asset prices move too much to be consistent with simple fundamentals models.[11] Economists have also begun to study the effect on asset prices of "noise traders:" investors who trade simply for the sake of trading, or who trade on what they (irrationally) believe to be valid information.[12]

Some of this work addresses the popular concern that increased trading has helped promote greater volatility in financial markets. French and Roll (1986), for example, have found that the variance of stock market prices is substantially higher when the market is open rather than when it is closed. This is true even for those days on which the market is closed but normal or larger than normal amounts of information are released (e.g., election days).

Looking at exchange rate data, one is immediately skeptical of any long-term relationship between trading volume and volatility. Indeed, there is little evidence that exchange rate volatility is markedly higher today than over the past fifteen years. Table 8.4 presents simple calculations of the annual volatility of the dollar against the pound, DM, and yen over the floating rate period. There is little evidence of any upward trend in volatility to match the growth in trading volume.

Perhaps, however, there is a great deal of high-frequency correlation between trading and volatility which gets lost when looking at longer-period averages. Because it is so difficult to measure trading in foreign-exchange markets, there have been no studies of the relationship between volume of trade and exchange rate volatility. This gap can be filled, however, by examining trading in exchange rate futures, for which records of trading volume and transactions prices are available. By using transactions prices and trading volumes, we can gain a better sense for whether there is any basis to the allegations that trading volume itself generates exchange rate volatility.

For a closer look at this question, we obtained transactions data on both price changes and the number of contracts traded over fifteen-minute intervals in five foreign-exchange futures contracts (the pound, Canadian dollar, Swiss franc, deutsche mark, and yen) each trading day during the period 1984–1987. These are the highest-frequency exchange rate time series that I have seen used. Table 8.5 presents summary statistics from these data. The lower part of the table shows the average number of futures contracts traded every fifteen minutes. As

Table 8.4   **Volatility of the Dollar Against Selected Currencies (in percent per annum)**

	Currency		
Year	Pound	DM	Yen
1973	7.57	13.26	10.47
1974	7.20	8.07	7.05
1975	7.98	10.53	2.21
1976	8.37	4.75	5.27
1977	8.92	7.36	9.96
1978	11.70	13.11	17.38
1979	11.68	14.27	13.17
1980	11.35	9.01	10.99
1981	9.67	10.30	15.19
1982	10.07	7.30	13.00
1983	8.61	11.63	7.61
1984	16.62	12.26	5.78
1985	12.21	15.93	12.29
1986	9.03	8.30	10.55
1987	8.60	8.07	9.38
1988	14.73	13.55	15.66

Note: Volatility measures the standard deviation of monthly data, multiplied by 12 and expressed as a percentage.

Table 8.5   **Volatility and the Volume of Trade in Exchange Rate Futures**

	1984	1985	1986	1987	Average % Increase 1984–87
Volatility ($\times 10^8$)					
Pound	194	525	244	166	−3.9
Canadian dollar	22	46	43	35	11.6
Swiss franc	184	393	328	252	7.9
Deutsche mark	232	337	299	200	−3.7
Yen	106	170	243	201	16.0
Volume of Trade					
Pound	10.1	17.9	14.5	12.2	4.7
Canadian dollar	4.5	5.6	7.1	7.0	11.0
Swiss franc	26.4	29.7	11.9	32.1	4.9
Deutsche mark	27.7	36.6	41.9	43.0	11.0
Yen	14.4	15.3	27.1	34.2	21.6

Note: Futures' prices are from the Chicago Monetary Exchange. The data are sampled every fifteen minutes, beginning at 7:30 am until 12:30 pm each trading day. Annual estimates are averages over all trading days. Volatility is the average variance of daily futures' price changes, computed over the fifteen-minute intervals. Volume is the average number of futures contracts traded every fifteen minutes.

one might expect, trading volume grew steadily over the sample period. For some currencies, growth was very rapid: volume of trade in yen grew the fastest of any currency, at an average annual rate of 22 percent.

In the upper part of the table, we record the average variance of the futures prices over each year. Here the results are more mixed than in the lower part of the table. The variance grew most rapidly again for the yen, rising at an average annual rate of 16 percent. But in two of the five currencies, including the DM, the variability of futures prices actually declined. The simple correlation between variability and volume of trade across these currencies (allowing each currency to have its own mean) is positive, but not statistically greater than zero. There is thus only slight evidence that high-frequency volatility has increased with the volume of trade.

There are, however, several problems to bear in mind when interpreting the numbers in these last two tables. First, a positive relationship between volatility and volume of trade need not imply that trading itself *causes* greater volatility. We cannot give a causal interpretation to positive correlations because we expect that information about fundamentals could increase both trading and volatility. The usual presumption behind information-based correlations is that an improvement in the information content of prices allows more efficient risk sharing, regardless of its effect on volatility. But new investors with new information may also bring new noise to prices, so that increases in trading, volatility, and the flow of information may still be associated with a reduction in welfare.[13] Second, our measure of volume is the number of contracts traded, and not the dollar value of those contracts. Depending on one's model of how trading and volatility interact, one may wish to measure the dollar volume of trade instead. Third, futures contracts are derivative, in that sense that futures prices are constrained by the behavior of the actual spot exchange rate and interest differentials. Even if trading does itself generate volatility, we might not see any such relationship in table 8.5. If the futures rate fluctuates for reasons other than futures trading (perhaps because of trading in the spot market that is uncorrelated with trading in futures) then we would expect variance to increase only on average with an increase in futures trading.

One way to get around this latter problem is to regress the squared price change for each fifteen-minute interval on the volume of trade over that interval. In doing this, we interpret the squared price change as a noisy estimate of the variance. This assumption would be problematic for standard time series samples, where the data are sampled less finely. Changing expected returns could easily account for a large portion of the variation in such series. But in finely sampled data, the stochastic component should dominate expected price changes.[14] Thus high-frequency squared price changes are very nearly unbiased estimates of the next interval's conditional variance. The high frequency of our time series is advantageous for another reason: for each currency we have at least 22,377 degrees of freedom!

The results of regressions of the log of the squared price change on the log of volume are presented in table 8.6. In contrast to the secular averages in the previous table, here the estimates indicate that volatility and volume of trade are positively related. All the coefficients are many standard errors from zero. There is some evidence, however, that the relationship between volatility and volume of trade is not stable. When we run the samples by year, as in table 8.7, we find that for several currencies in 1984 and 1985 the coefficient is negative, although it is not statistically different from zero. For all currencies in 1986 and 1987, the relationship is strongly positive.

Finally, we look at the average number of transactions and the average volatility by time of day. Figure 8.3 shows the graphs of these series. Both volatility and volume are high at the beginning of the day, then show a steady downward trend until they reach a low point at lunch time. After lunch, traders come back for an hour or so of vigorous trading, which reaches a peak at the close of the futures market. Volatility behaves similarly. It would seem hard to explain this pattern in daily volatility by arguing that the flow of information into the markets falls at lunch time or rises strongly during the last hour of trading. On the other hand, if much of the information reflected in prices must first be processed slowly by investors, then one might expect to see a decline in volatility during lunch and a rise thereafter. Of course, these daily patterns are also consistent with the noise-trading hypothesis, which would say that there should not be much volatility when traders are busy eating.

Overall, the positive relationship between volatility and the volume of trade is stronger for very high frequency fluctuations than for the lower-frequency secular averages reported in tables 8.4 and 8.5. Why should trading itself generate additional short-term volatility? We mentioned earlier that trading could be greater when more information is reaching the market. A second explanation would be that traders have short-run "bandwagon expectations," in which a current price increase by itself generates expectations of further price increases. Trading on the basis of bandwagon expectations, which was the concern of Nurkse (1944), would today qualify as noise trading. If financial

Table 8.6   **Regressions of Volatility on Volume of Trade**

Currency	Years	a	b	t-test $(b=0)$	DF	DW	R^2	F-value
Pound	1984–87	131	11.01	8.00	24,235	2.01	0.00	64
Canadian dollar	1984–87	−4	6.73	27.86	23,326	1.95	0.03	776
Swiss franc	1984–87	135	4.16	5.91	24,111	1.99	0.00	34
Deutsche mark	1984–87	208	2.33	3.22	24,260	1.98	0.00	11
Yen	1984–87	13	7.32	13.04	24,284	2.01	0.01	170

Note: Futures' prices are from the Chicago Monetary Exchange. The data are sampled every fifteen minutes, beginning at 7:30 am until 12:30 pm each trading day. Volatility is the average variance of daily futures' price changes, computed over the fifteen-minute intervals. Volume is the average number of futures contracts traded every fifteen minutes.

Table 8.7   **Regressions of Volatility on Volume of Trade**

Currency	Years	a	b	t-test $(b=0)$	DF	DW	R^2	F-value
Pound	1984	174	2.0	1.29	6,069	1.99	0.00	1.7
	1985	619	−5.2	−1.27	6,045	1.98	0.00	1.6
	1986	−71	21.7	13.80	6,045	2.05	0.03	190
	1987	−90	21.0	15.66	6,070	2.03	0.04	245
Canadian dollar	1984	9	2.9	9.89	6,044	1.95	0.02	98
	1985	21	4.4	6.70	6,070	1.90	0.01	45
	1986	−14	8.2	17.03	5,822	1.99	0.05	290
	1987	−27	8.8	20.23	5,384	1.94	0.07	409
Swiss franc	1984	195	−0.4	−0.46	5,895	1.99	0.00	0.2
	1985	581	−5.1	−2.16	6,070	1.96	0.00	4.7
	1986	−93	10.1	9.45	6,070	2.03	0.01	89
	1987	−95	8.1	10.31	6,070	2.01	0.02	106
Deutsche mark	1984	298	−2.5	−2.03	6,069	1.95	0.00	4.1
	1985	485	−5.0	−1.96	6,070	1.98	0.00	3.9
	1986	209	7.6	5.30	6,070	1.98	0.00	28
	1987	−114	9.8	12.94	6,045	1.94	0.03	167
Yen	1984	53	3.6	3.81	6,069	1.96	0.00	14.52
	1985	168	0.2	0.07	6,070	1.99	0.00	0.0
	1986	−144	14.3	11.49	6,070	2.04	0.02	132
	1987	−69	7.9	10.32	6,069	2.01	0.02	106.6

Note: Futures' prices are from the Chicago Monetary Exchange. The data are sampled every fifteen minutes, beginning at 7:30 am until 12:30 pm each trading day. Volatility is the average variance of daily futures' price changes, computed over the fifteen-minute intervals. Volume is the average number of futures contracts traded every fifteen minutes.

market innovations, such as lower transaction costs, increase the frequency of such trades, then bandwagon expectations may destabilize prices.

While Nurkse's concern has long been familiar, it is only recently that have we become better able to test it. The problem has been finding a valid measure of the (unobservable) expected future spot rate. The usual presumption is that exchange rate expectations can be extracted from ex post spot rate realizations, but this strategy may not work in testing for bandwagon expectations. After all, these expectations may not be rational, or they may be rational but disguised by peso problems or nonstationarity in the ex post spot rate. The other traditional measure of expected future rates, the forward rate, is contaminated by the exchange risk premium. A third alternative, survey data on exchange rate expectations, are not subject to these problems, and in any case provide new information about the behavior of the market's unobservable expectations.

On the issue of bandwagon expectations, the surveys give a very strong answer. Over short horizons of one week and one month, there are statistically significant bandwagon tendencies: investors tend to predict that current exchange rate changes will be extrapolated, and that current movements away

deutsche mark average daily volatility

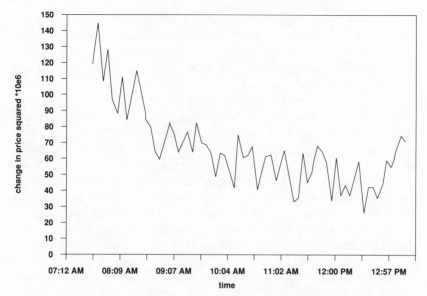

deutsche mark average daily volume

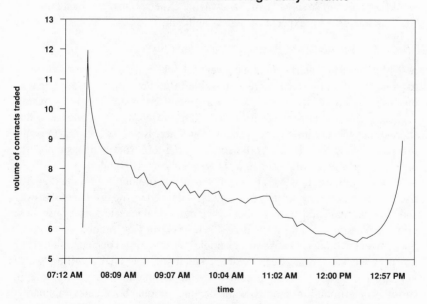

Fig. 8.3   **Deutsche mark futures' volatility and trading volume, 1984–1987**

from plausible long-run equilibrium values will continue.[15] Froot and Ito (1989), for example, show that a 10 percent exchange rate appreciation over the past week leads investors to expect on average a 1.5 percent further appreciation over the following week. Interestingly, however, the bandwagon effect is reversed for longer-term forecasts. At horizons of twelve months, for example, a current appreciation of 10 percent generates expectations of a 3.2 percent subsequent *depreciation*.

The contrasting behavior of expectations at different forecast horizons is difficult to square with the predictions of any single model. Froot and Ito (1989) test to see whether short-run and long-run expectations are consistent with a single, autoregressive model. They reject this hypothesis. In addition, they find that a current, positive exchange rate shock leads agents to expect a higher long-run future spot rate when iterating forward their short-term expectations than when thinking directly about the long run. In this sense short-horizon expectations may overreact to current exchange rate changes.

One way of interpreting these results is to think of agents using different models to forecast the spot rate at different horizons. Frankel and Froot (1988) discuss a case in which short-term expectations come out of "chartist" models, which are based on information only about past spot rates, whereas long-term expectations come from a "fundamentalist" model which ignores past exchange rates and uses the information in present and future fundamentals. This kind of theoretical explanation combined with the results above would suggest that short-term bandwagon expectations are destabilizing, whereas longer-term expectations are stabilizing.

8.1.3   Corporations and Exchange Rate Volatility

Within this framework, popular concerns about financial innovations leading to greater volatility seem more believable. But note that not all financial innovations and agents are subject to this line of criticism. The above results suggest that short-term volatility and trading are positively related and that short-term expectations may be destabilizing. There is no evidence that the same is true over long-term horizons. Indeed, the long-term survey data support the opposite contention, that trading at longer horizons is stabilizing.

Corporations are, however, precisely the agents responsible for the dramatic rise in longer-horizon currency trading, as evidenced by the growth of the swap and international bond markets. Banks and individual investors rarely use these primary markets, trading instead at shorter horizons on secondary markets. Spot currency traders at banks, for example, typically hold open positions only for short periods of time. Because of the paucity of other agents willing to take long positions, global corporations provide a unique, stabilizing role in currency determination. Indeed, while the international bond and swap market were in their infancy in the late 1970s, McKinnon (1979) identified a problem of "insufficient speculation." He recognized that while there were plenty of agents willing to trade at short horizons, few at that time took long-term positions. Financial innovations that encourage longer-term trading would appear to strengthen the role of fundamentals in determining exchange rates.

Of course, this view does not imply that all innovations are for the better. Policymakers eager to restrict noise trading must be careful not to undo the benefits from speculation based on stabilizing expectations. The evidence in this section suggests that, to the extent that noise trading is a problem, it affects short-horizon trades more than long-horizon trades.

To the extent that financial innovations have allowed multinationals and large domestic corporations to trade more at longer horizons, these innovations may have a stabilizing effect on the exchange rate. Corporations appear more able than private individuals or small companies to take advantage of imperfections in international capital markets and more likely to base their decisions on longer-term fundamentals. The arguments that exchange rates are too volatile may have some validity, but there is no evidence to support the contention that financial behavior of multinationals has contributed to excessive volatility.

A number of economists advocate the imposition of "Tobin" taxes on exchange rate transactions. It is important to note that if such taxes are applied to transactions in the international bond and swap markets, they will put U.S. firms at a cost-of-capital disadvantage, making it difficult to raise money in one currency and to spend it in another. As U.S. firms already complain that the U.S. tax law and institutional structure of U.S. capital markets places them at a cost-of-capital disadvantage, such a tax might be very unpopular. And to the extent that it discourages firms from issuing or swapping long-term securities, it may *reduce* the amount of stabilizing speculation.

8.2 Multinationals' Foreign Investment Decisions

As we mentioned earlier, there is a second channel by which multinationals influence exchange rates: through their real investment decisions. In this section we briefly review these effects.

Consider for a moment a multinational based in the United Kingdom which has a new low-cost technology for casting engine blocks. The company recognizes there is a great demand for this technology in the United States and may choose to purchase facilities near U.S. auto manufacturers in order to produce the engine blocks locally. There are clearly fixed, nonrecoverable costs for the company to set up a new production site in the United States. Denote these (dollar) costs by F, which might include establishing contacts with U.S. raw materials suppliers, shipping companies, local unions, costs of hiring top management, etc. Expressed in pounds, these costs are Fe, the dollar cost multiplied by the real price of the dollar in terms of the pound. Clearly, if Fe is too high the firm would not wish to produce its product in the United

States. It might elect instead to produce the engine blocks in the United Kingdom and export them, for which the firm incurs the fixed and nonrecoverable cost X.

The firm's decision to produce in the U.S. can affect exchange rates through a flow effect of increased domestic spending. Under a Keynesian model in which productive resources are not used to full capacity, if the firm adds to production in the United States, the result is an increase in U.S. investment spending, or a positive shock to the IS curve. The increase in spending tends to raise output and interest rates and to appreciate the dollar. Notice that if the U.K. firm were to purchase control of an existing engine block facility in the United States, however, investment spending would not rise. There would be no effect on the dollar.

The first point here is that FDI spent on new investments helps stabilize the real exchange rate. If there is a sudden real depreciation of the dollar—enough to generate expectations of future real appreciation—real interest rates in the United States will be low, and foreign firms will take advantage of this by investing Fe in order to produce in the U.S. Firms already exporting to the United States may wish to take advantage of the low real interest rates by shifting some of their production into the United States. While low real interest rates are an incentive for all agents to invest in the United States, the large differences in real interest rates across countries suggest that these incentives are not immediately arbitraged away. The presence of more multinationals on the margin of investing can only help eliminate these differentials. Notice also that improvements in communications technology, air transportation, etc., may lead to reductions in the fixed costs of establishing a foreign production site. Such technical progress would tend to enhance multinationals' stabilizing effects on exchange rate fluctuations.

The second point concerns the volatility of future exchange rates. Lately, a number of authors have focused on how uncertainty about future exchange rates affects the decisions to export.[16] If our U.K. firm had chosen to export to the United States, a large depreciation of the dollar would make the firm uncompetitive enough to sustain losses and even to stop exporting. If future exchange rates are uncertain, there is always a risk that exporting from the United Kingdom will not be a profitable strategy. The riskier are future exchange rates, the more reticent is the firm to commit to spending X in order to begin exporting. Krugman (1988) points out that this effect may feed back to magnify the volatility of the exchange rate. As the exchange rate is more volatile, firms are more reluctant to begin exporting. But as firms are more reluctant to export, the exchange rate must move by more to change the trade balance by a given amount. Thus, under uncertainty the exchange rate equilibrating function fulfilled by trade flows is reduced.

Foreign direct investment, however, is not as sensitive to uncertainty about future exchange rates. When our U.K. firm produces in the United States, it earns a profit, which from the U.K. firm's point of view is subject to exchange rate risk. If the U.K. firm produces in the United Kingdom, then its entire gross revenues, earned in the United States, are subject to exchange risk. But profits are only a tiny fraction of gross revenue. Thus the firm's production location decision will be much less affected by uncertainty in the exchange rate than is its decision to trade as long as Fe is comparable to X. When the United States becomes a low-cost place to produce, foreign firms will take the opportunity to move more of their production there, even when the exchange rate is very volatile. The lower are the costs of relocating production, F, the larger this effect is likely to be. Unlike trade flows, FDI's stabilizing influence on exchange rates is unlikely to be badly eroded by exchange rate uncertainty.

8.3   Net Capital Flows and Foreign Direct Investment

Charles Kindleberger once said that multinationals are about direct investment and not about international financial flows. Yet there are a number of reasons why the separation is artificial. So far we have followed proposition 1 of MM in that we have assumed firms' investment and financing decisions are completely separate. In practice, however, investment and financing decisions are rarely independent. Costs of capital across home and host countries, across firms, and across investment projects can and do vary. These differences can lead to important international financial flows. In this section we discuss two types of distortions which link investments and financing: segmentation of capital markets and taxes. We then turn to assess the importance of these distortions in the recent experience of the United States.

When investment and financing decisions are linked, multinationals will have a portfolio effect on exchange rates. To see this in our previous example, suppose that the United Kingdom changed its tax rules to make FDI tax preferred, and suppose that the firm's cheapest source of financial capital is cash or liquid assets that it has on hand. Foreign demand for U.S.–based production facilities would increase relative to U.S. demand for those facilities. The increase in demand for U.S. assets will appreciate the dollar provided that the price of the plants, equipment, and real estate in the United States are relatively sticky. Notice that, unlike the flow effect above, this effect does not depend on new production facilities being built. The greater demand to buy existing U.S. facilities will itself tend to appreciate the dollar. Finally, notice that the power and presence of a multinational will determine the importance of this effect.

8.3.1   Capital Market Integration, The Cost of Capital, and Investment

If capital markets are segmented, firms will have different costs of capital depending on where they are located and to whom they sell their securities. Much as in the Eurobond example above, firms which can raise money from unsatisfied clienteles will have a lower cost of capital than other firms. In countries with closed domestic capital markets, we would therefore expect to see a positive relationship between FDI and direct investment inflows in the balance of payments.

Consider a small country which is completely closed to FDI and foreign portfolio capital. What criteria will a firm operating in that country use to determine the investment projects it should undertake? If it can issue securities only to domestic residents, then the firm's cost of capital will be determined in part by the domestic capital market. Because domestic residents are not as well diversified as foreign investors (who have access to the world capital market), domestic residents will demand a higher return than foreign investors. Global firms which have access to international capital markets will have a lower cost of capital, and therefore will undertake more investment projects.

An example may help to show this effect. Under the Capital Asset Pricing Model (CAPM) and assuming no taxes, a firm's cost of capital is equal to the riskless rate plus a term measuring the firm's systematic risk:

$$(6) \qquad\qquad E(r) = r_f + \rho \Omega \omega,$$

where r_f is the riskless rate of return, ρ is the market price of risk (equivalent to the coefficient of relative risk aversion), Ω is the $N \times N$ covariance matrix of security returns, and ω is an $N \times 1$ vector of market portfolio weights.[17] The relevant set of N securities included in equation (6) will depend on which investors are purchasing the firm's securities. We assume that domestic residents hold N^d securities in their portfolios and that world residents hold a disjoint set of N^w securities.

For simplicity, we let each asset comprise an equal share of domestic and world portfolios. In order to obtain ballpark estimates of the cost of capital, we use the fact that the average return covariance of two securities from the same country is about 1 percent (per year), and the average own variance of returns is about 15 percent. Based on these numbers and equation (6), the firm's cost of capital from domestic residents is

$$(7) \qquad\qquad E(r) = r_f + \frac{\rho}{N^d}[0.01(N^d - 1) + 0.15].$$

Under the assumptions that ρ, the coefficient of relative risk aversion is 2 and that $r_f = 0.07$, equation (7) implies that the cost of capital from domestic residents is 11.8 percent for $N^d = 10$ and 10.1 percent for $N^d = 25$.

The cost of capital for world residents can be calculated in the same way. There are only two changes. First is that the average covariance between securities across countries is lower, about 0.5 percent. Second, world residents can hold better diversified portfolios. The firm's cost of capital in the world market would then be 8.3 percent if $N^w = 100$ and 8.0 percent if $N^w = \infty$. A global firm with access to the world capital market would find projects with returns between 8 and 10 percent to have positive net present value (NPV), whereas the purely domestic firm would find them to have negative NPV. Thus access to the world capital market is likely to lower a firm's cost of capital and increase investment when capital markets are segmented.

In this way, both the globalization of firms and the liberalization of domestic financial markets will tend to raise domestic investment. As with any other positive goods market shock, the effect is to generate a real appreciation. In this case, however, the increase in investment spending is associated with a capital inflow. Countries with floating currencies will experience a rise in interest rates (for a given monetary policy) and a currency appreciation. For fixed rate countries, the mechanism is that of the "Dutch disease": an increase in domestic spending leads to higher interest rates and a balance of payments surplus, which in turn raises the domestic price level. Either way, as the barriers of a restricted domestic capital market fall, real appreciation is likely to be the result.

Of course, globalization is a slow process, reflecting the inexorable evolution of technology and the reduction in costs of moving production sites. Financial market liberalization, by contrast, can be sudden and deliberate. Thus countries that have liberalized rapidly have seen dramatic reductions in the cost of capital, and have witnessed simultaneous investment booms. In Chile, for example, investment went from 17 percent of GNP in 1979 to 24 percent two years later as the result of the liberalization of its domestic financial markets and capital account. For Chile, as for several other developing countries, the rapid change was debilitating, as the real appreciation lead to expectations of depreciation, and therefore to even higher domestic interest rates.

8.3.2   Exchange Rates, Taxation, and Investment

Financing and investment decisions inevitably become blurred in the face of corporate taxation. In this field, multinationals operate in an extremely complex environment and spend a great deal of resources in tax planning. Taxes create distortions in international financial markets by affecting both the after-tax cash flows and the after-tax costs of raising funds for one national relative to another. Because tax effects are project- and financial-instrument-specific, small changes in the tax code can lead to large changes in firms' behavior. As improvements in technology, transportation, and communications make multinationals more mobile internationally, home and host country corporate tax codes necessarily become more powerful government instruments for influencing foreign investment by domestic multinationals as well as domestic investment by foreign multinationals.[18] In this section we give a brief overview of how corporate tax codes affect multinationals' incentives for FDI.

The most obvious effect on firms' location choices comes from differing marginal tax rates across countries. By locating their headquarters in low-tax rate "havens," some firms can pay far less income tax on earnings repatriated from foreign affiliates. As one might expect, there is enormous variation across countries in effective corporate income taxation.[19] Multinational corporations in tax havens such as Bermuda paid an average effective tax of 0.5 percent of income in 1982, while those in Panama paid an average of 19 percent. These effective tax rates compare very favorably with the average rate across all countries of about 39 percent, and the 36 percent effective rate in the United States.

The evidence that multinationals can increasingly take advantage of international tax havens is presented in table 8.8.[20] The share of income of foreign affiliates of U.S. corporations that is earned in tax havens has almost doubled between 1968 and 1982, rising to about 20 percent of total before-tax income. It is also clear from the table that multinationals across different industries differ in their ability to exploit the advantages of tax havens.

One might guess that much of this income shifting is a result of creative accounting, and that it does not primarily represent an increase in physical investment in these countries. However, gross private fixed investment did rise in most of the tax haven countries from 1968 to 1982, on average by 3.5 percent of GNP. Yet in absolute terms, this does not represent a large amount of investment.

It is likely that other tax practices have a greater impact on the choice of location for subsidiary affiliates. The most overt attempts to encourage foreign direct investment come from explicit subsidies and project-specific tax breaks. Host government financial incentive packages for investment are extremely common. For example, when Volkswagen decided to locate assembly operations in the United States, it received subsidies valued at over $50 million from local, state, and federal governments, as well as a $1.00 per hour wage concession from the U.A.W., which was worth an additional $40 million. The subsidies included municipal interest tax subsidies, foreign trade-zone tax subsidies, and CETA grants.[21] Not all subsidies to investment and project financing require negotiation, however. The province of Quebec in Canada, for example, allows a 10 percent tax credit on salaries paid to research workers. Another example is access to low-interest borrowing, which is a common subsidy to multinational investment in less-developed countries.

Table 8.8   Fraction of Before-Tax Earnings of Foreign Affiliates of U.S. Multinationals Located in Tax Havens

Industry	1968	1972	1980	1982
All Industries	11.0	12.8	14.0	20.2
Finance, insurance and real estate	30.4	35.5	42.5	NA
Wholesale trade	21.5	34.1	22.4	NA
Services	19.2	19.2	19.8	NA
Other industries	7.3	6.2	6.2	NA

Source: Kenadjian (1986).

Direct subsidization of investment, either explicitly or through lower marginal tax rates is an overt means of altering incentives. There are, however, more subtle and potentially more important ways that taxes can effect multinational investment decisions. For example, the United States and many other developed countries grant to foreign affiliates of home corporations a tax credit on foreign income taxes paid. To a first approximation, the foreign tax credit (FTC) may be thought of as adding to the incentives for home corporations to invest abroad. However, this is only a first approximation because the incentive to invest in any given host country is a function of both the home and host countries' corporate income tax codes. When the host and home countries define income differently, taxes paid may not result in taxes credited.[22]

These tax credits have several important effects on multinationals and governments. First, governments interested in foreign direct investment have an incentive to levy high income taxes—in order to provide foreign firms with a larger FTC—while at the same time offering offsetting non–income-based subsidies on investment. These subsidies may either lower the cost of capital for the investment project, or may directly reduce the after-tax cost of investment. Countries (such as some in Western Europe) which rely heavily on value-added taxes (VATs) effectively reduce the incentives for foreign investment, since VATs are not usually refundable through foreign tax credits.

Second, FTCs bias foreign corporations' incentives toward investment in heavily income-taxed investments. The U.S. affiliate of a foreign corporation can get no foreign tax credit on domestic investments that are sheltered from income taxes. Yet, because these investments are preferred by domestic investors, they have lower rates of return. Thus if the foreign affiliate invests in tax-preferred items, it pays an *implicit* tax. International economists will recognize this as an example of comparative advantage: because of the foregone FTC, tax-preferred investments have a *relatively* higher opportunity cost to foreign investors than to domestic investors.

One implication of the FTC is that changes in the domestic tax code which discourage domestic investment in a certain type of asset, encourage foreign investment in that same asset. For example, the U.S. Tax Reform Act (TRA) of 1986 removes several investment tax credits and highly accelerated depreciation rates. For U.S. corporations this makes many investment projects less attractive in comparison with passive investments (such as CDs). Yet the incentives for foreign multinationals to undertake those investment projects improve. Scholes and Wolfson (1988) present data which indicate that in the four quarters following the 1986 TRA, mergers and acquisitions in the United States by foreigners ran at an annual rate of $46 billion.[23] In the year prior to the tax reform act, mergers and acquisitions by foreigners came to only $12 billion. Over the same period, mergers and acquisitions of U.S. companies by U.S. residents *fell* by $33 billion, or about 16.5 percent. This would suggest that the change in taxes improved the relative profitability of takeovers to foreigners while lowering it for domestic residents. It is striking that, although the tax changes were in part intended to discourage mergers and acquisitions, overall M&A activity increased by $1 billion in the year following the reform. Whether a foreign firm should borrow from its parent or itself in the U.S. market will also be determined by relative tax preferences. If firms find assets within the firm to be a cheaper source of financing than selling securities on the open market or borrowing from banks would be, then we would expect such an increase in M&A activity to be associated with capital inflows of direct investment.

In addition to receiving a FTC on income earned abroad, U.S. multinationals may defer U.S. taxes on certain types of foreign-earned income until it is repatriated to the U.S. parent. Specifically, if majority-owned foreign affiliates of U.S. corporations reinvest their foreign earnings in active investments in host countries, where tax rates are often lower than in the United States, they need not pay U.S. income taxes, and can therefore shelter their interest earnings from U.S. taxes. This means that passive investments have high implicit tax rates for foreign affiliates of U.S. corporations. This distinction between passive and active investments, made in Subpart F of the U.S. tax code, was enacted in 1962. A number of other countries have comparable measures.

The policy of deferred domestic taxation combined with the FTC also creates an incentive for U.S. multinationals to repatriate earnings from high-tax countries and actively to reinvest earnings from low-tax countries. In these ways, the U.S. tax laws skew the incentives across foreign investment opportunities as well as the incentives for foreign versus domestic investment. The picture is further complicated, of course, once one takes into account the distortions created by foreign tax codes.

The Tax Reform Act of 1986 clearly creates major changes in incentives for investment and capital inflows by foreign affiliates of U.S. multinationals. And the 1986 TRA is already the fourth major U.S. tax reform bill in the 1980s! Add to this frequent changes in the tax laws of a multitude of countries in which multinationals operate, and it is clear that relative investment incentives in different countries move frequently due to changes in taxes. Each industrial country's tax changes may now influence the investment decisions of all other countries' multinational foreign affiliates.

8.3.3   Foreign Direct Investment Flows into the U.S.

For most international economists, it is difficult to believe that changes in taxation or in other capital market distortions can explain more than a tiny fraction of either the composition of U.S. capital inflows or the dollar's unprecedented swings in the 1980s. Other observers, however, have been more bold. The dollar's appreciation in the early 1980s is sometimes ascribed to the U.S. becoming a "safe haven" for investment and to the passage of the 1981

Economic Recovery Tax Act (ERTA) which purportedly raised the return on physical investments in the U.S.[24] Economists have tended to discount these explanations because during the dollar's appreciation there was little sign of a boom in investment spending.

This rules out much of the flow effect on exchange rates discussed above. However, if there are substantial adjustment costs or other costs to increasing the capital stock, existing assets will provide a higher return than new assets do until their prices fully adjust. Indeed, ERTA is frequently cited for having given U.S. firms an incentive to "churn" their assets, and is often credited with the subsequent boom in takeover activity by U.S. firms.[25] In addition, the 1984 repeal of interest withholding taxes on U.S. corporate bonds issued abroad and the simultaneous switch to bearer-bond status for U.S. Treasury bonds are often credited with causing further dollar appreciation. It is interesting to note that the difference between U.S. and foreign interest rates fell during this period, which corresponds with the predictions of this tax-change view of the dollar.

Data on FDI can shed light on whether capital inflows (and therefore potentially the exchange rate) were affected by major tax changes. Notice that the FDI data measure net purchases of new *and existing* assets. Thus, we might expect tax changes which affect old but not new asset values to show up in the balance of payments data even if those changes have little effect on investment in the national income accounts. The FDI data, however, do a poor job of measuring what we would like to know to gauge the ultimate effect of tax changes on the exchange rate. This would require information on the net increase in dollar exposure by foreign and U.S. multinationals.[26]

Figure 8.4 shows FDI inflows into the United States in relation to U.S. GNP. It is clear that the inflow has increased substantially in the 1980s and is particularly strong during periods of dollar depreciation. The generally higher inflows of the 1980s coincide with the widening overall capital inflow into the United States. Note that there is a discernible increase beginning in the fourth quarter of 1986, when the 1986 TRA was passed. (Recall that the TRA lowered foreign multinationals' relative effective tax rate on active U.S. investments). In addition, there is a drop in the FDI inflow in 1981 when the ERTA was passed. By the same arguments we used earlier, ERTA was likely to have *raised* foreign multinationals' relative effective tax on active U.S. investments.

The major impression created by figure 8.4, however, is that of a strong upward trend. The increase in foreign ownership of U.S. corporations has led to much public controversy. Figure 8.5 shows that much of the commotion is misplaced. The FDI inflow here is measured as a fraction of the total foreign capital inflow into the United States. The tendency toward greater FDI inflows is no longer apparent (except for the spurt around 1980, which is primarily due to a drying up of foreign private capital inflows). Indeed, it is clear that the enormous U.S. current account deficits of the mid-1980s (and possibly the

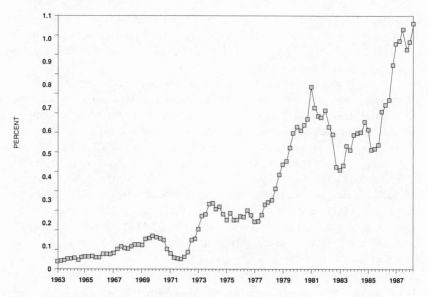

Fig. 8.4   Foreign direct investment inflows into the U.S. (as a percent of U.S. GNP)

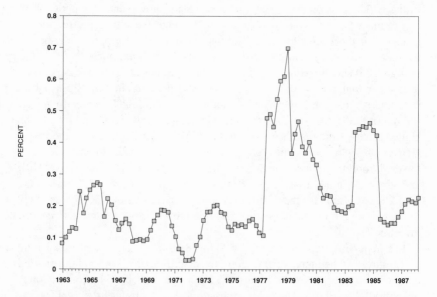

Fig. 8.5   Foreign direct investment inflows into the U.S. (as a fraction of total foreign capital inflows)

1981 tax change) are associated with a change in the composition of inflows toward portfolio investment and away from direct investment. FDI inflows have not kept pace with purchases of U.S. bonds by foreigners.

Naturally, some argue that the U.S. external deficits should have been financed entirely by borrowing instead of by the sale of U.S. corporate control. They think that the FDI inflow should not vary with total U.S. borrowing. Malcolm Forbes is on the record as saying, "It's one thing for Japanese and Germans and others to buy U.S. Government bonds to finance our huge trade imbalances . . . but it's a whole and totally impermissible other thing for them to use their vast billions of dollars to buy great chunks of America's big businesses. . . ."[27] Even though the stock of FDI in the United States has risen rapidly—going from 2 to 6 percent of GNP from 1979–87—it is still below the level of many other countries in which the United States is the major foreign investor.

Next we turn to U.S. FDI outflows. Figure 8.6 shows U.S. FDI abroad as a fraction of total U.S. private capital outflows. The steady downward trend is again a source of concern to some. But note the contrast with figure 8.7, which shows U.S. FDI abroad as a percentage of U.S. GNP. Strikingly, the FDI outflow is, by this measure, larger than twenty-five years ago. The conclusion is that U.S. direct investment abroad has suffered no secular decline. The downward trend seen in figure 8.6 is instead an indication that U.S. residents are taking advantage of foreign financial market liberalization in order to diversify their portfolio holdings.

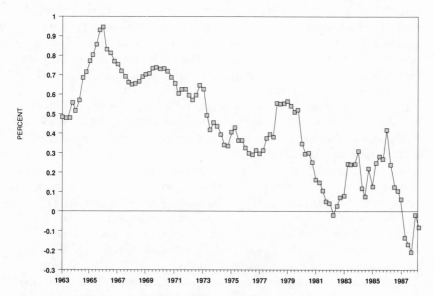

Fig. 8.6   U.S. direct investment outflows (as a fraction of total U.S. capital inflows)

Fig. 8.7   U.S. direct investment outflows (as a percent of U.S. GNP)

Figure 8.7 has two other important implications. First, note that there is a large drop in FDI outflows beginning in 1981. We might expect this from the ERTA changes, which increased U.S. multinationals' relative effective tax rate on foreign investment compared with domestic investment. The Deficit Reduction Act of 1984 eliminated some of this by increasing the depreciable lives of certain assets and by removing the opportunity to postpone the recapture of past depreciation through the use of installment sales.[28] Second, note that the 1986 TRA led to a rapid resumption of high U.S. FDI outflows. This reflects the increase in the relative return to U.S. multinationals of investing in their foreign affiliates.

It is worth mentioning that this corporate tax view of capital flows also has something to say about the welfare effects of FDI. If taxes are in fact responsible for the recent increase in foreign ownership of U.S. businesses, it is the foreign taxpayer, not the U.S. taxpayer, who loses. In shifting toward more heavily taxed U.S. investments, foreign firms add to U.S. Treasury receipts. Because U.S. firms are shifting their investments abroad, this helps offset lower tax revenues from U.S. firms. At the same time, foreign treasuries see their revenues fall, as home-based multinationals qualify for more generous foreign tax credits. Foreign firms' activities are thus subsidized by their own nationals, and the subsidy, in turn, is absorbed by the U.S. Treasury! Foreign taxpayers may end up paying to reduce the U.S. budget deficit.

In sum, it appears that both U.S. direct investment inflows and outflows may be strongly affected by corporate tax changes. More work is needed in this area, as it would be interesting to study earlier tax changes. But it may be that we have entered a new era for the importance of taxes in determining international capital flows. International companies are more mobile than ever before. With the innovations in financial markets, they can respond more rapidly and effectively to profitable investment opportunities. Whether it is a matter of buying a few shares in GM or all of Firestone Tire and Rubber (purchased by the Japanese-owned Bridgestone Corporation for $2.6 billion early in 1988), more information and capital resources are at the disposal of many investors worldwide. The same tax distortions which used to be dismissed as small and unimportant, may now appear large and critical for multinational investment. It would probably be wise to give more forethought to international capital flows when designing corporate tax policies. We have entered an age in which the financial multipliers of tax policy changes may be large.

8.4 Conclusion and Summary

Does the presence of large international corporations make the exchange rate more variable and difficult to control? This paper examines the potential effects that such corporations have on exchange rates and international capital flows. Section 8.1 of the paper looks at financial market innovations that have affected large corporations. It addresses the concerns of those observers who argue that financial innovations have had adverse effects on exchange rate volatility. There is little evidence of such adverse effects, however. First, to the extent that Modigliani-Miller holds, changes in the capital structures of international firms should have no effect on underlying risks or exchange rates. Second, the most important financial innovations for large firms are new markets for securitized corporate borrowing and security swaps. These facilitate trading at longer horizons. The paper reviews, and finds no evidence that supports, the hypothesis that these particular innovations have tended to destabilize exchange rates.

Sections 8.2 and 8.3 of the paper look at how multinationals' international investment activities might conceivably affect exchange rates and capital flows. One important route is through capital market imperfections. These imperfections can create a difference between the cost of capital to certain multinationals and to purely domestic firms. The paper argues that cost-of-capital differentials may help explain international flows of direct investment. It also argues that the tax systems in industrialized countries may be an important source of cost-of-capital differentials. This part of the paper discusses evidence which suggests that changes in corporate tax codes in the 1980s have had a visible impact on U.S. direct investment inflows and outflows. There is little evidence, however, that these capital flows have been important for exchange rate determination.

Notes

1. See Lipsey (1988) for a survey of U.S. multinational trade and investment.

2. It is interesting to note that it took economists a long time to understand this apparently obvious point. Mehra (1974) was the first to prove that the MM propositions also hold for a two-country capital market with stochastic exchange rates.

3. Notice that borrowing and lending is not the only way for the investor to achieve payoffs equivalent to $E_\$$. He could take a long position in a DM futures contract, which would replicate borrowing $D_\$$ dollars and lending the equivalent dollar amount of DM.

4. See Frankel (1982), Froot (1988), Froot and Frankel (1989), and Hodrick (1987).

5. In going from equation (1) to equation (2) we use the fact that for normally distributed random variables, $\text{cov}[f(x),y] = f'(x)\text{cov}(x,y)$. See Rubinstein (1976). We would get the same result even without normality if trading takes place continuously.

6. For a complete survey of international financial innovation, see Levich (1988).

7. These restrictions included penalties on U.S. banks for new loans made to foreigners and mandatory controls on capital transfers for U.S. corporations to their foreign affiliates. The controls discouraged both foreign borrowing from U.S. sources and repatriation of U.S. profits from foreign sources.

8. Mahajan and Fraser (1986) also find the average differential to be negative. In their 1975–83 sample, however, the differential is not statistically different from zero.

9. See *Institutional Investor* (1984, 1985).

10. See Cooper (1986) for an in-depth discussion of financial market innovation.

11. See, for example, Shiller (1981), Campbell and Shiller (1986), and Froot (1988). Of course, these findings can never be conclusive because fundamentals may be moving in ways not captured by the models being tested, biasing the results toward finding "excessive" volatility.

12. See, for example, Black (1986).

13. See Stein (1987), who presents a model in which the introduction of rational speculators destabilizes prices and lowers the welfare of other agents in the model.

14. Continuous-time stochastic processes are of unbounded variation, which means that as the sampling interval shrinks to zero, the fraction of price variation due to stochastic changes converges to one.

15. See Frankel and Froot (1988) for tests of these propositions.

16. See Baldwin and Krugman (1987) and Krugman (1988).

17. Equation (6) can be rewritten in the more familiar CAPM form as follows. Multiplying equation (6) by ω', the vector of portfolio weights, gives $E(r_m) = r_f + \rho\omega'\Omega\omega$. Using this expression, equation (6) becomes

$$E(r) - r_f = \frac{\Omega\omega}{\omega'\Omega\omega}[E(r_m) - r_f] = \beta[E(r_m) - r_f],$$

where β_i is the usual covariance of the ith asset with the market divided by the variance of the market.

18. For an interesting discussion of these issues see Blumenthal (1987).

19. See the discussion in Hines (1988), from which some of the following material is drawn.

20. In this table, countries designated as tax havens are the Bahamas, the Netherlands Antilles, Bermuda, Panama, Hong Kong, Liberia, Luxembourg, and Switzerland.

21. See Baldwin (1986) for a detailed analysis of the Volkswagen case.

22. Canada, for example, permits generous depreciation allowances on fixed investment. Because the U.S. law is stricter, a portion of a Canadian affiliates' income would not be considered income in the United States, and therefore the FTC for

investments in Canada is less valuable than it would be for investments in other countries. Even leaving these factors out, the ultimate effects on foreign investment of foreign tax are sensitive to a variety of assumptions. See Hartman (1985) and Hines (1988).

23. This is the total value of publicly traded stock purchased by foreigners in mergers and acquisitions of U.S. companies. To the extent that some of this was borrowed from third parties, the amount of FDI recorded in the balance of payments is smaller.

24. Canto (1988) goes so far as to argue that changes in marginal tax rates explain the dollar's entire 1981–84 appreciation, part of its 1985–87 depreciation, and all of its mid-1988 appreciation.

25. Mergers and acquisitions by and of U.S. firms doubled between 1980 and 1981. See Gilson, Scholes, and Wolfson (1987).

26. The FDI data on inflows report increases in foreign ownership of U.S. establishments that are either owned or acquired by foreigners. An establishment is considered foreign owned if a foreign entity owns more than 10 percent. Increases in ownership are defined net of all borrowing, unless the borrowing is done through the foreign parent. Tax changes will not create capital inflows to finance foreign direct investment if the cost of capital to foreign firms is lowest in the United States.

27. Quoted in Tolchin (1988).

28. See Scholes and Wolfson (1988).

References

Baldwin, C. 1986. The capital factor: Competing for capital in a global environment. In M. Porter, ed., *Competition in global industries,* 185–224. (Boston: Harvard Business School Press).

Baldwin, R., and P. Krugman. 1987. Persistent trade effects of large exchange rate shocks. MIT. Mimeograph.

Black, F. 1986. Noise, *Journal of Finance* 41: 529–43.

Blumenthal, M. 1987. Root Lectures, Council on Foreign Relations.

Campbell, J., and R. Shiller. 1986. The dividend-price ratio and expectations of future dividends and discount factors. NBER Working Paper no. 2100. Cambridge, MA: National Bureau of Economic Research.

Canto, V. 1988. Tax rates move currencies, and there's no easy fix. *New York Times,* September 23.

Caves, R. 1982. *Multinational Enterprise and Economic Analysis* (London: Cambridge University Press).

Cooper, I. 1986. Innovations: New market instruments. *Oxford Review of Economic Policy* 2: 1–17.

Frankel, J. 1982. In search of the exchange risk premium: A six currency test of mean-variance optimization. *Journal of International Money and Finance* 1: 255–74.

Frankel, J., and K. Froot. 1988. Chartists fundamentalists and the demand for dollars. In T. Courakis and M. Taylor, eds. *Policy issues for interdependent economies,* (London: Macmillan).

French, K., and R. Roll. 1986. Stock return variances: The arrival of information and the reaction of traders. *Journal of Financial Economics* 17: 5–26.

Froot, K. 1988. Tests of excess forecast volatility in the foreign exchange and stock markets. MIT. Mimeograph.

Froot, K., and J. Frankel. 1989. Forward discount bias: Is it an exchange risk premium? *Quarterly Journal of Economics* 104 (February): 139–61.

Froot, K., and T. Ito. 1989. On the consistency of short-run and long-run exchange rate expectations. *Journal of International Money and Finance* 8 (December): 487–510.

Gilson, R., M. Scholes, and M. Wolfson. 1987. Taxation and the dynamics of corporate control: The uneasy case for tax-motivated acquisitions. In J. Coffee, L. Lowenstein, and S. Rose-Ackerman, eds. *Knights, raiders and targets: The impact of the hostile takeover* (London: Oxford University Press).

Goodhart, C. 1987. The foreign exchange market: A random walk with a dragging anchor. London School of Economics. Typescript.

Hartman, D. 1985. Tax policy and foreign direct investment. *Journal of Public Economics* 26: 107–21.

Hines, J. 1988. Taxation and U.S. multinational investment. In L. Summers, ed. *Tax policy and the economy, 2.* (Cambridge: MIT Press).

Hodrick, R. 1987. *The empirical evidence on the efficiency of forward and futures foreign exchange markets* (Chur, Switzerland: Harwood).

Hymer, S. H. 1976. The international operations of multinational firms: A study of direct foreign investment. Cambridge, MA: MIT Press. (Ph.D. Diss., MIT, 1960.)

Institutional Investor. 1984. Clouds over morning-to-midnight defeasance. (June): 37–40.

————. 1985. Borrowing as a profit center. (August): 211–14.

Kenadjian, B. 1986. Levels and significance of tax haven use by controlled foreign corporations. U.S. Treasury. Mimeograph.

Kidwell, D., M. Marr, and G. Thompson. 1985. Eurodollar bonds: Alternative financing for U.S. companies. *Financial Management* (Winter): 18–27.

Kim, Y. C., and R. Stulz. 1988. The Eurobond market and corporate financial policy: A test of the clientele hypothesis. *Journal of Financial Economics* 22 (December): 189–206.

Kindleberger, C. 1969. *American business abroad: Six lectures on direct investment* (New Haven: Yale University Press).

Krugman, P. 1988. *Exchange rate instability* (Cambridge: MIT Press).

Levich, R. 1988. Financial innovations in international financial markets. In M. Feldstein, ed. *The United States in the world economy,* 215–56. (Chicago: University of Chicago Press).

Lipsey, R. 1988. Changing patterns of international investment in and by the U.S. In M. Feldstein, ed. *The United States in the world economy,* 475–544. (Chicago: University of Chicago Press).

McKinnon, R. 1979. *Money in international exchange: The convertible currency system.* (London: Oxford University Press).

Mahajan, A., and D. Fraser. 1986. Dollar Eurobonds and U.S. bond pricing. *Journal of International Business Studies* (Summer): 21–36.

Mehra, R. 1974. On the financing and investment decisions of multinational firms in the presence of exchange risk. *Journal of Financial and Quantitative Analysis* 13: 227–44.

Modigliani, F., and M. Miller. 1958. The cost of capital, corporation finance and the theory of investment. *American Economic Review* 48: 261–97.

Nurkse, R. 1944. *International Currency Experience* (Geneva, Switzerland: League of Nations).

Rubinstein, M. 1976. The valuation of uncertain income streams and the pricing of options. *Bell Journal of Economics* 7 (Autumn): 407–25.

Scholes, M., and M. Wolfson. 1988. The effects of changes in tax laws on corporate reorganization activity. Stanford University. Mimeograph.

Shiller, R. J. 1981. Do stock prices move too much to be justified by subsequent changes in dividends? *American Economic Review* 71: 421–36.

Stein, J. 1987. Informational externalities and welfare-reducing speculation. *Journal of Political Economy* 95: 1123–45.

Tolchin, M. 1988. Foreigners' investing: A warning. *New York Times*, February 22.

Comment   Geoffrey Carliner

Since the end of fixed exchange rates in the early 1970s, the dollar has fluctuated dramatically in relation to other major currencies. Especially during the 1980s, the real as well as the nominal value of the dollar has varied sharply. Partly as a result, the U.S. trade deficit has become a serious problem; finance ministers from the G–7 countries have met regularly to discuss exchange rate coordination; and economists have written volumes like the present one to review past attempts at coordination and examine possible future efforts by major countries to keep their currencies in line.

One common response to critics of the floating rate system is that international capital flows are now too large for a fixed rate system to function successfully. In the 1960s virtually all countries had controls on capital flows, and defending currencies against speculative attacks was within the power of central banks. In the 1980s, according to some supporters of the floating rate system, capital markets in the industrial economies are so integrated that a fixed rate system is no longer possible.

It is clear from Ken Froot's analysis that multinationals, acting as producers of goods and services in many countries, have not played a large part in the exchange rate fluctuations of the 1980s. If anything, their foreign direct investments have tended to stabilize the long-run value of the dollar. In any event, foreign direct investment by multinationals is dwarfed by international flows of portfolio capital. If international capital flows have in fact destabilized exchange rates or made fixed rate systems unworkable, it is clearly the actions of financial institutions rather than multinationals that are responsible.

One fact cited by Froot and by Goodhart (1987) brings this point home: 90 percent of the trading in foreign-exchange markets is between banks, and only 10 percent is between banks and their customers. It is this huge flow of assets across international borders, done primarily by banks for their own account, that makes a fixed exchange rate system so hard to imagine.

Other financial institutions besides banks have also become important players in foreign-exchange markets during the past decade. Thanks to capital market liberalizations, Japanese insurance companies and pension funds have joined American mutual funds, Swiss banks, and Dutch investment trusts in the buying and selling of foreign portfolio capital. Ten years ago there were tight limits on the percentage of assets which Japanese fund managers could

Geoffrey Carliner is the Executive Director of the National Bureau of Economic Research.

invest abroad. Today these limits are much higher. Ten years ago, U.S. mutual funds had a much smaller share of U.S. financial assets, and they invested only a tiny fraction of their portfolios abroad. Today, U.S. mutual funds have a larger share of total financial assets, and a significantly higher fraction is in foreign stocks and bonds.

It is true that multinationals can speculate in foreign-exchange markets along with financial institutions. The actions of Exxon and Pepsico in Eurobond markets, cited by Froot, are good examples. By moving their liquid assets from one country to another in response to interest differentials and expected exchange rate movements, multinationals as well as banks and other financial institutions now make the job of maintaining fixed exchange rates far more difficult. However, when they engage in these transactions, they are no different from other owners of financial assets and are not acting as multinationals, in Froot's words, as companies which manage production facilities in more than one country.

Foreign investments by multinationals may in fact respond to exchange rate fluctuations, but in a way that would dampen rather than amplify these fluctuations. In another paper with Stein (1989), Froot reports that FDI into the United States increased by $5 billion for every 10 percent fall in the value of the dollar between 1973 and 1988. The dollar's decline is thus associated with an increase in demand for dollars by multinationals who wish to buy nonfinancial U.S. assets. This increase in demand for dollars by multinationals will of course tend to offset the decline in the dollar's value. Froot and Stein suggest that this increase in FDI is the result of the greater ability of foreign firms to obtain external financing for their investments when the dollar value of their equity rises as a result of the fall in the dollar exchange rate.

When multinationals enter foreign-currency markets in their role as producers, either to invest abroad or to repatriate earnings, they are likely to be motivated by factors other than exchange rate speculation or to lean against it. Hines and Hubbard (1990) have shown that tax considerations dominate the timing of repatriation of foreign profits by U.S. multinationals. Under U.S. law, profits earned abroad are not taxed until they are repatriated. Hines and Hubbard found that U.S. multinationals waited to bring their overseas profits home until they could use foreign tax credits to minimize the taxes owed to the U.S. government. Repatriation was thus not sensitive to fluctuations in the value of the dollar but rather depended on their profits and tax liabilities at home and abroad.

As Froot points out in the present paper, the possibilities of international coordination of tax policies may be at least as great as the possibilities for international coordination of exchange rates. Without coordination, multinationals and other owners of capital can exploit international differences in tax codes to minimize their taxes. Countries that are too small to be important producers or consumers of the products of multinationals can serve as tax havens that allow these firms to avoid taxes in all countries. A failure to coordinate among countries can even lead to tax competition of the sort that has sometime plagued groups of states in the United States.

Froot's paper conclusively answers the question which he set out to answer: multinational corporations acting as producers of goods and services in more than one country do *not* tend to increase exchange rate fluctuations. If anything, they tend to dampen these fluctuations. Rather, it is the loosening of capital controls and the growth of financial institutions that has made international exchange rate coordination more difficult if not impossible. However, the growth of multinationals does raise questions about the need for international coordination of tax policies. Those issues certainly deserve some of the attention which exchange rate coordination has received during recent years.

References

Froot, Kenneth, and Jeremy Stein. 1989. Exchange rates and foreign direct investment: An imperfect capital markets approach. NBER Working Paper No. 2914. Cambridge, MA: National Bureau of Economic Research.
Goodhart, C. 1987. The foreign exchange market: A random walk with a dragging anchor. London School of Economics. Typescript.
Hines, James, Jr., and R. Glenn Hubbard. 1990. Coming home to America: Dividend repatriations by U. S. multinationals. In A. Razin and J. Slemrod, eds., *Taxation in the global economy,* Chicago: University of Chicago Press.

Comment   J. S. Flemming

This wide-ranging paper touches on many related issues to which it contributes either analytical insights or novel data. It thus clarifies areas which are subject to widespread confusion, mystery, and prejudice. Its range does however diminish the structure of the argument and the coherence of its conclusions which are scattered through the text.

I have half a dozen comments, some on what Kenneth Froot has said and two on themes he might have been expected to address but did not—at least explicitly.

Among the financial developments of recent years has been an increase in securitization as the LDC debt problem reduced the credit worthiness of many banks relative to their corporate customers. This has led to disintermediation as the margin available to banks narrowed or disappeared. Notice, however, that a guarantee even from an inferior source adds to the value of any security as long as there is a chance that the guarantor will survive some events leading to default by the primary issuer.

J. S. Flemming is an Executive Director of the Bank of England.

This is the basis of the acceptance business on which the London merchant banks were built and also plays an important role in explaining modern currency and interest rate swaps.

Froot argues correctly that exchange rate instability militates more strongly against trade than foreign direct investment, but he does not draw out the point that much of the undeterred FDI displaces the deterred trade. Moreover, FDI itself is likely to be reduced to the extent that in the absence of exchange risk a U.K. firm might have planned to meet Pacific demand from a U.S. plant.

Again, in the risk area, the comparison of open and closed economies is not straightforward. In a closed economy with limited scope for diversification, people may save more and depress the return on safe (or indeed any given risk level of) investment below that available elsewhere, contrary to Froot's implicit assumption of a uniform safe rate.

It is sometimes suggested that because multinational corporations are more sensitive to relative costs in, for example, their sourcing decisions than other firms are, they contribute to closer adherence to PPP. Though they may be assumed to have the relevant information, so may international buying agencies, and multinational corporations' plants in different countries are as subject to the costs of adjustment of switching production as any others. Moreover, to the extent that they have market power, they may be even better placed to discriminate in their pricing between different markets—as the automobile industry in particular shows.

On the more general question whether financial innovation by enhancing hedging opportunities reduces the effectiveness of interest and exchange rate policies, I think that a negative answer would be consistent with the thrust of Froot's arguments. Such instruments may eliminate the income effects of unexpected developments but do nothing to blunt their substitution effects.

9   Adequacy of International Transactions and Position Data for Policy Coordination

Lois Stekler

The use of international policy coordination to limit exchange rate fluctuations assumes that there are generally agreed upon measures of disequilibruim. Frequently mentioned in this context are current accounts and international indebtedness. The focus of this paper is the adequacy of data on current accounts and international investment positions as measures of the need for policy adjustments and coordination. Since I am most familiar with U.S. data, much of the discussion will focus on the U.S. current account and position.

There are several reasons for questioning the adequacy of current account and position data for use as measures of disequilibruim requiring international policy adjustments and coordination. High on this list has been the growth during the past decade in two discrepancies: the global current account discrepancy and the statistical discrepancy in the U.S. international transactions accounts.

9.1   Global Current Account Discrepancy

If data collection were completely accurate, each export recorded by one country would be matched by an equal import recorded by another country; the sum of all trade and services transactions for the whole world would equal zero. In practice, they do not sum to zero; reported imports of goods and services exceed reported exports. Moreover, as shown in table 9.1, this discrepancy has been very large in the 1980s and, although down substantially from the peak of $106 billion reached in 1982, it shows little sign of disappearing. The largest problems appear to be in the services accounts. When account is taken of the

Lois Stekler is an Economist at the Board of Governors of the Federal Reserve System.
Opinions expressed in this paper are those of the author and should not be attributed to any other individual or organization.

Table 9.1 Global Current Account Discrepancy

	1980	1981	1982	1983	1984	1985	1986	1987	1988*	1989*
Balance on Current Account[a]										
Industrial countries	-58.8	-17.0	-20.9	-18.5	-57.7	-50.8	-19.3	-49.4	-49.8	-51.1
Developing countries	30.6	-48.6	-86.9	-64.0	-33.5	-24.3	-38.9	4.4	-7.9	-8.4
Other countries[b]	0.8	-3.0	2.1	3.0	5.1	1.7	0.8	0.4	0.2	-0.3
Total[c]	-27.3	-68.6	-105.7	-79.5	-86.1	-73.5	-57.3	-44.6	-57.5	-59.8
Total by Selected Category										
Trade balance	30.9	18.1	-1.5	3.3	9.6	9.3	5.9	35.6	34.8	39.3
Timing[d]	11.0	-3.5	-9.4	1.0	-1.0	12.9	8.5	20.0	18.0	16.0
Residual asymmetry	19.9	21.6	7.9	2.3	10.6	-3.6	-2.5	15.6	16.8	23.3
Balance on services	-43.6	-74.5	-89.7	-72.8	-86.2	-72.4	-51.3	-64.0	-77.4	-83.6
(% of service payments)	-5.8	-8.7	-10.5	-9.3	-10.5	-8.8	-5.8	-6.1	-6.6	-6.7
Private transfers, net	-0.1	0.2	-1.6	—	2.2	1.4	4.1	6.2	5.7	6.4
Official transfers, net	-14.5	-12.5	-12.9	-10.1	-11.7	-11.7	-16.0	-22.3	-20.7	-21.9

Note: In billions of dollars.

Source: IMF (1988, 143).

[a]Including official transfers.

[b]Covers estimated balances on current transactions only in convertible currencies of the U.S.S.R. and nonmember countries of Eastern Europe.

[c]Reflects errors, omissions, and asymmetries in reported balance of payments statistics on current account, plus balances with countries not included.

[d]Staff estimates of the difference between the beginning-of-year and end-of-year "float," that is, the value of those exports that have not yet been recorded as imports (usually because the goods are in transit or because of delays in the processing of the documentation). The estimates should be viewed as only rough orders of magnitude.

*IMF projections.

fact that shipping goods takes time and that exports at the end of one year may be recorded as imports in the next year, the residual asymmetry in the trade balance is positive and relatively small. The large negative discrepancy appears to be mainly the result of services transactions.

In response to the growing global discrepancy, the IMF set up a working party to investigate the reasons for its growth and to assess its implications for the usefulness of countries' current account positions as indicators of the need for policy adjustments. The working party concentrated on five areas: direct investment income, portfolio investment income, offshore financial centers and financial innovations, shipping and transportation, and unrequited transfers.

The working party concluded that the most important source of the global discrepancy was portfolio investment income and that the overriding factor was the emergence of a large body of cross-border assets recognized by the debtor countries but not by the creditors, coupled with a higher level of interest rates after 1979 (IMF 1987, 12). Working party members reached this conclusion by comparing reported credits and debits with estimates based upon independent information on outstanding stocks of cross-border assets and liabilities and estimates of appropriate yields. In particular, heavy reliance was placed on the banking data reported to the Bank for International Settlements (BIS).

The resulting adjustments to portfolio investment income were widespread; the working party added net credits to the current accounts of most world areas. Table 9.2 reproduces the working party's allocation of the services and transfer discrepancy, by country groups, for 1983. For a more detailed analysis, the interested reader is referred to the report of the working party (IMF 1987). In conclusion, the working party judged that the additions to countries' net current account receipts were not so concentrated in any single country or group of countries as to invalidate the basic thrust of analyses drawn from the uncorrected figures.

9.2   U.S. Statistical Discrepancy

In contrast to the global discrepancy investigated by the IMF, the U.S. statistical discrepancy need not reflect errors and omissions in the reporting of current account transactions. In principle, the sum of all transactions in the U.S. balance of payments accounts, a double-entry bookkeeping system, should equal zero; for each transaction there should be two equal entries of opposite sign. In practice, the recorded accounts never sum exactly to zero because the data that would reflect the debit and credit counterparts of each single transaction generally are obtained from different sources. A positive statistical discrepancy represents some combination of net unrecorded exports of goods and services to foreigners and net unreported capital inflows from abroad.

Table 9.2   Allocation of Services and Transfer Discrepancy, 1983

Country Group	Income on Investments				Shipment and Transport	Other Services	Transfers	Total Current Account, Excluding Merchandise
	Reinvested earnings	Other direct investment income	Nondirect investment income	Total				
Industrial countries	−5.3	+4.4	+13.9	+13.0	+1.0	—	—	+14.0
Middle East oil exporters	−0.1	+4.0	+2.0	+5.9	+7.6	—	−2.0	+11.5
Offshore banking centers	−1.9	−3.7	+6.0	+0.4	+2.5	—	—	+2.9
Other developing countries	−3.1	+0.6	+5.5	+3.0	+10.4	—	+3.4	+16.8
Eastern European countries	—	—	−3.7	−3.7	+0.8	—	—	−2.9
International organizations	—	—	+3.1	+3.1	—	−7.0	+7.0	+3.1
Unallocated	—	—	+5.9	+5.9	+6.7	—	—	+12.6
Total	−10.4	+5.3	+32.8	+27.7	+29.0	−7.0	+8.4	+58.1

Note: In billions of dollars.

Source: IMF (1987, 109).

The growth of the statistical discrepancy in the U.S. international transactions accounts is a relatively recent development. In both the 1950s and the 1960s the statistical discrepancy was close to zero (see fig. 9.1). In contrast, during the early 1970s there were substantial net unrecorded outflows or payments. Since 1974 a positive statistical discrepancy indicating net unrecorded receipts or inflows has developed. This increase in magnitude is not just the result of the inflation of nominal values. Consider, for example, the ratio of the statistical discrepancy to the value of trade (the average of recorded exports and imports of goods and services). The mean absolute value of this ratio was 0.02 in the 1950s and the 1960s, but 0.05 in the 1970s and 0.06 in the 1980s. The peak values for this ratio in the postwar period were 0.14 in 1971 and 0.10 in 1982.

9.2.1 Possible Explanations

Early Focus on Capital Flows

In the early 1980s, it was assumed that the sudden increase in the positive discrepancy was largely accounted for by unrecorded capital flows. The wide quarterly swings in the size of the statistical discrepancy also supported that conclusion. It was recognized that errors and omissions occurred in the

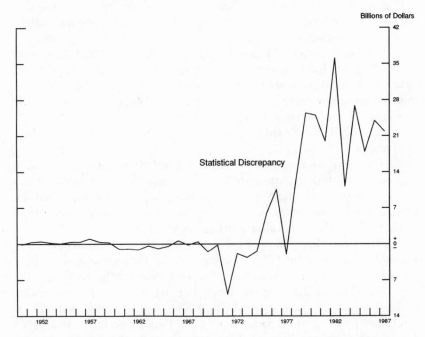

Fig. 9.1   Statistical discrepancy in U.S. international transactions accounts
Source: Survey of Current Business.

reporting of trade transactions, but there seemed little reason to assume that these errors would suddenly increase or that they would vary widely from quarter to quarter.

Previous periods of relatively large positive statistical discrepancies had coincided with unsettled political and economic conditions abroad. The ratio of the value of the statistical discrepancy to trade was about as high as or higher than the 1979–80 levels (0.08) in certain Depression years (1934, 1935, and 1937), in the early years of World War II (1939–41), and in 1948. It seemed reasonable to assume that these earlier episodes were associated with the flight of capital to a safe haven in the United States in forms that were not fully reported, either because these investors wanted to remain anonymous or because the reporting system failed to catch many small investors. The only other year since World War II when the statistical discrepancy was relatively large, although negative, was 1971. It seemed plausible to assume that expectations of dollar depreciation plus certain capital export restraints had led to unrecorded capital outflows in that year. The revolution in Iran in 1978 and the second oil crisis, combined with the rapid accumulation of wealth in OPEC hands and the U.S. freeze of Iranian assets, were all considered potential contributing factors to the unrecorded inflows in 1979 and 1980.

Evidence of Unreported Capital Flows

In general, it is not possible to check the data on U.S. capital flows used in the international transactions accounts against data on the same transactions from other sources. Most countries do not collect detailed information on capital flows, by country. Moreover, even where they do, there is little basis for deciding which data are correct. In addition, analysis is complicated by the central role of financial centers like London, which do not collect data on transactions by foreigners in foreign securities. For example, in the U.S. data, new issues of Eurobonds by U.S. corporations show up as sales of securities to underwriters in the United Kingdom, but the U.K. data would not include these transactions.

Data comparisons are possible with the few countries that collect detailed data on capital flows broken down by country and for certain bank transactions. In both cases, these data comparisons suggest that there may be substantial errors and omissions in the data on U.S. international capital flows included in the U.S. international transactions accounts.

Much has been made in the press in recent years about apparent discrepancies between U.S. and Japanese data on Japanese purchases of U.S. Treasury securities. Unfortunately, precise comparisons are not possible on the basis of published data because these data are aggregated in somewhat different ways.[1] The U.S. data indicate that residents of Japan (both official and private) purchased net virtually no U.S. Treasury securities in 1986 or 1987 and that, with purchases of other bonds and stocks, Japanese investments in U.S. securities amounted to approximately $13 billion in 1986 and $14 billion in 1987. Japanese data indicate private Japanese residents alone purchased net $49 billion in U.S. securities in 1986 and $37 billion in 1987. Anecdotal evidence would seem to support the Japanese data, but this impression is largely based upon the participation of the U.S. offices of Japanese-owned securities firms in the U.S. Treasury auctions. These offices did not report significant net sales of Treasury securities to Japan in these years.

It is likely that the discrepancy between U.S. and Japanese data on securities purchases reflects inadequacies in both reporting systems. Confusion about reporting responsibility is likely to occur in the U.S. system when the U.S. offices of Japanese firms place orders for securities for their head offices. The seller of the securities may not know that the purchaser is the foreign office, while the U.S. office of the Japanese firm may not report the sale because, technically, they never owned the securities. However, confusion is also possible in the Japanese reports of transactions by country. Transactions may be reported according to the nationality of the debtor, where the security is listed, or according to the residence of the transactor. Only if the data are reported on the last basis would it be consistent with the U.S. data and, therefore, a check on U.S. data accuracy. In the U.S. data, Japanese purchases of U.S. Treasury securities in the London market or purchases of Eurobonds issued by U.S. corporations would not be recorded as sales to Japan.

In addition to comparisons of U.S. data with data collected by other countries for balance of payments purposes, it is also possible to compare U.S. data with data collected by bank regulatory authorities. The BIS receives reports from a large number of countries on banks' claims on and liabilities to bank and nonbank residents of many countries. (These data on cross-border bank transactions are also published in modified form by the IMF.) In theory, the claims of banks in a foreign country on U.S. banks should match the liabilities of U.S. banks to banks in that country. In practice, precise comparisons are difficult because of differences in definitions. Many foreign countries include in their reports holdings by banks of securities issued by U.S. banks; U.S. banks exclude securities from their reported liabilities. (Changing the U.S. reports to include these would be difficult because the banks have little information on who holds their securities.) U.S. banks include in their reports custody holdings of negotiable instruments such as bankers' acceptances and commercial paper, which need not be the liabilities of banks in the United States. In addition, they report as custody liabilities, loans to U.S. nonbanks that are booked at their offices outside the United States. In foreign reports, these would be included in claims on U.S. nonbanks. The BIS and the IMF are currently working on comparisons of countries' data and attempting to explain the reasons for discrepancies.

Finally, some comparisons are possible between the U.S. international transactions data and data collected by the Federal Reserve Board on U.S. nonbanks' borrowing from and deposits at banks outside the United States. A special survey covering the end of 1982, completed by the Federal Reserve with the cooperation of foreign governments, indicated that the U.S. international transactions data understated dollar deposits abroad of U.S. nonbank residents by about $75 billion and claims of banks abroad on U.S. nonbanks by about $25 billion. A clarification by the U.S. Treasury of reporting responsibility in mid-1986 led to a significant improvement in coverage of bank loans to U.S. nonbanks in the U.S. data, although the question of when these capital inflows occurred was left unanswered and some inflows still appear to be omitted. However, the large omission of deposits outside the United States has not been dealt with. The Federal Reserve now regularly collects data on such deposits for inclusion in M3, but these data are not used in the U.S. international transactions accounts because of unresolved problems of double-counting and the lack of geographic information. Comparison of Federal Reserve data with the U.S. international transactions data indicates that substantial capital flows continue to be omitted. BIS data on banks' liabilities to U.S. nonbanks are roughly comparable to the Federal Reserve data.

There are a substantial number of reasons to believe that inadequacies in the reporting of U.S. capital flows are likely to increase in coming years. Growing securitization of international capital flows has shifted transactions off the balance sheets of banks, who tend to be relatively accurate reporters. In addition, the growing sophistication of U.S. corporations and individuals has increased the volume of transactions directly with intermediaries located outside the United States (and beyond the reach of U.S. reporting requirements). In either case, it is much easier to monitor reporting by a few large banks than to gather accurate information from thousands of corporations and wealthy investors. Moreover, technological changes and innovations require constant monitoring and efforts to clear up questions of reporting responsibilities that were not foreseen when report forms were designed.

Inadequacies of Data on Investment Income

If the data on U.S. capital flows are inadequate, then certain components of investment income will be inadequate as well. There are no direct reports of income on private portfolio claims and liabilities and only partial reports on U.S. government interest payments to foreigners. These income flows are estimated by the Department of Commerce from information on the level of assets and estimated rates of return. Estimates of the level of assets depend, in turn, on periodic benchmark surveys combined with subsequent recorded capital flows and rough valuation adjustments. Benchmark surveys of foreign portfolio investments in the United States are conducted regularly, but the last survey of U.S. portfolio assets abroad dates from World War II. Errors in valuation adjustments made since that date could potentially cumulate to a substantial sum. In addition, omission of capital flows from the reporting system, such as the increase in U.S. nonbanks' Eurodollar deposits discussed above, would lead to the understatement of portfolio investment income. Based on alternative (higher) estimates of U.S. nonbanks deposits at banks abroad and liabilities to banks abroad, the IMF working party estimated that U.S. net investment income was underestimated by about $4 billion in 1983. Since 1983, Treasury International Capital (TIC) reporting of liabilities to banks abroad has been improved, but reporting of claims has not, so current U.S. net investment income is probably underestimated by several billions more.

Errors will also be introduced into the estimates of portfolio investment income if the Commerce Departments' estimates of rates of return are inaccurate. The Commerce Department does periodically review the rates they use with major banks and other financial institutions in an attempt to keep up with the evolution of financial markets. However, there are inevitable problems; to illustrate, the role of the prime rate in bank lending has diminished dramatically in recent years, and the spread over LIBOR (London interbank offer rate) paid by particular countries may vary. In addition, the capital flows data frequently aggregate a mixture of instruments that pay differing rates of return; little information is available on how they should be weighted. For example, data on debt securities with maturities of more than one year are aggregated. However, the interest on thirty-year bonds can differ substantially from the rate on two-year notes that are due in thirty days. Moreover, fees on off-balance sheet transactions are becoming increasingly important to banks; efforts are currently underway to improve estimates of income associated with these transactions. In conclusion, despite the best efforts of the Department of Commerce, there are, undoubtedly, inaccuracies in the rates of return they use to estimate portfolio investment income. However, it is not clear that there would be any systematic bias in these errors, leading to a consistent over- or underestimation of receipts or payments.

In contrast to private portfolio receipts and payments, direct investment receipts and payments are directly reported by businesses. The reporting system is extensive, and missing reporters are likely to be small investors, so that only small amounts would be unaccounted for. However, the very low rate of return on assets reported by foreign direct investors in the United States does raise questions. Much foreign investment in the United States (as well as U.S. direct investment abroad) is in the form of wholly owned subsidiaries; companies try to minimize their tax burdens by using intercompany transactions to shift profits from high to low tax jurisdictions. The IRS recently reached an agreement to collect substantial back taxes from Toyota and Nissan on the grounds that they understated their U.S. profits by overcharging their affiliates for imported cars. If they had declared the same inflated value for the cars when they were imported, this would just shift payments from services to merchandise trade and not contribute to the statistical discrepancy. However, apparently it was common practice to declare a lower value for customs purposes than was used in calculating profits (contributing a negative value to the statistical discrepancy); the IRS has issued a rule in 1987 ending this practice by foreign investors in the United States. U.S. direct investors abroad have similar incentives to shift profits to lower tax jurisdictions, overstating direct investment receipts. However, this would have little impact on the statistical discrepancy unless they declared one price for exports to their affiliates in U.S. export documents and used another in calculating the profits of their affiliates. (The failure of multinational companies to adequately charge their foreign affiliates for R&D expenditures, central administration costs, etc., would just shift receipts from services to direct investment, and not affect the net current account.)

Inadequacy of Data on Other Services and Unilateral Transfers

The growing importance of services in the U.S. economy has led to efforts over the last decade to improve the coverage of services in the U.S. international transactions accounts. However, many inadequacies remain. The Department of Commerce has just conducted a special survey of a wide variety of service transactions with foreigners that are currently not covered, including sales of information, computer and data processing services, legal and accounting services, etc. Depending on the results, regular surveys may be instituted to cover the most important types of service transactions. In addition, the coverage of medical services provided to foreigners was added in 1987, and estimates are now included for fees earned by brokers and dealers on stock and bond transactions. Many gaps remain; the Commerce Department is currently working on ways to estimate education expenditures of foreign students in the United States and U.S. students abroad.

In addition to inadequacies in the coverage of many service transactions, the current estimates of immigrants transfers (which include only information on immigrants from Canada) undoubtedly underestimate the total (Frankel and Long 1985). For a country like the United States, with a tradition of welcoming large numbers of immigrants, the omission of immigrants transfers from the international transactions accounts could contribute significantly to the positive statistical discrepancy (see Frankel and Long 1985).

Inadequacy of Data on Trade

It is generally assumed that the U.S. data on trade are reasonably accurate and that errors and omissions in these data could not explain wide swings in the statistical discrepancy from quarter to quarter. However, because imports are frequently subject to duties or quotas, they are likely to be more carefully tracked than exports. This point is illustrated by the results of the regular reconciliation meetings of U.S. and Canadian statisticians. Comparison of Canadian with U.S. customs data has led the Department of Commerce to increase U.S. exports in the published accounts by between $6 and $10 billion (or between 2.5 and 4.7 percent of the compiled total) in the years 1985–87. However, the underreporting of exports to other countries is probably not as significant because, unlike the case with Canada, the compiled data do not depend on compliance with requirements that truckers place export documents in unmanned drop-boxes at large numbers of border crossings.

Another potential cause for concern is that fact that a significant part of U.S. trade is accounted for by transactions between multinational firms and their affiliates. Transactions between U.S. corporations and their majority-owned foreign affiliates accounted for approximately 25 percent of U.S. merchandise exports and 15 percent of U.S. merchandise imports in 1986. Transactions between foreign companies and their U.S. affiliates accounted approximately for an additional 10 percent of U.S. exports and 25 percent of U.S. imports in 1986. No information is available on what part of this trade is with wholly owned affiliates, but in cases where transactions are between parts of the same firm, prices charged affiliates or declared for customs purposes may not accurately reflect market values. Presumably, the declared values of imports subject to customs duties are carefully monitored, but the values declared on other transactions are probably not scrutinized as carefully, and may deviate substantially from market value.

Conclusions on the Adequacy of Reporting Systems

In conclusion, detailed examination of the U.S. international transactions accounts reveals many components that are inadequately covered or where the data appear to be inaccurate. Efforts are underway to improve the data, but results in many cases would require significant expenditures of money and increases in reporting burdens. Moreover, many improvements would not necessarily reduce the large positive statistical discrepancies observed in recent years.

9.2.2 Statistical Analysis

In addition to examining the adequacy of data on components of the U.S. international transactions accounts, it is possible to explore the sources of the statistical discrepancy in the accounts by examining correlations with other data.

In order to explore whether the statistical discrepancy behaves like unrecorded net capital inflows, I have looked at the correlation with recorded net capital inflows, components of recorded inflows, and variables that are conventionally used to explain capital flows such as interest rate differentials, expected exchange rate changes, and LDC capital flight.

It should be recognized that the insights obtained from correlations between the statistical discrepancy and recorded net capital inflows or components of recorded inflows are limited. Lack of correlation between the statistical discrepancy and a particular component of the balance of payments accounts does not prove that there are not substantial errors and omissions in reporting of that component. The correlation would be high only if a stable fraction of the balance of payments component were unreported. Moreover, since the balance of payments accounts are a double entry system, any correlation between the statistical discrepancy and a particular component of the accounts could be interpreted in two ways: either reporting of that component is inadequate or reporting of the other side of the transaction is inadequate. Sign does not necessarily indicate which interpretation is correct; for example, a negative correlation of the statistical discrepancy with foreign purchases of corporate securities could indicate either that sales of securities were being missed or that the reporting of the assets that investors were switching out of in order to pay for the securities was inadequate. In addition, the correlation results must be treated with caution because the estimates have been unstable; the addition or elimination of a few observations can change the results.

With these caveats in mind, table 9.3 shows the results of regression with various components of the international transactions accounts. All components were net to avoid spurious correlation because both the statistical discrepancy and almost everything else has gotten larger since 1970. Multiple regressions were not tried because the statistical discrepancy is, by definition, equal to the sum of the other components in the U.S. international transactions accounts with the reverse sign. The statistical discrepancy appears to be positively correlated with net direct investment inflows (row 6), but negatively related to other capital inflows (row 7), particularly bank reported inflows (row 8). One hypothesis that would be consistent with these results is that capital flows involving banks are more accurately reported than other flows, and when flows shift to other channels, errors and omissions rise.

Table 9.3 also shows the results of a regression relating the statistical discrepancy to variables that might be used to explain net capital flows (row 12): the differential between U.S. and weighted average foreign long-term interest rates and expected exchange rate changes (where it is assumed that actual exchange rate changes were correctly expected). These variables do not explain much of the variation in the statistical discrepancy, but it does appear that the statistical discrepancy rises when U.S. interest rates rise relative to foreign interest rates.

The next regression (row 13) in table 9.3 relates the statistical discrepancy to one measure of capital flight from Latin America and the Philippines. Capital flight is crudely measured as equal to the gross external debt of these countries plus the inflow of net foreign direct investment minus the current account deficit minus the change in external assets of the central bank and the commercial banks. The R^2 in this equation is not comparable to those in the other regressions because the data are annual rather than quarterly. However, the correlation appears strong and the coefficient appears high, implying that about half of every dollar of capital flight from these countries ended up in unrecorded U.S. capital inflows.

In conclusion, although these regression results must be viewed only as suggestive because of the dangers of spurious correlations, they do seem to

Table 9.3   **Statistical Discrepancy Regressions**

Explanatory Variable	Coefficient	T-Stat.	R^2
A. Components of U.S. International Transactions (1970Q1–1987Q4)			
1. Trade balance	−0.13	−2.51	.11
2. Services balance	0.32	1.54	.06
3. Net investment income	0.43	1.60	.06
4. Other service income	0.53	0.90	.05
5. Current account balance	−0.10	−2.02	.09
6. Net direct investment capital inflow	0.37	2.23	.10
7. Net other private capital inflows	−0.16	−2.94	.12
8. Bank reported	−0.18	−2.66	.12
9. Nonbank reported	−0.04	−0.36	.04
10. Net official capital inflow	−0.09	−1.13	.05
11. Foreign official inflow	−0.12	−1.28	.06
B. Variables Used to Explain Capital Flows (1974Q1–1987Q4)			
12. Constant	3.9	6.01	
U.S.–Foreign interest differential[a]	1.1	2.66	.10
Exchange rate change[b]	16.7	1.03	
C. Capital Flight (1978–1987)			
13. Constant	15.0	6.27	.71
Capital flight[c]	.57	3.30	
D. U.S. Interest Rate Level (1970Q1–1987Q4)			
14. Constant	−1.4	−.78	.11
U.S. Treasury bill rate[d]	.6	2.63	

Note: All regressions were OLS with Cochrane-Orcutt correction. Data were in billions of dollars. Annual data were used in the capital flight regressions, quarterly data in all others (not including the seasonal discrepancy adjustment).

[a]Interest rate on ten-year U.S. Treasury bonds minus the trade-weighted average of rates on ten-year government bonds for the G-10 countries.

[b]Change in the Federal Reserve trade-weighted index of the value of the dollar against G-10 currencies, $(I_t - I_{t-1})/I_{t-1}$.

[c]Capital flight from ten Latin American countries and the Philippines. Equal to the gross external debt plus the inflow of net foreign direct investment minus the current account deficit, minus the change in external assets of the central banks and the commercial banks.

[d]U.S. Treasury bill rate: three-month, secondary market.

support the view that at least part of the statistical discrepancy in the U.S. international transactions accounts is the result of errors and omissions in the reporting of capital flows.

Table 9.3 also reports the results of regressions relating the statistical discrepancy to components of the current account. There appears to be a negative relationship between the trade balance and the discrepancy (row 1). One possible explanation is that a fraction of the capital inflow necessary to finance the trade deficit is unreported. There is a positive, but not statistically significant relationship with the services balance (row 2). This positive relationship is supported by a regression relating the statistical discrepancy to the level of U.S. interest rates (row 14); if interest income were being underreported, the amounts involved would tend to increase as interest rates rose.

9.2.3   Conclusions on the U.S. Statistical Discrepancy

There are strong reasons to suspect errors and omissions in the reporting of both current and capital account transactions in the U.S. data. Inspection of the reporting systems and correlations between the statistical discrepancy and various variables confirm these suspicions. However, it is very difficult to quantify the contribution of current account versus capital account transactions to the statistical discrepancy. It would seem safe to assume, however, that the shift of the U.S. current account from near balance in the first three years of the 1980s to deficits of around $150 billion in recent years cannot be accounted for by errors and omissions; the direction of change is clear, although the exact magnitude of the deficit could be significantly below $150 billion.

9.3   International Investment Position Data: Global

Net debtor positions as well as current accounts are frequently mentioned as indicators of sustainability and the need for policy adjustments. Unlike the current account data, which are readily available for a large number of countries on a consistent basis from IMF sources, data on international investment positions must be collected from national sources. The difficulties of measuring a country's net investment position will become apparent in the next section of the paper, where the U.S. net investment position is examined in detail. Moreover, since there are no commonly agreed upon guidelines on how assets and liabilities should be valued, it is unlikely, even if data were available from all countries, that the sum of all countries' positions would equal zero.

With this caveat in mind, table 9.4 shows net external assets (excluding gold) for the seven major industrial countries and IMF projections for 1987 through 1989 (IMF 1988, 89). Over the next few years, these countries as a group are expected to move into a large negative position. According to the IMF (1988, 90):

Given that the recorded debt stock of the capital importing countries, which amounted to $1200 billion at the end of 1987, is unlikely to be fully matched by the assets of the smaller industrial countries and the capital exporting countries in the Middle East, the data presented here would seem to confirm the existence of a very large amount of cross-border assets recognized by debtor countries but which do not seem to be reflected in the statistics of creditor countries.

Table 9.4   Major Industrial Countries: Net External Assets, Excluding Gold, 1980–1989 (end of period, in billions of dollars)

	1980	1981	1982	1983	1984	1985	1986	1987[a]	1988[a]	1989[a]
Canada	−88.4	−111.5	−106.5	−112.6	−114.3	−122.1	−142.1	−149.3	−160.0	−171.7
United States	95.1	129.9	125.9	78.5	−7.5	−123.0	−274.7	−435.4	−576.5	−710.3
Japan	10.5	9.9	23.7	36.4	73.5	128.9	179.3	266.0	343.8	419.2
France	—	—	−11.8	−20.7	−22.2	−11.4	1.0	−3.4	−6.3	−9.6
Federal Republic of Germany	26.1	20.1	27.2	27.4	34.1	58.6	106.3	150.5	191.9	232.6
Italy	−1.1	−14.7	−20.9	−18.1	−18.2	−32.1	−34.0	−34.0	−35.0	−36.9
United Kingdom	27.2	47.6	56.0	69.2	84.5	105.4	162.3	159.5	152.2	143.0
Total	69.4	81.3	93.6	60.1	29.9	4.3	−1.9	−46.1	−89.9	−133.7

Source: IMF (1988, 89).

[a]IMF staff estimates and projections, excluding valuation effects and based on *World Economic Outlook* baseline assumptions of constant real exchange rates and interest rates.

This theme is examined in more detail in the *Report on the World Current Account Discrepancy* (IMF 1987). The IMF working party concluded that the underreporting of assets was widespread across countries; in particular, estimates of the international claims and liabilities of nonbanks appear to be deficient. Some idea of magnitudes can be inferred from the other side of transactions: bank records of claims on and liabilities to nonbank foreigners. The reasons for the inadequacy of data on nonbanks assets and liabilities vary but include evasion of taxes and exchange controls and ignorance of reporting requirements. This problem has been exacerbated in recent years by the securitization of international lending; information on issuers of securities in international bond markets is readily available, but little information is available on the purchasers of these securities.

In conclusion, it appears that there is significant underreporting of claims in many countries' net investment position data. However, forecasts of current accounts are likely to provide a reasonable indication of directions of change and, in many cases, of future trends in investment income payments. Moreover, in the case of highly indebted countries that have experienced significant capital flight, the fact that some residents of the country have assets hidden abroad and are earning income on these assets may be of little use if these assets are beyond government control.

9.4   U.S. Net International Investment Position

According to the Department of Commerce, foreign assets in the United States exceeded U.S. assets abroad by approximately $368 billion at the end of 1987 (see table 9.5). This net debtor position is a recent development; from World War I through 1984, the United States was a net creditor to the rest of the world, with the net asset position reaching a peak of $141 billion in 1981. The sharp reversal in recent years is a result of the large net capital inflows associated with growing U.S. current account deficits. Valuation changes estimated by the Department of Commerce play some role in explaining changes in position from year to year, but, in recent years, these valuation changes have been small relative to recorded capital flows.

As acknowledged by the Department of Commerce, these data are a rough indicator and not a precise statistical measure of U.S. net indebtedness to foreigners because of errors and omissions in the U.S. international transactions data and because of valuation problems.

9.4.1   Errors and Omissions

As discussed earlier, the statistical discrepancy in the U.S. international transactions accounts has been large and positive for the past decade, indicating some combination of omitted net exports of goods and services and omitted net capital inflows. In fact, cumulative net unrecorded transactions

Table 9.5   **International Investment Position of the United States at Year End (in billions of dollars)**

Row	Type of Investment	1975	1980	1985	1986	1987
1	Net international investment position of the United States	74	106	−111	−269	−368
2	U.S. assets abroad	295	607	950	1,071	1,168
3	Official reserve assets	16	27	43	49	46
4	Government assets, other than official	42	64	88	90	88
5	Private assets	237	517	819	933	1,034
6	Direct investment abroad	124	215	230	260	309
7	Foreign securities	35	63	113	133	147
8	Bonds	25	43	73	82	91
9	Corporate stocks	10	19	40	51	56
10	Claims on unaffiliated foreigners reported by U.S. nonbanking concerns	18	35	29	33	30
11	Claims reported by U.S. banks	60	204	447	507	548
12	Foreign assets in the United States	221	501	1,061	1,341	1,536
13	Official assets in the U.S.	87	176	203	242	283
14	Other assets in the United States	134	325	858	1,099	1,253
15	Direct investment in the United States	28	83	185	220	262
16	U.S. Treasury securities	4	16	84	91	78
17	U.S. securities other than U.S. Treasury securities	46	74	206	309	344
18	Corporate and other bonds	10	10	82	142	171
19	Corporate stocks	36	65	124	167	173
20	U.S. liabilities to unaffiliated foreigners reported by U.S. nonbanking concerns	14	30	29	27	29
21	U.S. liabilities reported by U.S. banks, not included elsewhere	42	121	354	452	539

Source: Survey of Current Business (June 1988): 78.

between 1959 and 1987 amounted to over $190 billion. Since the published net investment data rely only on recorded capital flows, the real net investment position could be more negative.

On the other hand, alternative sources of data indicate that U.S. nonbanks' deposits at banks outside the United States are seriously underestimated in the position data. As of the end of 1987, Federal Reserve data indicate that these deposits are at least $70 billion larger than the amount included in the position data.

9.4.2   Valuation Problems

Apart from stocks and bonds, the Department of Commerce does not attempt to revalue assets according to market prices. And even in the case of stocks and bonds, the valuation methods may be subject to substantial errors.

Securities

The Treasury Department conducts periodic benchmark surveys of the value of foreign holdings of U.S. stocks and bonds (rows 16 through 19 in table 9.5). In between these surveys, reliance must be placed on data collected on new transactions and estimates of the change in value of previous holdings (based on movements in stock market price indices and interest rate movements). In estimating the investment position, BEA is currently using data from the 1978 benchmark survey; however, 1984 data will be available soon. Estimates of changes in value are necessarily crude since foreigners' holdings of stocks may differ in composition from the stocks included in various market averages and since little information is available on the term structure of foreigners' holdings of bonds.

For U.S. holdings of foreign stocks and bonds (rows 8 and 9), the latest benchmark survey was conducted during World War II; no survey has been conducted since then because of the tremendous difficulty and expense of obtaining accurate data. As a result, the current estimate of holdings is based upon data on transactions since World War II and valuation adjustments based on foreign stock market indices, and interest rate and exchange rate movements. The task of valuing U.S. holdings of foreign securities is made even more difficult by the fact that purchases and sales data are collected on the basis of the nationality of the transactor, and not the issuer; transactions through financial centers like London need not reflect purchases or sales of U.K. securities. As a result, it certainly is possible that the errors in the estimated valuation adjustments to U.S. holdings of foreign securities could have cumulated to a substantial sum since World War II.

Gold

U.S. official reserve holdings of gold (included in row 3) are valued at the official price ($42.22 per ounce), while the market price is about 10 times higher. U.S. assets would be about $100 billion larger if gold were valued at current market prices.

Direct Investment

In addition, direct investment claims (row 6) and liabilities (row 15) are at book value. It seems likely that this valuation understates the market value of U.S. direct investment abroad by more than it understates the value of foreign direct investment in the United States because foreign direct investment in the United States is, on average, more recent than U.S. direct investment abroad. One way of crudely estimating market value would be to assume that the market value of investments (measured in dollars) increases proportionately with inflation and exchange rate changes (Helkie and Stekler 1987). Starting with the book value of direct investment assets in 1964, inflating each year by a weighted average foreign price index adjusted for exchange rate changes and then adding the new capital outflow yields an estimate of the value of U.S. direct investment assets of about $700 billion at the end of 1987. Using the same methodology, estimated foreign direct investment in the United States would be $350 billion, and the net position would be $350 billion, $300 billion larger than the net included by the Department of Commerce.

Comparison of the size of direct investment receipts and payments suggests that the market value of U.S. assets abroad may exceed the market value of foreign assets here by even more. The ratio of reported receipts to payments in recent years has been about 3 to 1, in contrast to the 2 to 1 ratio estimated above. However, this ratio calculated using receipts and payments may be distorted by temporary factors which inflate or depress earnings; if generally perceived as temporary, they would have a limited effect on the market value of assets. In addition, many affiliates of foreign companies in the United States and foreign affiliates of U.S. companies are wholly owned subsidiaries; the parent companies enjoy considerable latitude in determining charges for transactions with their subsidiaries, and tax considerations may play a significant role in determining where profits are reported.

Bank Claims and Liabilities

Bank-reported claims on and liabilities to foreigners (rows 11 and 21 in table 9.5) are also at book value. No adjustment is made, for example, for the market value of loans to countries experiencing debt servicing problems (as long as the banks continue to carry the loans on their books at full value).

9.4.3   Conclusions

The net international investment position of the United States, as published by the Department of Commerce, is subject to a substantial margin of error because of the errors and omissions in the U.S. international transactions accounts and because of valuation problems. However, given the magnitude of recent U.S. current account deficits, there is little doubt that the published data correctly indicate the direction and rough magnitude of change.

9.5   Usefulness of Current Account and Position Data as Indicators of Disequilibrium

Even if data were completely accurate, a given current account and investment position may not clearly indicate the need for policy changes because of lags in the adjustment process or underlying long-run trends.

9.5.1   Lags

The problem with using observed current account positions as an indicator of disequilibrium requiring policy adjustments can be illustrated by considering the current U.S. situation. Estimates of whether substantial further depreciation of the dollar is necessary to correct the U.S. current account deficit depend crucially on whether all or only part of the impact of the depreciation of the dollar from its high of February 1985 has been realized. Given current techniques for estimating the length and shape of lagged adjustments, it is possible for different econometricians to arrive at very different conclusions using the same data. This problem has been discussed extensively elsewhere, for example, at the January 1987 Brookings workshop on the U.S. external deficit, and I do not intend to repeat it (see Bryant, Holtham, and Hooper 1988, 101–39).

9.5.2   Underlying Long-Run Trends

Another problem with using current account or investment position data as an indicator of required policy adjustments is the need to take into account underlying trends. For example, it may be appropriate for a country with a rapidly aging population to run current account surpluses and accumulate assets in preparation for future years when a large retired population must be supported. There are many additional factors which might mean that it would be unwise to identify current account balance with equilibrium and current account surpluses or deficits with disequilibrium. I plan to focus on only one of these: the implications for future U.S. net investment income of the growing U.S. net international indebtedness.

Many observers have concluded that the United States will have to run substantial trade surpluses in the future to cover large net payments of investment income on the U.S. net debtor position. Crude estimates are arrived at by assuming that the U.S. net debt will accumulate to $1 trillion and by assuming an interest rate, for example, 7 percent, producing an estimate of around $70 billion per year in net interest payments. These back-of-the-envelope calculations probably substantially overstate the net interest payments that are likely to be associated with a recorded U.S. net investment position of that size.

The reasons for this are twofold: first, the rate of return on U.S. assets abroad tends to be higher than the rate of return on foreign assets in the United States, and, second, while U.S. liabilities are growing more rapidly than U.S. assets, both are likely to continue to trend upwards. The combined effect of these factors is illustrated by the fact that net investment income was positive in 1987 despite a sizable net debtor position. U.S. net investment income would tend to increase if our net debtor position were not growing.

Relative Rates of Return

Two questions are apparent: is this differential in rates of return likely to persist in the future and does it represent a real difference or just a recorded difference in rates of return? Turning first to direct investment, table 9.6 shows the rate of return on direct investment as published by the Department of Commerce. Because the direct investment position used in these calculations is measured at book value, and since direct investment in the United States is, on average, more recent than U.S. direct investment abroad, the value of U.S.

Table 9.6   **Implicit Rates of Return on U.S. Direct Investments**

	Claims		Liabilities	
	Dept. of Commerce Basis	Adjusted	Dept. of Commerce Basis	Adjusted
1980	18.4	9.06	15.4	7.11
1981	14.4	6.92	9.8	5.13
1982	9.9	5.24	2.6	1.88
1983	9.5	5.87	4.3	2.66
1984	10.2	6.65	6.1	4.32
1985	14.8	6.28	3.5	2.99
1986	15.7	5.46	2.7	2.66
1987	18.4	5.95	4.4	3.24

direct investment abroad is more seriously understated because of inflation than the value of foreign direct investment in the United States. If the rates of return are recalculated using Department of Commerce capital flows data, adjusted for inflation and exchange rate changes (also shown in the table), the differences are reduced substantially, but some margin remains.

Some differential might be expected on the grounds that some U.S. direct investment abroad is located in countries where political and economic risks are significant. However, a major part of the differential is probably the result of tax incentives which lead multinational firms to use transfer prices to shift reported profits to lower tax jurisdictions abroad. Although U.S. corporate tax rates were lowered recently relative to other industrial countries, they still remain above rates in various tax havens. The incentive to report profits abroad will probably persist, inflating reported receipts on U.S. direct investment abroad and depressing payments on foreign direct investment in the United States. Balancing this distortion of the direct investment accounts is the underreporting of exports of goods and services by U.S. corporations to their affiliates abroad and the overstatement of the imports of goods and services by the U.S. affiliates of foreign companies. These understatements of net credits on other current account items are likely to grow as direct investment in and out of the United States continues to expand, so errors in the returns on direct investment are likely to be matched by equal and opposite errors in other current account items.

Turning now to portfolio investment income, table 9.7 shows the average rates of return implicit in the data published by the Department of Commerce on income and position. The implicit rate for private payments has been consistently below the rate for government payments and private receipts. There are several explanations for this. First, at the end of 1987, foreign holdings of U.S. equities amounted to $173 billion, somewhat less than 20 percent of the U.S. private sector's portfolio liabilities to foreigners, while U.S. holdings of foreign equities amounted to only $56 billion, less than 10 percent of U.S.

Table 9.7   **Implicit Rates of Return on U.S. Portfolio Investments**

	Claims		Liabilities	
	Private	Govt.	Private	Govt.
1980	12.20	3.55	8.49	9.18
1981	15.00	4.31	10.20	10.99
1982	12.79	4.48	9.30	11.33
1983	9.71	4.84	6.89	9.95
1984	10.63	4.96	7.82	10.11
1985	8.76	4.87	6.41	9.40
1986	7.30	5.20	5.40	8.40
1987	6.74	4.24	5.43	8.11

private portfolio claims on foreigners. Since dividends generally provide only a part of the expected return on equities, and since capital gains on stocks are excluded from the balance of payments accounts, the average rate of return on both portfolio claims and liabilities is brought down, but the impact is larger on the payments side.

Second, the bulk of U.S. portfolio claims and liabilities are reported by banks: about three-quarters of private claims and three-fifths of private liabilities. As intermediaries, banks make profits by earning more on their assets than they pay on their liabilities.[2] In addition, the Department of Commerce includes in receipts of income on U.S. assets abroad estimates of fees earned by banks in the United States for various services provided to foreigners. In response to pressures to improve capital adequacy, major U.S. banks have slowed the growth of their balance sheets and have focused increased attention on profitable off-balance-sheet transactions. Fees from these off-balance-sheet services to foreigners are likely to continue to grow in the future.

Finally, U.S. nonbanks are likely to be paid a higher rate of return on their dollar deposits abroad than foreigners are paid on their bank deposits in the United States because of the absence of reserve requirements and deposit insurance charges in the Eurodollar market.

Growth of Gross Claims and Liabilities

Despite the shift to a net debtor position, U.S. assets abroad have continued to grow, illustrating the continuing internationalization of financial markets and the use of U.S. financial institutions as intermediaries by foreigners. As can be seen in figure 9.2, the rate of growth of U.S. portfolio claims on foreigners has slowed in recent years, as the U.S. current account deficit has grown. However, the deceleration is exaggerated by the rapid growth of bank claims in 1981 and 1982; in these years banks shifted business from the books of their affiliates outside the United States to their newly established International Banking Facilities (IBFs). The slower growth of bank claims in recent years also has been associated with the debt crisis and efforts to improve capital adequacy as well as a slowdown in inflation. As a result, one might expect the

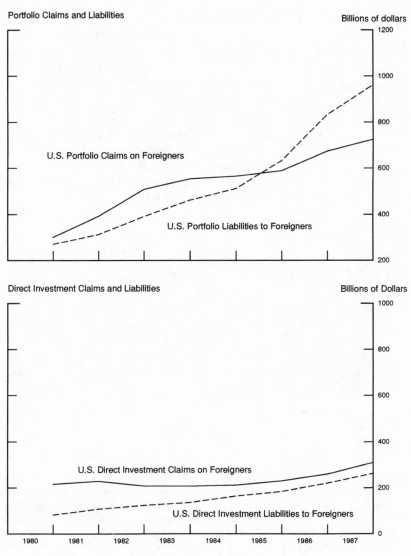

Fig. 9.2   U.S. international investment position

rate of growth of U.S. private portfolio claims on foreigners to remain somewhat below the average for the 1970s and early 1980s, but to remain significant.

U.S. direct investment assets abroad have also continued to grow in recent years, although the year to year changes are sensitive to fluctuations in economic activity (and currency translation effects). U.S.–based firms are likely to continue to invest in growing economies abroad and the pressures of international competition are likely to continue the trend toward global sourcing and expansion of production facilities in countries with lower costs.

Implications for U.S. Net Investment Income

The simulations done with the Multicountry Model of the Federal Reserve Board for the Brookings Conference on the U.S. Current Account (January 1987) illustrate the implications of continuing growth of U.S. gross claims on foreigners for future net investment income. Between 1986 and 1991, the U.S. net investment position declines by $746 billion, from −$280 billion to −$1026 billion. However, U.S. net investment income declines only by $23 billion, from $22 billion to −$1 billion. These numbers are just illustrative; they should not be interpreted as a forecast because the underlying assumptions are somewhat arbitrary and have, in many cases, been overtaken by more recent developments. But they do illustrate the point that underlying trends must be taken into account, along with current account positions, in analyzing necessary policy adjustments.

9.6 Conclusions

The data on U.S. and other countries' current accounts and international investment positions appear to be subject to a considerable margin of error. However, large shifts in recorded data are unlikely to be illusory. There is little doubt that the United States has been running massive current account deficits in recent years and that the rest of the world has accumulated large claims on the United States as a result. While the data may be accurate enough to discern broad trends, current account and net investment positions do not always yield unambiguous signals of the need for policy adjustments. This is illustrated by the current debate over the appropriate exchange rates for the U.S. dollar.

Notes

1. The published U.S. data aggregate official and private purchases of U.S. Treasury or other securities by Japan, while the Japanese data exclude central bank purchases of securities and do not distinguish between U.S. Treasuries and other long-term bonds.

2. The IMF working party on the statistical discrepancy in world current account balances used a spread of 250 basis points between the rate earned on bank claims on nonbanks and the rate paid on liabilities to nonbanks; the spread on interbank transactions is much smaller.

References

Bryant, Ralph, Gerald Holtham, and Peter Hooper, eds. 1988. *External deficits and the dollar*. Washington, DC: Brookings Institution.

Frankel, Allen, and Alice Long. 1985. The treatment of immigrants' transfers in U.S. international transactions data. Washington DC: Federal Reserve Board. Unpublished memo, January 3.

Helkie, William, and Lois Stekler. 1987. *Modeling investment income and other services in the U.S. international transactions accounts.* International Finance Discussion Paper no. 319 (December). Washington, DC.

IMF. 1987. *Report on the World Current Account Discrepancy.* Washington DC: IMF, September.

IMF. 1988. *World Economic Outlook*, (April). Washington DC: IMF.

Krueger, Russell C. 1988. U.S. international transactions, first quarter 1988. In U.S. Department of Commerce, *Survey of Current Business* (June). Washington, DC.

Scholl, Russell. 1988. The international investment position of the United States in 1987. In U.S. Department of Commerce, *Survey of Current Business.* Washington, DC.

Contributors

C. Fred Bergsten
Director
Institute for International Economics
11 Dupont Circle NW
Washington, DC 20036

William H. Branson
Woodrow Wilson School
Princeton University
Princeton, NJ 08544

Ralph C. Bryant
Brookings Institution
1775 Massachusetts Avenue, NW
Washington, DC 20036

Geoffrey Carliner
Executive Director
National Bureau of Economic Research
1050 Massachusetts Avenue
Cambridge, MA 02138

Richard N. Cooper
Harvard Institute for International
    Development
1737 Cambridge Street, Room 403
Cambridge, MA 02138

Martin Feldstein
President and Chief Executive Officer
National Bureau of Economic Research
1050 Massachusetts Avenue
Cambridge, MA 02138

Stanley Fischer
The World Bank
S-9035
1818 H Street, NW
Washington, DC 20433

J. S. Flemming
Executive Director
Bank of England
Threadneedle Street
London, EC2R 8AH,
    England

David Folkerts-Landau
Central Banking Depart-
    ment
International Monetary Fund
700 19th Street, NW
Washington, DC 20431

Jeffrey A. Frankel
Department of Economics
University of California
Evans Hall
Berkeley, CA 94720

Jacob A. Frenkel
Economic Counsellor and Director,
    Research Department
International Monetary Fund
700 19th Street, NW
Washington, DC 20431

Kenneth A. Froot
Graduate School of Business
Harvard University
Soldiers Field
Boston, MA 02163

Hans Genberg
Graduate Institute of International
    Studies
Case Postale 36
132, Rue de Lausanne
CH-1211 Geneva 21
Switzerland

Francesco Giavazzi
Dipartmento di Scienze Economiche
Universita di Bologna
Strada Maggiore 45
Bologna, Italy

Alberto Giovannini
Graduate School of Business
Columbia University
622 Uris Hall
New York, NY 10027

Morris Goldstein
Research Department
International Monetary Fund
700 19th Street, NW
Washington, DC 20431

Peter B. Kenen
International Finance Section
Department of Economics
Princeton University
Dickinson Hall
Princeton, NJ 08544

Paul R. Krugman
Department of Economics
Massachusetts Institute of
    Technology
50 Memorial Drive
Cambridge, MA 02139

Richard C. Marston
Wharton School
University of Pennsylvania
2300 Steinberg-Dietrich Hall
Philadelphia, PA 19104

Paul R. Masson
Research Department
International Monetary Fund
700 19th Street, NW
Washington, DC 20431

Michael Mussa
Graduate School of Business
University of Chicago
1101 E. 58th Street
Chicago, IL 60637

Shuntaro Namba
Chief, Research Division II
Institute for Monetary and Economic
    Studies
The Bank of Japan
CPO Box 203
Tokyo 100–91, Japan

Maurice Obstfeld
Department of Economics
University of California
Evans Hall
Berkeley, CA 94720

Francesco Papadia
Research Department
Banca d'Italia
Casella Postale 2484
Via Nazionale, 91
00100 Roma, Italy

Douglas D. Purvis
Department of Economics
Queen's University
Kingston, Ontario K7L 3N6
Canada

Wolfgang Rieke
Head, International Department
Deutsche Bundesbank
Postfach 10 06 02
6000 Frankfurt 1
Federal Republic of Germany

Lois Stekler
Board of Governors of the Federal
    Reserve System
20th & C Streets, NW
Washington, DC 20551

Author Index

Subject Index